Authorized Self-Study Guide

Interconnecting Cisco Network Devices, Part 1 (ICND1)

Second Edition

Steve McQuerry,
CCIE No. 6108

Cisco Press

800 East 96th Street
Indianapolis, Indiana 46240 USA

Interconnecting Cisco Network Devices, Part 1 (ICND1)
Second Edition

Steve McQuerry, CCIE No. 6108

Copyright© 2008 Cisco Systems, Inc.

Cisco Press logo is a trademark of Cisco Systems, Inc.

Published by:
Cisco Press
800 East 96th Street
Indianapolis, IN 46240 USA

Printed in the United States of America

First Printing   December 2007

Library of Congress Cataloging-in-Publication Data:

McQuerry, Steve.

Authorized self-study guide : interconnecting Cisco network devices.

Part 1 (ICND1) / Steve McQuerry. —2nd ed.

   p. cm.

Includes index.

ISBN 978-1-58705-462-4 (hbk.)

1. Internetworking (Telecommunication)—Examinations—Study guides. 2. Computer networks—Problems, exercises, etc. 3. Telecommunications engineers—Certification—Examinations—Study guides. I. Title. II. Title: Interconnecting Cisco network devices, part 1 (ICND1).

TK5105.5.M3399 2007
004.6—dc22

2007043780

ISBN-13: 978-1-58705-462-4
ISBN-10: 1-58705-462-0

This book is part of the Cisco Networking Academy® series from Cisco Press. The products in this series support and complement the Cisco Networking Academy curriculum. If you are using this book outside the Networking Academy, then you are not preparing with a Cisco trained and authorized Networking Academy provider.

For more information on the Cisco Networking Academy or to locate a Networking Academy, please visit www.cisco.com/edu.

CISCO.

Warning and Disclaimer

Feedback Information

At Cisco Press, our goal is to create in-depth technical books of the highest quality and value. Each book is crafted with care and precision, undergoing rigorous development that involves the unique expertise of members from the professional technical community.

Readers' feedback is a natural continuation of this process. If you have any comments regarding how we could improve the quality of this book, or otherwise alter it to better suit your needs, you can contact us through email at feedback@ciscopress.com. Please make sure to include the book title and ISBN in your message.

We greatly appreciate your assistance.

Corporate and Government Sales

The publisher offers excellent discounts on this book when ordered in quantity for bulk purchases or special sales, which may include electronic versions and/or custom covers and content particular to your business, training goals, marketing focus, and branding interests. For more information, please contact:

U.S. Corporate and Government Sales   1-800-382-3419   corpsales@pearsontechgroup.com

For sales outside the United States, please contact:
International Sales   international@pearsoned.com

Trademark Acknowledgments

All terms mentioned in this book that are known to be trademarks or service marks have been appropriately capitalized. Cisco Press or Cisco Systems, Inc., cannot attest to the accuracy of this information. Use of a term in this book should not be regarded as affecting the validity of any trademark or service mark.

Publisher	Paul Boger
Associate Publisher	Dave Dusthimer
Cisco Representative	Anthony Wolfenden
Cisco Press Program Manager	Jeff Brady
Executive Editor	Brett Bartow
Managing Editor	Patrick Kanouse
Development Editor	Ginny Bess Munroe
Copy Editor	Kevin Kent and Written Elegance, Inc.
Technical Editors	Matthew C. Brussel
	Tami Day-Orsatti
	Kevin Wallace
Editorial Assistant	Vanessa Evans
Designer	Louisa Adair
Composition	ICC Macmillan Inc.
Indexer	Tim Wright
Proofreader	Water Crest Publishing

Americas Headquarters	Asia Pacific Headquarters	Europe Headquarters
Cisco Systems, Inc.	Cisco Systems, Inc.	Cisco Systems International BV
170 West Tasman Drive	168 Robinson Road	Haarlerbergpark
San Jose, CA 95134-1706	#28-01 Capital Tower	Haarlerbergweg 13-19
USA	Singapore 068912	1101 CH Amsterdam
www.cisco.com	www.cisco.com	The Netherlands
Tel: 408 526-4000	Tel: +65 6317 7777	www-europe.cisco.com
800 553-NETS (6387)	Fax: +65 6317 7799	Tel: +31 0 800 020 0791
Fax: 408 527-0883		Fax: +31 0 20 357 1100

Cisco has more than 200 offices worldwide. Addresses, phone numbers, and fax numbers are listed on the Cisco Website at **www.cisco.com/go/offices.**

About the Author

Steve McQuerry, CCIE No. 6108, is a consulting systems engineer with Cisco Systems focused on data center architecture. Steve works with enterprise customers in the midwestern United States to help them plan their data center architectures. Steve has been an active member of the internetworking community since 1991 and has held multiple certifications from Novell, Microsoft, and Cisco. Prior to joining Cisco, Steve worked as an independent contractor with Global Knowledge, where he taught and developed coursework around Cisco technologies and certifications.

About the Technical Reviewers

Matthew C. Brussel is currently leading accelerated certification training courses for Training Camps that specialize in MCSE: Security 2003, MCDST XP, A+, Net+, Security+, CCNA, CCDA, and others. After studying IT, economics, and accounting in college, Matthew has been an IT consultant, pre-sales engineer, and IT trainer in various capacities for over 20 years. He has worked as a traditional trainer and as an accelerated technical certification boot camp trainer for well over the last 10 years. Matthew also contributes to custom content and exam prep study guides and participates in various technical writing and technical editing projects. Previously, Matthew worked as an IT consultant for over 10 years in Portsmouth, RI; Stamford, CT; Greenwich, CT; and New York City. Now traveling to Training Camp sites all across America, he currently resides in central Florida. He has over 70 technical certifications and exams to his credit, including Microsoft MCT, MCSE 2003 with Security and Messaging, CCNA, CCDA, A+, Network+, I-Net+, Security+, and CTT+ (Written). Matthew can be reached at MattBrussel@gmail.com.

Tami Day-Orsatti, CCSI, CCDP, CCNP, CISSP, ECI, EMCPA, MCT, MCSE: 2000/2003 Security, is an IT networking, security, and data storage instructor for T^2 IT Training. She is responsible for the delivery of authorized Cisco, (ISC)^2, EMC, and Microsoft classes. She has over 23 years in the IT industry working with many different types of organizations (private business, city and federal government, and DoD), providing project management and senior-level network and security technical skills in the design and implementation of complex computing environments. She maintains active memberships in local and national organizations such as (ISC)^2, ISSA, and SANS.

Kevin Wallace, CCIE No. 7945, is a certified Cisco instructor and a full-time instructor of Cisco courses. With 18 years of Cisco networking experience, Kevin has been a network design specialist for The Walt Disney World Resort and a network manager for Eastern Kentucky University. Kevin holds a bachelor's of science degree in electrical engineering from the University of Kentucky. Kevin is also a CCVP, CCSP, CCNP, and CCDP, and he holds multiple Cisco IP communication and security specializations. Additionally, Kevin has authored several books for Cisco Press, including *CCNP Video Mentor*, *Voice over IP First-Step*, and *Cisco Voice over IP*, Second Edition.

Dedication

This work is dedicated to my family. Becky, as the years go by, I love you more. Thank you for your support and understanding. Katie, your work ethic has always amazed me. As you prepare to move into the next phase of your life, remember your goals and keep working hard and you can achieve anything. Logan, you have never believed there was anything you couldn't do. Keep that drive and spirit and there will be no limit to what you can accomplish. Cameron, you have a keen sense of curiosity that reminds me of myself as a child. Use that thirst for understanding and learning, and you will be successful in all your endeavors.

Acknowledgments

There are a great number of people that go into publishing a work like this, and I would like to take this space to thank everyone who was involved with this project.

Thanks to the ICND course developers. Most of this book is the product of their hard work.

Thanks to the technical editors, Tami Day-Orsatti, Kevin Wallace, and Matt Brussel, for looking over this work and helping maintain its technical integrity.

Thanks to all the real publishing professionals at Cisco Press. This is a group of people that I have had the pleasure of working with since 1998, and it has been a joy and honor. Thanks to Brett Bartow for allowing me the opportunity to write for Cisco Press once again and to Chris Cleveland for gently reminding me how to write again after a three-year break. It's defiantly not as easy as riding a bike. Thanks to Ginny Bess Munroe for keeping the work flowing and dealing with my bad jokes. Also to Kevin Kent and John Edwards (Written Elegance), you are the best in the industry.

Thanks to my manager at Cisco, Darrin Thomason, for trusting me to keep all my other projects managed while working on this project in my spare time. (Wait, do we have spare time at Cisco?)

Thanks to my customers, colleagues, and former students. Your questions, comments, and challenges have helped me to continue to learn and helped teach me how to pass that information to others.

Thanks to my family, for their patience and understanding during this project and all my projects.

Most importantly, I would like to thank God, for giving me the skills, talents, and opportunity to work in such a challenging and exciting profession.

This Book Is Safari Enabled

The Safari™ Enabled icon on the cover of your favorite technology book means the book is available through Safari Bookshelf. When you buy this book, you get free access to the online edition for 45 days.

Safari Bookshelf is an electronic reference library that lets you easily search thousands of technical books, find code samples, download chapters, and access technical information whenever and wherever you need it.

To gain 45-day Safari Enabled access to this book

- Go to http://www.ciscopress.com/safarienabled.

- Complete the brief registration form.

- Enter the coupon code GQLK-NEAM-LVB1-X9NY-A24D.

If you have difficulty registering on Safari Bookshelf or accessing the online edition, please e-mail customer-service@safaribooksonline.com.

Contents at a Glance

Contents

Icons Used in This Book

 Router

 Switch

 Bridge

 IP Telephony Router

 IP Phone

 DSU/CSU

 uBR910 Cable DSU

 Hub

 100BaseT Hub

 Repeater

 Network Cloud

 Access Server

 Access Point

 Database

 Modem

 Server

 Host

 PC

 Laptop

 Printer

 Headquarters

 Branch Office

 Home Office

Command Syntax Conventions

The conventions used to present command syntax in this book are the same conventions used in the IOS Command Reference. The Command Reference describes these conventions as follows:

- **Boldface** indicates commands and keywords that are entered literally as shown. In actual configuration examples and output (not general command syntax), boldface indicates commands that are manually input by the user (such as a **show** command).

- *Italics* indicate arguments for which you supply actual values.

- Vertical bars (|) separate alternative, mutually exclusive elements.

- Square brackets [ ] indicate optional elements.

- Braces { } indicate a required choice.

- Braces within brackets [{ }] indicate a required choice within an optional element.

Foreword

Cisco Certification Self-Study Guides are excellent self-study resources for networking professionals to maintain and increase internetworking skills and to prepare for Cisco Career Certification exams. Cisco Career Certifications are recognized worldwide and provide valuable, measurable rewards to networking professionals and their employers.

Cisco Press exam certification guides and preparation materials offer exceptional—and flexible—access to the knowledge and information required to stay current in one's field of expertise, or to gain new skills. Whether used to increase internetworking skills or as a supplement to a formal certification preparation course, these materials offer networking professionals the information and knowledge required to perform on-the-job tasks proficiently.

Developed in conjunction with the Cisco certifications and training team, Cisco Press books are the only self-study books authorized by Cisco. They offer students a series of exam practice tools and resource materials to help ensure that learners fully grasp the concepts and information presented.

Additional authorized Cisco instructor-led courses, e-learning, labs, and simulations are available exclusively from Cisco Learning Solutions Partners worldwide. To learn more, visit http://www.cisco.com/go/training/.

I hope you will find this guide to be an essential part of your exam preparation and professional development, as well as a valuable addition to your personal library.

Drew Rosen
Manager, Learning and Development
Learning@Cisco
November 2007

Introduction

Since the introduction of the personal computer in the early 1970s, businesses have found more uses and applications for technology in the workplace. With the introduction of local-area networks, file sharing, and print sharing in the 1980s, it became obvious that distributed computing was no longer a passing fad. By the 1990s, computers became less expensive, and innovations such as the Internet enabled everyone to connect to computer services worldwide. Computing services have become large and distributed. The days of punch cards and green-bar paper are behind us, and a new generation of computing experts is being asked to keep this distributed technology operational. These experts are destined to have a new set of issues and problems to deal with, the most complex of them being connectivity and compatibility between differing systems and devices.

The primary challenge with data networking today is to link multiple devices' protocols and sites with maximum effectiveness and ease of use for end users. Of course, this must all be accomplished in a cost-effective way. Cisco offers a variety of products to give network managers and analysts the ability to face and solve the challenges of internetworking.

In an effort to ensure that these networking professionals have the knowledge to perform these arduous tasks, Cisco has developed a series of courses and certifications that act as benchmarks for internetworking professionals. These courses help internetworking professionals learn the fundamentals of internetworking technologies along with skills in configuring and installing Cisco products. The certification exams are designed to be a litmus test for the skills required to perform at various levels of internetworking. The Cisco certifications range from the associate level (CCNA), through the professional level (CCNP), to the expert level (CCIE).

The Interconnecting Cisco Network Devices 1 (ICND1) course is one of two recommended training classes for CCNA preparation. As a self-study complement to the course, this book helps to ground individuals in the fundamentals of switches and routed internetworks. It presents the concepts, commands, and practices required to configure Cisco switches and routers to operate in corporate internetworks. You will be introduced to all the basic concepts and configuration procedures required to build a multiswitch, multirouter, and multigroup internetwork that uses LAN and WAN interfaces for the most commonly used routing and routed protocols. ICND1 provides the installation and configuration information that network administrators require to install and configure Cisco products.

This book is the first part of a two-part, introductory-level series and is recommended for individuals who have one to three years of internetworking experience, are familiar with basic internetworking concepts, and have basic experience with TCP/IP. While this self-study book is designed for those who are pursuing the CCNA certification, it is also useful for network administrators responsible for implementing and managing small- and medium-sized business networks. Network support staff who perform a help-desk role in a medium- or enterprise-sized company will find this a valuable resource. Finally, Cisco customers or channel resellers and network technicians entering the internetworking industry who are new to Cisco products can benefit from the contents of this book.

Goals

The goals of this book are twofold. First, it is intended as a self-study resource that covers the subjects on the 640-822 (ICND1) exam as well as the ICND1 material of the 640-802 (CCNA) exam. Second, like the certification itself, the book should help you become literate in the use of switches, routers, and the associated protocols and technologies. Using these skills, someone who completes the book and the CCNA certification should be able to select, connect, and configure Cisco devices in an internetworking environment. In particular, the book covers the basic steps and processes involved with moving data through the network using routing and Layer 2 switching.

> **NOTE** To become CCNA certified, you must pass separate ICND1 and ICND2 exams or pass a single CCNA exam that tests on the topics from both ICND1 and ICND2.

Readers interested in more information about the CCNA certification should consult the Cisco website at http://www.cisco.com/web/learning/index.html. To schedule a Cisco certification test, contact Pearson Vue on the web at http://www.pearsonvue.com/cisco/.

Chapter Organization

This book is divided into six chapters and is designed to be read in order because many chapters build on content from previous chapters.

- Chapter 1, "Building a Simple Network," describes the principles on which basic networks operate. This chapter helps build a foundational understanding that is used throughout the other chapters of the book.

- Chapter 2, "Ethernet LANs," explores the operation and configuration of LANs, including the challenges associated with these networks, and describes how network devices are used to eliminate these problems focusing on Layer 2 switching.

- Chapter 3, "Wireless LANs," describes how to extend the boundaries of network connectivity through wireless connectivity. It describes the business drivers and standards that affect wireless LAN implementation. It also discusses WLAN security issues and threat mitigation.

- Chapter 4, "LAN Connections," looks at how a router provides connectivity between the different networks in an internetwork. This chapter also describes IP addressing number conversion and basic routing configuration skills.

- Chapter 5, "WAN Connections," discusses the connectivity required for sites that are across wide geographic areas. It discusses interconnectivity using point-to-point links as well as DSL and cable services. The chapter also discusses how to configure Network Address Translation (NAT).

- Chapter 6, "Network Environment Management," discusses how to use Cisco IOS commands to determine the layout of a Cisco network topology. It also describes how to manage the router startup as well as how to work with IOS configuration files and Cisco IOS images.

- Appendix, "Answers to Chapter Review Questions," provides answers to the review questions at the end of each chapter.

Features

This book features actual router and switch output to aid in the discussion of the configuration of these devices. Many examples, illustrations, and notes are spread throughout the text. In addition, you can find many references to standards, documents, books, and websites to help you understand networking concepts. At the end of each chapter, your comprehension and knowledge are tested by review questions prepared by a certified Cisco Systems instructor.

> **NOTE** The operating system used in this book is Cisco IOS Software Release 12.4 for the routers, and Cisco Catalyst 2960 is based on Cisco IOS Software Release 12.2.

This chapter includes the following sections:

CHAPTER 1

Building a Simple Network

When you are building a network, the tasks and components can sometimes be overwhelming. The key to understanding how to build a computer network lies in understanding the foundations of network communications. The key to building a complex network involves gaining an understanding of the physical and logical components of a simple point-to-point network. To become proficient in networking, you must gain knowledge of why networks are built and the protocols used in modern network designs. This chapter explores the basics of networking and provides a solid foundation on which to build a comprehensive knowledge of networking technology.

Chapter Objectives

Upon completing this chapter, you will be able to create a simple point-to-point network and describe network components and functions. These abilities include meeting these objectives:

- Identify the benefits of computer networks and how they function

- Identify common threats to a network and threat-mitigation methods

- Identify and compare the Open System Interconnection (OSI) and TCP/IP layered models that control host-to-host communications

- Describe IP address classification and how a host can obtain an address

- Describe the process that TCP uses to establish a reliable connection

- Describe the host-to-host packet delivery process

- Describe how Ethernet operates at Layer 1 and Layer 2 of the OSI model

- Explain how to connect to an Ethernet LAN

Exploring the Functions of Networking

To understand how networks function, you need to become familiar with the basic elements of a network. This chapter explains networks by introducing fundamental computer and network concepts and the characteristics, functions, benefits, metrics, and attributes used to describe network features and performance. This chapter also introduces the Open System Interconnection (OSI) reference model, data communications terms and concepts, and the TCP/IP protocol, which serves as the de facto standard for most of today's computer networks. Finally, this chapter provides you with an opportunity to connect two PCs in a point-to-point serial network.

What Is a Network?

The first task in understanding how to build a computer network is defining what a network is and understanding how it is used to help a business meet its objectives. A network is a connected collection of devices and end systems, such as computers and servers, that can communicate with each other.

Networks carry data in many types of environments, including homes, small businesses, and large enterprises. In a large enterprise, a number of locations might need to communicate with each other, and you can describe those locations as follows:

■ **Main office:** A main office is a site where everyone is connected via a network and where the bulk of corporate information is located. A main office can have hundreds or even thousands of people who depend on network access to do their jobs. A main office might use several connected networks, which can span many floors in an office building or cover a campus that contains several buildings.

■ **Remote locations:** A variety of remote access locations use networks to connect to the main office or to each other.

— **Branch offices:** In branch offices, smaller groups of people work and communicate with each other via a network. Although some corporate information might be stored at a branch office, it is more likely that branch offices have local network resources, such as printers, but must access information directly from the main office.

— **Home offices:** When individuals work from home, the location is called a home office. Home office workers often require on-demand connections to the main or branch offices to access information or to use network resources such as file servers.

— **Mobile users:** Mobile users connect to the main office network while at the main office, at the branch office, or traveling. The network access needs of mobile users are based on where the mobile users are located.

Figure 1-1 shows some of the common locations of networks that can be used to connect users to business applications.

Figure 1-1 *Network Locations*

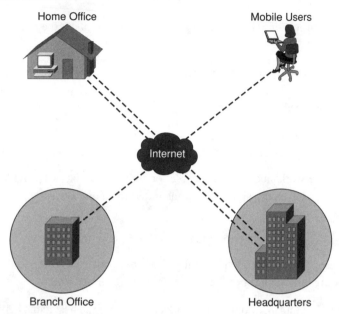

Many different types and locations of networks exist. You might use a network in your home or home office to communicate via the Internet, to locate information, to place orders for merchandise, and to send messages to friends. You might have work in a small office that is set up with a network that connects other computers and printers in the office. You might work in a large enterprise in which many computers, printers, storage devices, and servers communicate and store information from many departments over large geographic areas. All of these networks share many common components.

Common Physical Components of a Network

The physical components are the hardware devices that are interconnected to form a computer network. Depending on the size of the network, the number and size of these components varies, but most computer networks consist of the basic components shown in Figure 1-2.

Figure 1-2 *Common Network Components*

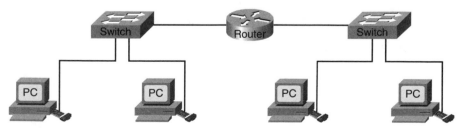

These are the four major categories of physical components in a computer network:

■ **Personal computers (PCs):** The PCs serve as endpoints in the network, sending and receiving data.

■ **Interconnections:** The interconnections consist of components that provide a means for data to travel from one point to another point in the network. This category includes components such as the following:

— Network interface cards (NICs) that translate the data produced by the computer into a format that can be transmitted over the local network

— Network media, such as cables or wireless media, that provide the means by which the signals are transmitted from one networked device to another

— Connectors that provide the connection points for the media

■ **Switches:** Switches are devices that provide network attachment to the end systems and intelligent switching of the data within the local network.

■ **Routers:** Routers interconnect networks and choose the best paths between networks.

Interpreting a Network Diagram

When designing and describing a computer network, you use a drawing or diagram to describe the physical components and how they are interconnected.

The network diagram uses common symbols to capture information related to the network for planning, reference, and troubleshooting purposes. The amount of information and the details of that information differ from organization to organization. The network topology is commonly represented by a series of lines and icons. Figure 1-3 shows a typical network diagram.

In this diagram:

■ A cloud represents the Internet or WAN connection.

■ A cylinder with arrows represents a router.

■ A rectangular box with arrows represents a workgroup switch.

■ A tower PC represents a server.

■ A laptop or computer and monitor represent an end user PC.

- A straight line represents an Ethernet link.

- A Z-shaped line represents a serial link.

Figure 1-3 *Typical Network Diagram*

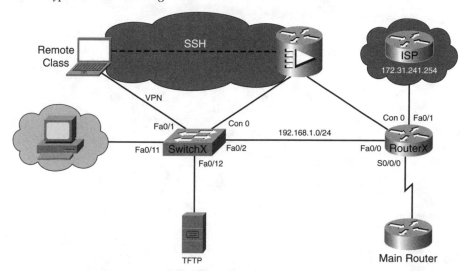

Other information can be included as space allows. For example, it is sometimes desirable to identify the interface on a device in the format of s0/0/0 for a serial interface or fa0/0 for a Fast Ethernet interface. It is also common to include the network address of the segment in the format such as 10.1.1.0/24, where 10.1.1.0 indicates the network address and /24 indicates the subnet mask.

Resource-Sharing Functions and Benefits

The main functions of computer networks in business today are to simplify and streamline business processes through the use of data and application sharing. Networks enable end users to share both information and hardware resources. By providing this interconnection between the users and common sets of data, businesses can make more efficient use of their resources. The major resources that are shared in a computer network include the following:

- **Data and applications:** When users are connected through a network, they can share files and even software application programs, making data more easily available and promoting more efficient collaboration on work projects.

- **Physical resources:** The resources that can be shared include both input devices, such as cameras, and output devices, such as printers.

■ **Network storage:** Today the network makes storage available to users in several ways. Direct attached storage (DAS) directly connects physical storage to a PC or a shared server. Network attached storage (NAS) makes storage available through a special network appliance. Finally, storage area networks (SAN) provide a network of storage devices.

■ **Backup devices:** A network can also include backup devices, such as tape drives, that provide a central means to save files from multiple computers. Network storage is also used to provide archive capability, business continuance, and disaster recovery.

Figure 1-4 shows some common shared resources.

Figure 1-4   *Shared Resources*

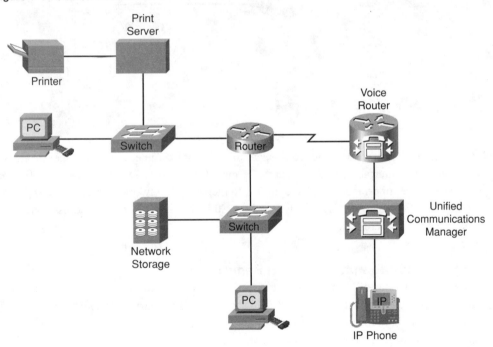

The overall benefit to users who are connected by a network is an efficiency of operation through commonly available components used in everyday tasks, sharing files, printing, and storing data. This efficiency results in reduced expenditures and increased productivity.

In recent years, the open access to devices that was once pervasive in networking has been replaced with a need for caution. There have been many well-advertised acts of "cyber vandalism," in which both end systems and network devices have been broken into; therefore, the need for network security has to be balanced with the need for connectivity.

Network User Applications

The key to utilizing multiple resources on a data network is having applications that are aware of these communication mechanisms. Although many applications are available for users in a network environment, some applications are common to nearly all users.

The most common network user applications include the following:

- **E-mail:** E-mail is a valuable application for most network users. Users can communicate information (messages and files) electronically in a timely manner, to not only other users in the same network but also other users outside the network (suppliers, information resources, and customers, for example). Examples of e-mail programs include Microsoft Outlook and Eudora by Qualcomm.

- **Web browser:** A web browser enables access to the Internet through a common interface. The Internet provides a wealth of information and has become vital to the productivity of both home and business users. Communicating with suppliers and customers, handling orders and fulfillment, and locating information are now routinely done electronically over the Internet, which saves time and increases overall productivity. The most commonly used browsers are Microsoft Internet Explorer, Netscape Navigator, Mozilla, and Firefox.

- **Instant messaging:** Instant messaging started in the personal user-to-user space; however, it soon provided considerable benefit in the corporate world. Now many instant messaging applications, such as those provided by AOL and Yahoo!, provide data encryption and logging, features essential for corporate use.

- **Collaboration:** Working together as individuals or groups is greatly facilitated when the collaborators are on a network. Individuals creating separate parts of an annual report or a business plan, for example, can either transmit their data files to a central resource for compilation or use a workgroup software application to create and modify the entire document, without any exchange of paper. One of the best-known traditional collaboration software programs is Lotus Notes. A more modern web-based collaboration application is a wiki.

- **Database:** This type of application enables users on a network to store information in central locations (such as storage devices) so that others on the network can easily retrieve selected information in the formats that are most useful to them. Some of the most common databases used in enterprises today are Oracle and Microsoft SQL Server.

The Impact of User Applications on the Network

The key to user applications is that they enable users to be connected to one another through the various types of software. As a business begins to rely on these applications as part of the day-to-day business process, the network that the applications operate in becomes a critical part of the business. A special relationship exists between these applications and the network. The applications can affect network performance, and network performance can affect applications. Therefore, you need to understand some common interactions between user applications and the network. Figure 1-5 characterizes some of the interactions for different types of applications.

Figure 1-5 *Application Interaction*

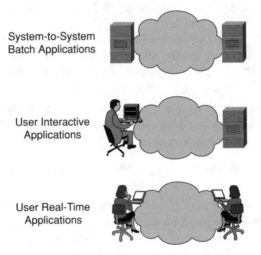

Historically, when the interaction between the network and the applications that ran on the network was considered, bandwidth was the main concern. Batch applications such as FTP, TFTP, and inventory updates, which simply used the network to transfer bulk data between systems, would be initiated by a user and then run to completion by the software with no further direct human interaction. Bandwidth was important but not critical because little human interaction occurred. As long as the time the application took to complete did not become excessive, no one really cared.

Interactive applications, such as Enterprise Resource Planning (ERP) software, perform tasks, such as inventory inquiries and database updates, that require more human interaction. The user requests some type of information from the server and then waits for a reply. With these types of applications, bandwidth becomes more important because users are intolerant of slow responses. However, application response is not solely dependant on the bandwidth of the network; the server and storage devices also play a part. However, in cases where the network becomes a problem, other features such as quality of service (QoS) can alleviate some bandwidth limitations by giving the traffic from interactive applications preference over batch applications.

Another type of application that can be affected heavily by the network is a real-time application. Like interactive applications, real-time applications such as Voice over IP (VoIP) and video applications involve human interaction. Because of the amount of information that is transmitted, bandwidth is critical. In addition, because these applications are time-critical, latency (delay through the network) is critical. Even variations in the amount of latency (jitter) can affect the application. Not only is proper bandwidth mandatory, but QoS is also mandatory. VoIP and video applications must be given the highest priority.

In today's environment, the end user is bombarded with ads indicating how much money can be saved by converting to VoIP and how installation is as easy as dropping a VoIP router into the network. Although this is often true in the home network, it can result in disaster in a small office network. Applications that used to work start to run so slowly that they are unusable, for example, when someone is on the phone, and voice quality is poor. This type of implementation does not provide enough bandwidth to the Internet, nor does it provide a proper QoS scheme.

Both issues can be overcome with proper network design.

Characteristics of a Network

Many characteristics are commonly used to describe and compare various network designs. When you are determining how to build a network, each of these characteristics must be considered along with the applications that will be running on the network. The key to building the best network is to achieve a balance of these characteristics.

Networks can be described and compared according to network performance and structure, as follows:

- **Speed:** Speed is a measure of how fast data is transmitted over the network. A more precise term would be data rate.

- **Cost:** Cost indicates the general cost of components, installation, and maintenance of the network.

- **Security:** Security indicates how secure the network is, including the data that is transmitted over the network. The subject of security is important and constantly evolving. You should consider security whenever you take actions that affect the network.

■   **Availability:** Availability is a measure of the probability that the network will be available for use when required. For networks that are meant to be used 24 hours a day, 7 days a week, 365 days a year, availability is calculated by dividing the time it is actually available by the total time in a year and then multiplying by 100 to get a percentage.

For example, if a network is unavailable for 15 minutes a year because of network outages, its percentage availability can be calculated as follows:

([Number of minutes in a year – downtime] / [Number of minutes in a year]) * 100 = Percentage availability

([525600 – 15] / [525600]) * 100 = 99.9971

■   **Scalability:** Scalability indicates how well the network can accommodate more users and data transmission requirements. If a network is designed and optimized for just the current requirements, it can be very expensive and difficult to meet new needs when the network grows.

■   **Reliability:** Reliability indicates the dependability of the components (routers, switches, PCs, and so on) that make up the network. Reliability is often measured as a probability of failure, or mean time between failures (MTBF).

■   **Topology:** Networks have two types of topologies: the physical topology, which is the arrangement of the cable, network devices, and end systems (PCs and servers), and the logical topology, which is the path that the data signals take through the physical topology.

These characteristics and attributes provide a means to compare different networking solutions. Increasingly, features such as security, availability, scalability, and reliability have become the focus of many network designs because of the importance of the network to the business process.

Physical Versus Logical Topologies

Building a reliable and scalable network depends on the physical and logical topology. Topology defines the interconnection method used between devices including the layout of the cabling and the primary and backup paths used in data transmissions. As previously mentioned, each type of network has both a physical and a logical topology.

Physical Topologies

The physical topology of a network refers to the physical layout of the devices and cabling. You must match the appropriate physical topology to the type of cabling that will be installed. Therefore, understanding the type of cabling used is important to understanding each type of physical topology. Here are the three primary categories of physical topologies:

■ **Bus:** Computers and other network devices are cabled together in a line.

■ **Ring:** Computers and other network devices are cabled together with the last device connected to the first to form a circle, or ring. This category includes both ring and dual-ring topologies.

■ **Star:** A central cabling device connects the computers and other network devices. This category includes both star and extended-star topologies.

Figure 1-6 shows some common physical topologies used in networking.

Figure 1-6 *Common Physical Topologies*

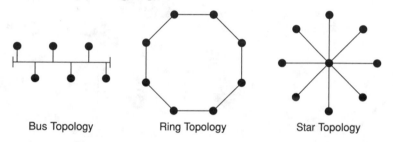

Bus Topology   Ring Topology   Star Topology

Logical Topologies

The logical topology of a network refers to the logical paths that the signals use to travel from one point on the network to another—that is, the way in which data accesses the network media and transmits packets across it.

The physical and logical topologies of a network can be the same. For example, in a network physically shaped as a linear bus, the data travels along the length of the cable. Therefore, the network has both a physical bus topology and a logical bus topology.

On the other hand, a network can have quite different physical and logical topologies. For example, a physical topology in the shape of a star, in which cable segments connect all computers to a central hub, can have a logical ring topology. Remember that in a ring, the data travels from one computer to the next, and inside the hub, the wiring connections are such that the signal actually travels around in a circle from one port to the next, creating a logical ring. Therefore, you cannot always predict how data travels in a network simply by observing its physical layout.

Star topology is by far the most common implementation of LANs today. Ethernet uses a logical bus topology in either a physical bus or a physical star. An Ethernet hub is an example of a physical star topology with a logical bus topology.

Figure 1-7 shows some common logical topologies used in networking.

Figure 1-7   *Common Logical Topologies*

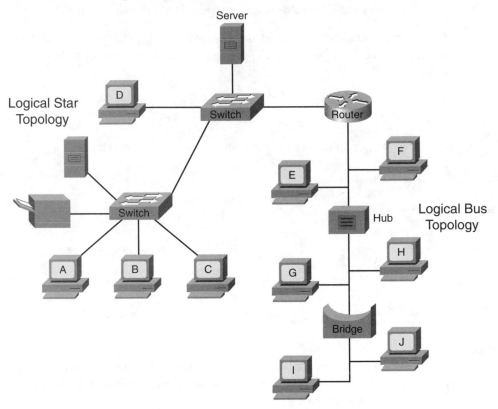

Bus Topology

The bus topology is commonly referred to as a linear bus; all of the devices on a bus topology are effectively connected by one single cable.

As illustrated in Figure 1-8, in a bus topology, a cable proceeds from one computer to the next like a bus line going through a city. The main cable segment must end with a terminator that absorbs the signal when it reaches the end of the line or wire. If no terminator exists, the electrical signal representing the data bounces back at the end of the wire, causing errors in the network. An example of a physical bus topology is a Thicknet Ethernet cable running through the length of a building with devices taped into it, though this is an antiquated connection method that is no longer used. An example of a logical bus topology is an Ethernet hub.

Figure 1-8   *Bus Topology*

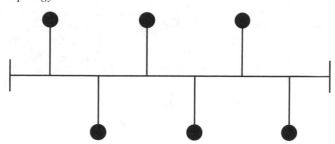

Star and Extended-Star Topologies

The star topology is the most common physical topology in Ethernet LANs. When a star network is expanded to include an additional network device that is connected to the main network devices, the topology is referred to as an extended-star topology. The following sections describe both the star and extended-star topologies.

Star Topology

When installed, the star topology resembles spokes in a bicycle wheel. It is made up of a central connection point that is a device, such as a hub, switch, or router, where all the cabling segments actually meet. Each device on the network is connected to the central device with its own cable.

Although a physical star topology costs more to implement than the physical bus topology, the advantages of a physical star topology make it worth the additional cost. Each device is connected to the central device with its own wire, so that if that cable has a problem, only that one device is affected, and the rest of the network remains operational. This benefit is important and is the reason why almost every newly designed Ethernet LAN has a physical star topology. Figure 1-9 depicts a star topology with all transmissions going through a single point.

Extended-Star Topology

A common deployment of an extended-star topology is in a hierarchical design such as a WAN or an Enterprise or a Campus LAN. Figure 1-10 shows the topology of an extended star.

Figure 1-9   *Star Topology*

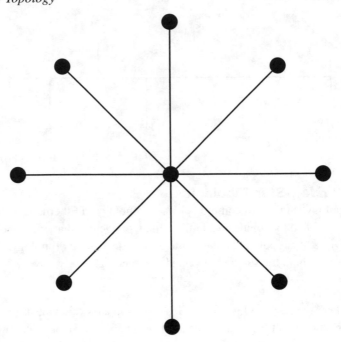

Figure 1-10   *Extended Star Topology*

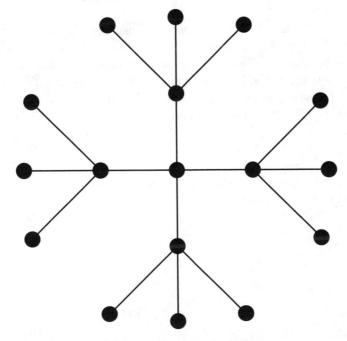

The problem with the pure extended-star topology is that if the central node point fails, large portions of the network can become isolated. For this reason, most extended-star topologies employ a redundant connection to a separate set of connection devices to prevent isolation in the event of a device failure.

Ring Topologies

As the name implies, in a ring topology all the devices on a network are connected in the form of a ring or circle. Unlike the physical bus topology, a ring type of topology has no beginning or end that needs to be terminated. Data is transmitted in a way that is different from the logical bus topology. In one implementation, a "token" travels around the ring, stopping at each device. If a device wants to transmit data, it adds that data and the destination address to the token. The token then continues around the ring until it finds the destination device, which takes the data out of the token. The advantage of using this type of method is that no collisions of data packets occur. Two types of ring topology exist: single-ring and dual-ring.

Single-Ring Topology

In a single-ring topology, all the devices on the network share a single cable, and the data travels in one direction only. Each device waits its turn to send data over the network. The single ring, however, is susceptible to a single failure, stopping the entire ring from functioning. Figure 1-11 shows the traffic flow in a single-ring topology.

Figure 1-11   *Traffic Flow in a Single-Ring Topology*

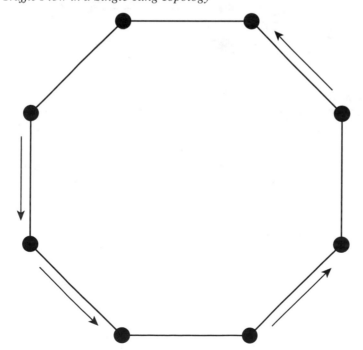

Dual-Ring Topology

In a dual-ring topology, two rings allow data to be sent in both directions. This setup creates redundancy (fault tolerance), meaning that if one ring fails, data can be transmitted on the other ring. Figure 1-12 shows the traffic flow in a typical dual-ring topology.

Figure 1-12   *Traffic Flow in a Dual-Ring Topology*

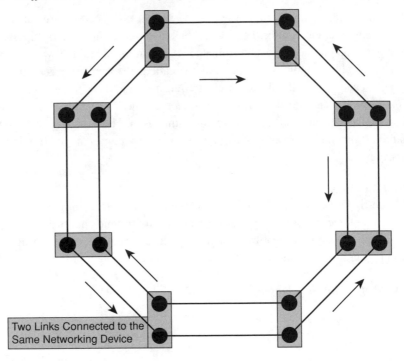

Mesh and Partial-Mesh Topologies

Another type of topology that is similar to the star topology is mesh topology. Mesh topology provides redundancy between devices in a star topology. A network can be fully meshed or partially meshed depending on the level of redundancy needed. This type of topology helps improve network availability and reliability. However, it increases cost and can limit scalability, so you need to exercise care when meshing.

Full-Mesh Topology

The full-mesh topology connects all devices (or nodes) to one another for redundancy and fault tolerance. Implementing a full-mesh topology is expensive and difficult. This method is the most resistant to failures because the failure of any single link does not affect reachability in the network.

Figure 1-13 shows the connections in a full-mesh topology.

Figure 1-13   *Full-Mesh Topology*

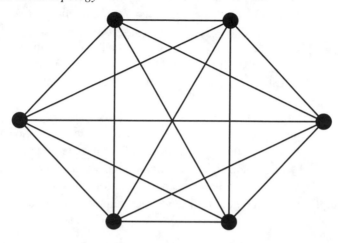

Partial-Mesh Topology

In a partial-mesh topology, at least one device maintains multiple connections to all other devices, without having all other devices fully meshed. This method trades off the cost of meshing all devices by allowing the network designer to choose which nodes are the most critical and appropriately interconnect them.

Figure 1-14 shows an example of a partial-mesh topology.

Figure 1-14   *Partial-Mesh Topology*

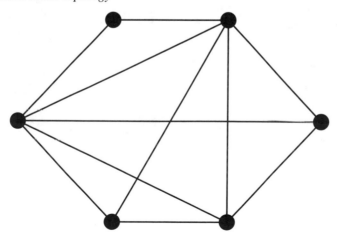

Connection to the Internet

Another key component for most business users today is a connection to the Internet. An Internet connection is a WAN connection, but small- to medium-sized computer networks can use various methods and topologies to interconnect to the Internet.

You have three common methods of connecting the small office to the Internet. Digital subscriber line (DSL) uses the existing telephone lines as the infrastructure to carry the signal. Cable uses the cable television (CATV) infrastructure. Serial uses the classic digital local loops.

In the case of DSL and cable, the incoming lines are terminated into a modem that converts the incoming digital encoding into a digital format for the router to process. In the case of serial this is done by channel service unit (CSU)/digital service unit (DSU). In all three cases (DSL, cable, and serial), the digital output is sent to a router that is part of the customer premises equipment (CPE). Figure 1-15 shows the equipment placement for these different connection methods.

Figure 1-15 *Common Internet Connections Methods*

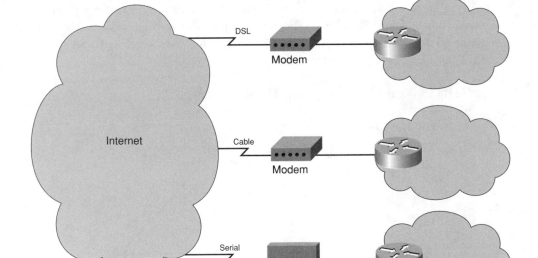

Summary of Exploring the Functions of Networking

The key purpose of this section was to get a basic understanding of the key components in a computer network and how the network is used by business. The main points are as follows:

- A network is a connected collection of computing devices that communicate with each other to carry data in homes, small businesses, and enterprise environments.

- You have four major categories of physical components in a computer network: the computer, interconnections, switches, and routers.

- The major resources that are shared in a computer network include data and applications, physical resources, storage devices, and backup devices.

- The most common network user applications include e-mail, web browsers, instant messaging, collaboration, and databases.

- The terms that describe networks include characteristics around network performance and structure such as speed, cost, security, availability, scalability, reliability, and topology.

- A physical topology describes the layout for wiring the physical devices, while a logical topology describes how information flows to devices within the networks.

- In a physical bus topology, a single cable connects all the devices together.

- In a physical star topology, each device in the network is connected to central device with its own cable.

- When a star network is expanded to include additional networking devices that are connected to the main networking device, it is called an extended-star topology.

- In a ring topology, all the hosts are connected to one another in the form of a ring or circle. A dual-ring topology provides a second ring for redundancy.

- A full-mesh topology connects all devices to each other for redundancy, while a partial-mesh topology provides multiple connections for only some devices.

Securing the Network

Security is a fundamental component of every network design. When planning, building, and operating a network, you should understand the importance of a strong security policy. How important is it to have a strong network security policy? The Computer Security Institute (CSI) produced a report from the "Computer Crime and Security Survey" that provided an updated look at the impact of computer crime in the United States. One of the major participants was the San Francisco Federal Bureau of Investigation (FBI) Computer Intrusion Squad. Based on responses from over 700 computer security practitioners in U.S. corporations, government agencies, financial institutions, medical institutions, and universities, the survey confirms that the threat from computer crime and other information security breaches continues unabated and that the financial toll is mounting.

The application of an effective security policy is the most important step that an organization must take to protect itself. An effective security policy is the foundation for all of the activities undertaken to secure network resources.

Need for Network Security

In the past, hackers were highly skilled programmers who understood the intricacies of computer communications and how to exploit vulnerabilities. Today almost anyone can become a hacker by downloading tools from the Internet. These sophisticated attack tools and generally open networks have generated an increased need for network security and dynamic security policies.

The easiest way to protect a network from an outside attack is to close it off completely from the outside world. A closed network provides connectivity only to trusted known parties and sites; a closed network does not allow a connection to public networks. Figure 1-16 shows an example of a closed network.

Because they have no Internet connectivity, networks designed in this way can be considered safe from Internet attacks. However, internal threats still exist. The CSI in San Francisco, California, estimates that 60 to 80 percent of network misuse comes from inside the enterprise where the misuse has taken place.

Today, corporate networks require access to the Internet and other public networks. Most of these networks have several access points to public and other private networks, as shown in Figure 1-17. Securing open networks is important.

Figure 1-16 *Closed Network*

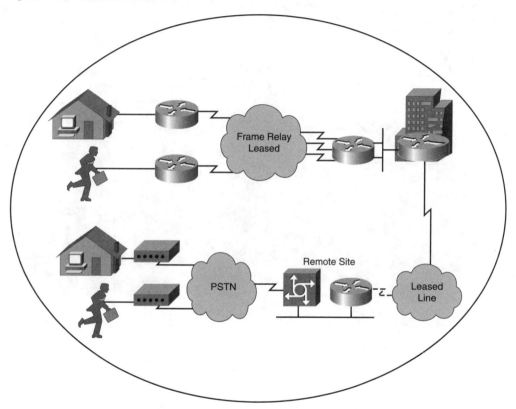

As previously mentioned, one of the challenges to security is that hacking a network has become easier for those with little or no computer skills. Figure 1-18 illustrates how the increasing sophistication of hacking tools and the decreasing skill needed to use these tools have combined to pose increasing threats to open networks.

Figure 1-17 *Open Network*

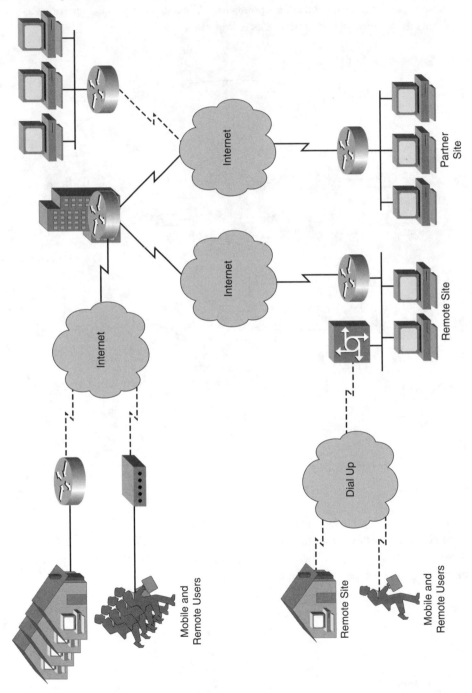

Figure 1-18 *Hacking Skills Matrix*

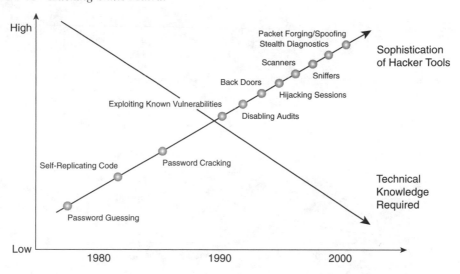

With the development of large open networks, security threats have increased significantly in the past 20 years. Hackers have discovered more network vulnerabilities, and because you can now download applications that require little or no hacking knowledge to implement, applications intended for troubleshooting and maintaining and optimizing networks can, in the wrong hands, be used maliciously and pose severe threats.

Balancing Network Security Requirements

The overall security challenge is to find a balance between two important needs: open networks to support evolving business requirements and freedom-of-information initiatives versus the protection of private, personal, and strategic business information. Figure 1-19 shows the relationship between expanding the business value and increasing security risks.

Security has moved to the forefront of network management and implementation. The survival of many businesses depends on allowing open access to network resources and ensuring that data and resources are as secure as possible. The escalating importance of e-business and the need for private data to traverse potentially unsafe public networks both increase the need for the development and implementation of a corporate-wide network security policy. Establishing a network security policy should be the first step in changing a network over to a secure infrastructure.

Figure 1-19 *Security Challenge*

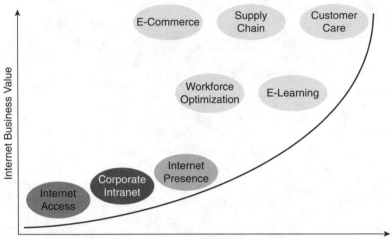

The Internet has created expectations for a company to build stronger relationships with customers, suppliers, partners, and employees. E-business challenges companies to become more agile and competitive. The benefit of this challenge is that new applications for e-commerce, supply chain management, customer care, workforce optimization, and e-learning have been created. These applications streamline and improve processes, lowering costs while increasing turnaround times and user satisfaction.

As enterprise network managers open their networks to more users and applications, they also expose the networks to greater risks. The result has been an increase in business security requirements. Security must be included as a fundamental component of any e-business strategy.

E-business requires mission-critical networks that can accommodate ever-increasing constituencies and ever-increasing demands on capacity and performance. These networks also need to handle voice, video, and data traffic as networks converge into multiservice environments.

Adversaries, Hacker Motivations, and Classes of Attack

To defend against attacks on information and information systems, organizations must define the threat in these three terms:

- **Adversaries:** Potential adversaries might include nation-states, terrorists, criminals, hackers, disgruntled employees, and corporate competitors.

- **Hacker motivations:** Hackers' motivations might include intelligence gathering, the theft of intellectual property, denial of service (DoS), the embarrassment of the company or clients, or the challenge of exploiting a notable target.

- **Classes of attack:** Classes of attack might include passive monitoring of communications, active network attacks, close-in attacks, exploitation by insiders, and attacks through the service provider.

Information systems and networks offer attractive targets and should be resistant to attack from the full range of threat agents, from hackers to nation-states. A system must be able to limit damage and recover rapidly when attacks occur.

Classes of Attack

There are five classes of attack:

- **Passive:** Passive attacks include traffic analysis, monitoring of unprotected communications, decrypting weakly encrypted traffic, and capturing authentication information such as passwords. Passive interception of network operations enables adversaries to see upcoming actions. Passive attacks result in the disclosure of information or data files to an attacker without the consent or knowledge of the user. Examples include the disclosure of personal information such as credit card numbers and medical files.

- **Active:** Active attacks include attempts to circumvent or break protection features, to introduce malicious code, and to steal or modify information. These attacks are mounted against a network backbone, exploit information in transit, electronically penetrate an enclave, or attack an authorized remote user during an attempt to connect to an enclave. Active attacks result in the disclosure or dissemination of data files, DoS, or modification of data.

- **Close-in:** Close-in attacks consist of regular individuals attaining close physical proximity to networks, systems, or facilities for the purpose of modifying, gathering, or denying access to information. Close physical proximity is achieved through surreptitious entry into the network, open access, or both.

- **Insider:** Insider attacks can be malicious or nonmalicious. Malicious insiders intentionally eavesdrop, steal, or damage information; use information in a fraudulent manner; or deny access to other authorized users. Nonmalicious attacks typically result from carelessness, lack of knowledge, or intentional circumvention of security for such reasons as performing a task.

- **Distributed:** Distribution attacks focus on the malicious modification of hardware or software at the factory or during distribution. These attacks introduce malicious code such as a back door to a product to gain unauthorized access to information or to a system function at a later date.

Mitigating Common Threats

Improper and incomplete network device installation is an often-overlooked security threat that, if left unaddressed, can have dire results. Software-based security measures alone cannot prevent premeditated or even accidental network damage caused by poor installation. The following sections describe how to mitigate common security threats to Cisco routers and switches.

Physical Installations

Hardware threats involve threats of physical damage to the router or switch hardware. Mission-critical Cisco network equipment should be located in wiring closets or in computer or telecommunications rooms that meet these minimum requirements:

- The room must be locked with only authorized personnel allowed access.

- The room should not be accessible via a dropped ceiling, raised floor, window, ductwork, or point of entry other than the secured access point.

- If possible, use electronic access control with all entry attempts logged by security systems and monitored by security personnel.

- If possible, security personnel should monitor activity via security cameras with automatic recording.

Environmental threats, such as temperature extremes (too hot or too cold) or humidity extremes (too wet or too dry), also require mitigation. Take these actions to limit environmental damage to Cisco network devices:

- Supply the room with dependable temperature and humidity control systems. Always verify the recommended environmental parameters of the Cisco network equipment with the supplied product documentation.

- Remove any sources of electrostatic and magnetic interference in the room.

- If possible, remotely monitor and alarm the environmental parameters of the room.

Electrical threats, such as voltage spikes, insufficient supply voltage (brownouts), unconditioned power (noise), and total power loss, can be limited by adhering to these guidelines:

- Install uninterruptible power supply (UPS) systems for mission-critical Cisco network devices.

- Install backup generator systems for mission-critical supplies.

- Plan for and initiate regular UPS or generator testing and maintenance procedures based on the manufacturer-suggested preventative maintenance schedule.

- Install redundant power supplies on critical devices.

- Monitor and alarm power-related parameters at the power supply and device levels.

Maintenance threats include poor handling of key electronic components, electrostatic discharge (ESD), lack of critical spares, poor cabling, poor labeling, and so on. Maintenance-related threats are a broad category that includes many items. Follow the general rules listed here to prevent maintenance-related threats:

- Clearly label all equipment cabling and secure the cabling to equipment racks to prevent accidental damage, disconnection, or incorrect termination.

- Use cable runs, raceways, or both to traverse rack-to-ceiling or rack-to-rack connections.

- Always follow ESD procedures when replacing or working with internal router and switch device components.

- Maintain a stock of critical spares for emergency use.

- Do not leave a console connected to and logged into any console port. Always log off administrative interfaces when leaving a station.

- Do not rely upon a locked room as the only necessary protection for a device. Always remember that no room is ever totally secure. After intruders are inside a secure room, nothing is left to stop them from connecting a terminal to the console port of a Cisco router or switch.

Reconnaissance Attacks

Reconnaissance is the unauthorized discovery and mapping of systems, services, or vulnerabilities. Reconnaissance is also known as information gathering and, in most cases, precedes an actual access or DoS attack. First, the malicious intruder typically conducts a ping sweep of the target network to determine which IP addresses are alive. Then the intruder determines which services or ports are active on the live IP addresses. From this information, the intruder queries the ports to determine the type and version of the application and operating system running on the target host.

Reconnaissance is somewhat analogous to a thief investigating a neighborhood for vulnerable homes, such as an unoccupied residence or a house with an easy-to-open door or window. In many cases, intruders look for vulnerable services that they can exploit later when less likelihood that anyone is looking exists.

Access Attacks

Access attacks exploit known vulnerabilities in authentication services, FTP services, and web services to gain entry to web accounts, confidential databases, and other sensitive information.

Password Attacks

A password attack usually refers to repeated attempts to identify a user account, password, or both. These repeated attempts are called brute-force attacks. Password attacks are implemented using other methods, too, including Trojan horse programs, IP spoofing, and packet sniffers.

A security risk lies in the fact that passwords are stored as plaintext. You need to encrypt passwords to overcome risks. On most systems, passwords are processed through an encryption algorithm that generates a one-way hash on passwords. You cannot reverse a one-way hash back to its original text. Most systems do not decrypt the stored password during authentication; they store the one-way hash. During the login process, you supply an account and password, and the password encryption algorithm generates a one-way hash. The algorithm compares this hash to the hash stored on the system. If the hashes are the same, the algorithm assumes that the user supplied the proper password.

Remember that passing the password through an algorithm results in a password hash. The hash is not the encrypted password, but rather a result of the algorithm. The strength of the hash is that the hash value can be recreated only with the original user and password information and that retrieving the original information from the hash is impossible. This strength makes hashes perfect for encoding passwords for storage. In granting authorization, the hashes, rather than the plain password, are calculated and compared.

Password attack threat-mitigation methods include these guidelines:

■ Do not allow users to have the same password on multiple systems. Most users have the same password for each system they access, as well as for their personal systems.

■ Disable accounts after a specific number of unsuccessful logins. This practice helps to prevent continuous password attempts.

■ Do not use plaintext passwords. Use either a one-time password (OTP) or an encrypted password.

■ Use strong passwords. Strong passwords are at least eight characters long and contain uppercase letters, lowercase letters, numbers, and special characters. Many systems now provide strong password support and can restrict users to strong passwords only.

Summary of Securing the Network

Security is an important part of any computer network. When you are building a network, a strong security policy should be part of the foundation. The following items represent a summary of considerations for building a strong security policy:

- Sophisticated attack tools and open networks continue to generate an increased need for network security policies and infrastructure to protect organizations from internally and externally based attacks.

- Organizations must balance network security needs against e-business processes, legal issues, and government policies. Establishing a network security policy is the first step in changing a network over to a secure infrastructure.

- The strategy of information assurance affects network architecture.

- Providing physical installation security for network devices is very important.

- Network devices should be protected against password attacks through controlled access methods and strong passwords.

References

For additional information regarding network security, refer to these resources:

- Much of the material in this lesson comes from readily available documents provided by many government agencies.

- The Information Assurance Technical Framework Forum (IATFF) is a National Security Agency (NSA)–sponsored outreach activity created to foster dialog aimed at seeking solutions for information assurance problems. The IATFF website can be found at http://www.iatf.net.

Understanding the Host-to-Host Communications Model

The Open Systems Interconnection (OSI) reference model was created to help define how network processes function in general, including the various components of networks and transmission of data. Understanding the structure and purpose of the OSI model is central to understanding how one host communicates with another. This section introduces the OSI model and describes each of its layers. Remember that this is a reference model to provide a framework for building protocols and to help people understand the process around network communications and not a communications standard in itself.

> **NOTE**   This section is a discussion of the OSI reference model and not the OSI protocol.

No matter what type of connectivity, operating system, or network services interconnect computers and computer networks, the fact still remains that for these devices to communicate, some rules must exist. Like any system of communication, rules govern how the communication must take place. Also, some medium for the communication to take place over exists. For example, a language has rules for the formation of sentences using basic words. This language can be used for verbal communication, using air as the medium, or written communication, using paper as the medium.

Most languages have rules that specify how words are put together and then how they are spoken or written. In many western languages, words are written from left to right, but in some eastern languages words are written from right to left or even top to bottom. To be able to effectively communicate, you must understand how to read the words and in what order to read them.

Many of the computers and operating systems within an organization are manufactured by different companies and use different types of programs to operate; however, if these systems are going to communicate with one another, they must use a common set of rules for data communications. The rules that define how systems talk to one another are called *protocols.*

Many internetworking protocols can be used to establish communications paths between systems, and each of these protocols provides very similar functions. To provide a way to establish some common and open rules for building a data communications protocol, the International Organization for Standardization (ISO) created the OSI reference model.

The following sections describe the purpose of the OSI reference model and the TCP/IP protocol stack. You also learn how the OSI reference model facilitates data communication.

OSI Reference Model

The OSI reference model is the primary model for network communications. The early development of LANs, MANs, and WANs was chaotic in many ways. The early 1980s saw tremendous increases in the number and sizes of networks. As companies realized that they could save money and gain productivity by using networking technology, they added networks and expanded existing networks as rapidly as new network technologies and products were introduced.

By the mid-1980s, companies began to experience difficulties from all the expansions they had made. It became more difficult for networks using different specifications and implementations to communicate with each other. The companies realized that they needed to move away from proprietary networking systems, those systems that are privately developed, owned, and controlled.

> **NOTE** In the computer industry, proprietary is the opposite of open. Proprietary means that one company or a small group of companies controls all usage of the technology. Open means that free usage of the technology is available to the public.

To address the problem of networks being incompatible and unable to communicate with each other, the ISO researched different network schemes. As a result of this research, the ISO created a model that would help vendors create networks that would be compatible with, and operate with, other networks.

The OSI reference model, released in 1984, was the descriptive scheme that the ISO created. It provided vendors with a set of standards that ensured greater compatibility and interoperability between the various types of network technologies produced by companies around the world. Although other models exist, most network vendors today relate their products to the OSI reference model, especially when they want to educate customers on the use of their products. The OSI model is considered the best tool available for teaching people about sending and receiving data on a network.

The OSI reference model has seven layers, as shown in Figure 1-20, each illustrating a particular network function. This separation of networking functions is called layering. The OSI reference model defines the network functions that occur at each layer. More importantly, the OSI reference model facilitates an understanding of how information travels throughout a network. In addition, the OSI reference model describes how data travels from application programs (for example, spreadsheets), through a network medium, to an application program located in another computer, even if the sender and receiver are connected using different network media.

Figure 1-20 *OSI Reference Model*

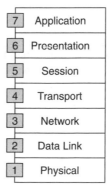

Dividing the network into these seven layers provides these advantages:

- **Reduces complexity**: It breaks network communication into smaller, simpler parts.

- **Standardizes interfaces**: It standardizes network components to allow multiple vendor development and support.

- **Facilitates modular engineering**: It allows different types of network hardware and software to communicate with each other.

- **Ensures interoperable technology**: It prevents changes in one layer from affecting the other layers, allowing for quicker development.

- **Accelerates evolution**: It provides for effective updates and improvements to individual components without affecting other components or having to rewrite the entire protocol.

- **Simplifies teaching and learning**: It breaks network communication into smaller components to make learning easier.

The practice of moving information between computers is divided into seven techniques in the OSI reference model.

Each OSI layer contains a set of functions performed by programs to enable data to travel from a source to a destination on a network. The following sections provide brief descriptions of each layer in the OSI reference model.

Layer 7: The Application Layer

The application layer is the OSI layer that is closest to the user. This layer provides network services to the user's applications. It differs from the other layers in that it does not provide services to any other OSI layer, but only to applications outside the OSI reference model. The application layer establishes the availability of intended communication partners and synchronizes and establishes agreement on procedures for error recovery and control of data integrity.

Layer 6: The Presentation Layer

The presentation layer ensures the information that the application layer of one system sends out is readable by the application layer of another system. For example, a PC program communicates with another computer, one using extended binary coded decimal interchange code (EBCDIC) and the other using ASCII to represent the same characters. If necessary, the presentation layer might be able to translate between multiple data formats by using a common format.

Layer 5: The Session Layer

The session layer establishes, manages, and terminates sessions between two communicating hosts. It provides its services to the presentation layer. The session layer also synchronizes dialogue between the presentation layers of the two hosts and manages their data exchange. For example, web servers have many users, so many communication processes are open at a given time. Therefore, keeping track of which user communicates on which path is important. In addition to session regulation, the session layer offers provisions for efficient data transfer, class of service, and exception reporting of session layer, presentation layer, and application layer problems.

Layer 4: The Transport Layer

The transport layer segments data from the sending host's system and reassembles the data into a data stream on the receiving host's system. For example, business users in large corporations often transfer large files from field locations to a corporate site. Reliable delivery of the files is important, so the transport layer breaks down large files into smaller segments that are less likely to incur transmission problems.

The boundary between the transport layer and the session layer can be thought of as the boundary between application protocols and data-flow protocols. Whereas the application, presentation, and session layers are concerned with application issues, the lower four layers are concerned with data-transport issues.

The transport layer attempts to provide a data-transport service that shields the upper layers from transport implementation details. Specifically, issues such as reliability of transport between two hosts are the concern of the transport layer. In providing communication service, the transport layer establishes, maintains, and properly terminates virtual circuits. Transport error detection and recovery and information flow control provide reliable service.

Layer 3: The Network Layer

The network layer provides connectivity and path selection between two host systems that might be located on geographically separated networks. The growth of the Internet has increased the number of users accessing information from sites around the world, and the network layer manages this connectivity.

Layer 2: The Data Link Layer

The data link layer defines how data is formatted for transmission and how access to the network is controlled. This layer is responsible for defining how devices on a common media communicate with one another, including addressing and control signaling between devices.

Layer 1: The Physical Layer

The physical layer defines the electrical, mechanical, procedural, and functional specifications for activating, maintaining, and deactivating the physical link between end systems. Characteristics such as voltage levels, timing of voltage changes, physical data rates, maximum transmission distances, physical connectors, and other similar attributes are defined by physical layer specifications.

Data Communications Process

All communications on a network originate at a source and are sent to a destination. A networking protocol using all or some of the layers listed in the OSI reference model move data between devices. Recall that Layer 7 is the part of the protocol that communicates with the application, and Layer 1 is the part of a protocol that communicates with the media. A data frame is able to travel across a computer network because of the layers of the protocol. The process of moving data from one device in a network is accomplished by passing information from applications down the protocol stack, adding an appropriate header at each layer of the model. This method of passing data down the stack and adding headers and trailers is called encapsulation. After the data is encapsulated and passed across the network, the receiving device removes the information added, using the messages in the header as directions as to how to pass the data up the stack to the appropriate application.

Data encapsulation is an important concept to networks. It is the function of like layers on each device, called *peer layers*, to communicate critical parameters such as addressing and control information.

Although encapsulation seems like an abstract concept, it is actually quite simple. Imagine that you want to send a coffee mug to a friend in another city. How will the mug get there? Basically, it will be transported on the road or through the air. You can't go outside and set the mug on the road or throw it up in the air and expect it to get there. You need a service to pick it up and deliver it. So, you call your favorite parcel carrier and give them the mug. But, that's not all. Here's the complete process:

Step 1 Pack the mug in a box.

Step 2 Place an address label on the box so the carrier knows where to deliver it.

Step 3 Give the box to a parcel carrier.

Step 4 The carrier drives it down the road toward its final destination.

This process is similar to the encapsulation method that protocol stacks use to send data across networks. After the package arrives, your friend has to reverse the process. He takes the package from the carrier, reads the label to see who it's from, and finally opens the box and removes the mug. The reverse of the encapsulation process is known as de-encapsulation. The next sections describe the encapsulation and de-encapsulation processes.

Encapsulation

As indicated in the previous section, encapsulation on a data network is similar to the process of sending that mug. However, instead of sending a coffee mug to a friend, you send information from an application from one device to another. The information sent on a network is referred to as data or data packets.

Encapsulation wraps data with the necessary protocol information before network transit. Therefore, as the data moves down through the layers of the OSI reference model, each OSI layer adds a header (and a trailer, if applicable) to the data before passing it down to a lower layer. The headers and trailers contain control information for the network devices and receiver to ensure proper delivery of the data and to ensure that the receiver can correctly interpret the data.

Figure 1-21 illustrates how encapsulation occurs. It shows the manner in which data travels through the layers. These steps occur to encapsulate data:

Step 1   The user data is sent from an application to the application layer.

Step 2   The application layer adds the application layer header (Layer 7 header) to the user data. The Layer 7 header and the original user data become the data that is passed down to the presentation layer.

Step 3   The presentation layer adds the presentation layer header (Layer 6 header) to the data. This then becomes the data that is passed down to the session layer.

Step 4   The session layer adds the session layer header (Layer 5 header) to the data. This then becomes the data that is passed down to the transport layer.

Step 5   The transport layer adds the transport layer header (Layer 4 header) to the data. This then becomes the data that is passed down to the network layer.

Step 6   The network layer adds the network layer header (Layer 3 header) to the data. This then becomes the data that is passed down to the data link layer.

Step 7   The data link layer adds the data link layer header and trailer (Layer 2 header and trailer) to the data. A Layer 2 trailer is usually the frame check sequence (FCS), which is used by the receiver to detect whether the data is in error. This then becomes the data that is passed down to the physical layer.

Step 8   The physical layer then transmits the bits onto the network media as defined by the media type.

Figure 1-21   *Data Encapsulation*

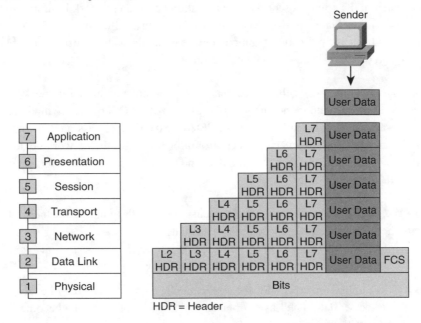

HDR = Header

De-Encapsulation

When the remote device receives a sequence of bits, the physical layer at the remote device passes the bits to the data link layer for manipulation. The data link layer performs the following process, referred to as de-encapsulation:

Step 1   It checks the data link trailer (the FCS) to see if the data is in error.

Step 2   If the data is in error, it is discarded.

Step 3   If the data is not in error, the data link layer reads and interprets the control information in the data link header.

Step 4   It strips the data link header and trailer and then passes the remaining data up to the network layer based on the control information in the data link header.

Each subsequent layer performs a similar de-encapsulation process, as shown in Figure 1-22.

Think of de-encapsulation as the process of reading the address on a package to see whether it is for you and then opening and removing the contents of the package if it is addressed to you.

Figure 1-22 *De-Encapsulation*

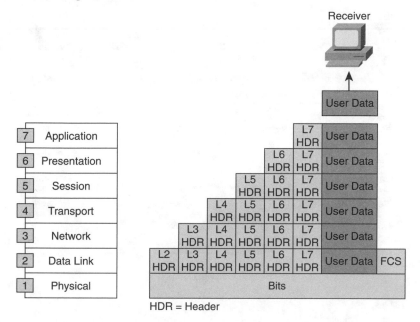

HDR = Header

Peer-to-Peer Communication

For data to travel from the source to the destination, each layer of the OSI reference model at the source must communicate with its peer layer at the destination. This form of communication is referred to as *peer-to-peer communication*. During this process, the protocols at each layer exchange information, called *protocol data units (PDU)*, between peer layers, as shown in Figure 1-23.

Data packets on a network originate at a source and then travel to a destination. Each layer depends on the service function of the OSI layer below it. To provide this service, the lower layer uses encapsulation to put the PDU from the upper layer into its data field. It then adds whatever headers the layer needs to perform its function. As the data moves down through Layers 7 through 5 of the OSI reference model, additional headers are added. The grouping of data at the Layer 4 PDU is called a segment.

The network layer provides a service to the transport layer, and the transport layer presents data to the internetwork subsystem. The network layer moves the data through the internetwork by encapsulating the data and attaching a header to create a datagram (the Layer 3 PDU). The header contains information required to complete the transfer, such as source and destination logical addresses.

Figure 1-23   *Peer-to-Peer Communication*

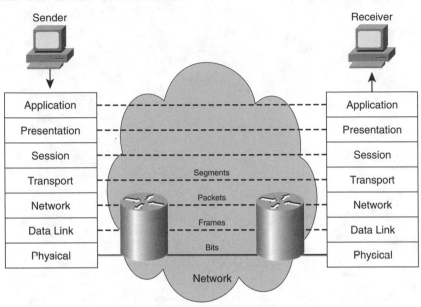

The data link layer provides a service to the network layer by encapsulating the network layer datagram in a frame (the Layer 2 PDU). The frame header contains the physical addresses required to complete the data link functions, and the frame trailer contains the FCS.

The physical layer provides a service to the data link layer, encoding the data link frame into a pattern of 1s and 0s (bits) for transmission on the medium (usually a wire) at Layer 1.

Network devices such as hubs, switches, and routers work at the lower three layers. Hubs are at Layer 1, switches are at Layer 2, and routers are at Layer 3.

The TCP/IP Protocol Stack

The TCP/IP suite is a layered model similar to the OSI reference model. Its name is actually a combination of two individual protocols, Transmission Control Protocol (TCP) and Internet Protocol (IP). It is divided into layers, each of which performs specific functions in the data communication process.

Both the OSI model and the TCP/IP stack were developed by different organizations at approximately the same time as a means to organize and communicate the components that guide the transmission of data.

Although the OSI reference model is universally recognized, the historical and technical open standard of the Internet is the TCP/IP protocol stack. The TCP/IP protocol stack, shown in Figure 1-24, varies slightly from the OSI reference model.

Figure 1-24 *TCP/IP Protocol Stack*

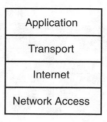

The TCP/IP protocol stack has four layers. Note that although some of the layers in the TCP/IP protocol stack have the same names as layers in the OSI reference model, the layers have different functions in each model, as is described in the following list:

■ **Application layer**: The application layer handles high-level protocols, including issues of representation, encoding, and dialog control. The TCP/IP model combines all application-related issues into one layer and ensures that this data is properly packaged for the next layer.

■ **Transport layer**: The transport layer deals with QoS issues of reliability, flow control, and error correction. One of its protocols, TCP, provides for reliable network communications.

■ **Internet layer**: The purpose of the Internet layer is to send source datagrams from any network on the internetwork and have them arrive at the destination, regardless of the path they took to get there.

■ **Network access layer**: The name of this layer is broad and somewhat confusing. It is also called the host-to-network layer. It includes the LAN and WAN protocols and all the details in the OSI physical and data link layers.

OSI Model Versus TCP/IP Stack

Both similarities and differences exist between the TCP/IP protocol stack and the OSI reference model. Figure 1-25 offers a side-by-side comparison of the two models.

Similarities between the TCP/IP protocol stack and the OSI reference model include the following:

■ Both have application layers, though they include different services.

■ Both have comparable transport and network layers.

■ Both assume packet-switched technology, not circuit-switched. (Analog telephone calls are an example of circuit-switched technology.)

Figure 1-25   *OSI Model Versus TCP/IP*

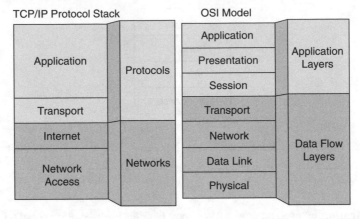

The differences that exist between the TCP/IP protocol stack and the OSI reference model include the following:

■   TCP/IP combines the presentation and session layers into its application layer.

■   TCP/IP combines the OSI data link and physical layers into the network access layer.

TCP/IP protocols are the standards around which the Internet developed, so the TCP/IP protocol stack gains credibility just because of its protocols. In contrast, networks are not typically built on the OSI reference model, even though the OSI reference model is used as a guide.

Summary of Understanding the Host-to-Host Communications Model

This following summarizes the host-to-host communications model key points:

■   The OSI reference model defines the network functions that occur at each layer.

■   The physical layer defines the electrical, mechanical, procedural, and functional specifications for activating, maintaining, and deactivating the physical link between end systems.

■   The data link layer defines how data is formatted for transmission.

■   The network layer provides connectivity and path selection between two host systems that might be located on geographically separated networks.

■   The transport layer segments data from the system of the sending host and reassembles the data into a data stream on the system of the receiving host.

- The session layer establishes, manages, and terminates sessions between two communicating hosts.

- The presentation layer ensures that the information sent at the application layer of one system is readable by the application layer of another system.

- The application layer provides network services, such as e-mail, file transfer, and web services, to applications of the users.

- The information sent on a network is referred to as data or data packets. If one computer wants to send data to another computer, the data must first be packaged by a process called encapsulation.

- When the remote device receives a sequence of bits, the physical layer at the remote devices passes the bits of data up the protocol stack for manipulation. This process is referred to as de-encapsulation.

- TCP/IP is now the most widely used protocol for a number of reasons, including its flexible addressing scheme, usability by most operating systems and platforms, its many tools and utilities, and the need to be connected to the Internet.

- The components of the TCP/IP stack are the network access, Internet, transport, and application layers.

- The OSI reference model and the TCP/IP stack are similar in structure and function, with correlation at the physical, data link, network, and transport layers. The OSI reference model divides the application layer of the TCP/IP stack into three separate layers.

Understanding TCP/IP's Internet Layer

Among the protocols included in the TCP/IP protocol stack are a network layer protocol and a transport layer protocol. The internetworking layer handles the routing of packets of data by using IP addresses to identify each device on the network. Each computer, router, printer, or any other device attached to a network has its own unique IP address that routes packets of data.

Each IP address has a specific structure, and various classes of IP addresses exist. In addition, subnetworks and subnet masks play a role in IP addressing schemes, and different routing functions and protocols are involved in transmitting data from one network node to another using IP addresses.

The various aspects of IP addressing include calculations for constructing an IP address, classes of IP addresses designated for specific routing purposes, and public versus private

IP addresses. Also, two different types of IP addresses exist: IP version 4 (IPv4) and IP version 6 (IPv6). The 32-bit IPv4 address type is currently the most common, but the 128-bit IPv6 address is also in use and will probably become the more common address type over time. This lesson describes 32-bit IPv4 addressing, except where IPv6 is explicitly identified.

How do end systems initially obtain their IP address information? Although manual assignment of IP address information is possible, it does not scale and is a barrier to deployment and maintenance of networks. Therefore, protocols for the automatic assignment of IP address information have evolved and now provide this essential function without end user intervention. This lesson describes how IP address protocols function.

IP Network Addressing

Just as you use addresses to identify the specific locations of homes and businesses so that mail can reach them efficiently, you use IP addresses to identify the location of specific devices on a network so that data can be sent correctly to those locations. IP addressing has various aspects, including the calculations for constructing an IP address, the classes of IP addresses designated for specific routing purposes, and public versus private IP addresses.

Learning how IP addresses are structured and how they function in the operation of a network provides an understanding of how data is transmitted through Layer 3 internetworking devices using TCP/IP. To facilitate the routing of packets over a network, the TCP/IP protocol suite uses a 32-bit logical address known as an IP address. This address must be unique for each device in the internetwork.

The header of the Internet layer of TCP/IP is known as the IP header. Figure 1-26 shows the layout of the IP header.

Figure 1-26 *IP Header*

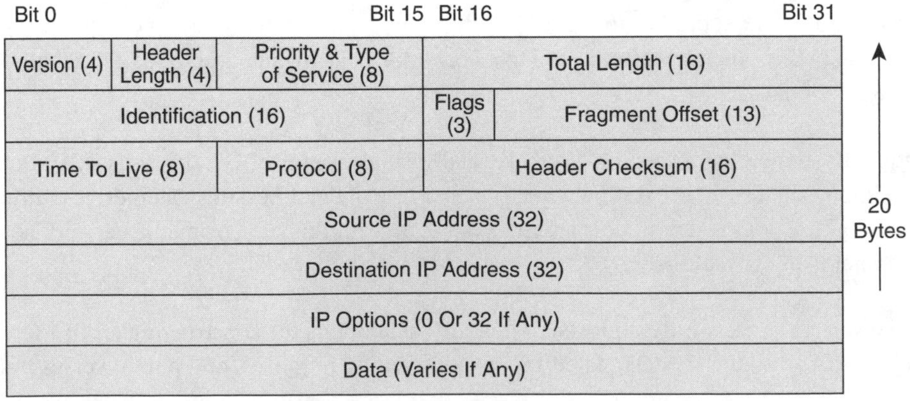

Note that each IP datagram carries this header, which includes a source IP address and destination IP address that identify the source and destination network and host.

An IP address is a hierarchical address, and it consists of two parts:

■ The high order, or leftmost, bits specify the network address component (network ID) of the address.

■ The low order, or rightmost, bits specify the host address component (host ID) of the address.

Every physical or virtual LAN on the corporate internetwork is seen as a single network that must be reached before an individual host within that company can be contacted. Each LAN has a unique network address. The hosts that populate that network share those same bits, but each host is identified by the uniqueness of the remaining bits. Like a group of houses along the same road, the street address is the same, but the house number is unique.

Figure 1-27 illustrates a sample IP addressing scheme in an internetwork.

Figure 1-27 *IP Addressing*

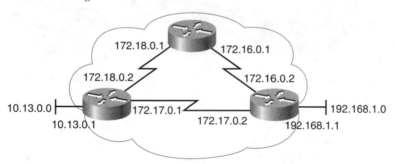

The IP address is 32 bits in length and is binary in nature, but it is expressed in a format that can be easily understood by the human brain. Basically, the 32 bits are broken into 4 sections of 8 bits each, known as *octets* or bytes. Each of these octets is then converted into decimal numbers between 0 and 255, and each octet is separated from the following one by dots. Figure 1-28 illustrates the format of an IP address using 172.16.122.204 as an example.

Figure 1-28 *IP Address Format*

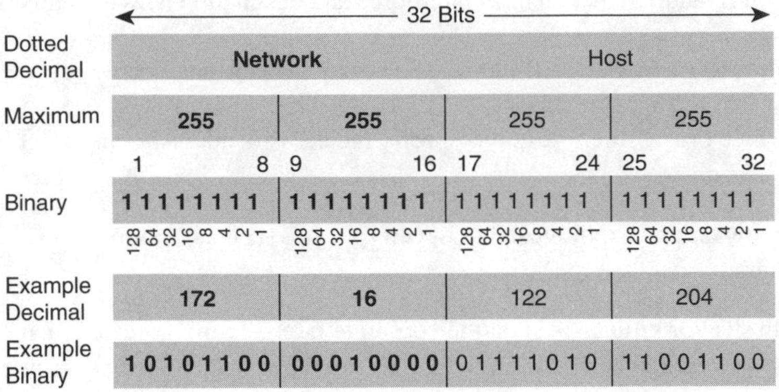

The IP address format is known as dotted decimal notation. Figure 1-28 shows how the dotted decimal address is derived from the 32-bit binary value:

■ Sample address: 172.16.122.204.

■ Each bit in the octet has a binary weight (such as 128, 64, 32, 16, 8, 4, 2, and 1), and when all the bits are on, the sum is 255.

■ The minimum decimal value for an octet is 0; it contains all 0s.

■ The maximum decimal value for an octet is 255; it contains all 1s.

While many computers might share the same network address, combining the network address with a host address uniquely identifies any device connected to the network.

IP Address Classes

When IP was first developed, no classes of addresses existed, because it was assumed that 254 networks would be more than enough for an internetwork of academic, military, and research computers.

As the number of networks grew, the IP addresses were broken into categories called classes to accommodate different sizes of networks and to aid in identifying them. These classes are illustrated in Figure 1-29.

Assigning IP addresses to classes is known as classful addressing. The allocation of addresses is managed by a central authority, the American Registry for Internet Numbers (ARIN), which you can go to at http://www.arin.net for more information about network numbers.

Figure 1-29 *Address Classes*

	8 Bits	8 Bits	8 Bits	8 Bits
Class A:	**Network**	Host	Host	Host
Class B:	**Network**	**Network**	Host	Host
Class C:	**Network**	**Network**	**Network**	Host
Class D:	Multicast			
Class E:	Research			

Five IP address classes are used, as follows:

- **Class A:** The Class A address category was designed to support extremely large networks. A Class A address uses only the first octet to indicate the network address. The remaining three octets are used for host addresses.

  The first bit of a Class A address is always 0; therefore, the lowest number that can be represented is 00000000 (decimal 0), and the highest number that can be represented is 01111111 (decimal 127). However, these two network numbers, 0 and 127, are reserved and cannot be used as a network address. Any address that starts with a value between 1 and 126 in the first octet, then, is a Class A address.

  > **NOTE** The 127.0.0.0 network is reserved for loopback testing (routers or local machines can use this address to send packets to themselves). Therefore, it cannot be assigned to a network.

- **Class B:** The Class B address category was designed to support the needs of moderate- to large-sized networks. A Class B address uses two of the four octets to indicate the network address. The other two octets specify host addresses.

  The first 2 bits of the first octet of a Class B address are always binary 10. The remaining 6 bits might be populated with either 1s or 0s. Therefore, the lowest number that can be represented with a Class B address is 10000000 (decimal 128), and the highest number that can be represented is 10111111 (decimal 191). Any address that starts with a value in the range of 128 to 191 in the first octet is a Class B address.

- **Class C:** The Class C address category is the most commonly used of the original address classes. This address category was intended to support a lot of small networks.

  A Class C address begins with binary 110. Therefore, the lowest number that can be represented is 11000000 (decimal 192), and the highest number that can be represented is 11011111 (decimal 223). If an address contains a number in the range of 192 to 223 in the first octet, it is a Class C address.

■ **Class D:** The Class D address category was created to enable multicasting in an IP address. A multicast address is a unique network address that directs packets with that destination address to predefined groups of IP addresses. Therefore, a single station can simultaneously transmit a single stream of datagrams to multiple recipients.

The Class D address category, much like the other address categories, is mathematically constrained. The first 4 bits of a Class D address must be 1110. Therefore, the first octet range for Class D addresses is 11100000 to 11101111, or 224 to 239. An IP address that starts with a value in the range of 224 to 239 in the first octet is a Class D address.

As illustrated in Figure 1-30, Class D addresses (multicast addresses) include the following range of network numbers: 224.0.0.0 to 239.255.255.255.

■ **Class E:** Although a Class E address category has been defined, the Internet Engineering Task Force (IETF) reserves the addresses in this class for its own research. Therefore, no Class E addresses have been released for use in the Internet. The first 4 bits of a Class E address are always set to 1111. Therefore, the first octet range for Class E addresses is 11110000 to 11111111, or 240 to 255.

Figure 1-30 *Multicast Addresses*

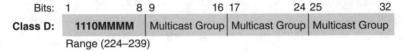

Within each class, the IP address is divided into a network address (or network identifier, network ID) and the host address (or host identifier, host ID). The number of networks and hosts vary by class. A bit or bit sequence at the start of each address, known as the high order bits, determines the class of the address, as shown in Figure 1-31.

Figure 1-31 *Address Classification*

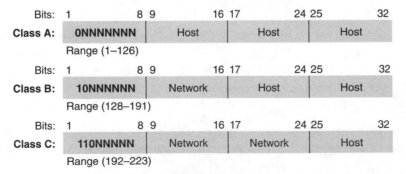

Figure 1-31 shows how the bits in the first octet identify the address class. The router uses the first bits to identify how many bits it must match to interpret the network portion of the address (based on the standard address class). Table 1-1 lists the characteristics of Class A, B, and C addresses that address network devices.

Table 1-1 *IP Address Classes*

Class A Address	Class B Address	Class C Address
The first bit is 0.	The first 2 bits are 10.	The first 3 bits are 110.
Range of network numbers: 1.0.0.0 to 126.0.0.0.	Range of network numbers: 128.0.0.0 to 191.255.0.0.	Range of network numbers: 192.0.0.0 to 223.255.255.0.
Number of possible networks: 127 (1 through 126 are usable; 127 is reserved).	Number of possible networks: 16,384.	Number of possible networks: 2,097,152.
Number of possible values in the host portion: 16,777,216.*	Number of possible values in the host portion: 65,536. *	Number of possible values in the host portion: 256.*

*The number of usable hosts is two less than the total number possible because the host portion must be nonzero and cannot be all 1s.

Network and Broadcast Addresses

Certain IP addresses are reserved and cannot be assigned to individual devices on a network. These reserved addresses include a network address, which identifies the network itself, and a broadcast address, which is used for broadcasting packets to all the devices on a network.

An IP address that has binary 0s in all host bit positions is reserved for the network address. Therefore, as a Class A network example, 10.0.0.0 is the IP address of the network containing the host 10.1.2.3. A router uses the network IP address when it searches its IP route table for the destination network location. As a Class B network example, the IP address 172.16.0.0 is a network address, as shown in the Figure 1-32.

Figure 1-32 *Network Address*

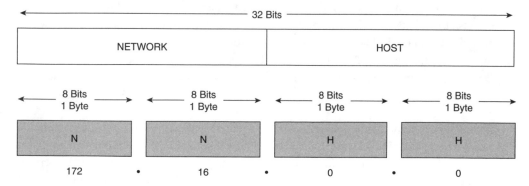

Network Address (Host Bits = All 0s)

The decimal numbers that fill the first two octets in a Class B network address are assigned. The last two octets contain 0s because those 16 bits are for host numbers and are used for devices that are attached to the network. The IP address in the example (172.16.0.0) is reserved for the network address; it is never used as an address for any device that is attached to it. An example of an IP address for a device on the 172.16.0.0 network would be 172.16.16.1. In this example, 172.16 is the network-address portion and 16.1 is the host-address portion.

If you wanted to send data to all the devices on a network, you would need to use a network broadcast address. Broadcast IP addresses end with binary 1s in the entire host part of the address (the host field), as shown in Figure 1-33.

For the network in the example (172.16.0.0), in which the last 16 bits make up the host field (or host part of the address), the broadcast that is sent out to all devices on that network includes a destination address of 172.16.255.255.

Figure 1-33 *Network Broadcast Address*

Network Address (Host Bits = All 0s)

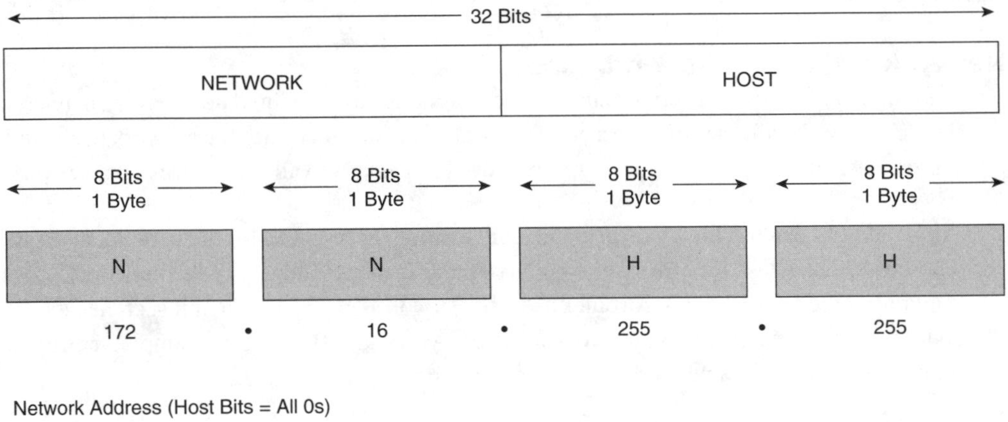

The network broadcast is also known as a directed broadcast and is capable of being routed, because the longest match in the routing table would match the network bits. Because the host bits would not be known, the router would forward this out all the interfaces that were members of the major 172.16.0.0 network. Directed broadcast can be used to perform a DoS attack against routed networks. This behavior is not the default for Cisco routers, however.

If an IP device wants to communicate with all devices on all networks, it sets the destination address to all 1s (255.255.255.255) and transmits the packet. This address can be used, for example, by hosts that do not know their network number and are asking some server for it, as with Reverse Address Resolution Protocol (RARP) or DHCP. This form of broadcast is never capable of being routed, because RFC 1812 prohibits the forwarding of an all networks broadcast. For this reason, an all networks broadcast is called a *local broadcast* because it stays local to the LAN segment or VLAN.

The network portion of an IP address is also referred to as the network ID. It is important because hosts on a network can only directly communicate with devices in the same network. If they need to communicate with devices with interfaces assigned to some other network ID, a Layer 3 internetworking device that can route data between the networks is needed. This is true even when the devices share the same physical media segment or VLAN.

A network ID enables a router to put a packet onto the appropriate network segment. The host ID helps the router deliver the Layer 2 frame, encapsulating the packet to a specific host on the network. As a result, the IP address is mapped to the correct MAC address, which is needed by the Layer 2 process on the router to address the frame.

Specific guidelines exist for assigning IP addresses in a network. First, each device or interface must have a nonzero host number. Figure 1-34 shows devices and routers with IP addresses assigned.

Figure 1-34 *Host Addresses*

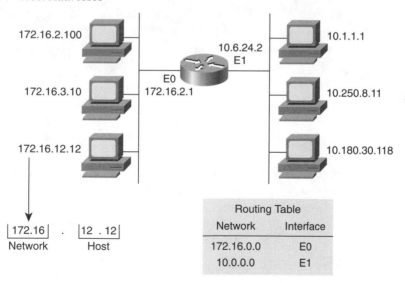

Each wire is identified with the network address. This value is not assigned, but it is assumed. A value of 0 means "this network" or "the wire itself" (for example, 172.16.0.0). This is the information used by the router to identify each network. The routing table contains entries for network or wire addresses; it usually does not contain any information about hosts.

As soon as the network portion is determined by the classification, you can determine the total number of hosts on the network by summing all available 1 and 0 combinations of the remaining address bits and subtracting 2. You must subtract 2 because an address consisting of all 0 bits specifies the network, and an address of all 1 bits is used for network broadcasts.

The same result can be derived by using the following formula:

$$2^N - 2 \text{ (where N is the number of bits in the host portion)}$$

Figure 1-35 illustrates a Class B network, 172.16.0.0. In a Class B network, 16 bits are used for the host portion. Applying the formula $2^N - 2$ (in this case, $2^{16} - 2 = 65,534$) results in 65,534 usable host addresses.

All classful addresses have only a network portion and host portion. So, the router(s) within the internetwork know it only as a single network, and no detailed knowledge of the internal hosts is required. All datagrams addressed to network 172.16.0.0 are treated the same, regardless of the third and fourth octets of the address.

Figure 1-35 *Determining the Available Host Addresses*

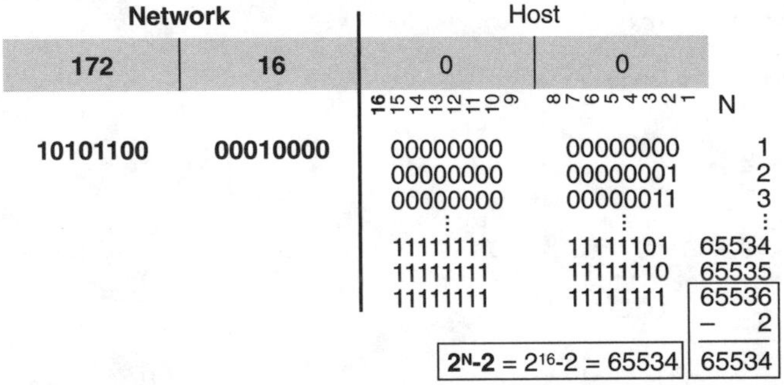

Each class of a network allows a fixed number of hosts. In a Class A network, the first octet is assigned for the network, leaving the last three octets to be assigned to hosts. The first host address in each network (all 0s) is reserved for the actual network address, and the final host address in each network (all 1s) is reserved for broadcasts. The maximum number of hosts in a Class A network is $2^{24} - 2$ (subtracting the network and broadcast reserved addresses), or 16,777,214.

In a Class B network, the first two octets are assigned for the network, leaving the final two octets to be assigned to hosts. The maximum number of hosts in a Class B network is $2^{16} - 2$, or 65,534.

In a Class C network, the first three octets are assigned for the network. This leaves the final octet to be assigned to hosts, so the maximum number of hosts is $2^8 - 2$, or 254.

Just as local broadcasts and directed broadcasts are special network addresses, you also find a special host address known as the loopback address that is used to test the TCP/IP stack on a host. This address is 127.0.0.1.

Another common special host address that many people run into is the autoconfiguration IP address assigned when neither a statically nor a dynamically configured IP address is found on startup. Hosts supporting IPv4 link-local addresses (RFC 3927) generate an address in the 169.254.X.X/16 prefix range. The address can be used only for local network connectivity and operates with many caveats, one of which is that it is not routed. These addresses are usually encountered when a host fails to obtain an address via startup using DHCP.

Public and Private IP Addresses

Some networks connect to each other through the Internet, whereas others are private. Public and private IP addresses are required, therefore, for both of these network types.

Internet stability depends directly on the uniqueness of publicly used network addresses. Therefore, some mechanism is needed to ensure that addresses are, in fact, unique. This responsibility originally rested within an organization known as the InterNIC (Internet Network Information Center). This organization was succeeded by the Internet Assigned Numbers Authority (IANA). IANA carefully manages the remaining supply of IP addresses to ensure that duplication of publicly used addresses does not occur. Such duplication would cause instability in the Internet and compromise its capability to deliver datagrams to networks using the duplicated addresses.

To obtain an IP address or block of addresses, you must contact an Internet service provider (ISP). The ISP allocates addresses from the range assigned by their upstream registry or their appropriate regional registry, which is managed by IANA, as follows:

- Asia Pacific Network Information Center (APNIC)

- American Registry for Internet Numbers (ARIN)

- Réseaux IP Europens Network Coordination Centre (RIPE NCC)

With the rapid growth of the Internet, public IP addresses began to run out, so new addressing schemes such as classless interdomain routing (CIDR) and IPv6 were developed to help solve the problem. CIDR and IPv6 are discussed later in this chapter in the "Address Exhaustion" section.

Although Internet hosts require a globally unique IP address, private hosts that are not connected to the Internet can use any valid address, as long as it is unique within the private network. Because many private networks exist alongside public networks, grabbing "just any address" is strongly discouraged. Therefore, the IETF defined 3 blocks of IP addresses (1 Class A network, 16 Class B networks, and 256 Class C networks) in RFC 1918 for private, internal use. Addresses in this range are not routed on the Internet backbone, as shown in Table 1-2. Internet routers are configured to discard private addresses as defined by RFC 1918.

Table 1-2 *Private IP Addresses*

Class	RFC 1918 Internal Address Range
A	10.0.0.0 to 10.255.255.255
B	172.16.0.0 to 172.31.255.255
C	192.168.0.0 to 192.168.255.255

If you are addressing a nonpublic intranet, these private addresses can be used instead of globally unique addresses. If you want to connect a network using private addresses to the Internet, however, it is necessary to translate the private addresses to public addresses. This translation process is referred to as Network Address Translation (NAT). A router is often the network device that performs NAT.

Address Exhaustion

The growth of the Internet has resulted in enormous demands for IP addresses. This section describes the capabilities of IPv4 in relation to that demand.

When TCP/IP was first introduced in the 1980s, it relied on a two-level addressing scheme, which at the time offered adequate scalability. The architects of TCP/IP could not have predicted that their protocol would eventually sustain a global network of information, commerce, and entertainment. Twenty years ago, IPv4 offered an addressing strategy that, although scalable for a time, eventually resulted in an inefficient allocation of addresses.

The Class A and B addresses make up 75 percent of the IPv4 address space, but a relative handful of organizations (fewer than 17,000) can be assigned a Class A or B network number. Class C network addresses are far more numerous than Class A and B addresses, although they account for only 12.5 percent of the possible 4 billion IP addresses, as shown in Figure 1-36.

Unfortunately, Class C addresses are limited to 254 hosts, which does not meet the needs of larger organizations that cannot acquire a Class A or B address.

Figure 1-36 *IP Address Allocation*

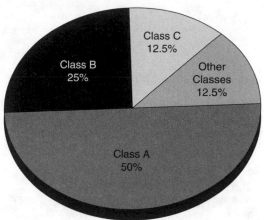

As early as 1992, the IETF identified two specific concerns:

■ The Class B address category was on the verge of depletion, and the remaining, unassigned IPv4 network addresses were nearly depleted at the time.

■ As more Class C networks came online to accommodate the rapid and substantial increase in the size of the Internet, the resulting flood of new network information threatened the capability of Internet routers to cope effectively.

Over the past 20 years, numerous extensions to IPv4 have been developed to improve the efficiency with which the 32-bit address space can be used.

In addition, an even more extendable and scalable version of IP, IPv6, has been defined and developed. An IPv6 address is a 128-bit binary value, which can be displayed as 32 hexadecimal digits. It provides 3.4×10^{38} IP addresses. This version of IP should provide sufficient addresses for future Internet growth needs. Table 1-3 compares IPv4 and IPv6 addresses.

Table 1-3 *IPv6 Addresses*

Version	IPv4	IPv6
Number of octets	4 octcts	16 octets
Binary representation of address	11000000.10101000.110010 01.01110001	11010001.11011100.11001001.0111 0001.11010001.11011100.11001100 1.01110001.11010001.11011100.110 01001.01110001.11010001.1101110 0.11001001.01110001

continues

Table 1-3 *IPv6 Addresses (Continued)*

Version	IPv4	IPv6
Notation of address	192.168.201.113	A524:72D3:2C80:DD02:0029:EC7A:002B:EA73
Total number of addresses available	4,294,467,295 IP addresses	3.4×10^{38} IP addresses

After years of planning and development, IPv6 is slowly being implemented in select networks. Eventually, IPv6 might replace IPv4 as the dominant internetwork protocol.

Another solution to the shortage of public IP addresses is a different kind of routing. CIDR is a new addressing scheme for the Internet that allows for more efficient allocation of IP addresses than the old Class A, B, and C address scheme allows.

First introduced in 1993 and later deployed in 1994, CIDR dramatically improved the scalability and efficiency of IPv4 in the following ways:

■ It replaced classful addressing with a more flexible and less wasteful scheme.

■ It provided enhanced route aggregation, also known as supernetting. As the Internet grows, routers on the Internet require huge memory tables to store all the routing information. Supernetting helps reduce the size of router memory tables by combining and summarizing multiple routing information entries into one single entry. This reduces the size of router memory tables and also allows for faster table lookup.

A CIDR network address looks like this:

192.168.54.0/23

The 192.168.54.0 is the network address itself and the /23 means that the first 23 bits are the network part of the address, leaving the last 9 bits for specific host addresses. The effect of CIDR is to aggregate, or combine, multiple classful networks into a single larger network. This aggregation reduces the number of entries required in the IP routing tables and allows the provisioning a larger number of hosts within the network. Both are done without using a network ID from the next larger classful address group.

With the CIDR approach, if you need more than 254 host addresses, you can be assigned a /23 address instead of wasting a whole Class B address that supports 65,534 hosts.

Figure 1-37 shows an example of using CIDR. Company XYZ asks for an address block from its ISP, not a central authority. The ISP evaluates company XYZ's needs and allocates address space from its own large *CIDR block* of addresses. CIDR blocks can be, and are, assigned by the regional authorities to governments, service providers, enterprises, and organizations.

Figure 1-37   *CIDR Addressing*

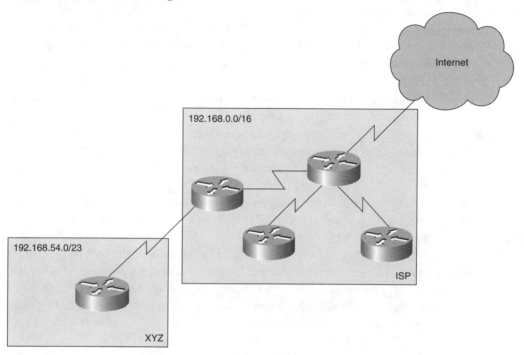

> **NOTE**   Figure 1-37 shows an example using private IP addresses as defined in RFC 1918. These addresses would never be used by an ISP for CIDR, but they are shown here merely as an illustration. Public addresses are not used in this example for security reasons.

In this example, the ISP owns the 192.168.0.0/16 address block. The ISP announces only this single 192.168.0.0/16 address to the Internet (even though this address block actually consists of many Class C networks). The ISP assigns the smaller 192.168.54.0/23 address block within the larger 192.168.0.0/16 address block to the XYZ company. This assignment allows the XYZ company to have a network that can have up to 510 hosts ($2^9 - 2 = 510$), or that network can be subdivided into multiple smaller subnets by the XYZ company.

Providers assume the burden of managing address space in a classless system. With this system, Internet routers keep only one summary route, or supernet route, to the provider's network, and only the individual provider keeps routes that are more specific to its own customer networks. This method drastically reduces the size of internetwork routing tables.

Dynamic Host Configuration Protocol

Host addresses are assigned to devices either manually or automatically. Automated methods make administration of devices easier, so they are the ones most often employed. Several automated methods that use protocols for assigning IP addresses exist, and DHCP is the most popular of those methods.

DHCP is a protocol used to assign IP addresses automatically and to set TCP/IP stack configuration parameters, such as the subnet mask, default router, and Domain Name System (DNS) servers for a host. DHCP is also used to provide other configuration information as necessary, including the length of time the address has been allocated to the host. DHCP consists of two components: a protocol for delivering host-specific configuration parameters from a DHCP server to a host and a mechanism for allocating network addresses to hosts. DCHP addresses are usually obtained on startup, and Figure 1-38 shows the communication that takes place to obtain the address.

Using DHCP, a host can obtain an IP address quickly and dynamically. All that is required is a defined range of IP addresses on a DHCP server. As hosts come online, they contact the DHCP server and request address information. The DHCP server selects an address and allocates it to that host. The address is only "leased" to the host, so the host periodically contacts the DHCP server to extend the lease. This lease mechanism ensures that hosts that have been moved or are switched off for extended periods of time do not hold on to addresses that they are not using. The addresses are returned to the address pool by the DHCP server to be reallocated as necessary.

DHCP is a protocol specified by RFC 2131, superseding RFC 1541. DHCP is based on the Bootstrap Protocol (BOOTP), which it has effectively superseded.

IP addresses can also be assigned statically by configuring the host manually.

Domain Name System

Another important parameter used in TCP/IP is DNS. DNS is a mechanism for converting symbolic names into IP addresses. The DNS application frees users of IP networks from the burden of having to remember IP addresses. Without this freedom, the Internet would *not* be as popular or as usable as it is.

The DNS address is a server that provides the DNS services. The address is typically assigned during the DCHP address assignment or can be assigned manually.

Figure 1-38 *DHCP Request*

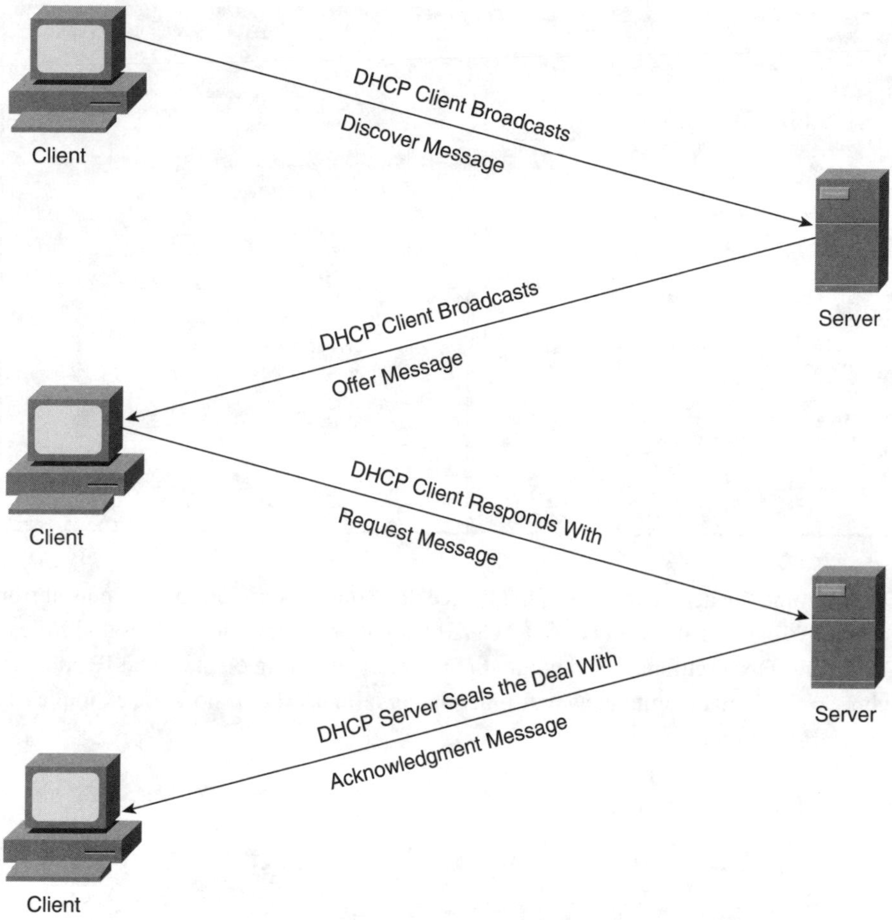

Using Common Host Tools to Determine the IP Address of a Host

Most operating systems provide a series of tools that can be used to verify host addresses and DNS addresses

For a Microsoft Windows device the Network Connections tab under System setup enables you to set and view the IP address configured on the PC. As shown in Figure 1-39, this PC is configured to obtain the address from a DHCP server.

Figure 1-39 *TCP/IP Properties*

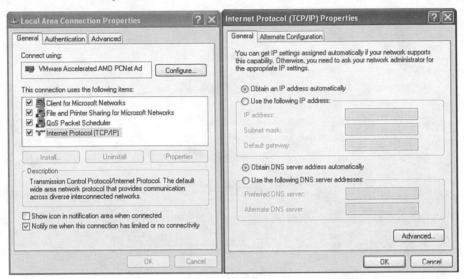

To determine the actual address of the device, the command **ipconfig** can be used from the command line to display all current TCP/IP network configuration values and refresh DHCP and DNS settings. Used without parameters, **ipconfig** displays the IP address, subnet mask, and default gateway for all adapters. Figure 1-40 shows an example of an IPCONFIG output.

Figure 1-40 *IPCONFIG Output*

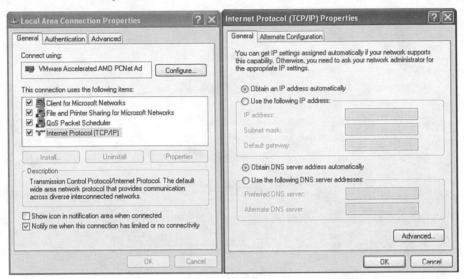

You can run **ipconfig** with various flags to determine exactly what output should be displayed. The syntax flags are as follows:

```
ipconfig [/all] [/renew [Adapter]] [/release [Adapter]] [/flushdns] [/displaydns]
    [/registerdns] [/showclassid Adapter] [/setclassid Adapter [ClassID]]
```

The parameters are as follows:

- **/all:** Displays the full TCP/IP configuration for all adapters. Without this parameter, **ipconfig** displays only the IP address, subnet mask, and default gateway values for each adapter. Adapters can represent physical interfaces, such as installed network adapters, or logical interfaces, such as dialup connections.

- **/renew** [*Adapter*]**:** Renews DHCP configuration for all adapters (if an adapter is not specified) or for a specific adapter if the *Adapter* parameter is included. This parameter is available only on computers with adapters that are configured to obtain an IP address automatically. To specify an adapter name, type the adapter name that appears when you use **ipconfig** without parameters.

- **/release** [*Adapter*]**:** Sends a DHCPRELEASE message to the DHCP server to release the current DHCP configuration and discard the IP address configuration for either all adapters (if an adapter is not specified) or for a specific adapter if the *Adapter* parameter is included. This parameter disables TCP/IP for adapters configured to obtain an IP address automatically. To specify an adapter name, type the adapter name that appears when you use **ipconfig** without parameters.

- **/flushdns:** Flushes and resets the contents of the DNS client resolver cache. During DNS troubleshooting, you can use this procedure to discard negative cache entries from the cache, as well as any other entries that have been added dynamically.

- **/displaydns:** Displays the contents of the DNS client resolver cache, which includes both entries preloaded from the local hosts file and any recently obtained resource records for name queries resolved by the computer. The DNS client service uses this information to resolve frequently queried names quickly, before querying its configured DNS servers.

- **/registerdns:** Initiates manual dynamic registration for the DNS names and IP addresses that are configured at a computer. You can use this parameter to troubleshoot a failed DNS name registration or resolve a dynamic update problem between a client and the DNS server without rebooting the client computer. The DNS settings in the advanced properties of the TCP/IP protocol determine which names are registered in DNS.

■ **/showclassid** *Adapter***:** Displays the DHCP class ID for a specified adapter. To see the DHCP class ID for all adapters, use the asterisk (*) wildcard character in place of *Adapter*. This parameter is available only on computers with adapters that are configured to obtain an IP address automatically.

■ **/setclassid** *Adapter* [*ClassID*]**:** Configures the DHCP class ID for a specified adapter. To set the DHCP class ID for all adapters, use the asterisk (*) wildcard character in place of *Adapter*. This parameter is available only on computers with adapters that are configured to obtain an IP address automatically. If a DHCP class ID is not specified, the current class ID is removed.

■ **/?:** Displays help at the command prompt.

Summary of TCP/IP's Internet Layer

The following list summarizes key points about TCP/IP's Internet layer:

■ IP network addresses consist of two parts: the network ID and the host ID.

■ IPv4 addresses have 32 bits that are divided into octets and are generally shown in dotted decimal form (for example, 192.168.54.18).

■ IPv4 addresses are divided into A, B, and C classes to be assigned to user devices.

■ Classes D and E are used for multicast and research, respectively.

■ The first few bits of an address determine the class.

■ Certain IP addresses (network and broadcast) are reserved and cannot be assigned to individual network devices.

■ Internet hosts require a unique public IP address, but private hosts can have any valid private address that is unique within the private network.

■ DCHP assigns IP addresses and parameters to host devices automatically.

■ DNS is a TCP/IP application that resolves domain names like Cisco.com into IP addresses to be used by the application.

■ Hosts provide tools that can be used to verify the IP addresses of the device. Windows tools are Network Connections and IPCONFIG.

Understanding TCP/IP's Transport and Application Layers

When computers communicate with one another, certain rules, or protocols, are required to allow them to transmit and receive data in an orderly fashion. Throughout the world, the most widely adopted protocol suite is TCP/IP. Understanding how TCP/IP functions is important for a larger understanding of how data is transmitted in network environments.

The way in which IP delivers a packet of data across a network is a fundamental concept in the TCP/IP architecture used in large networks. Understanding how data is transmitted via IP is central to understanding how the TCP/IP suite of protocols functions overall. This, in turn, adds to an understanding of how data that is communicated across networks can be prioritized, restricted, secured, optimized, and maintained. This lesson describes the sequence of steps in IP packet delivery and the concepts and structures involved, such as packets, datagrams, and protocol fields, to provide a view of how data is transmitted over large networks.

For the Internet and internal networks to function correctly, data must be delivered reliably. You can ensure reliable delivery of data through development of the application and by using the services provided by the network protocol. In the OSI reference model, the transport layer manages the process of reliable data delivery. The transport layer hides details of any network-dependent information from the higher layers by providing transparent data transfer. The User Datagram Protocol (UDP) and TCP operate between the transport layer and the application layer. Learning how UDP and TCP function between the network layer and the application layer provides a more complete understanding of how data is transmitted in a TCP/IP networking environment. This section describes the function of the transport layer and how UDP and TCP operate.

The Transport Layer

Residing between the application and network layers, the transport layer, Layer 4, is in the core of the TCP/IP layered network architecture. The transport layer has the critical role of providing communication services directly to the application processes running on different hosts. Learning how the transport layer functions provides an understanding of how data is transmitted in a TCP/IP networking environment.

The transport layer protocol places a header on data that is received from the application layer. The purpose of this protocol is to identify the application from which the data was received and create segments to be passed down to the Internet layer. Some transport layer protocols also perform two additional functions: flow control (provided by sliding windows) and reliability (provided by sequence numbers and acknowledgments). Flow control is a mechanism that enables the communicating hosts to negotiate how much data is transmitted each time. Reliability provides a mechanism for guaranteeing the delivery of each packet.

Two protocols are provided at the transport layer:

- **TCP:** A connection-oriented, reliable protocol. In a connection-oriented environment, a connection is established between both ends before transfer of information can begin. TCP is responsible for breaking messages into segments, reassembling them at the destination station, resending anything that is not received, and reassembling messages from the segments. TCP supplies a virtual circuit between end user applications.

- **UDP:** A connectionless and unacknowledged protocol. Although UDP is responsible for transmitting messages, no checking for segment delivery is provided at this layer. UDP depends on upper-layer protocols for reliability.

When devices communicate with one another, they exchange a series of messages. To understand and act on these messages, devices must agree on the format and the order of the messages exchanged, as well as the actions taken on the transmission or receipt of a message.

An example of a how a protocol can be used to provide this functionality is a conversation exchange between a student and a teacher in a classroom:

1. The teacher is lecturing on a particular subject. The teacher stops to ask, "Are there any questions?" This question is a broadcast message to all students.

2. You raise your hand. This action is an implicit message back to the teacher.

3. The teacher responds with "Yes, what is your question?" Here, the teacher has acknowledged your message and signals you to send your next message.

4. You ask your question. You transmit your message to the teacher.

5. The teacher hears your question and answers it. The teacher receives your message and transmits a reply back to you.

6. You nod to the teacher that you understand the answer. You acknowledge receipt of the message from the teacher.

7. The teacher asks if everything is all clear.

The transmission and receipt of messages and a set of conventional actions taken when sending and receiving these messages are at the heart of this question-and-answer protocol.

TCP provides transparent transfer of data between end systems using the services of the network layer below to move packets between the two communicating systems. TCP is a transport layer protocol. IP is a network layer protocol.

Similar to the OSI reference model, TCP/IP separates a full network protocol suite into a number of tasks. Each layer corresponds to a different facet of communication. Conceptually, you can envision TCP/IP as a protocol stack.

The services provided by TCP run in the host computers at either end of a connection, not in the network. Therefore, TCP is a protocol for managing end-to-end connections. Because end-to-end connections can exist across a series of point-to-point connections, these end-to-end connections are called *virtual circuits*. The characteristics of TCP are as follows:

- **Connection-oriented:** Two computers set up a connection to exchange data. The end systems synchronize with one another to manage packet flows and adapt to congestion in the network.

- **Full-duplex operation:** A TCP connection is a pair of virtual circuits, one in each direction. Only the two synchronized end systems can use the connection.

- **Error checking:** A checksum technique verifies that packets are not corrupted.

- **Sequencing:** Packets are numbered so that the destination can reorder packets and determine if a packet is missing.

- **Acknowledgments:** Upon receipt of one or more packets, the receiver returns an acknowledgment to the sender indicating that it received the packets. If packets are not acknowledged, the sender can retransmit the packets or terminate the connection if the sender thinks the receiver is no longer on the connection.

- **Flow control:** If the sender is overflowing the buffer of the receiver by transmitting too quickly, the receiver drops packets. Failed acknowledgments alert the sender to slow down or stop sending. The receiver can also lower the flow to slow the sender down.

- **Packet recovery services:** The receiver can request retransmission of a packet. If packet receipt is not acknowledged, the sender resends the packets.

TCP is a reliable transport layer protocol. Reliable data delivery services are critical for applications such as file transfers, database services, transaction processing, and other mission-critical applications in which delivery of every packet must be guaranteed.

An analogy to TCP protocol services would be sending certified mail through the postal service. For example, someone who lives in Lexington, Kentucky, wants to send this book to a friend in New York City, New York, but for some reason, the postal service handles only letters. The sender could rip the pages out and put each one in a separate envelope. To ensure the receiver reassembles the book correctly, the sender numbers each envelope. Then, the sender addresses the envelopes and sends the first envelope certified mail. The postal service delivers the first envelope by any truck and any route. Upon delivery of that envelope, the carrier must get a signature from the receiver and return that certificate of delivery to the sender.

The sender mails several envelopes on the same day. The postal service again delivers each envelope by any truck using any route. The sender returns to the post office each day sending several envelopes each requiring a return receipt. The receiver signs a separate receipt for each envelope in the batch as they are received. If one envelope is lost in transit, the sender would not receive a certificate of delivery for that numbered envelope. The sender might have already sent the pages that follow the missing one, but would still be able to resend the missing page. After receiving all the envelopes, the receiver puts the pages in the right order and pastes them back together to make the book. TCP provides these levels of services.

UDP is another transport layer protocol that was added to the TCP/IP protocol suite. This transport layer protocol uses a smaller header and does not provide the reliability available with TCP.

The early IP suite consisted only of TCP and IP, although IP was not differentiated as a separate service. However, some end user applications needed timeliness rather than accuracy. In other words, speed was more important than packet recovery. In real-time voice or video transfers, a few lost packets are tolerable. Recovering packets creates excessive overhead that reduces performance.

To accommodate this type of traffic, TCP architects redesigned the protocol suite to include UDP. The basic addressing and packet-forwarding service in the network layer was IP. TCP and UDP are in the transport layer on top of IP, and both use IP services.

UDP offers only minimal, nonguaranteed transport services and gives applications direct access to the IP layer. UDP is used by applications that do not require the level of service of TCP or that want to use communications services such as multicast or broadcast delivery, not available from TCP.

An analogy of the UDP protocol services would be using the postal service to send fliers notifying all of your neighbors of your garage sale. In this example, you make a flier advertising the day, time, and location of your garage sale. You address each flier with the specific name and address of each neighbor within a 2-mile radius of your house. The postal service delivers each flier by any truck and any route. However, it is not important if a flier is lost in transit or if a neighbor acknowledges receipt of the flier.

TCP/IP Applications

In addition to including the IP, TCP, and UDP protocols, the TCP/IP protocol suite also includes applications that support other services such as file transfer, e-mail, and remote login. Some of the applications that TCP/IP supports include the following:

- **FTP:** FTP is a reliable, connection-oriented service that uses TCP to transfer files between systems that support FTP. FTP supports bidirectional binary and ASCII file transfers.

- **TFTP:** TFTP is an application that uses UDP. Routers use TFTP to transfer configuration files and Cisco IOS images and to transfer files between systems that support TFTP.

- **Terminal Emulation (Telnet):** Telnet provides the capability to remotely access another computer. Telnet enables a user to log on to a remote host and execute commands.

- **E-mail (SMTP):** Simple Mail Transfer Protocol allows users to send and receive messages to e-mail applications throughout the internetwork.

Transport Layer Functionality

The transport layer hides details of any network-dependent information from the higher layers by providing transparent data transfer. Learning how the TCP/IP transport layer and the TCP and UDP protocols function provides a more complete understanding of how data is transmitted with these protocols in a TCP/IP networking environment.

Transport services enable users to segment and reassemble several upper-layer applications onto the same transport layer data stream. This transport layer data stream provides end-to-end transport services. The transport layer data stream constitutes a logical connection between the endpoints of the internetwork, the originating or sending host and the destination or receiving host.

A user of a reliable transport layer service must establish a connection-oriented session with its peer system. For reliable data transfer to begin, both the sending and the receiving applications inform their respective operating systems that a connection is to be initiated, as shown in Figure 1-41.

One machine initiates a connection that must be accepted by the other. Protocol software modules in the two operating systems communicate by sending messages across the network to verify that the transfer is authorized and that both sides are ready.

Figure 1-41 *Network Connection*

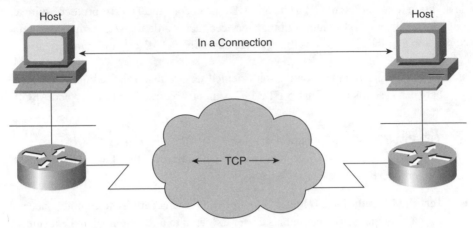

After successful synchronization has occurred, the two end systems have established a connection, and data transfer can begin. During transfer, the two machines continue to verify that the connection is still valid.

Encapsulation is the process by which data is prepared for transmission in a TCP/IP network environment. This section describes the encapsulation of data in the TCP/IP stack.

The data container looks different at each layer, and at each layer the container goes by a different name, as shown in Figure 1-42.

Figure 1-42 *Names for Encapsulated Data by Layer*

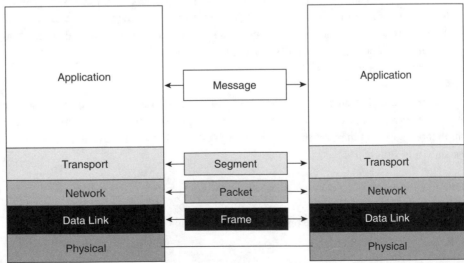

The names for the data containers created at each layer are as follows:

- **Message:** The data container created at the application layer is called a message.

- **Segment or datagram:** The data container created at the transport layer, which encapsulates the application layer message, is called a segment if it comes from the transport layer's TCP protocol. If the data container comes from the transport layer's UDP protocol, it is called a datagram.

- **Packet:** The data container at the network layer, which encapsulates the transport layer segment, is called a packet.

- **Frame:** The data container at the data link layer, which encapsulates the packet, is called a frame. This frame is then turned into a bit stream at the physical layer.

A segment or packet is the unit of end-to-end transmission containing a transport header and the data from the above protocols. In general, in discussion about transmitting information from one node to another, the term *packet* is used loosely to refer to a piece of data. However, this book refers to data formed in the transport layer as a segment, data at the network layer as a datagram or packet, and data at the link layer as a frame.

To provide communications between the segments, each protocol uses a particular header, as discussed in the next section.

TCP/UDP Header Format

TCP is known as a connection-oriented protocol because the end stations are aware of each other and are constantly communicating about the connection. A classic nontechnical example of connection-oriented communication is a telephone conversation between two people. First, a protocol lets the participants know that they have connected and can begin communicating. This protocol is analogous to an initial conversation of "Hello."

UDP is known as a connectionless protocol. An example of a connectionless conversation is the normal delivery of U.S. postal service. You place the letter in the mail and hope that it gets delivered. Figure 1-43 illustrates the TCP segment header format, the field definitions of which are described in Table 1-4. These fields provide the communication between end stations to control the conversation.

Figure 1-43 *TCP Header Format*

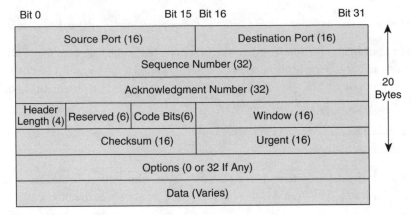

Table 1-4 *TCP Header Field Descriptions*

TCP Header Field	Description	Number of Bits
Source Port	Number of the calling port	16 bits
Destination Port	Number of the called port	16 bits
Sequence Number	Number used to ensure correct sequencing of the arriving data	32 bits
Acknowledgment Number	Next expected TCP octet	32 bits
Header Length	Number of 32-bit words in the header	4 bits
Reserved	Set to zero	6 bits
Code Bits	Control functions such as setup and termination of a session	6 bits
Window	Number of octets that the device is willing to accept	16 bits
Checksum	Calculated checksum of the header and data fields	16 bits
Urgent	Indicates the end of the urgent data	16 bits
Options	One currently defined: maximum TCP segment size	0 or 32 bits, if any
Data	Upper-layer protocol data	Varies

Figure 1-44 shows a data capture of an Ethernet frame with the TCP header field expanded.

Figure 1-44 *TCP Header*

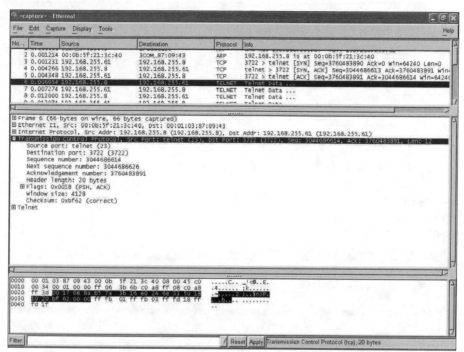

The TCP header is 20 bytes. Transporting multiple packets with small data fields results in less efficient use of available bandwidth than transporting the same amount of data with fewer, larger packets. This situation is like placing several small objects into several boxes, which could hold more than one object, and shipping each box individually instead of filling one box completely with all of the objects and sending only that box to deliver all the objects.

Figure 1-45 illustrates the UDP segment header format, the field definitions for which are described in Table 1-5. The UDP header length is always 64 bits.

Figure 1-45 *UDP Header*

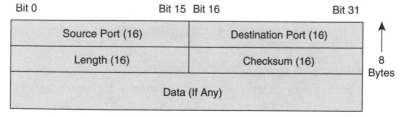

No Sequence Or Acknowledgment Fields

Table 1-5 *UDP Header Field Descriptions*

UDP Header Field	Description	Number of Bits
Source Port	Number of the calling port	16 bits
Destination Port	Number of the called port	16 bits
Length	Length of UDP header and UDP data	16 bits
Checksum	Calculated checksum of the header and data fields	16 bits
Data	Upper-layer protocol data	Varies

Figure 1-46 shows a data capture of an Ethernet frame with the UDP header field expanded.

Protocols that use UDP include TFTP, SNMP, Network File System (NFS), and DNS.

Figure 1-46 *UDP Header*

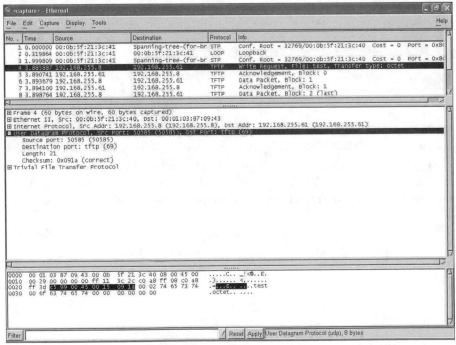

How TCP and UDP Use Port Numbers

Both TCP and UDP use port numbers to pass information to the upper layers. Port numbers keep track of different conversations crossing the network at the same time. Figure 1-47 defines some of the port numbers as used by TCP and UDP.

Figure 1-47 *Port Numbers*

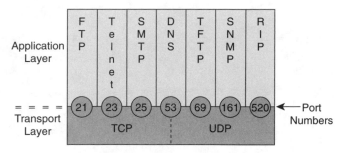

Application software developers agree to use well-known port numbers that are controlled by the IANA. For example, any conversation bound for the FTP application uses the standard port number 21. Conversations that do not involve an application with a well-known port number are assigned port numbers randomly chosen from within a specific range instead. These port numbers are used as source and destination addresses in the TCP segment.

Some ports are reserved in both TCP and UDP, but applications might not be written to support them. Port numbers have the following assigned ranges:

■ Numbers below 1024 are considered well-known or assigned ports.

■ Numbers 1024 and above are dynamically assigned ports.

■ Registered ports are those registered for vendor-specific applications. Most are above 1024.

> **NOTE**   Some applications, such as DNS, use both transport layer protocols. DNS uses UDP for name resolution and TCP for server zone transfers.

Figure 1-48 shows how well-known port numbers are used by hosts to connect to the application on the end station. It also illustrates the selection of a source port so that the end station knows how to communicate with the client application.

RFC 1700, "Assigned Numbers," defines all the well-known port numbers for TCP/IP. For a listing of current port numbers, refer to the IANA website at http://www.iana.org.

End systems use port numbers to select the proper application. Originating source port numbers are dynamically assigned by the source host, some number greater than 1023.

Figure 1-48   *Port Number Example*

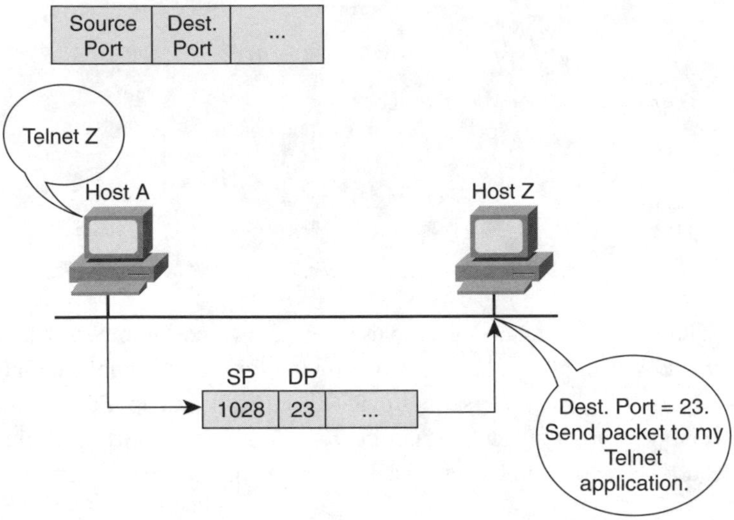

Establishing a TCP Connection: The Three-Way Handshake

TCP is connection-oriented, so it requires connection establishment before data transfer begins. For a connection to be established or initialized, the two hosts must synchronize on each other's initial sequence numbers (ISN). Synchronization is done in an exchange of connection-establishing segments carrying a control bit called SYN (for synchronize) and the initial sequence numbers. As shorthand, segments carrying the SYN bit are also called "SYNs." Hence, the solution requires a suitable mechanism for picking an initial sequence number and a slightly involved handshake to exchange the ISN.

The synchronization requires each side to send its own initial sequence number and to receive a confirmation of its successful transmission within the acknowledgment (ACK) from the other side. Here is the sequence of events:

1. **Host A** to **Host B SYN**: My sequence number is 100, ACK number is 0, and ACK bit is not set. SYN bit is set.

2. **Host A** to **Host B SYN, ACK**: I expect to see 101 next, my sequence number is 300, and ACK bit is set. Host B to Host A SYN bit is set.

3. **Host A** to **Host B ACK**: I expect to see 301 next, my sequence number is 101, and ACK bit is set. SYN bit is not set.

> **NOTE**   The initial sequence numbers are actually large random numbers chosen by each host.

This exchange is called the three-way handshake and is illustrated in Figure 1-49.

Figure 1-49   *Three-Way Handshake*

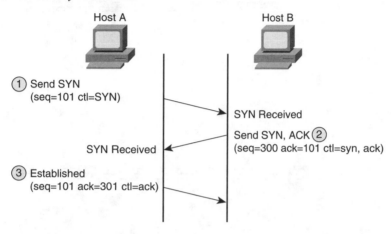

Figure 1-50 shows a data capture of the three-way handshake. Notice the sequence numbers in the three frames.

A three-way handshake is necessary because sequence numbers are not tied to a global clock in the network, and IP stacks might have different mechanisms for picking the ISN. Because the receiver of the first SYN has no way of knowing whether the segment was an old delayed one, unless it remembers the last sequence number used on the connection (which is not always possible), it must ask the sender to verify this SYN. Figure 1-51 illustrates the acknowledgment process.

The window size determines how much data, in bytes, the receiving station accepts at one time before an acknowledgment is returned. With a window size of 1 byte (as shown in Figure 1-51), each segment must be acknowledged before another segment is transmitted. This results in inefficient use of bandwidth by the hosts.

Figure 1-50 *Capture of Three-Way Handshake*

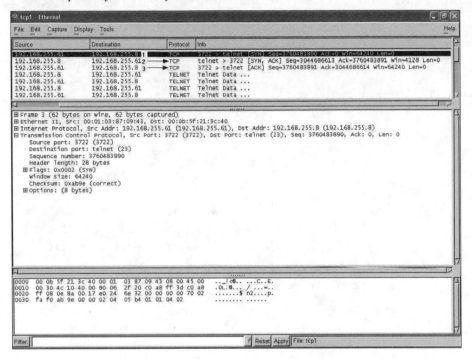

Figure 1-51 *Simple Acknowledgment*

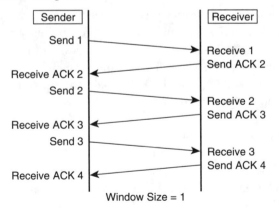

TCP provides sequencing of segments with a forward reference acknowledgment. Each datagram is numbered before transmission. At the receiving station, TCP reassembles the segments into a complete message. If a sequence number is missing in the series, that segment is retransmitted. If segments are not acknowledged within a given time period, that results in retransmission. Figure 1-52 illustrates the role that acknowledgment numbers play when datagrams are transmitted.

Figure 1-52 *Acknowledgment Numbers*

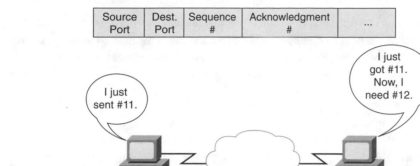

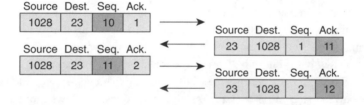

Session Multiplexing

Session multiplexing is an activity by which a single computer, with a single IP address, is able to have multiple sessions occur simultaneously. A session is created when a source machine needs to send data to a destination machine. Most often, this involves a reply, but a reply is not mandatory. The session is created and controlled within the IP network application, which contains the functionality of OSI Layers 5 through 7.

A best-effort session is very simple. The session parameters are sent to UDP. A best-effort session sends data to the indicated IP address using the port numbers provided. Each transmission is a separate event, and no memory or association between transmissions is retained.

When using the reliable TCP service, a connection must first be established between the sender and the receiver before any data can be transmitted. TCP opens a connection and negotiates connection parameters with the destination. During data flow, TCP maintains reliable delivery of the data and, when complete, closes the connection.

For example, you enter a URL for Yahoo! into the address line in the Internet Explorer window, and the Yahoo! site corresponding to the URL appears. With the Yahoo! site open, you can open the browser again in another window and type in another URL (for example,

Google). You can open another browser window and type the URL for Cisco.com, and it will open. Three sites are open using only one IP connection, because the session layer is sorting the separate requests based on the port number.

Segmentation

TCP takes data chunks from the application layers and prepares them for shipment onto the network. Each chunk is broken up into smaller segments that fit the maximum transmission unit (MTU) of the underlying network layers. UDP, being simpler, does no checking or negotiating and expects the application process to give it data that works.

Flow Control for TCP/UDP

To govern the flow of data between devices, TCP uses a flow control mechanism. The receiving TCP reports a "window" to the sending TCP. This window specifies the number of bytes, starting with the acknowledgment number, that the receiving TCP is currently prepared to receive.

TCP window sizes are variable during the lifetime of a connection. Each acknowledgment contains a window advertisement that indicates how many bytes the receiver can accept. TCP also maintains a congestion control window that is normally the same size as the receiver's window but is cut in half when a segment is lost (for example, when you have congestion). This approach permits the window to be expanded or contracted as necessary to manage buffer space and processing. A larger window size allows more data to be processed.

> **NOTE**   TCP window size is documented in RFC 793, "Transmission Control Protocol," and RFC 813, "Window and Acknowledgment Strategy in TCP," which you can find at http://www.ietf.org/rfc.html.

In Figure 1-53, the sender sends three 1-byte packets before expecting an ACK. The receiver can handle a window size of only 2 bytes (because of available memory). So, it drops packet 3, specifies 3 as the next byte to be received, and specifies a window size of 2. The sender resends packet 2 and also sends the next 1-byte packet, but still specifies its window size of 3. (For example, it can still accept three 1-byte packets.) The receiver acknowledges bytes 3 and 4 by requesting byte 5 and continuing to specify a window size of 2 bytes.

Many of the functions described in these sections, such as windowing and sequencing, have no meaning in UDP. Recall that UDP has no fields for sequence numbers or window sizes. Application layer protocols can provide for reliability. UDP is designed for applications that provide their own error recovery process. It trades reliability for speed.

Figure 1-53 *TCP Windowing*

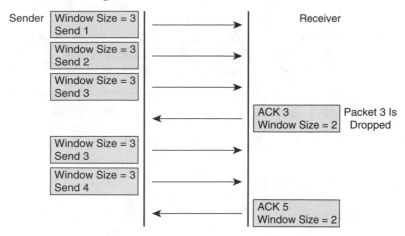

TCP, UDP, and IP and their headers are key in the communications between networks. Layer 3 devices use an internetwork protocol like TCP/IP to provide communications between remote systems.

Acknowledgment

TCP performs sequencing of segments with a forward reference acknowledgment. A forward reference acknowledgment comes from the receiving device and tells the sending device which segment the receiving device is expecting to receive next.

For the purpose of this lesson, the complex operation of TCP is simplified in a number of ways. Simple incremental numbers are used as the sequence numbers and acknowledgments, although in reality the sequence numbers track the number of bytes received. In a TCP simple acknowledgment, the sending computer transmits a segment, starts a timer, and waits for acknowledgment before transmitting the next segment. If the timer expires before receipt of the segment is acknowledged, the sending computer retransmits the segment and starts the timer again.

Imagine that each segment is numbered before transmission (remember that it is really the number of bytes that are tracked). At the receiving station, TCP reassembles the segments into a complete message. If a sequence number is missing in the series, that segment and all subsequent segments can be retransmitted. The steps involved with the acknowledgment process are as follows:

Step 1   The sender and receiver agree that each segment must be acknowledged before another can be sent. This occurs during the connection setup procedure by setting the window size to 1.

Step 2   The sender transmits segment 1 to the receiver. The sender starts a timer and waits for acknowledgment from the receiver.

Step 3   The receiver receives segment 1 and returns ACK = 2. The receiver acknowledges the successful receipt of the previous segment by stating the expected next segment number.

Step 4   The sender receives ACK = 2 and transmits segment 2 to the receiver. The sender starts a timer and waits for acknowledgment from the receiver.

Step 5   The receiver receives segment 2 and returns ACK = 3. The receiver acknowledges the successful receipt of the previous segment.

Step 6   The sender receives ACK = 3 and transmits segment 4 to the receiver. This process continues until all data is sent.

Windowing

The TCP window controls the transmission rate at a level where receiver congestion and data loss do not occur.

Fixed Windowing

In the most basic form of reliable, connection-oriented data transfers, ignoring network congestion issues, the recipient acknowledges the receipt of each data segment to ensure the integrity of the transmission. However, if the sender must wait for an acknowledgment after sending each segment, throughput is low, depending on the round-trip time (RTT) between sending data and receiving the acknowledgment.

Most connection-oriented, reliable protocols allow more than one segment to be outstanding at a time. This approach can work because time is available after the sender completes a segment transmission and before the sender processes any acknowledgment of receipt. During this interval, the sender can transmit more data, provided the window at the receiver is large enough to handle more than one segment at a time. The window is the number of data segments the sender is allowed to send without getting acknowledgment from the receiver, as shown in Figure 1-54.

Windowing enables a specified number of unacknowledged segments to be sent to the receiver, thereby reducing latency. Latency in this instance refers to the amount of time it takes for data to be sent and the acknowledgment to be returned.

Example: Throwing a Ball

Think of two people standing 50 feet apart. One person throws a football to the other, and that portion of the trip takes 3 seconds. The second person receives the football, throws a ball back (acknowledgment), and that portion of the trip takes 3 seconds. The round trip takes a total of 6 seconds. To do this process 3 times would take a total of 18 seconds. Now imagine that the first person has three balls and throws them one after the other. This part of the trip still takes 3 seconds. The second person throws back one ball to acknowledge the receipt of the third ball, and that portion of the trip again takes 3 seconds. The round trip takes a total of 6 seconds. (Of course, this ignores processing time and so on.)

Figure 1-54   *Fixed Windowing*

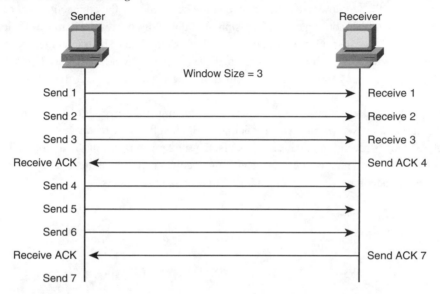

The following steps describe the windowing process in a TCP connection:

Step 1   The sender and receiver set an initial window size: three segments before an acknowledgment must be sent. This occurs during the connection setup procedure.

Step 2   The sender transmits segments 1, 2, and 3 to the receiver. The sender transmits the segments, starts a timer, and waits for acknowledgment from the receiver.

Step 3   The receiver receives segments 1, 2, and 3 and returns ACK = 4. The receiver acknowledges the successful receipt of the previous segments.

Step 4   The sender receives ACK = 4 and transmits segments 4, 5, and 6 to the receiver. The sender transmits the segments, starts a timer, and waits for acknowledgment from the receiver.

Step 5   The receiver receives segments 4, 5, and 6 and returns ACK = 7. The receiver acknowledges the successful receipt of the previous segments.

The numbers used in this example are simplified for ease of understanding. These numbers actually represent octets (bytes) and would be increasing in much larger numbers representing the contents of TCP segments, not the segments themselves.

TCP Sliding Windowing

TCP uses a sliding window technique to specify the number of segments, starting with the acknowledgment number that the receiver can accept.

In fixed windowing, the window size is established and does not change. In sliding windowing, the window size is negotiated at the beginning of the connection and can change dynamically during the TCP session. A sliding window results in more efficient use of bandwidth because a larger window size allows more data to be transmitted pending acknowledgment. Also, if a receiver reduces the advertised window size to 0, this effectively stops any further transmissions until a new window greater than 0 is sent.

In Figure 1-55, the window size is 3. The sender can transmit three segments to the receiver. At that point, the sender must wait for acknowledgment from the receiver. After the receiver acknowledges receipt of the three segments, the sender can transmit three more. However, if resources at the receiver become scarce, the receiver can reduce the window size so that it does not become overwhelmed and have to drop data segments.

Figure 1-55 *Sliding Windowing*

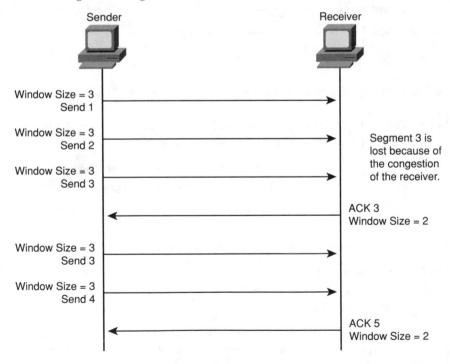

Each acknowledgment transmitted by the receiver contains a window advertisement that indicates the number of bytes the receiver can accept (the window size). This allows the window to be expanded or contracted as necessary to manage buffer space and processing.

TCP maintains a separate congestion window size (CWS) parameter, which is normally the same size as the window size of the receiver, but the CWS is cut in half when segments are lost. Segment loss is perceived as network congestion. TCP invokes sophisticated back off and restart algorithms so that it does not contribute to network congestion. The following steps are taken during a sliding window operation:

Step 1   The sender and the receiver exchange their initial window size values. In this example, the window size is 3 segments before an acknowledgment must be sent. This occurs during the connection setup procedure.

Step 2   The sender transmits segments 1, 2, and 3 to the receiver. The sender waits for an acknowledgment from the receiver after sending segment 3.

Step 3   The receiver receives segments 1 and 2, but now can handle a window size of only 2 (ACK = 3 WS = 2). The receiver's processing might slow down for many reasons, such as when the CPU is searching a database or downloading a large graphic file.

Step 4   The sender transmits segments 3 and 4. The sender waits for an acknowledgment from the receiver after sending segment 5, when it still has two outstanding segments.

Step 5   The receiver acknowledges receipt of segments 3 and 4, but still maintains a window size of 2 (ACK = 5 WS = 2). The receiver acknowledges the successful receipt of segments 3 and 4 by requesting transmission of segment 5.

Maximize Throughput

The congestion windowing algorithm manages the rate of sent data. This minimizes both data drop and the time spent recovering dropped data; therefore, efficiency is improved.

Global Synchronization

While the congestion windowing algorithm improves efficiency in general, it can also have an extremely negative effect on efficiency by causing global synchronization of the TCP process. Global synchronization is when all the same senders use the same algorithm and their behavior synchronizes. The senders all perceive the same congestion and all back off at the same time. Then, because the senders are all using the same algorithm, they all come back at the same time, which creates waves of congestion.

Summary of Understanding TCP/IP's Transport and Application Layers

The following are the key points that were discussed in this section:

- UDP is a protocol that operates at the transport layer and provides applications with access to the network layer without the overhead and reliability mechanisms of TCP. UDP is a connectionless, best-effort delivery protocol.

- TCP is a protocol that operates at the transport layer and provides applications with access to the network layer. TCP is connection-oriented, provides error checking, delivers data reliably, operates in full-duplex mode, and provides some data recovery functions.

- TCP/IP supports a number of applications, including FTP, TFTP, and Telnet.

- IP uses a protocol number in the datagram header to identify which protocol to use for a particular datagram.

- Port numbers map Layer 4 to an application.

- If you use TCP as the transport layer protocol, before applications can transfer data, both sending and receiving applications inform their respective operating systems that a connection will be initiated. After synchronization has occurred, the two end systems have established a connection and data transfer can begin.

- Flow control avoids the problem of a transmitting host overflowing the buffers in the receiving host and slowing network performance.

- TCP provides sequencing of segments with a forward reference acknowledgement. When a single segment is sent, receipt is acknowledged, and the next segment is then sent.

- TCP window size decreases the transmission rate to a level at which congestion and data loss do not occur. The TCP window size allows for a specified number of unacknowledged segments to be sent.

- A fixed window is a window with an unchanging size that can accommodate a specific flow of segments.

- A TCP sliding window is a window that can change size dynamically to accommodate the flow of segments.

- TCP provides the sequencing of segments by providing sequence numbers and acknowledgment numbers in the TCP headers.

Exploring the Packet Delivery Process

The previous sections discussed the elements that govern host-to-host communications. You also need to understand how these elements interact. This section covers host-to-host communications by providing a graphic representation.

Layer 1 Devices and Their Functions

Layer 1 defines the electrical, mechanical, procedural, and functional specifications for activating, maintaining, and deactivating the physical link between end systems. Some common examples are Ethernet segments and serial links like Frame Relay and T1.

Repeaters that provide signal amplification are also considered Layer 1 devices. Figure 1-56 shows some common Layer 1 devices.

Figure 1-56 *Layer 1 Devices*

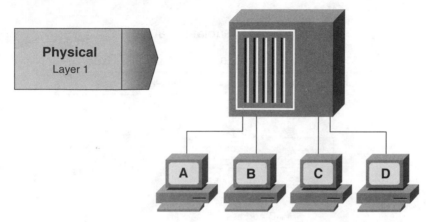

The physical interface on the NIC can also be considered part of Layer 1.

Layer 2 Devices and Their Functions

Layer 2 defines how data is formatted for transmission and how access to the physical media is controlled. These devices also provide an interface between the Layer 2 device and the physical media. Some common examples are a NIC installed in a host, bridge, or switch. Figure 1-57 shows an example of Layer 2 devices.

Figure 1-57 *Layer 2 Devices*

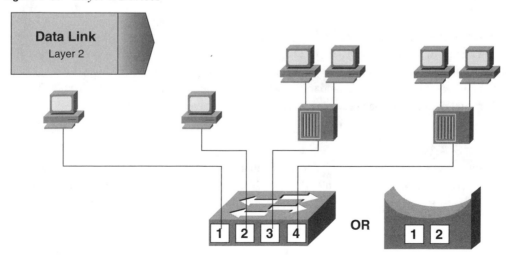

Layer 2 Addressing

Host communications require a Layer 2 address. Figure 1-58 shows an example of a MAC address for a Layer 2 Ethernet frame.

Figure 1-58   *Ethernet MAC Address*

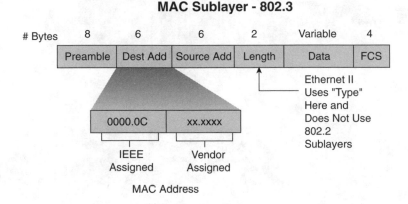

When the host-to-host communications were first developed, several network layer protocols were called network operating systems (NOS). Early NOS were NetWare, IP, ISO, and Banyan-Vines. It became apparent that a need for a Layer 2 address that was independent of the NOS existed, so the MAC address was created.

MAC addresses are assigned to end devices such as hosts. In most cases, Layer 2 network devices such as bridges and switches are not assigned a MAC address. However, in some special cases, switches might be assigned an address.

Layer 3 Devices and Their Functions

The network layer provides connectivity and path selection between two host systems that might be located on geographically separated networks. In the case of a host, this is the path between the data link layer and the upper layers of the NOS. In the case of a router, it is the actual path across the network. Figure 1-59 shows Layer 3 devices.

Layer 3 Addressing

Each NOS has its own Layer 3 address format. For example, the OSI reference model uses a network service access point (NSAP), while TCP/IP uses an IP address. This course focuses on TCP/IP. Figure 1-60 shows an example of Layer 3 addressing.

Figure 1-59 *Layer 3 Devices*

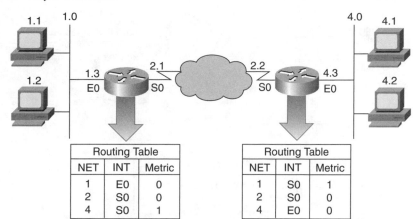

Figure 1-60 *Layer 3 Addressing*

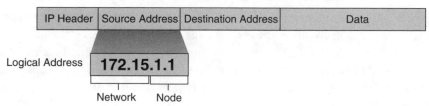

Mapping Layer 2 Addressing to Layer 3 Addressing

For IP communication on Ethernet-connected networks to take place, the logical (IP) address needs to be bound to the physical (MAC) address of its destination. This process is carried out by the Address Resolution Protocol (ARP). Figure 1-61 shows an example of mapping a Layer 2 address to a Layer 3 address.

To send data to a destination, a host on an Ethernet network must know the physical (MAC) address of the destination. ARP provides the essential service of mapping IP addresses to physical addresses on a network.

Figure 1-61   *Mapping Layer 2 to Layer 3*

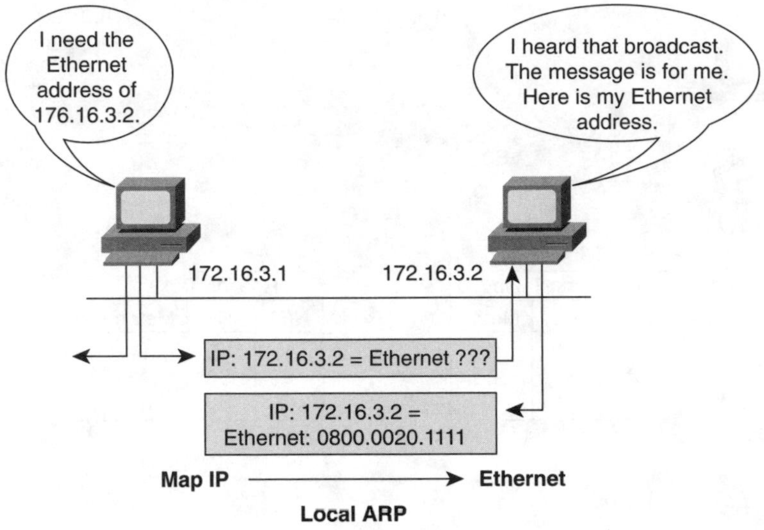

The term *address resolution* refers to the process of binding a network layer IP address of a remote device to its locally reachable, data link layer MAC address. The address is "resolved" when ARP broadcasts the known information (the target destination IP address and its own IP address). The broadcast is received by all devices on the Ethernet segment. When the target recognizes itself by reading the contents of the ARP request packet, it responds with the required MAC address in its ARP reply. The address resolution procedure is completed when the originator receives the reply packet (containing the required MAC address) from the target and updates the table containing all of the current bindings. (This table is usually called the ARP cache or ARP table.) The ARP table maintains a correlation between each IP address and its corresponding MAC address.

The bindings in the table are kept current by a process of aging out unused entries after a period of inactivity. The default time for this aging is usually 300 seconds (5 minutes), ensuring that the table does not contain information for systems that might be switched off or that have been moved.

ARP Table

The ARP table, or ARP cache, keeps a record of recent bindings of IP addresses to MAC addresses. Figure 1-62 shows an example of an ARP table.

Figure 1-62 *ARP Table*

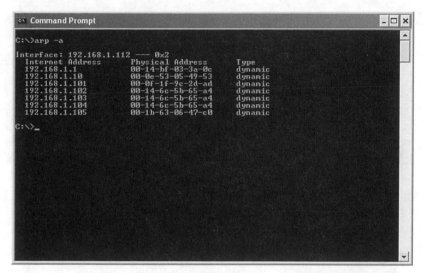

Each IP device on a network segment maintains an ARP table in its memory. This table maps the IP addresses of other devices on the network with their physical (MAC) addresses. When a host wants to transmit data to another host on the same network, it searches the ARP table to see if an entry exists. If an entry does exist, the host uses it, but if not, ARP is used to get an entry.

The ARP table is created and maintained dynamically, adding and changing address relationships as they are used on the local host. The entries in an ARP table usually expire after a period of time, by default 300 seconds; however, when the local host wants to transmit data again, the entry in the ARP table is regenerated through the ARP process.

Host-to-Host Packet Delivery

In Figure 1-63, an application on the host with a Layer 3 address of 192.168.3.1 wants to send some data to the host with a Layer 3 address of 192.168.3.2. The application wants to use a reliable connection. The application requests this service from the transport layer.

The transport layer selects TCP to set up the session. TCP initiates the session by passing a TCP header with the SYN bit set and the destination Layer 3 address (192.168.3.2) to the IP layer.

Figure 1-63 *Packet Delivery*

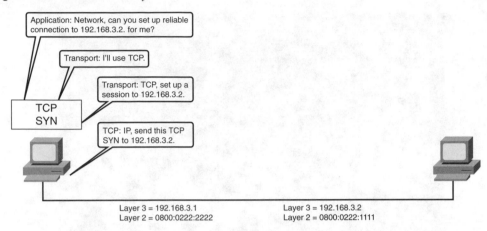

The IP layer encapsulates the TCP's SYN in a Layer 2 packet by prepending the local Layer 3 address and the Layer 3 address that IP received from TCP. IP then passes the packet to Layer 2. Figure 1-64 shows this operation.

Figure 1-64 *IP Layer Operation*

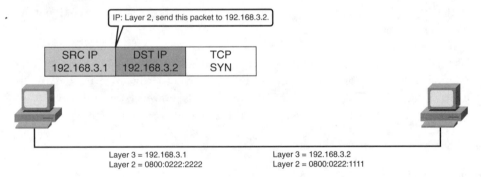

Layer 2 needs to encapsulate the Layer 3 packet into a Layer 2 frame. To do this, Layer 2 needs to map the Layer 3 destination address of the packet to its MAC address. It does this by requesting a mapping from the ARP program.

ARP checks its table. In this example, it is assumed that this host has not communicated with the other host, so you see no entry in the ARP table. This results in Layer 2 holding the packet until ARP can provide a mapping. Figure 1-65 shows this operation.

Figure 1-65 *ARP Table Lookup*

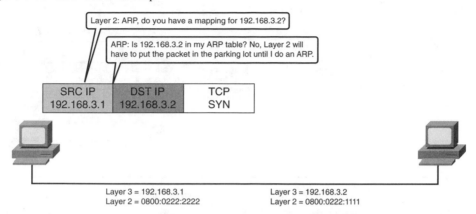

The ARP program builds an ARP request and passes it to Layer 2, telling Layer 2 to send the request to a broadcast (all Fs) address. Layer 2 encapsulates the ARP request in a Layer 2 frame using the broadcast address provided by ARP as the destination MAC address and the local MAC address as the source. Figures 1-66 and 1-67 show this operation.

Figure 1-66 *ARP Overview*

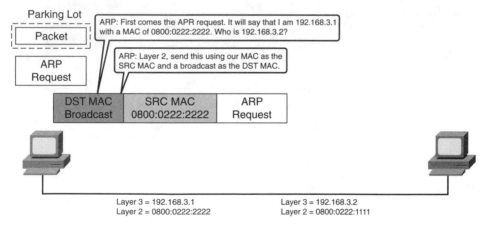

Figure 1-67 *ARP Request Sent*

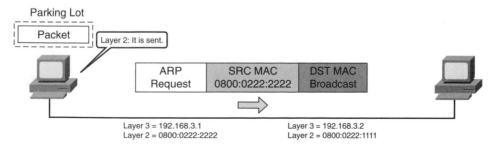

When host 192.168.3.2 receives the frame, it notes the broadcast address and strips the Layer 2 encapsulation. Figure 1-68 shows this operation.

Figure 1-68 *ARP Response Received*

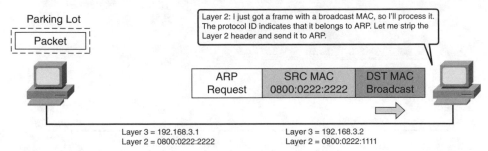

The remaining ARP request is passed to ARP. Figure 1-69 shows this operation.

Figure 1-69 *Layer 2 Passes to ARP*

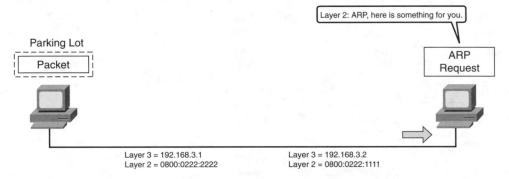

Using the information in the ARP request, ARP updates its table. Figure 1-70 shows this operation.

Figure 1-70 *ARP Adds Sending Information to Table*

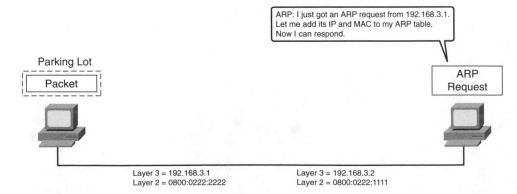

ARP builds a response and passes it to Layer 2, telling Layer 2 to send the response to MAC address 0800:0222:2222 (host 192.168.3.1). Figure 1-71 shows this operation.

Figure 1-71 *ARP Builds a Response*

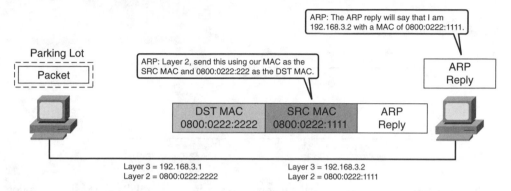

Layer 2 encapsulates the ARP in a Layer 2 frame using the destination MAC address provided by ARP and the local source MAC address. Figure 1-72 shows this operation.

Figure 1-72 *ARP Responds*

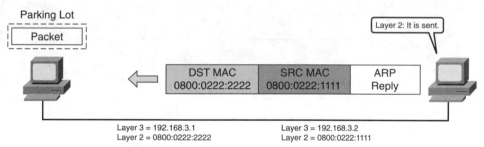

When host 192.168.3.1 receives the frame, it notes that the destination MAC address is the same as its own address. It strips the Layer 2 encapsulation. Figure 1-73 shows this operation.

Figure 1-73 *Layer 2 Recognizes MAC Address*

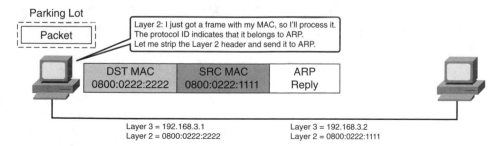

The remaining ARP reply is passed to ARP. Figure 1-74 shows this operation.

Figure 1-74 *Layer 2 Passes to ARP*

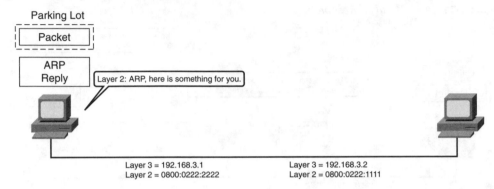

ARP updates its table and passes the mapping to Layer 2. Figure 1-75 shows this operation.

Figure 1-75 *ARP Updates the Table*

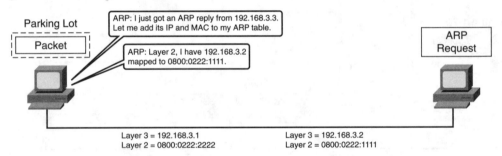

Layer 2 can now send the pending Layer 2 packet. Figure 1-76 shows this operation.

Figure 1-76 *Layer 2 Sends Packet Inside Frame to Start the Three-Way Handshake*

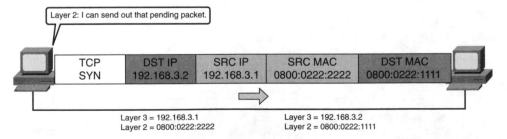

At host 192.168.3.2, the frame is passed up the stack where encapsulation is removed. The remaining protocol data unit (PDU) is passed to TCP. Figure 1-77 shows this operation.

Figure 1-77 *IP Packet Is Received*

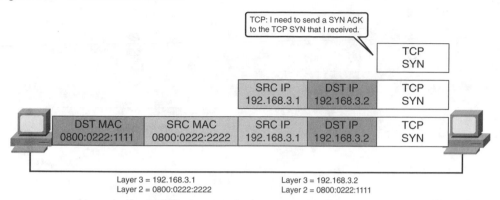

In response to the SYN, TCP passes a SYN ACK down the stack to be encapsulated. Figure 1-78 shows this operation.

Figure 1-78 *Receiver Acknowledges Frame*

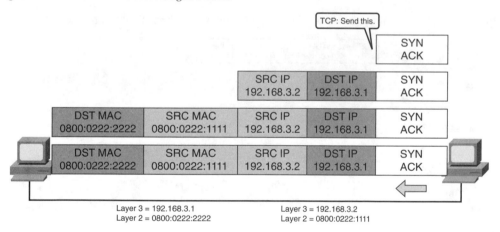

The sender receives the ACK along with a SYN from the receiver that it must respond to. This is shown in Figure 1-79.

Figure 1-79 *Sender Receives ACK*

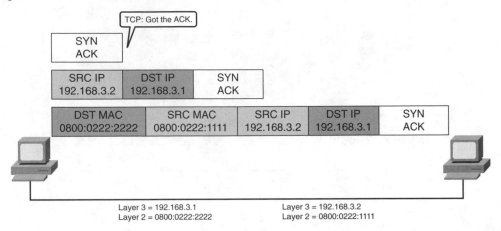

The sender sends the ACK to the receiver that it must respond to. This is shown in Figure 1-80.

Figure 1-80 *Sender Acknowledges ACK and Completes the Three-Way Handshake*

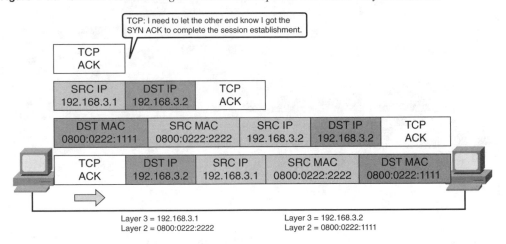

With the three-way handshake completed, TCP can inform the application that the session has been established. This is shown in Figure 1-81.

Figure 1-81   *Session Is Open*

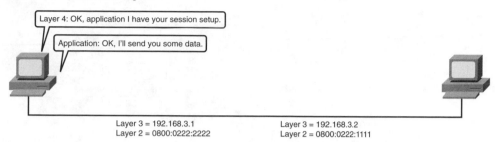

Now the application can send the data over the session, relying on TCP for error detection. Figures 1-82 through 1-84 show this operation.

Figure 1-82   *Data Flow Begins*

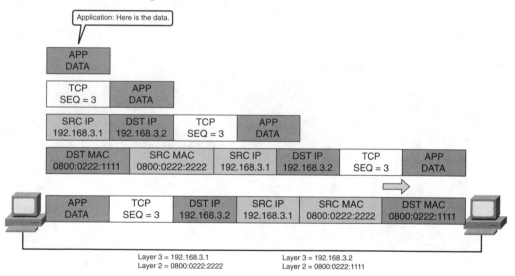

Figure 1-83 *Data Is Received*

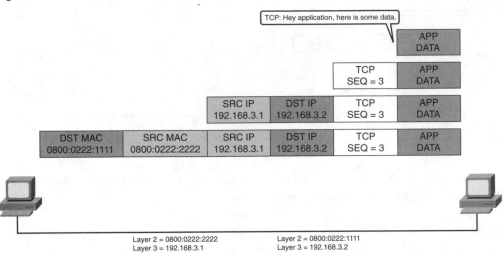

Figure 1-84 *Data Is Acknowledged*

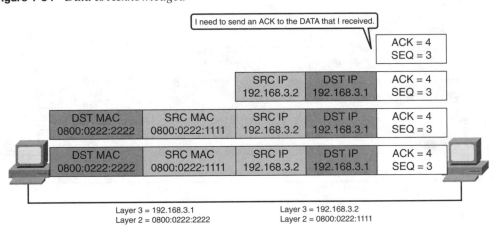

The data exchange continues until the application stops sending data.

Function of the Default Gateway

In the host-to-host packet delivery example, the host was able to use ARP to map a destination's MAC address to the destination's IP address. However, this option is available only if the two hosts are on the same network. If the two hosts are on different networks, the sending host must send the data to the default gateway, which forwards the data to the destination. Figure 1-85 shows role of the default gateway in data transfers.

Figure 1-85 *Role of the Default Gateway*

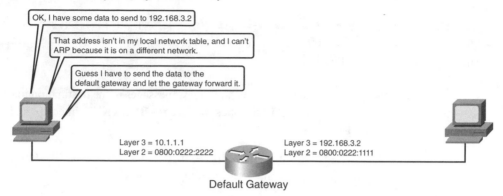

Using Common Host Tools to Determine the Path Between Two Hosts Across a Network

Ping is a computer network tool used to test whether a particular host is reachable across an IP network. Ping works by sending Internet Control Message Protocol (ICMP) "echo request" packets ("Ping?") to the target host and listening for ICMP "echo response" replies. Using interval timing and response rates, ping estimates the RTT (generally in milliseconds) and packet-loss rate between hosts. Figure 1-86 shows the ping output from a windows command line.

Figure 1-86 *Ping*

```
Command Prompt                                                    _ □ ×

C:\>ping example.com

Pinging example.com [192.168.1.1] with 32 bytes of data:

Reply from 192.168.1.1: bytes=32 time=5ms TTL=64
Reply from 192.168.1.1: bytes=32 time=8ms TTL=64
Reply from 192.168.1.1: bytes=32 time=3ms TTL=64
Reply from 192.168.1.1: bytes=32 time=9ms TTL=64

Ping statistics for 192.168.1.1:
    Packets: Sent = 4, Received = 4, Lost = 0 (0% loss),
Approximate round trip times in milli-seconds:
    Minimum = 3ms, Maximum = 9ms, Average = 6ms

C:\>
```

The syntax for a Windows ping is as follows:

```
ping [-t] [-a] [-n Count] [-l Size] [-f] [-i TTL] [-v TOS] [-r Count] [-s Count]
     [{-j HostList | -k HostList}] [-w Timeout] [TargetName]
```

The syntax flags are as follows:

- **-t:** Specifies that ping continue sending echo request messages to the destination until interrupted. To interrupt and display statistics, press **Ctrl-BREAK**. To interrupt and quit ping, press **Ctrl-C**.

- **-a:** Specifies that reverse name resolution is performed on the destination IP address. If this is successful, ping displays the corresponding hostname.

- **-n** *Count*: Specifies the number of echo request messages sent. The default is 4.

- **-l** *Size*: Specifies the length, in bytes, of the Data field in the echo request messages sent. The default is 32. The maximum size is 65,527.

- **-f:** Specifies that echo request messages are sent with the Don't Fragment flag in the IP header set to 1. The echo request message cannot be fragmented by routers in the path to the destination. This parameter is useful for troubleshooting path maximum transmission unit (PMTU) problems.

- **-i** *TTL*: Specifies the value of the Time-to-Live (TTL) field in the IP header for echo request messages sent. The default is the default TTL value for the host. For Windows XP hosts, this is typically 128. The maximum TTL is 255.

- **-v** *TOS*: Specifies the value of the Type of Service (TOS) field in the IP header for echo request messages sent. The default is 0. TOS is specified as a decimal value from 0 to 255.

- **-r** *Count*: Specifies that the Record Route option in the IP header is used to record the path taken by the echo request message and corresponding echo reply message. Each hop in the path uses an entry in the Record Route option. If possible, specify a *Count* that is equal to or greater than the number of hops between the source and destination. The *Count* must be a minimum of 1 and a maximum of 9.

- **-s** *Count*: Specifies that the Internet Timestamp option in the IP header is used to record the time of arrival for the echo request message and corresponding echo reply message for each hop. The *Count* must be a minimum of 1 and a maximum of 4.

- **-j** *HostList*: Specifies that the echo request messages use the Loose Source Route option in the IP header with the set of intermediate destinations specified in *HostList*. With loose source routing, successive intermediate destinations can be separated by one or multiple routers. The maximum number of addresses or names in the host list is nine. The *HostList* is a series of IP addresses (in dotted decimal notation) separated by spaces.

- **-k** *HostList*: Specifies that the echo request messages use the Strict Source Route option in the IP header with the set of intermediate destinations specified in *HostList*. With strict source routing, the next intermediate destination must be directly reachable (it must be a neighbor on an interface of the router). The maximum number of addresses or names in the host list is nine. The *HostList* is a series of IP addresses (in dotted decimal notation) separated by spaces.

- **-w** *Timeout*: Specifies the amount of time, in milliseconds, to wait for the echo reply message that corresponds to a given echo request message to be received. If the echo reply message is not received within the timeout, the "Request timed out" error message is displayed. The default timeout is 4000 (4 seconds).

- *TargetName*: Specifies the destination, which is identified by either IP address or host name.

- **/?**: Displays help at the command prompt.

The Windows **arp** command shown in Figure 1-87 displays and modifies entries in the ARP cache, which contains one or more tables that store IP addresses and their resolved Ethernet physical addresses. A separate table exists for each Ethernet or Token Ring network adapter installed on your computer. Used without parameters, **arp** displays help.

Figure 1-87   *Displaying the ARP Table*

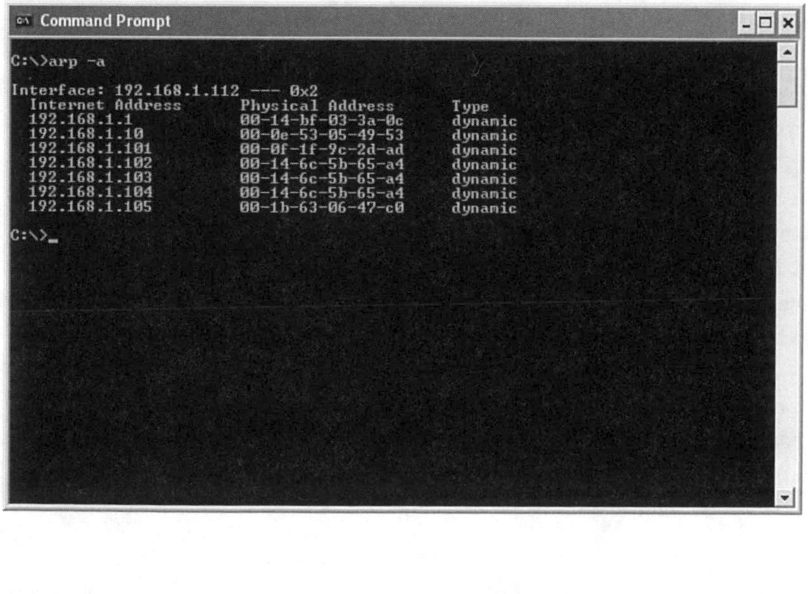

The syntax for the command is as follows:

```
arp [-a [InetAddr] [-N IfaceAddr]] [-g [InetAddr] [-N IfaceAddr]] [-d InetAddr
  [IfaceAddr]] [-s InetAddr EtherAddr [IfaceAddr]]
```

The following are the parameters associated with the windows ARP command:

- **-a** [*InetAddr*] [**-N** *IfaceAddr*]**:** Displays current ARP cache tables for all interfaces. To display the ARP cache entry for a specific IP address, use **arp -a** with the *InetAddr* parameter, where *InetAddr* is an IP address. To display the ARP cache table for a specific interface, use the **-N** *IfaceAddr* parameter where *IfaceAddr* is the IP address assigned to the interface. The **-N** parameter is case-sensitive.

- **-g** [*InetAddr*] [**-N** *IfaceAddr*]**:** Identical to **-a**.

- **-d** *InetAddr* [*IfaceAddr*]**:** Deletes an entry with a specific IP address, where *InetAddr* is the IP address. To delete an entry in a table for a specific interface, use the *IfaceAddr* parameter where *IfaceAddr* is the IP address assigned to the interface. To delete all entries, use the asterisk (*****) wildcard character in place of InetAddr.

- **-s** *InetAddr EtherAddr* [*IfaceAddr*]**:** Adds a static entry to the ARP cache that resolves the IP address *InetAddr* to the physical address *EtherAddr*. To add a static ARP cache entry to the table for a specific interface, use the *IfaceAddr* parameter where *IfaceAddr* is an IP address assigned to the interface.

- **/?:** Displays help at the command prompt.

The TRACERT (traceroute) diagnostic utility determines the route to a destination by sending ICMP echo packets to the destination. In these packets, TRACERT uses varying IP TTL values. Because each router along the path is required to decrement the packet's TTL by at least 1 before forwarding the packet, the TTL is effectively a hop counter. When the TTL on a packet reaches zero (0), the router sends an ICMP "Time Exceeded" message back to the source computer.

TRACERT sends the first echo packet with a TTL of 1 and increments the TTL by 1 on each subsequent transmission until the destination responds or until the maximum TTL is reached. The ICMP "Time Exceeded" messages that intermediate routers send back show the route. Note, however, that some routers silently drop packets with expired TTL values, and these packets are invisible to TRACERT.

TRACERT prints out an ordered list of the intermediate routers that return ICMP "Time Exceeded" messages. Using the **-d** option with the **tracert** command instructs TRACERT not to perform a DNS lookup on each IP address, so that TRACERT reports the IP address of the near-side interface of the routers. Figure 1-88 shows a traceroute to yahoo.com.

Figure 1-88 *Performing a Traceroute*

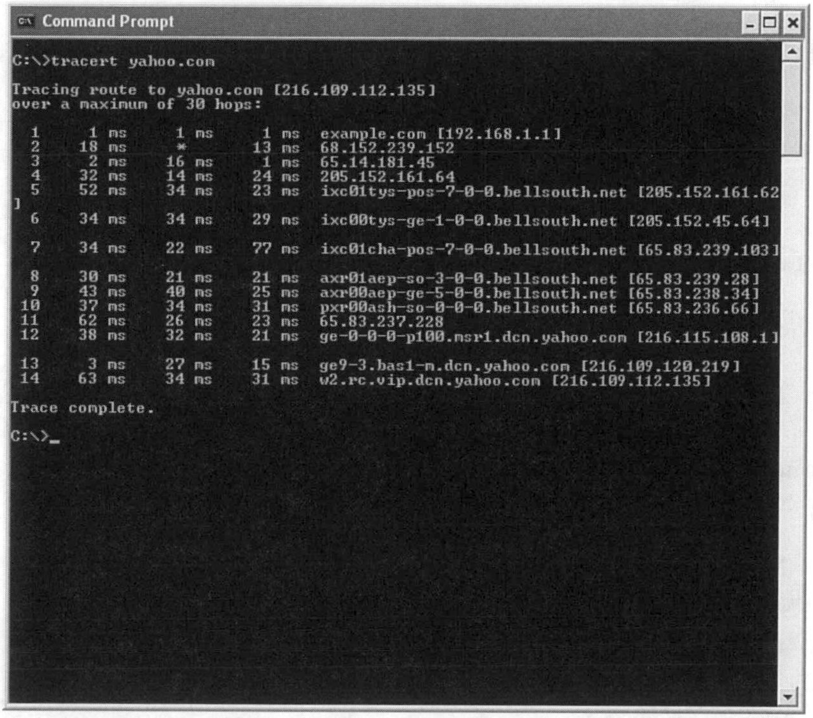

```
Command Prompt                                                    _ □ ✕

C:\>tracert yahoo.com

Tracing route to yahoo.com [216.109.112.135]
over a maximum of 30 hops:

  1     1 ms      1 ms      1 ms   example.com [192.168.1.1]
  2    18 ms      *        13 ms   68.152.239.152
  3     2 ms     16 ms      1 ms   65.14.181.45
  4    32 ms     14 ms     24 ms   205.152.161.64
  5    52 ms     34 ms     23 ms   ixc01tys-pos-7-0-0.bellsouth.net [205.152.161.62
]
  6    34 ms     34 ms     29 ms   ixc00tys-ge-1-0-0.bellsouth.net [205.152.45.64]

  7    34 ms     22 ms     77 ms   ixc01cha-pos-7-0-0.bellsouth.net [65.83.239.103]

  8    30 ms     21 ms     21 ms   axr01aep-so-3-0-0.bellsouth.net [65.83.239.28]
  9    43 ms     40 ms     25 ms   axr00aep-ge-5-0-0.bellsouth.net [65.83.238.34]
 10    37 ms     34 ms     31 ms   pxr00ash-so-0-0-0.bellsouth.net [65.83.236.66]
 11    62 ms     26 ms     23 ms   65.83.237.228
 12    38 ms     32 ms     21 ms   ge-0-0-0-p100.msr1.dcn.yahoo.com [216.115.108.1]

 13     3 ms     27 ms     15 ms   ge9-3.bas1-m.dcn.yahoo.com [216.109.120.219]
 14    63 ms     34 ms     31 ms   w2.rc.vip.dcn.yahoo.com [216.109.112.135]

Trace complete.

C:\>_
```

The syntax for a windows traceroute is as follows:

tracert -d -h *maximum_hops* -j *HostList* -w *Timeout target_host*

The following are the parameters associated with the windows traceroute command:

- **-d:** Specifies to not resolve addresses to hostnames

- **-h** *maximum_hops***:** Specifies the maximum number of hops to search for the target

- **-j** *HostList***:** Specifies loose source route along the host list

- **-w** *Timeout***:** Waits the number of milliseconds specified by timeout for each reply

- *target_host***:** Specifies the name or IP address of the target host

Summary of Exploring the Packet Delivery Process

The following summarizes the key points that were discussed in this lesson.

- Layer 1 devices provide the connection to the physical media and its encoding.

- Layer 2 devices provide an interface between the Layer 2 device and the physical media.

- Layer 2 addresses are MAC addresses.

- The network layer provides connectivity and path selection between two host systems.

- Layer 3 addresses provide identification of a network and a host, such as an IP address.

- Before a host can send data to another host, it must know the MAC address of the other device.

- ARP is a protocol that maps IP addresses to MAC addresses.

- TCP uses a three-way handshake to establish a session before sending data.

- Most operating systems offer tools to view the device ARP table as well as tools like ping and traceroute to test IP connectivity.

Understanding Ethernet

A LAN is a common type of network found in home offices, small businesses, and large enterprises. Understanding how a LAN functions, including network components, frames, Ethernet addresses, and operational characteristics, is important for an overall knowledge of networking technologies.

This lesson describes LANs and provides fundamental knowledge about LAN characteristics, components, and functions. It also describes the basic operations of an Ethernet LAN and how frames are transmitted over it.

The Definition of a LAN

A LAN is a network of computers and other components located relatively close together in a limited area. LANs can vary widely in their size. A LAN might consist of only two computers in a home office or small business, or it might include hundreds of computers in a large corporate office or multiple buildings. Figure 1-89 shows some examples of LANs.

A small home business or a small office environment could use a small LAN to connect two or more computers and to connect the computers to one or more shared peripheral devices such as printers. A large corporate office could use multiple LANs to accommodate hundreds of computers and shared peripheral devices, for departments such as finance or operations, spanning many floors in an office complex.

Figure 1-89 *LANs*

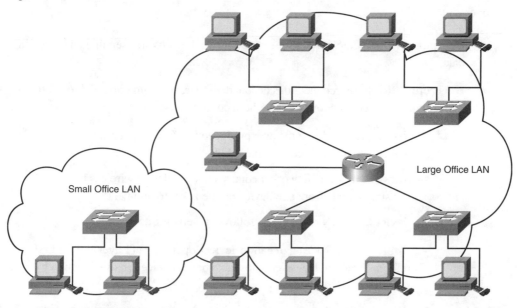

Components of a LAN

Every LAN has specific components, including hardware, interconnections, and software.
Figure 1-90 highlights the hardware components of a LAN

Figure 1-90 *LAN Components*

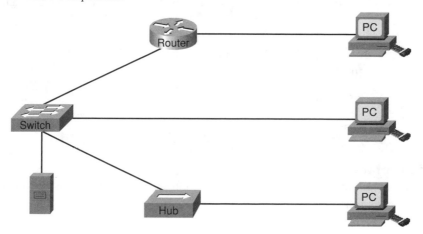

Regardless of the size of the LAN, it requires these fundamental components for its operation.

- **Computers:** Computers serve as the endpoints in the network, sending and receiving data.

- **Interconnections:** Interconnections enable data to travel from one point to another in the network. Interconnections include these components:

    — **NICs:** NICs translate the data produced by the computer into a format that can be transmitted over the LAN.

    — **Network media:** Network media, such as cables or wireless media, transmit signals from one device on the LAN to another.

- **Network devices:** A LAN requires the following network devices:

    — **Hubs:** Hubs provide aggregation devices operating at Layer 1 of the OSI reference model. However, hubs have been replaced in this function by switches.

    — **Ethernet switches:** Ethernet switches form the aggregation point for LANs. Ethernet switches operate at Layer 2 of the OSI reference model and provide intelligent distribution of frames within the LAN.

    — **Routers:** Routers, sometimes called gateways, provide a means to connect LAN segments. Routers operate at Layer 3 of the OSI reference model.

- **Protocols:** Protocols govern the way data is transmitted over a LAN and include the following:

    — Ethernet protocols

    — IP

    — ARP and RARP

    — DHCP

Functions of a LAN

LANs provide network users with communication and resource-sharing functions, including the following:

- **Data and applications:** When users are connected through a network, they can share files and even software application programs. This makes data more easily available and promotes more efficient collaboration on work projects.

■ **Resources:** The resources that can be shared include both input devices, such as cameras, and output devices, such as printers.

■ **Communication path to other networks:** If a resource is not available locally, the LAN, via a gateway, can provide connectivity to remote resources—for example, access to the web.

How Big Is a LAN?

A LAN can be configured in a variety of sizes, depending on the requirements of the environment in which it operates. Figure 1-91 contrasts LAN sizes.

Figure 1-91   *Sizes of a LAN*

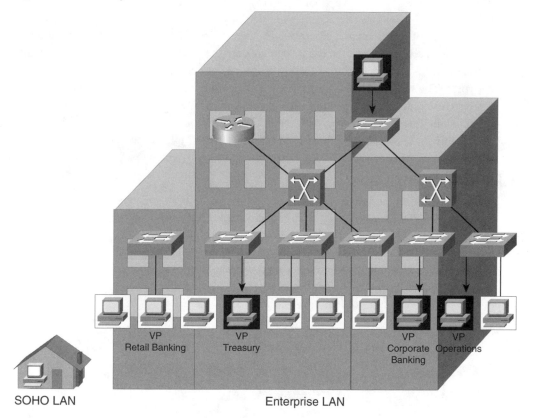

LANs can be of various sizes to fit different work requirements, including the following:

■ **Small office/home office (SOHO):** The SOHO environment typically has only a few computers and some peripherals such as printers.

■ **Enterprise:** The enterprise environment might include many separate LANs in a large office building or in different buildings on a corporate campus. In the enterprise environment, each LAN might contain hundreds of computers and peripherals in each LAN.

Ethernet

Ethernet is the most common type of LAN. It was originally developed in the 1970s by Digital Equipment Corporation (DEC), Intel, and Xerox and was called DIX Ethernet. It later came to be called thick Ethernet (because of the thickness of the cable used in this type of network), and it transmitted data at 10 megabits per second (Mbps). The standard for Ethernet was updated in the 1980s to add more capability, and the new version of Ethernet was referred to as Ethernet Version 2 (also called Ethernet II).

The Institute of Electrical and Electronic Engineers (IEEE) is a professional organization that defines network standards. IEEE standards are the predominant LAN standards in the world today. In the mid-1980s, an IEEE workgroup defined new standards for Ethernet-like networks. The set of standards they created was called Ethernet 802.3 and was based on the carrier sense multiple access with collision detection (CSMA/CD) process. Ethernet 802.3 specified the physical layer (Layer 1) and the MAC portion of the data link layer (Layer 2). Today, this set of standards is most often referred to as simply "Ethernet."

Ethernet LAN Standards

Ethernet LAN standards specify cabling and signaling at both the physical and data link layers of the OSI reference model. This topic describes Ethernet LAN standards at the data link layer.

Figure 1-92 shows how LAN protocols map to the OSI reference model.

Figure 1-92 *Ethernet Compared to the OSI Model*

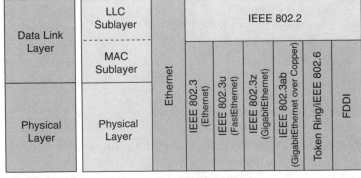

The IEEE divides the OSI data link layer into two separate sublayers:

- **Logical link control (LLC):** Transitions up to the network layer

- **MAC:** Transitions down to the physical layer

LLC Sublayer

The IEEE created the LLC sublayer to allow part of the data link layer to function independently from existing technologies. This layer provides versatility in services to the network layer protocols that are above it, while communicating effectively with the variety of MAC and Layer 1 technologies below it. The LLC, as a sublayer, participates in the encapsulation process.

An LLC header tells the data link layer what to do with a packet when it receives a frame. For example, a host receives a frame and then looks in the LLC header to understand that the packet is destined for the IP protocol at the network layer.

The original Ethernet header (prior to IEEE 802.2 and 802.3) did not use an LLC header. Instead, it used a type field in the Ethernet header to identify the Layer 3 protocol being carried in the Ethernet frame.

MAC Sublayer

The MAC sublayer deals with physical media access. The IEEE 802.3 MAC specification defines MAC addresses, which uniquely identify multiple devices at the data link layer. The MAC sublayer maintains a table of MAC addresses (physical addresses) of devices. To participate on the network, each device must have a unique MAC address.

The Role of CSMA/CD in Ethernet

Ethernet signals are transmitted to every station connected to the LAN, using a special set of rules to determine which station can "talk" at any particular time. This topic describes that set of rules.

Ethernet LANs manage the signals on a network by CSMA/CD, which is an important aspect of Ethernet. Figure 1-93 illustrates the CSMA/CD process.

In an Ethernet LAN, before transmitting, a computer first listens to the network media. If the media is idle, the computer sends its data. After a transmission has been sent, the computers on the network compete for the next available idle time to send another frame. This competition for idle time means that no one station has an advantage over another on the network.

Figure 1-93   *CSMA/CD*

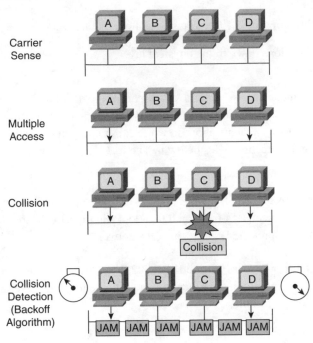

Stations on a CSMA/CD LAN can access the network at any time. Before sending data, CSMA/CD stations listen to the network to determine whether it is already in use. If it is, the CSMA/CD stations wait. If the network is not in use, the stations transmit. A collision occurs when two stations listen for network traffic, hear none, and transmit simultaneously (see the figure). In this case, both transmissions are damaged, and the stations must retransmit at some later time. CSMA/CD stations must be able to detect collisions to know that they must retransmit.

When a station transmits, the signal is referred to as a carrier. The NIC senses the carrier and consequently refrains from broadcasting a signal. If no carrier exists, a waiting station knows that it is free to transmit. This is the "carrier sense" part of the protocol.

The extent of the network segment over which collisions occur is referred to as the collision domain. The size of the collision domain has an impact on efficiency, and therefore on data throughput.

In the CSMA/CD process, priorities are not assigned to particular stations, so all stations on the network have equal access. This is the "multiple access" part of the protocol. If two or more stations attempt a transmission simultaneously, a collision occurs. The stations are alerted of the collision, and they execute a backoff algorithm that randomly schedules retransmission of the frame. This scenario prevents the machines from repeatedly attempting to transmit at the same time. Collisions are normally resolved in microseconds. This is the "collision detection" part of the protocol.

Ethernet Frames

Bits that are transmitted over an Ethernet LAN are organized into frames. In Ethernet terminology, the "container" into which data is placed for transmission is called a frame. The frame contains header information, trailer information, and the actual data that is being transmitted.

Figure 1-94 illustrates all of the fields that are in a MAC layer of the Ethernet frame, which include the following:

Figure 1-94 *Ethernet Frame*

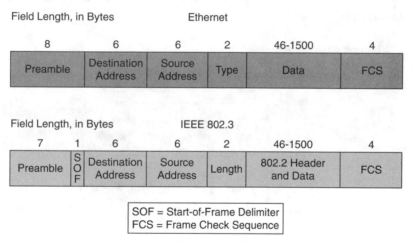

- **Preamble:** This field consists of 7 bytes of alternating 1s and 0s, which synchronize the signals of the communicating computers.

- **Start-of-frame (SOF) delimiter:** This field contains bits that signal the receiving computer that the transmission of the actual frame is about to start and that any data following is part of the packet.

- **Destination address:** This field contains the address of the NIC on the local network to which the packet is being sent.

- **Source address:** This field contains the address of the NIC of the sending computer.

- **Type/length:** In Ethernet II, this field contains a code that identifies the network layer protocol. In 802.3, this field specifies the length of the data field. The protocol information is contained in 802.2 fields, which are at the LLC layer. The newer 802.3 specifications have allowed the use of Ethertype protocol identifiers when not using the 802.2 field.

- **Data and pad:** This field contains the data that is received from the network layer on the transmitting computer. This data is then sent to the same protocol on the destination computer. If the data is too short, an adapter adds a string of extraneous bits to "pad" the field to its minimum length of 46 bytes.

- **Frame check sequence (FCS):** This field includes a checking mechanism to ensure that the packet of data has been transmitted without corruption.

Ethernet Frame Addressing

Communications in a network occur in three ways: unicast, broadcast, and multicast. Ethernet frames are addressed accordingly. Figure 1-95 shows forms of Ethernet communications.

Figure 1-95 *Ethernet Communications*

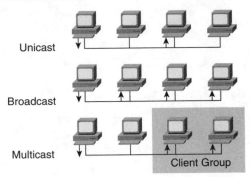

The three major types of network communications are as follows:

- **Unicast:** Communication in which a frame is sent from one host and addressed to one specific destination. In unicast transmission, you have just one sender and one receiver. Unicast transmission is the predominant form of transmission on LANs and within the Internet.

- **Broadcast:** Communication in which a frame is sent from one address to all other addresses. In this case, you have just one sender, but the information is sent to all connected receivers. Broadcast transmission is essential when sending the same message to all devices on the LAN.

- **Multicast:** Communication in which information is sent to a specific group of devices or clients. Unlike broadcast transmission, in multicast transmission clients must be members of a multicast group to receive the information.

Ethernet Addresses

The address used in an Ethernet LAN, which is associated with the network adapter, is the means by which data is directed to the proper receiving location. Figure 1-96 shows the format of an Ethernet address.

Figure 1-96 *Ethernet Addresses*

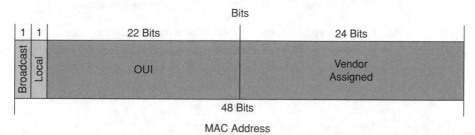

The address that is on the NIC is the MAC address, often referred to as the burned-in address (BIA), and some vendors allow the modification of this address to meet local needs. A 48-bit Ethernet MAC address has two components:

- **24-bit Organizational Unique Identifier (OUI):** The letter "O" identifies the manufacturer of the NIC card. The IEEE regulates the assignment of OUI numbers. Within the OUI, the two following bits have meaning only when used in the destination address:

    - **Broadcast or multicast bit:** This indicates to the receiving interface that the frame is destined for all or a group of end stations on the LAN segment.

    - **Locally administered address bit:** Normally the combination of OUI and a 24-bit station address is universally unique; however, if the address is modified locally, this bit should be set.

- **24-bit vendor-assigned end station address:** This uniquely identifies the Ethernet hardware.

MAC Addresses and Binary-Hexadecimal Numbers

The MAC address plays a specific role in the function of an Ethernet LAN. The MAC sublayer of the OSI data link layer handles physical addressing issues, and the physical address is a number in hexadecimal format that is actually burned into the NIC. This address is referred to as the MAC address, and it is expressed as groups of hexadecimal digits that are organized in pairs or quads, such as the following: 00:00:0c:43:2e:08 or 0000:0c43:2e08. Figure 1-97 shows the MAC address format compared to the MAC frame.

Figure 1-97 *Hexadecimal MAC Address*

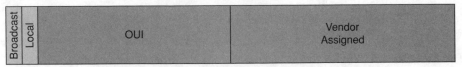

Each device on a LAN must have a unique MAC address to participate in the network. The MAC address identifies the location of a specific computer on a LAN. Unlike other kinds of addresses used in networks, the MAC address should *not* be changed unless you have some specific need.

Summary of Understanding Ethernet

The following summarizes the key points that were discussed in this lesson:

- A LAN is a network that is located in a limited area, with the computers and other components that are part of this network located relatively close together.

- Regardless of its size, several fundamental components are required for the operation of a LAN, including computers, interconnections, network devices, and protocols.

- LANs provide both communication and resource-sharing functions for their users and can be configured in various sizes, including both SOHO and enterprise environments.

- Ethernet was developed in the 1970s by DEC, Intel, and Xerox and was called DIX Ethernet. In the 1980s, an IEEE workgroup body defined a new Ethernet standard for public use, and it was called Ethernet 802.3 and Ethernet 802.2.

- Ethernet LAN standards specify cabling and signaling at both the physical and data link layers of the OSI model.

- Stations on a CSMA/CD LAN can access the network at any time before sending data. CSMA/CD stations listen to the network to determine whether it is already in use. If it is in use, they wait. If it is not in use, the stations transmit. A collision occurs when two stations listen for the network traffic, hear none, and transmit simultaneously.

- An Ethernet frame consists of fields, including preamble, start-of-frame delimiter, destination address, source address, type/length, data and pad, and frame check sequence.

- You find three major kinds of communications in networks: unicast, multicast, and broadcast.

- The address used in an Ethernet LAN is the means by which data is directed to the proper receiving location.

- The MAC sublayer handles physical addressing issues, and the physical address is a 48-bit number usually represented in hexadecimal format.

Connecting to an Ethernet LAN

In addition to understanding the components of an Ethernet LAN and the standards that govern its architecture, you need to understand the connection components of an Ethernet LAN. This lesson describes the connection components of an Ethernet LAN, including network interface cards (NIC) and cable.

Ethernet Network Interface Cards

A NIC is a printed circuit board that provides network communication capabilities to and from a personal computer on a network. Figure 1-98 shows an example of a NIC.

Figure 1-98 *Network Interface Card*

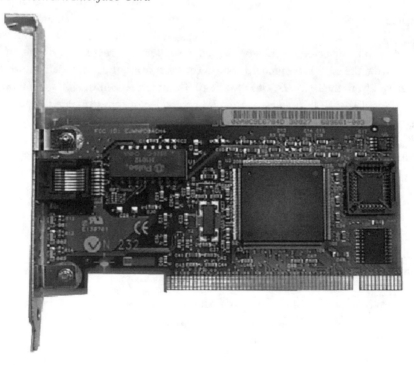

Also called a LAN adapter, the NIC plugs into a motherboard and provides a port for connecting to the network. The NIC constitutes the computer interface with the LAN.

The NIC communicates with the network through a serial connection, and with the computer through a parallel connection. When a NIC is installed in a computer, it requires an interrupt request line (IRQ), an input/output (I/O) address, a memory space within the operating system (such as DOS or Windows), and drivers (software) that allow it to perform its function. An IRQ is a signal that informs a CPU that an event needing its attention has occurred. An IRQ is sent over a hardware line to the microprocessor. An example of an interrupt request being issued is when a key is pressed on a keyboard, and the CPU must move the character from the keyboard to RAM. An I/O address is a location in memory used by an auxiliary device to enter data into or retrieve data from a computer.

The MAC address is burned onto each NIC by the manufacturer, providing a unique, physical network address.

Ethernet Media and Connection Requirements

Distance and time dictate the type of Ethernet connections required. This section describes the cable and connector specifications used to support Ethernet implementations.

The cable and connector specifications used to support Ethernet implementations are derived from the EIA/TIA standards body. The categories of cabling defined for Ethernet are derived from the EIA/TIA-568 (SP-2840) Commercial Building Telecommunications Wiring Standards. EIA/TIA specifies an RJ-45 connector for unshielded twisted-pair (UTP) cable.

The important difference to note is the media used for 10-Mbps Ethernet versus 100-Mbps Ethernet. In networks today, where you see a mix of 10- and 100-Mbps requirements, you must be aware of the need to change over to UTP Category 5 to support Fast Ethernet.

Connection Media

Several types of connection media can be used in an Ethernet LAN implementation. Figure 1-99 shows typical connection types.

The most common type of connection media is the RJ-45 connector and jack illustrated in Figure 1-99. The letters "RJ" stands for registered jack, and the number "45" refers to a specific physical connector that has 8 conductors.

A Gigabit Interface Converter (GBIC), shown in Figure 1-100, is a hot-swappable I/O device that plugs into a Gigabit Ethernet port. A key benefit of using a GBIC is that it is interchangeable, allowing you the flexibility to deploy other 1000BASE-X technology without having to change the physical interface or model on the router or switch. GBICs support UTP (copper) and fiber-optic media for Gigabit Ethernet transmission.

Figure 1-99 *Connection Types*

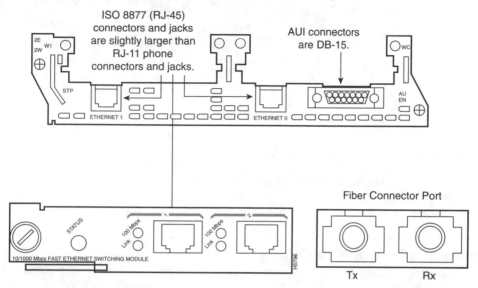

Figure 1-100 *1000Base-T GBIC*

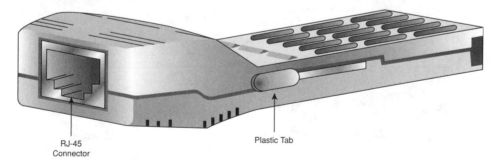

Typically, GBICs are used in the LAN for uplinks and are normally used for the backbone. GBICs are also seen in remote networks.

The fiber-optic GBIC, shown in Figure 1-101, is a transceiver that converts serial electric currents to optical signals and converts optical signals to digital electric currents.

Figure 1-101 *Fiber GBIC*

Optical GBICs include these types:

- Short wavelength (1000BASE-SX)

- Long wavelength/long haul (1000BASE-LX/LH)

- Extended distance (1000BASE-ZX)

Unshielded Twisted-Pair Cable

Twisted-pair is a copper wire–based cable that can be either shielded or unshielded. UTP cable is frequently used in LANs. Figure 1-102 shows an example of a UTP cable.

Figure 1-102 *UTP Cable*

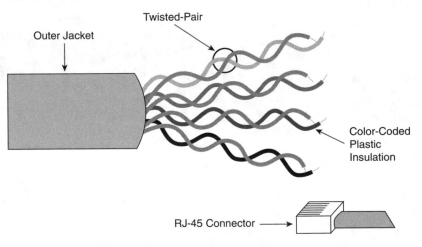

UTP cable is a four-pair wire. Each of the eight individual copper wires in UTP cable is covered by an insulating material. In addition, the wires in each pair are twisted around each other. The advantage of UTP cable is its ability to cancel interference, because the twisted-wire pairs limit signal degradation from electromagnetic interference (EMI) and radio frequency interference (RFI). To further reduce crosstalk between the pairs in UTP cable, the number of twists in the wire pairs varies. Both UTP and shielded twisted-pair (STP) cable must follow precise specifications regarding how many twists or braids are permitted per meter.

UTP cable is used in a variety of types of networks. When used as a network medium, UTP cable has 4 pairs of either 22- or 24-gauge copper wire. UTP used as a network medium has an impedance of 100 ohms, differentiating it from other types of twisted-pair wiring, such as that used for telephone wiring. Because UTP cable has an external diameter of approximately 0.43 cm, or 0.17 inches, its small size can be advantageous during installation. Also, because UTP can be used with most of the major network architectures, it continues to grow in popularity.

Here are the categories of UTP cable:

- **Category 1:** Used for telephone communications; not suitable for transmitting data

- **Category 2:** Capable of transmitting data at speeds of up to 4 Mbps

- **Category 3:** Used in 10BASE-T networks; can transmit data at speeds up to 10 Mbps

- **Category 4:** Used in Token Ring networks; can transmit data at speeds up to 16 Mbps

- **Category 5:** Capable of transmitting data at speeds up to 100 Mbps

- **Category 5e:** Used in networks running at speeds up to 1000 Mbps (1 Gbps)

- **Category 6:** Consists of 4 pairs of 24-gauge copper wires, which can transmit data at speeds of up to 1000 Mbps

The most commonly used categories in LAN environments today are Categories 1 (used primarily for telephony), 5, 5e, and 6.

UTP Implementation

For a UTP implementation in a LAN, you must determine the EIA/TIA type of cable needed and also whether to use a straight-through or crossover cable. This topic describes the characteristics and uses of straight-through and crossover cables, as well as the types of connectors used when UTP is implemented in a LAN. Figure 1-103 shows a RJ-45 connector.

Figure 1-103 *RJ-45 Connector*

If you look at the RJ-45 transparent-end connector, you can see eight colored wires, twisted into four pairs. Four of the wires (two pairs) carry the positive or true voltage and are considered "tip" (T1 through T4); the other four wires carry the inverse of false voltage grounded and are called "ring" (R1 through R4). *Tip* and *ring* are terms that originated in the early days of the telephone. Today, these terms refer to the positive and negative wires in a pair. The wires in the first pair in a cable or a connector are designated as T1 and R1, the second pair as T2 and R2, and so on.

The RJ-45 plug is the male component, crimped at the end of the cable. As you look at the male connector from the front, the pin locations are numbered from 8 on the left to 1 on the right. Figure 1-104 shows a RJ-45 jack.

The jack is the female component in a network device, wall, cubicle partition outlet, or patch panel.

In addition to identifying the correct EIA/TIA category of cable to use for a connecting device (depending on which standard is being used by the jack on the network device), you need to determine which of the following to use:

■   A straight-through cable (either T568A OR T568B at each end)

■   A crossover cable (T568A at one end; T568B at the other)

Figure 1-104 *RJ-45 Jack*

In Figure 1-105, the RJ-45 connectors on both ends of the cable show all the wires in the same order. If the two RJ-45 ends of a cable are held side-by-side in the same orientation, the colored wires (or strips or pins) can be seen at each connector end. If the order of the colored wires is the same at each end, the cable type is straight-through.

Figure 1-105 *Straight-Through Cable*

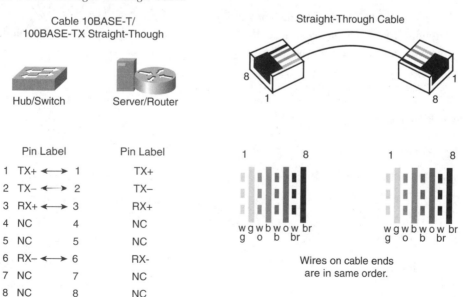

With crossover cables, the RJ-45 connectors on both ends show that some of the wires on one side of the cable are crossed to a different pin on the other side of the cable. Specifically, for Ethernet, pin 1 at one RJ-45 end should be connected to pin 3 at the other end. Pin 2 at one end should be connected to pin 6 at the other end, as shown in the Figure 1-106.

Figure 1-106   *Crossover Cable*

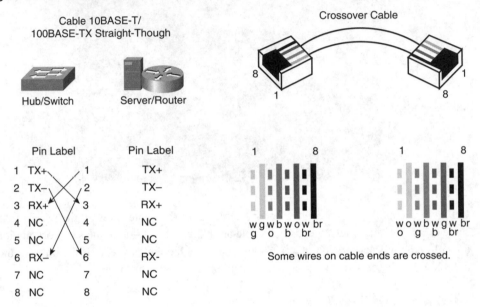

Figure 1-107 shows the guidelines for choosing which type of cable to use when interconnecting Cisco devices. In addition to verifying the category specification on the cable, you must determine when to use a straight-through or crossover cable.

Use straight-through cables for the following cabling:

- Switch to router

- Switch to PC or server

- Hub to PC or server

Use crossover cables for the following cabling:

- Switch to switch

- Switch to hub

- Hub to hub

- Router to router

- Router Ethernet port to PC NIC

- PC to PC

Figure 1-107 *When to Use a Straight-Through Cable Versus a Crossover Cable*

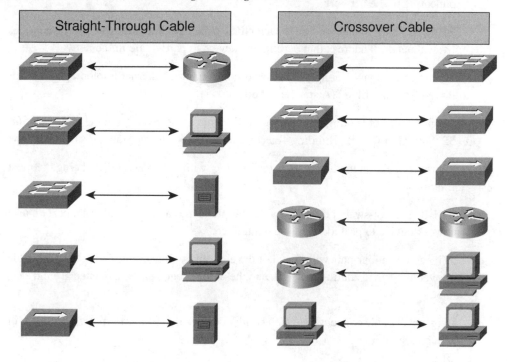

Figure 1-108 illustrates how a variety of UTP cable types might be required in a given network. Note that the category of UTP required is based on the type of Ethernet that you choose to implement.

Figure 1-108 *Using Varieties of UTP*

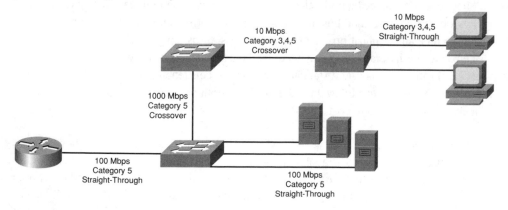

Summary of Connecting to an Ethernet LAN

This section summarizes the key points that were discussed in this lesson:

- A NIC or LAN adapter plugs into a motherboard and provides an interface for connecting to the network.

- The MAC address is burned onto each NIC by the manufacturer, providing a unique, physical network address that permits the device to participate in the network.

- The cable and connector specifications used to support Ethernet implementations are derived from the EIA/TIA standards body.

- The categories of cabling defined for the Ethernet are derived from the EIA/TIA-568 (SP2840) Commercial Building Telecommunications Wiring Standards.

- Several connection media are used for Ethernet with RJ-45 and GBIC being the most common.

- A GBIC is a hot-swappable I/O device that plugs into a Gigabit Ethernet port on a network device to provide a physical interface.

- UTP cable is a four-pair wire. Each of the eight individual copper wires in UTP cable is covered by an insulating material, and the wires in each pair are twisted around each other.

- A crossover cable connects between similar devices like router to router, PC to PC, or switch to switch.

- A straight-through cable connects between dissimilar devices like switch to router or PC to switch.

Chapter Summary

A network is a connected collection of devices that can communicate with each other. Networks in homes, small businesses, or large enterprises allow users to share resources such as data and applications (e-mail, web access, messaging, collaboration, and databases), peripherals, storage devices, and backup devices. Networks carry data (or data packets) following rules and standards called protocols, each with its own specialized function. Networks can be evaluated in terms of both performance and structure, using measures such as speed, cost, security, availability, scalability, reliability, and topology.

Ethernet is the most common type of LAN used today. Standards unique to Ethernet specify Ethernet LAN cabling and signaling at both the physical and data link layers of the OSI reference model. Bits that are transmitted over an Ethernet LAN are organized into frames. Ethernet LANs manage the signals on a network using a process called CSMA/CD.

The OSI reference model facilitates an understanding of how information travels through a network, by defining the network functions that occur at each layer.

Most networks operate under the rules defined by TCP/IP. TCP/IP defines a 32-bit address that is represented by 4 octets separated by a period. This host address can be manually configured or obtained from a DHCP server.

Review Questions

Use the questions here to review what you learned in this chapter. The correct answers and solutions are found in the appendix, "Answers to Chapter Review Questions."

1. Which three statements about networks are accurate? (Choose three.)

   a. Networks transmit data in many kinds of environments, including homes, small businesses, and large enterprises.

   b. A main office can have hundreds or even thousands of people who depend on network access to do their jobs.

   c. A network is a connected collection of devices that can communicate with each other.

   d. A main office usually has one large network to connect all users.

   e. The purpose of a network is to create a means to provide all workers with access to all information and components that are accessible by the network.

   f. Remote locations cannot connect to a main office through a network.

2. What is the purpose of a router?

   a. To interconnect networks and choose the best paths between them

   b. To provide the connection points for the media

   c. To serve as the endpoint in the network, sending and receiving data

   d. To provide the means by which the signals are transmitted from one networked device to another

3. What is the purpose of a switch?

   a. To connect separate networks and filter the traffic over those networks so that the data is transmitted through the most efficient route

   b. To choose the path over which data is sent to its destination

   c. To serve as the endpoint in the network, sending and receiving data

   d. To provide network attachment to the end systems and intelligent switching of the data within the local network

4. What is the purpose of network interconnections?

   a. To connect separate networks and filter the traffic over those networks so that the data is transmitted through the most efficient route

   b. To choose the path over which data is sent to its destination

   c. To provide a means for data to travel from one point to another in the network

   d. To provide network attachment to the end systems and intelligent switching of the data within the local network

5. Which resource is not sharable on a network?

   a. memory

   b. applications

   c. peripherals

   d. storage devices

6. Which three of the following are common network applications? (Choose three.)

   a. e-mail

   b. collaboration

   c. graphics creation

   d. databases

   e. word processing

   f. spreadsheets

7. Match each network characteristic to its definition.

   _____1. speed

   _____2. cost

   _____3. security

   _____4. availability

   _____5. scalability

   _____6. reliability

   _____7. topology

   a. Indicates how easily users can access the network

   b. Indicates how dependable the network is

   c. Indicates the protection level of the network itself and the data that is transmitted

d. Indicates how fast data is transmitted over the network

e. Indicates how well the network can accommodate more users or data transmission requirements

f. Indicates the structure of the network

g. Indicates the general price of components, installation, and maintenance of the network

8. Which statements about physical networking topologies are accurate? (Choose two.)

a. A physical topology defines the way in which the computers, printers, network devices, and other devices are connected.

b. There are two primary categories of physical topologies: bus and star.

c. A physical topology describes the paths that signals travel from one point on a network to another.

d. The choice of a physical topology is largely influenced by the type of data to be transmitted over the network.

9. Which statement about logical topologies is accurate?

a. A logical topology defines the way in which the computers, printers, network devices, and other devices are connected.

b. A logical topology depends solely on the type of computers to be included in the network.

c. A logical topology describes the paths that the signals travel from one point on a network to another.

d. A network cannot have different logical and physical topologies.

10. Match each topology type to its correct description.

_____1. All of the network devices connect directly to each other in a linear fashion.

_____2. All of the network devices are directly connected to one central point with no other connections between them.

_____3. All of the devices on a network are connected in the form of a circle.

_____4. Each device has a connection to all of the other devices.

_____5. At least one device maintains multiple connections to other devices.

_____6. This design adds redundancy to the network.

    a.   star

    b.   bus

    c.   mesh

    d.   ring

    e.   partial-mesh

    f.   dual-ring

11. Which two statements about wireless networks are accurate? (Choose two.)

    a.   Instead of cables, wireless communication uses RFs or infrared waves to transmit data.

    b.   To receive the signals from the access point, a computer needs to have a wireless adapter card or wireless NIC.

    c.   For wireless LANs, a key component is a router, which propagates signal distribution.

    d.   Wireless networks are not very common, and generally only large corporations use them.

12. What is the main threat to a closed network?

    a.   A deliberate attack from outside

    b.   A deliberate or accidental attack from inside

    c.   Misuse by customers

    d.   Misuse by employees

13. Which two factors have recently influenced the increase in threats from hackers? (Choose two.)

    a.   Hacker tools require more technical knowledge to use.

    b.   Hacker tools have become more sophisticated.

    c.   The number of reported security threats has remained constant year to year.

    d.   Hacker tools require less technical knowledge to use.

14. Which of the following four attacks are classified as access attacks? (Choose two.)

    a.   Password attacks

    b.   DDoS

    c.   Trojan horse

    d.   Love Bug

15. Which two statements about the purpose of the OSI model are accurate? (Choose two.)

    a. The OSI model defines the network functions that occur at each layer.

    b. The OSI model facilitates an understanding of how information travels throughout a network.

    c. The OSI model ensures reliable data delivery through its layered approach.

    d. The OSI model allows changes in one layer to affect the other layers.

16. Match each OSI layer to its function.

    _____1. physical

    _____2. data link

    _____3. network

    _____4. transport

    _____5. session

    _____6. presentation

    _____7. application

    a. Provides connectivity and path selection between two host systems that might be located on geographically separated networks

    b. Ensures that the information sent at the application layer of one system is readable by the application layer of another system

    c. Defines how data is formatted for transmission and how access to the network is controlled

    d. Segments data from the system of the sending host and reassembles the data into a data stream on the system of the receiving host

    e. Defines the electrical, mechanical, procedural, and functional specifications for activating, maintaining, and deactivating the physical link between end systems

    f. Provides network services to the applications of the user, such as e-mail, file transfer, and terminal emulation

    g. Establishes, manages, and terminates sessions between two communicating hosts and also synchronizes dialogue between the presentation layers of the two hosts and manages their data exchange

17. Arrange the steps of the data encapsulation process in the correct order.

    _____1. Step 1

    _____2. Step 2

_____3. Step 3

_____4. Step 4

_____5. Step 5

_____6. Step 6

_____7. Step 7

_____8. Step 8

a. The presentation layer adds the presentation layer header (Layer 6 header) to the data. This then becomes the data that is passed down to the session layer.

b. The session layer adds the session layer header (Layer 5 header) to the data. This then becomes the data that is passed down to the transport layer.

c. The application layer adds the application layer header (Layer 7 header) to the user data. The Layer 7 header and the original user data become the data that is passed down to the presentation layer.

d. The network layer adds the network layer header (Layer 3 header) to the data. This then becomes the data that is passed down to the data link layer.

e. The transport layer adds the transport layer header (Layer 4 header) to the data. This then becomes the data that is passed down to the network layer.

f. The user data is sent from an application to the application layer.

g. The data link layer adds the data link layer header and trailer (Layer 2 header and trailer) to the data. A Layer 2 trailer is usually the frame check sequence, which is used by the receiver to detect whether the data is in error. This then becomes the data that is passed down to the physical layer.

h. The physical layer then transmits the bits onto the network media.

18. At which layer does de-encapsulation first occur?

a. application

b. data link

c. network

d. transport

19. Match each layer with the function it performs in peer-to-peer communication.

_____1. network layer

_____2. data link layer

_____3. physical layer

   a. Encapsulates the network layer packet in a frame

   b. Moves the data through the internetwork by encapsulating the data and attaching a header to create a packet

   c. Encodes the data link frame into a pattern of 1s and 0s (bits) for transmission on the medium (usually a wire)

20. What is the function of a network protocol?

   a. Uses sets of rules that tell the services of a network what to do

   b. Ensures reliable delivery of data

   c. Routes data to its destination in the most efficient manner

   d. Is a set of functions that determine how data is defined

21. Match each TCP/IP stack layer to its function.

      ____1. Provides applications for file transfer, network troubleshooting, and Internet activities, and supports the network

      ____2. Defines how data is formatted for transmission and how access to the network is controlled

      ____3. Defines the electrical, mechanical, procedural, and functional specifications for activating, maintaining, and deactivating the physical link between end systems

      ____4. Provides routing of data from the source to a destination by defining the packet and addressing scheme, moving data between the data link and transport layers, routing packets of data to remote hosts, and performing fragmentation and reassembly of data packets

      ____5. Provides communication services directly to the application processes running on different network hosts

   a. physical layer

   b. data link layer

   c. Internet layer

   d. transport layer

   e. application layer

22. Which area of the OSI model and the TCP/IP stack is most diverse?

   a. network layer

   b. transport layer

   c.   application layer

   d.   data link layer

23. How many bits are in an IPv4 address?

   a.   16

   b.   32

   c.   48

   d.   64

   e.   128

24. In a Class B address, which of the octets are the host address portion and are assigned locally?

   a.   The first octet is assigned locally.

   b.   The first and second octets are assigned locally.

   c.   The second and third octets are assigned locally.

   d.   The third and fourth octets are assigned locally.

25. The address 172.16.128.17 is of which class?

   a.   Class A

   b.   Class B

   c.   Class C

   d.   Class D

26. Which of the following statements is true of a directed broadcast address?

   a.   A broadcast address is an address that has all 0s in the host field.

   b.   Any IP address in a network can be used as a broadcast address.

   c.   A directed broadcast address is an address that has all 1s in the host field.

   d.   None of the above is correct.

27. Which two of these addresses are private IP addresses? (Choose two.)

   a.   10.215.34.124

   b.   172.16.71.43

    c.   172.17.10.10

    d.   225.200.15.10

28. Which three statements about IP are accurate? (Choose three.)

    a.   IP is a connectionless protocol.

    b.   IP uses relational addressing.

    c.   IP delivers data reliably.

    d.   IP operates at Layer 2 of the TCP/IP stack and OSI model.

    e.   IP does not provide any recovery functions.

    f.   IP delivers data on a best-effort basis.

29. Which three statements about TCP are accurate? (Choose three.)

    a.   TCP operates at Layer 3 of the TCP/IP stack.

    b.   TCP is a connection-oriented protocol.

    c.   TCP provides no error checking.

    d.   TCP packets are numbered and sequenced so that the destination can reorder packets and determine if a packet is missing.

    e.   TCP provides no recovery service.

    f.   Upon receipt of one or more TCP packets, the receiver returns an acknowledgement to the sender indicating that it received the packets.

30. Which characteristic is similar between TCP and UDP?

    a.   Operates at Layer 4 (transport layer) of the OSI model and the TCP/IP stack

    b.   Capable of performing a very limited form of error checking

    c.   Provides service on a best-effort basis and does not guarantee packet delivery

    d.   Provides no special features that recover lost or corrupted packets

31. When a single computer with one IP address has several websites open at once, this is called _____.

    a.   windowing

    b.   session multiplexing

    c.   segmenting

    d.   connection-oriented protocol

32. TCP is best for which two of the following applications? (Choose two.) (Understanding TCP/IP's Transport and Application Layers)

    a. E-mail

    b. Voice streaming

    c. Downloading

    d. Video streaming

33. Which three of the following characteristics apply to UDP? (Choose three.)

    a. Packets are treated independently.

    b. Packet delivery is guaranteed.

    c. Packet delivery is not guaranteed.

    d. Lost or corrupted packets are not resent.

34. Which two of the following characteristics apply to TCP? (Choose two.)

    a. Packet delivery is not guaranteed.

    b. Lost or corrupted packets are not resent.

    c. Lost or corrupted packets are resent.

    d. TCP segment contains a sequence number and an acknowledgment number.

35. Proprietary applications use which kind of port?

    a. Dynamically assigned ports

    b. Well-known ports

    c. Registered ports

36. Ports that are used only for the duration of a specific session are called _____.

    a. dynamically assigned ports

    b. well-known ports

    c. registered ports

37. The source port in both a UDP header and a TCP header is a _____.

    a. 16-bit number of the called port

    b. 16-bit length of the header

    c. 16-bit sum of the header and data fields

    d. 16-bit number of the calling port

38. Which field in a TCP header ensures that data arrives in correct order?

  a. Acknowledgment number

  b. Sequence number

  c. Reserved

  d. Options

39. In a TCP connection setup, the initiating device sends which message?

  a. ACK

  b. Receive SYN

  c. Send SYN

40. Acknowledgment and windowing are two forms of _____.

  a. flow control

  b. TCP connection

  c. TCP sequencing

  d. reliable connections

41. Windowing provides which of the following services?

  a. The sender can multiplex.

  b. The receiver can have outstanding acknowledgments.

  c. The receiver can multiplex.

  d. The sender can transmit a specified number of unacknowledged segments.

42. Sequence numbers and acknowledgment numbers are found where?

  a. UDP header

  b. TCP header

  c. Initial sequence number

  d. Application layer

43. What organization is responsible for Ethernet standards?

  a. ISO

  b. IEEE

  c. EIA

  d. IEC

44. What are three characteristics of Ethernet 802.3? (Choose three.)

   a. Based on the CSMA/CD process

   b. Is a standard that has been replaced by Ethernet II

   c. Specifies the physical layer (Layer 1)

   d. Developed in the mid-1970s

   e. Specifies the MAC portion of the data link layer (Layer 2)

   f. Also referred to as thick Ethernet

45. Which statement about an Ethernet address is accurate?

   a. The address used in an Ethernet LAN directs data to the proper receiving location.

   b. The source address is the 4-byte hexadecimal address of the NIC on the computer that is generating the data packet.

   c. The destination address is the 8-byte hexadecimal address of the NIC on the LAN to which a data packet is being sent.

   d. Both the destination and source addresses consist of a 6-byte hexadecimal number.

46. Which statement about MAC addresses is accurate?

   a. A MAC address is a number in hexadecimal format that is physically located on the NIC.

   b. A MAC address is represented by binary digits that are organized in pairs.

   c. It is not necessary for a device to have a unique MAC address to participate in the network.

   d. The MAC address can never be changed.

47. Which statement about NICs is accurate?

   a. The NIC plugs into a USB port and provides a port for connecting to the network.

   b. The NIC communicates with the network through a serial connection and communicates with the computer through a parallel connection.

   c. The NIC communicates with the network through a parallel connection and communicates with the computer through a serial connection.

   d. An NIC is also referred to as a switch adapter.

48. Which minimum category of UTP is required for Ethernet 1000BASE-T?

   a. Category 3

   b. Category 4

   c. Category 5

   d. Category 5e

49. Match the UTP categories to the environments in which they are most commonly used.

       ____1. Category 1

       ____2. Category 2

       ____3. Category 3

       ____4. Category 4

       ____5. Category 5

       ____6. Category 5e

       ____7. Category 6

   a. Capable of transmitting data at speeds up to 100 Mbps

   b. Used in networks running at speeds up to 1000 Mbps (1 Gbps)

   c. Consists of 4 pairs of 24-gauge copper wires, which can transmit data at speeds up to 1000 Mbps

   d. Used for telephone communications; not suitable for transmitting data

   e. Used in Token Ring networks; can transmit data at speeds up to 16 Mbps

   f. Capable of transmitting data at speeds up to 4 Mbps

   g. Used in 10BASE-T networks; can transmit data at speeds up to 10 Mbps

50. Which three characteristics pertain to UTP? (Choose three.)

   a. UTP cable is an eight-pair wire.

   b. An insulating material covers each of the individual copper wires in UTP cable.

   c. The wires in each pair are wrapped around each other.

   d. There is limited signal degradation from EMI and RFI.

   e. There are seven categories of UTPa cable.

This chapter includes the following sections:

- Chapter Objectives

- Understanding the Challenges of Shared LANs

- Exploring the Packet Delivery Process

- Operating Cisco IOS Software

- Starting a Switch

- Understanding Switch Security

- Maximizing the Benefits of Switching

- Troubleshooting Switch Issues

- Chapter Summary

- Review Questions

CHAPTER 2

Ethernet LANs

This chapter describes the various types of Ethernet LAN topologies, details the challenges of shared LANs and how those challenges are solved with switched LAN technology, and describes ways in which LANs can be optimized.

Chapter Objectives

Upon completing this chapter, you will be able to expand an Ethernet LAN by adding a hub. This ability includes being able to meet the following objectives:

- Describe issues related to increasing traffic on an Ethernet LAN

- Identify switched LAN technology solutions to Ethernet networking issues

- Describe the host-to-host packet delivery process through a switch

- Describe the features and functions of the Cisco IOS Software command-line interface (CLI)

- Start an access layer switch and use the CLI to configure and monitor the switch

- Enable physical, access, and port-level security on a switch

- List the ways in which an Ethernet LAN can be optimized

- Describe methods of troubleshooting switch issues

Understanding the Challenges of Shared LANs

LANs are a relatively low-cost means of sharing expensive resources. LANs allow multiple users and devices in a relatively small geographic area to exchange files and messages and to access shared resources such as those provided by file servers. LANs have rapidly evolved into support systems that are critical to communications within an organization. The following sections describe the challenges that shared LANs face as they confront the increasing need for bandwidth and speed to satisfy the needs of multiple users and devices.

Ethernet LAN Segments

Segment length (the maximum length) is an important consideration when using Ethernet technology in a LAN. This topic describes segments and their limitations.

A segment is a network connection made by a single unbroken network cable. Ethernet cables and segments can span only a limited physical distance, beyond which transmissions will become degraded because of line noise, reduced signal strength, and failure to follow the carrier sense multiple access collision detect (CSMA/CD) specifications for collision detection.

Here are guidelines for understanding Ethernet cable specifications, using 10BASE-T as an example:

- 10 refers to the speed supported, in this case 10 Mbps.

- BASE means it is baseband Ethernet.

- T means twisted-pair cable, Category 5 or above.

Each connection specification distinguishes some characteristics. For example, 10BASE-FL would be 10 Mbps, baseband, over fiber-optic (FL indicates fiber link). Each type of Ethernet network also has a maximum segment length. Table 2-1 describes the different Ethernet specifications.

Table 2-1 *Ethernet Segment Distance Limitations*

Ethernet Specification	Description	Segment Length
10BASE-T	10-Mbps Ethernet over twisted-pair	100 m
10BASE-FL	10-Mbps over fiber-optic cable	2000 m
100BASE-TX	100-Mbps Ethernet over twisted-pair	100 m
100BASE-FX	Fast Ethernet, still 100-Mbps, over fiber-optic cable	400 m
1000BASE-T	Gigabit Ethernet, 1000-Mbps, over twisted-pair	100 m
1000BASE-LX	Gigabit Ethernet over fiber-optic cable	550 m if 62.5-micron (μ) or 50-μ multimode fiber; 10 km if 10-μ single-mode fiber
1000BASE-SX	Gigabit Ethernet over fiber-optic cable	250 m if 62.5-μ multimode fiber; 550 m if 50-μ multimode fiber
1000BASE-CX	Gigabit Ethernet over copper cabling	25 m

Extending a LAN Segment

You can add devices to an Ethernet LAN to extend segments. This topic describes how adding repeaters or hubs can overcome the distance limitation in an Ethernet LAN.

A repeater is a physical layer device that takes a signal from a device on the network and acts as an amplifier. Adding repeaters to a network extends the segments of the network so that data can be communicated successfully over longer distances. There are, however, limits on the number of repeaters that can be added to a network.

A hub, which also operates at the physical layer, is similar to a repeater. Figure 2-1 shows two users connected to a hub, each 100 meters from the hub and effectively 200 meters from one another.

Figure 2-1   *Extending the Segment Link with a Hub*

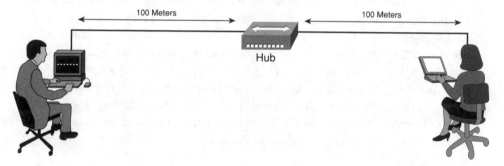

When a hub receives a transmission signal, it amplifies the signal and retransmits it. Unlike a repeater, however, a hub can have multiple ports to connect to a number of network devices; therefore, a hub retransmits the signal to every port to which a workstation or server is connected. Hubs do not read any of the data passing through them, and they are not aware of the source or destination of the frame. Essentially, a hub simply receives incoming bits, amplifies the electrical signal, and transmits these bits through all its ports to the other devices connected to the same hub.

A hub extends, but does not terminate, an Ethernet LAN. The bandwidth limitation of a shared technology remains. Although each device has its own cable that connects to the hub, all devices of a given Ethernet segment compete for the same amount of bandwidth.

Collisions

Collisions are part of the operation of Ethernet, occurring when two stations attempt to communicate at the same time. Because all the devices on a Layer 1 Ethernet segment share the bandwidth, only one device can transmit at a time. Because there is no control mechanism that states when a device can transmit, collisions can occur as shown in Figure 2-2.

Figure 2-2 *Ethernet Collision*

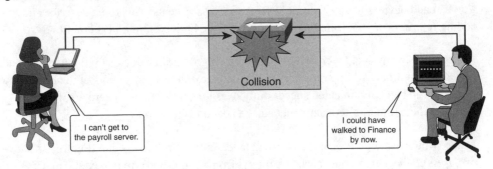

Collisions are by-products of the CSMA/CD method used by Ethernet. In a shared-bandwidth Ethernet network, when using hubs, many devices will share the same physical segment. Despite listening first, before they transmit, to see whether the media is free, multiple stations might still transmit simultaneously. If two or more stations on a shared media segment do transmit at the same time, a collision results, and the frames are destroyed. When the sending stations involved with the collision recognize the collision event, they will transmit a special "jam" signal, for a predetermined time, so that all devices on the shared segment will know that the frame has been corrupted, that a collision has occurred, and that all devices on the segment must stop communicating. The sending stations involved with the collision will then begin a random countdown timer that must be completed before attempting to retransmit the data.

As networks become larger, and devices each try to use more bandwidth, it becomes more likely that end devices will each attempt to transmit data simultaneously, and that will ultimately cause more collisions to occur. The more collisions that occur, the worse the congestion becomes, and the effective network throughput of actual data can become slow. Eventually, with sufficient collisions, the total throughput of actual "data" frames becomes almost nonexistent.

Adding a hub to an Ethernet LAN can overcome the segment length limits and the distances that a frame can travel over a single segment before the signal degrades, but Ethernet hubs cannot improve collision issues.

Collision Domains

In expanding an Ethernet LAN, to accommodate more devices with more bandwidth requirements, you can create separate physical network segments called collision domains so that collisions are limited to a single collision domain, rather than the entire network.

In traditional Ethernet segments, the network devices compete and contend for the same shared bandwidth, with all devices sharing a command media connection, only one single device is able to transmit data at a time. The network segments that share the same bandwidth are known as collision domains, because when two or more devices within that segment try to communicate at the same time, collisions can occur.

You can, however, use other network devices, operating at Layer 2 and above of the OSI model, to divide a network into segments and reduce the number of devices that are competing for bandwidth. Each new segment, then, results in a new collision domain. More bandwidth is available to the devices on a segment, and collisions in one collision domain do not interfere with the operation of the other segments. Figure 2-3 shows how a switch has been used to isolate each user and device into its own collision domain.

Figure 2-3 *Creating Multiple Collision Domains Using a Switch*

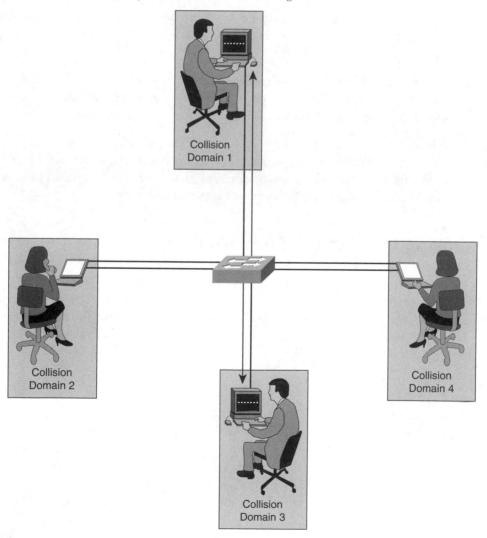

Summary of Ethernet Local-Area Networks

The key points that were discussed in the previous sections are as follows:

- A segment is a network connection made by a single unbroken network cable. Ethernet cables and segments can only span a limited physical distance, after which the transmissions become degraded.

- A hub works like a multiport repeater and can effectively extend a network segment by receiving the incoming frames, amplifying the electrical signals, and transmitting these frames back out through all ports to all devices that are connected to segments on the same Ethernet hub.

- If two or more stations connected to the same hub transmit at the same time, a collision results because of the half-duplex nature of the Ethernet 802.3 CSMA/CD specification.

- The network segments that share the same bandwidth are called collision domains because when two or more devices on the same segment both communicate and send data at the same time, collisions can occur within that shared segment.

- It is possible to use other network devices, operating at Layer 2 (or above) of the OSI model, to divide network segments and reduce the number of devices that are competing or contending for bandwidth on any given segment and to provide better throughput for end users and devices on each separate segment.

Exploring the Packet Delivery Process

The "Understanding the Host-to-Host Communications Model" section in Chapter 1, "Building a Simple Network," addressed host-to-host communications for a TCP connection in a single broadcast domain and introduced switches. The following sections provide a graphic representation of host-to-host communications through a switch. For network devices to communicate, they must have addresses that allow traffic to be sent to the appropriate workstation.

Layer 2 Addressing

As covered in Chapter 1, unique physical MAC addresses are assigned by the manufacturer to end Ethernet devices. Such devices are known as hosts, which in this context, is any device with an Ethernet network interface card (NIC). In most cases, Layer 2 network devices, like bridges and switches, are not assigned a different MAC address to every Ethernet port on the switch for the purpose of transmitting or forwarding traffic. These Layer 2 devices pass traffic, or forward frames, transparently at Layer 2 to the end devices.

Layer 3 Addressing

Some network operating systems (NOS) have their own Layer 3 address format. For example, the Novell IPX Protocol uses a network service address along with a host identifier. However, most operating systems today, Including Novell, can support TCP/IP, which uses a logical IP address at Layer 3 for host-to-host communication.

Host-to-Host Packet Delivery

Chapter 1 reviewed a host-to-host packet delivery for two devices in the same collision domain, that is, two devices connected to the same segment. As mentioned before, limitations to connecting all devices to the same segment include bandwidth limitations and distance limitations. To overcome these limitations, switches are used in networks to provide end-device connectivity. Switches operate at Layer 2 of the OSI model, and therefore host-to-host communication differs slightly at each layer. Figures 2-4 through 2-14 show graphical representations of host-to-host IP communications through a switch.

Figure 2-4 shows that host 192.168.3.1 has data that it wants to send to host 192.168.3.2. This application does not need a reliable connection, so it will use User Datagram Protocol (UDP) as the Layer 4 protocol.

Figure 2-4 *Host Sending Data*

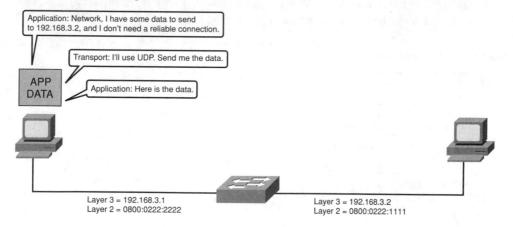

Because it is not necessary to set up a Layer 4 session with UDP, the UDP-based application can start sending data. UDP prepends a UDP header and passes the Layer 4 protocol data unit (PDU), which is called a segment at Layer 4, down to IP (at Layer 3) with instructions to send the PDU to 192.168.3.2. IP encapsulates the Layer 4 PDU in a Layer 3 PDU, where the PDU is referred to as a packet, and then passes it to Layer 2, where the PDU is then called a frame. This is illustrated in Figure 2-5.

Figure 2-5 *Data Encapsulation*

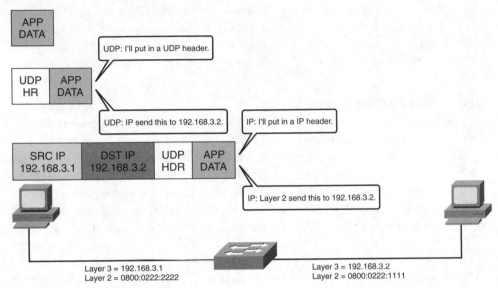

As with the example in Chapter 1, "Building a Simple Network," Address Resolution Protocol (ARP) does not have an entry in its MAC address table, so it must place the packet in the parking lot until it uses ARP to resolve the Layer 3 logical IP address to the Layer 2 physical MAC address. This is shown in Figure 2-6.

Figure 2-6 *Checking the ARP Table*

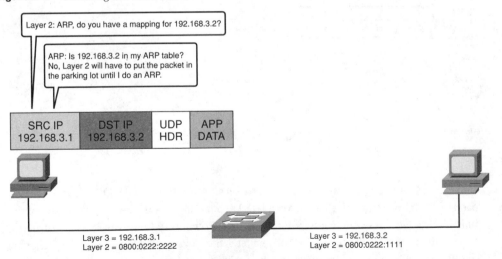

Host 192.168.3.1 sends out the ARP (broadcast) request to learn the MAC address of the device using the IP address 192.168.3.2. However, in this example, the ARP broadcast frame is received by the switch before it reaches the remote host, as illustrated in Figure 2-7.

Figure 2-7 *Sending the ARP Request*

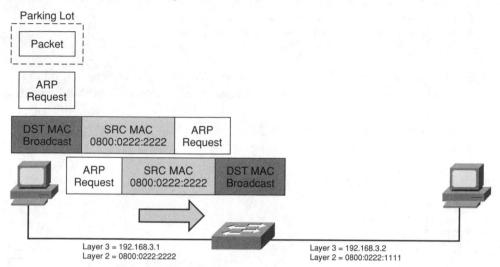

When the switch receives the frame, it needs to forward it out the proper port. However, in this example, neither the source nor the destination MAC address is in the switch's MAC address table. The switch can learn the port mapping for the source host by reading and learning the source MAC address in the frame, so the switch will add the source MAC address, and the port it learned it on, to the port mapping table, or MAC address table.

Now the switch knows the source MAC address and what port to use when attempting to reach that MAC address. For example, source MAC address is 0800:0222:2222 = out port 1.

But, because the switch does not know which port the destination MAC is connected to yet, and because it is doing an ARP broadcast, the destination address is a broadcast, so the switch has to flood the packet, now called a Layer 2 frame, out all ports except for the "source" port. This is shown in Figure 2-8.

Figure 2-8 *Switch Learning and Forwarding*

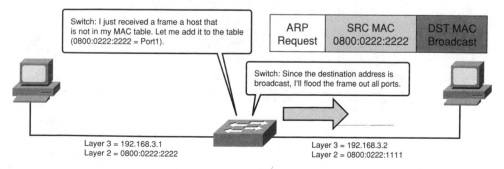

> **NOTE**   A broadcast packet will never be learned by a switch, and the frame will always
> be flooded out all the ports in the broadcast domain. Also, note that when forwarding
> a frame, the switch does not change the frame in any way.

The destination host (and all hosts except the source) receives the ARP request, via an ARP
broadcast. Then only the correct host, the one using the IP address 192.168.3.2, replies to
the ARP request directly to the specific MAC address of the source device, which it
learned—like the switch did—by reading the source MAC address in the original ARP
"broadcast" frame, as shown in Figures 2-9 and 2-10.

Figure 2-9   *Host Receives ARP Request*

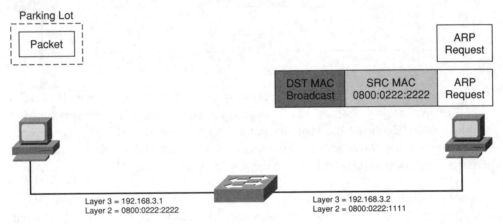

Figure 2-10   *Host Responds to ARP Request*

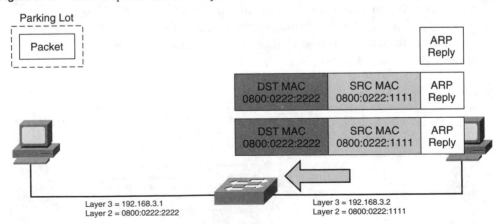

The switch learns the port mapping for the source host by reading the source MAC address in the ARP broadcast reply frame. So the switch adds this new source MAC address and the port that it learned it on to the port-mapping table or MAC address table.

In this case: 0800:0222:1111 = port 2.

Because the new destination MAC address being replied to was previously added to the switch's MAC table, the switch can now forward the reply frame back out port 1, and only out port 1, because it knows what port the desired MAC address "lives" on, or is connected to. This is shown in Figure 2-11.

Figure 2-11   *Host Receives ARP Response*

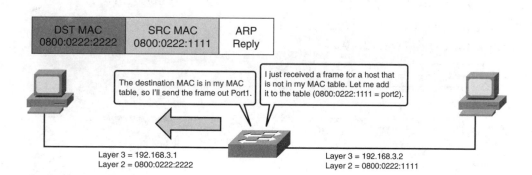

After the sender receives the ARP response, it populates its own ARP cache and then moves the packet out of the parking lot and places the appropriate Layer 2 destination MAC address on the frame for delivery, as shown in Figure 2-12.

As the data is sent to the switch, the switch recognizes that the destination MAC address of the receiver is connected out a particular port, and it sends only the frame out that port to the receiver, where it is received and deencapsulated. The switch also refreshes the timer in its port-mapping table for the sender. Figure 2-13 shows the frame being sent out the port to the receiver.

Figure 2-12 *Sender Builds Frame*

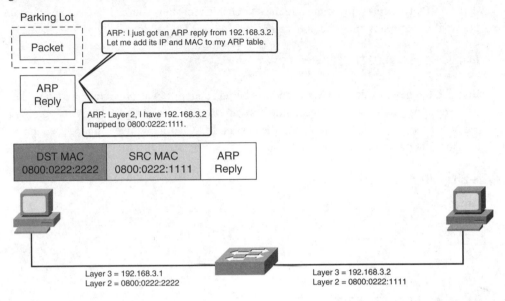

Figure 2-13 *Switch Forwards Frame*

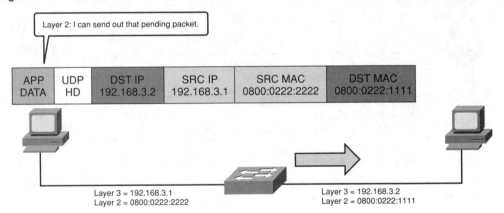

Summary of Exploring the Packet Delivery Process

The key points that were discussed in the previous sections are as follows:

- Operating systems use Layer 3 (IP) and Layer 2 (MAC) addresses to provide host-to-host communications.

- Layer 2 switches forward frames based on entries in the port-mapping MAC address table.

- Layer 2 switches learn the MAC addresses of devices that pass traffic through them to build the port-mapping table, and they learn MAC addresses by reading the source MAC address in a frame.

- If the destination MAC address is unknown, meaning not in the MAC address table of the switch, or if the destination MAC is a broadcast, the frame is "flooded," or sent out, all ports of the switch except for the source port.

- Layer 2 switches do not change the traffic in the frame in any way.

Operating Cisco IOS Software

Understanding the enterprise network environment provides a perspective about the need for greater functionality and control over network components, delivered through more sophisticated network devices such as switches. Cisco IOS Software is feature-rich network system software, providing network intelligence for business-critical solutions. The following sections compare the functionality of switches and devices in small office, home office (SOHO) network environments with network components in enterprise network environments, and describe Cisco IOS Software functions and operation.

Cisco IOS Software Features and Functions

Cisco IOS Software is the industry-leading and is the most widely deployed network system software. This topic describes the features and functions of Cisco IOS Software.

The Cisco IOS Software platform is implemented on most Cisco hardware platforms, including switches, routers, and similar Cisco IOS–based network devices. It is the embedded software architecture in all Cisco devices and is also the operating system of Cisco Catalyst switches.

Cisco IOS Software enables the following network services in Cisco products:

- Features to carry the chosen network protocols and functions.

- Connectivity enables high-speed traffic between devices.

- Security controls access and prohibit unauthorized network use.

- Scalability adds interfaces and capability as needed for network growth.

- Reliability ensures dependable access to networked resources.

The Cisco IOS Software command-line interface (CLI) is accessed through a console connection, a modem connection, or a Telnet session. Regardless of which connection method is used, access to the Cisco IOS Software CLI is generally referred to as an EXEC session.

Configuring Network Devices

The Cisco IOS CLI is used to communicate the configuration details that implement the network requirements of an organization. This topic describes the initial steps for starting and configuring a Cisco network device.

When a Cisco IOS device is started for the first time, its initial configuration with default settings is sufficient for it to operate at Layer 2. When a Cisco router is started for the first time, however, the device does not have sufficient information in its initial configuration to operate at Layer 3, because the device management requires IP address information on its router interfaces, at a minimum. However, when an "unconfigured" Cisco device starts for the first time, with no "startup configuration" settings, the IOS will prompt you for basic configuration information using an interactive dialog mode called setup mode.

This basic configuration sets up the device with the following information:

■ Protocol addressing and parameter settings, such as configuring the IP address and subnet mask on an interface

■ Options for administration and management, such as setting up passwords

In this section, a minimal device configuration for a switch is discussed. Changes to these minimal or default configurations to meet particular network requirements constitute many of the tasks of a network administrator. Figure 2-14 shows the basic startup steps for a Cisco router or switch.

Figure 2-14   *Switch and Router Startup Steps*

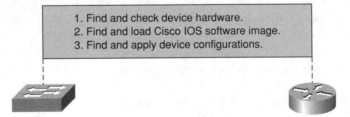

1. Find and check device hardware.
2. Find and load Cisco IOS software image.
3. Find and apply device configurations.

When a Cisco device starts up, the following three main operations are performed on the networking device:

1.   The device performs hardware-checking routines. A term often used to describe this initial set of routines is power-on self test (POST).

2.   After the hardware has been shown to be in good working order, the device performs system startup routines. These initiate the switch or device operating system IOS software.

3. After the operating system is loaded, the device tries to find and apply software configuration settings (later to be stored in the startup-config file) that establish the details needed for network operation.

Typically, a sequence of fallback routines provides software startup alternatives, if needed.

External Configuration Sources

A switch or device can be configured from sources that are external to the device. Figure 2-15 illustrates the many sources from which a Cisco device can obtain configuration settings.

Figure 2-15 *Sources for Router Configurations*

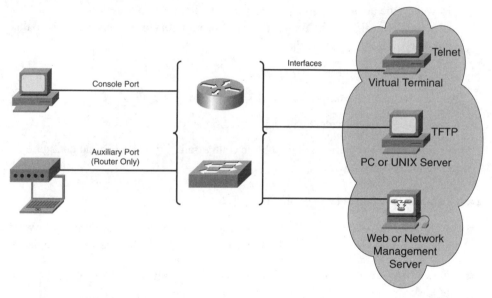

You can access a device directly or from a remote location without being physically connected to the device. You can connect directly by using a console cable connection to the console (CON) port, or you can connect from a remote location by dialing into a modem connected to the auxiliary (AUX) port on the device. After a Cisco device is properly configured, you can also make an over-the-network connection, through Telnet (to VTY ports). In general, the console port is recommended for initial configuration because it displays device startup messages, whereas the auxiliary port does not provide this information. A Cisco IOS device can be configured through the following connections:

■ **Console terminal:** Upon initial installation, you can configure networking devices from the console terminal, which is connected through the console port. You will need the following items to configure a Cisco device from the console port:

— RJ-45–to–RJ-45 rollover cable

— Personal computer (PC) or equivalent with "terminal" communications software configured with the following settings:

Speed: 9600 bits per second

Data bits: 8

Parity: None

Stop bit: 1

Flow control: None

- **Remote terminal:** To support a remote device, a modem connection to the auxiliary port of the device allows a remote device to be configured from a remote terminal. However, the auxiliary port of the device must first be configured for communication with the external modem. You need the following items to connect remotely to the auxiliary port on a Cisco device:

  — Straight-through serial cable

  — 14.4-kilobits-per-second (kbps) modem

  — PC or equivalent with suitable communications software

After initial startup and after an initial basic configuration, you access and configure the device in the following ways:

- Establish a terminal (vty) session using Telnet.

- Configure the device through the current connection, or download a previously written startup-config file from a Trivial File Transfer Protocol (TFTP) server on the network.

- Download a configuration file using a network management software application such as CiscoWorks.

> **NOTE**   Not all network devices have all the ports shown in Figure 2-15. For example, some Cisco SOHO devices do not have an auxiliary port.

Cisco IOS Command-Line Interface Functions

Cisco IOS Software uses a CLI through the console as its traditional environment to enter commands. While Cisco IOS Software is a core technology that extends across many products, its operation details vary on different internetworking devices. This section describes the functions of the Cisco IOS CLI.

The typical interface to a Cisco IOS device is through a console connection or a Telnet connection to the CLI. Figure 2-16 shows an administrator configuring a router and switch through a console connection.

Figure 2-16 *Administrator Connecting to the CLI*

To enter commands into the CLI, type or paste the entries within one of the several console command modes. Each command mode is indicated with a distinctive prompt. Pressing the **Enter** key instructs the device to parse and execute the command.

Cisco IOS Software uses a hierarchy of commands in its command-mode structure. Each command mode supports specific Cisco IOS commands related to a type of operation on the device.

As a security feature, Cisco IOS Software separates the EXEC sessions. EXEC sessions are basically any sessions you initiate through CON, AUX, or VTY connections. All such EXEC sessions are defined by, or put into, one the following two access levels:

- **User EXEC mode:** Allows a person to access only a limited number of basic monitoring commands (like **show** or other basic troubleshooting commands).

- **Privileged EXEC mode:** Allows a person to access all device commands, such as those used for configuration and management, and can be password protected to allow only authorized users to access the device at this "full-access" level. This mode is also called enable mode because you get to it with the **enable** command.

Entering the EXEC Modes

Cisco IOS Software supports two EXEC command modes: user EXEC mode and privileged EXEC mode. The following procedure outlines how to enable and enter the different EXEC modes on a Cisco switch or device:

Step 1   Log in to the device initially with a username and password (if login is configured for CON, AUX, or VTY connections). This brings the device to a user EXEC mode prompt. A prompt displays to signify the user EXEC mode. The right-facing arrow (>) in the prompt indicates that the device or switch is at the user EXEC level. Enter **exit** to close the session from the user EXEC mode.

Step 2   Enter the **?** command at the user EXEC level prompt to display command options available in the user EXEC mode. The **?** command in privileged EXEC mode reveals many more command options than it does at the user EXEC level. This feature is referred to as context-sensitive help.

User EXEC mode does not contain any commands that might control the operation of the device or switch. For example, user EXEC mode does not allow reloading or configuring of the device or switch.

Critical commands, such as **configuration** and **management**, require you to be in privileged EXEC (enable) mode.

To change to privileged EXEC mode from user EXEC mode, enter the **enable** command at the hostname> prompt. If an enable password or an enable secret password is configured, the switch or device will then prompt you for the required password.

NOTE   If both an enable password and a secret password are set, the secret password is the one that is required.

When the correct enable password is entered, the switch or device prompt changes from hostname> to hostname#, indicating that the user is now at the privileged EXEC mode level. Entering the **?** command at the privileged EXEC level will reveal many more command options than those available at the user EXEC mode level.

To return to the user EXEC level, enter the **disable** command at the hostname# prompt.

NOTE   For security reasons, a Cisco network device will not echo, or show on the screen, the password that is entered. However, if a network device is configured over a modem link, or if Telnet is used, the password is sent over the connection in plain text. Telnet by itself does not offer a method to secure packets that contain passwords or commands.

Secure Shell (SSH) Protocol, which runs on most Cisco devices, allows communication securely over insecure channels and provides strong authentication. SSH can be seen in this context as an encrypted form of Telnet. Refer to Cisco IOS documentation to learn how to use SSH.

Keyboard Help in the CLI

Cisco devices use Cisco IOS Software with extensive command-line input help facilities, including context-sensitive help. This topic describes the CLI keyboard help that is available on Cisco devices.

The Cisco IOS CLI on Cisco devices offers the following types of help:

■ **Word help:** Enter the character sequence of an incomplete command followed immediately by a question mark. Do not include a space before the question mark. The device will display a list of available commands that start with the characters that you entered. For example, enter the **sh?** command to get a list of commands that begin with the character sequence sh.

■ **Command syntax help:** Enter the **?** command to get command syntax help to see how to complete a command. Enter a question mark in place of a keyword or argument. Include a space before the question mark. The network device will then display a list of available command options, with <cr> standing for carriage return. For example, enter **show?** to get a list of the various command options supported by the **show** command.

> **NOTE**   Cisco devices and Catalyst switches have similar command-line help facilities. All the help facilities mentioned in this section for devices also apply to Catalyst switches, unless otherwise stated.

Special **Ctrl** and **Esc** key sequences, the **Tab** key, the up-arrow and down-arrow keys, and many others can reduce the need to reenter or type entire command strings. Cisco IOS Software provides several commands, keys, and characters to recall or complete command entries from a command history buffer that keeps the last several commands that you entered. These commands can be reused instead of reentered, if appropriate.

Console error messages help identify problems with an incorrect command entry. Error messages that might be encountered while using the CLI are shown in Table 2-2.

Table 2-2   *CLI Error Messages*

Error Message	Meaning	How to Get Help
% Ambiguous command: "show con"	You did not enter enough characters for your device to recognize the command.	Reenter the command followed by a question mark (**?**), *without* a space between the command and the question mark. The possible keywords that you can enter with the command are displayed.
% Incomplete command	You did not enter all the keywords or values required by this command.	Reenter the command followed by a question mark (**?**), *with* a space between the command and the question mark.
% Invalid input detected at '^' marker	You entered the command incorrectly. The caret (^) marks the point of the error.	Enter a question mark (**?**) to display all the commands or parameters that are available.

The command history buffer stores the commands that have been most recently entered. To see these commands, enter the Cisco IOS **show history** command.

You can use context-sensitive help to determine the syntax of a particular command. For example, if the device clock needs to be set but the clock command syntax is not known, the context-sensitive help provides a means to check the syntax for setting the clock.

If the word *clock* is entered but misspelled, the system performs a symbolic translation of the misspelled command as parsed by Cisco IOS Software. If no CLI command matches the string input, an error message is returned. If there is no Cisco IOS command that begins with the misspelled letters, by default, the device will interpret the misspelled command as a host name and attempt to resolve the host name to an IP address, and then try to telnet to that host.

Context-sensitive help will supply the entire command, even if you enter just the first part of the command, such as **cl?**.

If you enter the **clock** command but an error message indicating that the command is incomplete is displayed, enter the question mark (**?**) command (preceded by a space) to determine what arguments are required for completing the command sequence. In the **clock ?** example, the help output shows that the keyword **set** is required after **clock**.

If you now enter the command **clock set** and then press **Enter**, but another error message displays indicating that the command is still incomplete, press **Ctrl-P** (or the up-arrow key) to repeat the command entry. Then, add a space and enter the question mark (**?**) command to display a list of command arguments that are available at that point in the CLI for the given command.

After the last command recall, the administrator can use the question mark (**?**) command to reveal the additional arguments, which involve entering the current time using hours, minutes, and seconds.

After entering the current time, if you still see the Cisco IOS Software error message indicating that the command entered is incomplete, recall the command, add a space, and enter the question mark (**?**) to display a list of command arguments that are available at that point for the given command. In the example, enter the day, month, and year using the correct syntax, and then press **Enter** to execute the command.

Syntax checking uses the caret symbol (^) as an error-location indicator. The caret symbol appears at the point in the command string where an incorrect command, keyword, or argument has been entered. The error-location indicator and interactive help system provide a way to easily find and correct syntax errors. In the clock example, the caret symbol (^) indicates that the month was entered incorrectly. The parser is expecting the month to be spelled out.

Enhanced Editing Commands

The Cisco IOS CLI includes an enhanced editing mode that provides a set of editing key functions. Although the enhanced line-editing mode is automatically enabled, you can disable it. You should disable enhanced line editing if there are scripts that do not interact well when enhanced line editing is enabled. Use the **terminal editing** EXEC command to turn on advanced line-editing features and the **terminal no editing** EXEC command to disable advanced line-editing features.

Most commands are "undone," or turned off, by reentering the command with the word **no** in front of it. The **terminal** commands are one of the odd exceptions to the "no" rule. Notice that terminal editing is turned off by entering **terminal no editing** (instead of "no terminal editing").

One of the advanced line-editing features is to provide horizontal scrolling for commands that extend beyond a single line on the screen. When the cursor reaches the right margin, the command line shifts ten spaces to the left. The first ten characters of the line can no longer be seen, but you can scroll back to check the syntax at the beginning of the command.

The command entry extends beyond one line, and you can only see the end of the command string:

```
SwitchX> $ value for customers, employees, and partners.
```

The dollar sign ($) indicates that the line has been scrolled to the left. To scroll back, press **Ctrl-B** or the left-arrow key repeatedly until you are at the beginning of the command entry, or press **Ctrl-A** to return directly to the beginning of the line.

The key sequences are shortcuts or hot keys provided by the CLI. Use these key sequences to move the cursor around on the command line for corrections or changes.

Table 2-3 describes each of the shortcuts shown in Figure 2-16 and shows some additional shortcuts for command-line editing and controlling command entry.

Table 2-3 *Command-Line Editing Keys*

Command-Line Editing Key Sequence	Description
Ctrl-A	Moves the cursor to the beginning of the command line
Ctrl-E	Moves the cursor to the end of the command line
Esc-B	Moves the cursor back one word
Esc-F	Moves the cursor forward one word
Ctrl-B	Moves the cursor back one character
Ctrl-F	Moves the cursor forward one character
Ctrl-D	Deletes a single character to the left of the cursor
Backspace	Removes one character to the left of the cursor
Ctrl-R	Redisplays the current command line
Ctrl-U	Erases a line
Ctrl-W	Erases a word to the left of the cursor
Ctrl-Z	Ends configuration mode and returns directly to the privileged EXEC mode hostname# prompt
Tab	Completes a partially entered command if enough characters have been entered to make it unambiguous

NOTE   The **Esc** key is not functional on all terminals.

Command History

The Cisco CLI provides a history or record of commands that have been entered. This feature, called the command history buffer, is particularly useful in helping recall long or complex commands or entries.

With the command history feature, you can complete the following tasks:

■ Display the contents of the command buffer.

■ Set the command history buffer size.

■ Recall previously entered commands stored in the history buffer. There is a buffer for the EXEC mode and another buffer for the configuration mode.

By default, command history is enabled, and the system records the last ten command lines in its history buffer.

To change the number of command lines that the system will record and recall during the current terminal session only, use the **terminal history** command at the user EXEC mode prompt.

To recall commands in the history buffer beginning with the most recent command, press **Ctrl-P** or the up-arrow key. Repeat the key sequence to recall successively older commands.

To return to more recent commands in the history buffer, after recalling older commands by pressing **Ctrl-P** or the up-arrow key, press **Ctrl-N** or the down-arrow key. Repeat the key sequence to recall successively more recent commands.

On most computers, there are additional select and copy facilities available. You can copy a previous command string, paste or insert it as the current command entry, and then press **Enter**.

A Cisco router has the following four primary types of memory:

- **RAM:** Stores routing tables and the fast-switching cache. RAM holds the current running configuration file, the currently loaded IOS, and so on.

- **NVRAM:** Used for writable permanent storage of the startup configuration settings.

- **Flash:** Provides permanent storage of the Cisco IOS Software image file, backup configurations, and any other files through memory cards.

- **ROM:** Provides the POST routine and also provides a mini-IOS that can be used for troubleshooting and emergencies, such as when the stored IOS in flash is corrupted. The mini-IOS provided by ROM can also be for password recovery.

  ROM cannot be modified or copied to by device administrators.

The **show startup-config** command displays the saved startup configuration settings stored in NVRAM. The **show running-config** command displays the current configuration settings currently running in RAM. Figure 2-17 shows the location of the running and startup configuration files, along with where the setup utility copies the configuration.

Figure 2-17 *Location of Configuration Files*

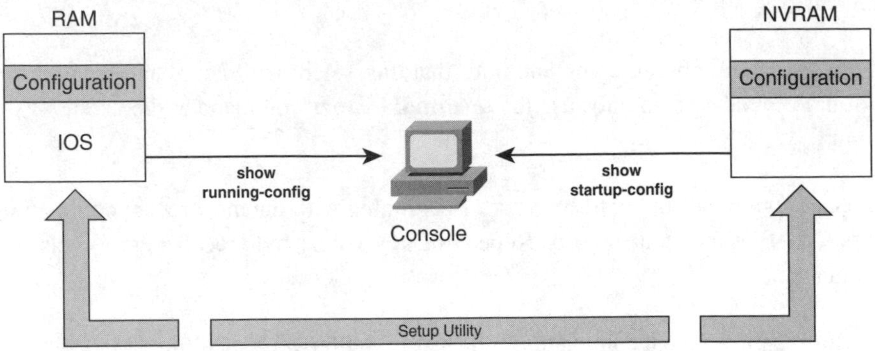

The **show running-config** command displays the current running configuration in RAM.

When you issue the **show running-config** command on a router, you will initially see "Building configuration . . . ." This output indicates that the running configuration is being built from the active configuration settings currently running and currently stored in RAM.

After the running configuration is built from RAM, the "Current configuration:" message appears, indicating that this is the current running configuration that is currently running in RAM.

The first line of the **show startup-config** command output indicates the amount of NVRAM used to store the configuration. For example, "Using 1359 out of 32762 bytes" indicates that the total size of the NVRAM is 32,762 bytes and the current configuration stored in NVRAM takes up 1359 bytes.

Summary of Operating Cisco IOS Software

The key points that were discussed in the previous sections are as follows:

- Cisco IOS Software is embedded software architecture in all the Cisco IOS devices and is also the operating system of Catalyst switches. Its functions include carrying the chosen network protocols, connectivity, security, scalability, and reliability.

- A switch or IOS device can be configured from a local terminal connected to the console (CON) port, from a remote terminal connected through a modem connection to the auxiliary (AUX) port, or through a Telnet (VTY) connection.

- The CLI is used by network administrators to monitor and configure various Cisco IOS devices. The CLI also offers a help facility to aid network administrators with the verification and configuration of commands.

- The CLI supports two EXEC modes: user EXEC mode and privileged EXEC mode. The privileged EXEC mode provides more functionality than the user EXEC mode, and privileged EXEC mode is also sometimes called enable mode.

- Cisco IOS devices use Cisco IOS Software with extensive command-line input help facilities, including context-sensitive help.

- The Cisco IOS CLI includes an enhanced editing mode that provides a set of editing key functions.

- A Cisco IOS device's CLI provides a history or record of the commands that have been entered.

Starting a Switch

A Cisco Catalyst switch goes through its startup routine when the switch is turned on. When the startup is complete, the initial software settings can be configured. Recognizing that the switch startup has completed without error is the first step in deploying a Catalyst switch. The switch must start successfully and have a default configuration to operate on the network. The following sections describe how the switch starts up and how to verify its initial operation.

Physical Startup of the Catalyst Switch

The startup of a Catalyst switch requires verifying the physical installation, powering up the switch, and viewing the Cisco IOS Software output on the console.

The initial startup of a Catalyst switch requires completion of the following steps:

Step 1   Before starting the switch, verify the following:

— All network cable connections are secure.

— Your terminal is connected to the console port.

— Your console terminal application, such as HyperTerminal, is selected.

Step 2   Attach the power cable plug to the switch power supply socket. The switch starts. There is no On/Off switch on some Catalyst switches, including the Cisco Catalyst 2960 series.

Step 3   Observe the boot sequence as follows:

— Look at the light emitting diodes (LED) on the switch chassis.

— Observe the Cisco IOS Software output text on the console.

> **NOTE**   This course describes the Catalyst 2960 series switch only. Switch information
> and configuration commands presented are specific to the Catalyst 2960 series. Your
> switch might differ.

Switch LED Indicators

The Catalyst switches have several status LEDs that are generally lit in green when the
switch functions normally but that turn amber when there is a malfunction. Figure 2-18
shows the locations of the LEDs on a Catalyst 2960 series switch.

Figure 2-18   *Catalyst 2960 LEDs*

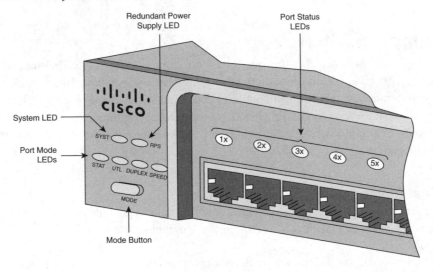

The LED locations on the Catalyst 2960-12 and 2960-24 are shown in the figure, and their
functions are explained in Table 2-4.

Table 2-4   *Switch LEDs*

Switch LED	Description
System LED	Off: System is not powered up.
	Green: System is powered and operational.
	Amber: System malfunction; one or more power-on self test (POST) errors occurred.

Table 2-4 *Switch LEDs (Continued)*

Switch LED	Description
Redundant power supply	Off: Redundant power supply is off or is not installed.
	Green: Redundant power supply is operational.
	Flashing green: Redundant power supply is connected but unavailable because it is providing power to another device.
	Amber: Redundant power supply is installed but not operational.
	Flashing amber: Internal power supply failed, and redundant power supply is providing power to the switch.

The port LED display modes are indicated in Table 2-5, with information about the various LED colors or lighting.

Table 2-5 *Port LED Modes*

Port LED Display Mode	Description
Port status (STAT LED on)	Off: No link is present.
	Green: Link is present but no activity.
	Flashing green: Link is present with traffic activity.
	Alternating green and amber: Link fault. Error frames can affect connectivity. Excessive collisions and cyclic redundancy check (CRC), alignment, and jabber errors are monitored for a link-fault indication.
	Amber: Port is not forwarding because the port was disabled by management, suspended because of an address violation, or suspended by Spanning Tree Protocol (STP) because of network loops.
Bandwidth utilization (UTL LED on)	Green: Current bandwidth utilization is displayed over the amber LED background on a logarithmic scale.
	Amber: Maximum backplane utilization occurred because the switch was powered on.

continues

Table 2-5 *Port LED Modes (Continued)*

Port LED Display Mode	Description
	Green and amber: Depends on model as follows:
	Catalyst 2960-12, 2960-24, 2960C-24, and 2960T-24 switches: If all LEDs are green, the switch uses 50 percent or more of the total bandwidth. If the far-right LED is off, the switch uses more than 25 percent but less than 50 percent of the total bandwidth, and so on. If only the far-left LED is green, the switch uses less than 0.0488 percent of the total bandwidth.
	Catalyst 2960G-12-EI switches: If all LEDs are green, the switch is using 50 percent or more of the total bandwidth. If the LED for the Gigabit Interface Converter (GBIC) module slot 2 is off, the switch uses more than 25 percent but less than 50 percent of the total bandwidth. If LEDs for both GBIC module slots are off, the switch uses less than 25 percent of the total bandwidth, and so on.
	Catalyst 2960G-24-EI and 2960G-24-EI-DC switches: If all LEDs are green, the switch is using 50 percent or more of the total bandwidth.
	GBIC module slot 2: If the LED is off, the switch uses more than 25 percent but less than 50 percent of the total bandwidth. If LEDs for both GBIC module slots are off, the switch is using less than 25 percent of the total bandwidth, and so on.
	Catalyst 2960G-48-EI switches: If all LEDs are green, the switch uses 50 percent or more of the total bandwidth. If the LED for the upper GBIC module slot is off, the switch uses more than 25 percent but less than 50 percent of the total bandwidth. If LEDs for both GBIC module slots are off, the switch uses less than 25 percent of the total bandwidth, and so on.
Full duplex mode (FDUP LED on)	Green: Ports are configured in full-duplex mode.
	Off: Ports are configured in half-duplex mode.
Speed mode (Speed LED on)	Flashing Green: Port is operating at 1 Gbps.
	Green: Port is operating at 100 Mbps.
	Off: Port is operating at 10 Mbps.

Viewing Initial Bootup Output from the Switch

During initial startup, if POST failures are detected, they are reported to the console. If POST completes successfully, you can configure the switch.

After POST completes successfully on a Catalyst 2960 switch, assuming that this is the first time you have powered on the switch, there is a prompt to enter the initial configuration setup mode for the switch. An automatic setup program can be used to assign the switch with basic IP information, host and cluster names, and passwords, and to create a default configuration for continued basic operation. Later, the CLI can be used to customize and secure the configuration. To run the setup program, access the switch from the PC terminal that was connected to the console port.

Complete the initial configuration by answering each question as it appears, as shown here:

```
             --- System Configuration Dialog ---
Would you like to enter the initial configuration dialog? [yes/no]: y
At any point you may enter a question mark '?' for help.
Use ctrl-c to abort configuration dialog at any prompt.
Default settings are in square brackets '[]'.
Basic management setup configures only enough connectivity
for management of the system, extended setup will ask you
to configure each interface on the system
Would you like to enter basic management setup? [yes/no]: no
First, would you like to see the current interface summary? [yes]: no
Configuring global parameters:
  Enter host name [Switch]: SwitchX
  The enable secret is a password used to protect access to
  privileged EXEC and configuration modes. This password,
    after entered, becomes encrypted in the configuration.
  Enter enable secret: secret_password
  The enable password is used when you do not specify an
  enable secret password, with some older software versions,
    and some boot images.
  Enter enable password: enable_password
  The virtual terminal password is used to protect
  access to the router over a network interface.
  Enter virtual terminal password: vty_password
  Configure SNMP Network Management? [no]: no
Configuring interface parameters:
Do you want to configure Vlan1 interface? [yes]: yes
  Configure IP on this interface? [yes]: yes
    IP address for this interface: 10.1.1.140
    Subnet mask for this interface [255.0.0.0] : 255.255.255.0
    Class A network is 10.0.0.0, 24 subnet bits; mask is /24
Do you want to configure FastEthernet0/1 interface? [yes]: n
..text omitted ..
Do you want to configure FastEthernet0/24 interface? [yes]: n
Would you like to enable as a cluster command switch? [yes/no]: n
```

After the required settings are entered, the setup program displays the configuration to be confirmed, as follows.

The following configuration command script was created:

```
hostname SwitchX
enable secret 5 $1$oV63$8z7cBuveTibpCn1Rf5uI01
enable password enable_password
line vty 0 15
password vty_password
no snmp-server
!
!
interface Vlan1
```

```
ip address 10.1.1.140 255.255.255.0
!
interface FastEthernet0/1
..text omitted..
interface FastEthernet0/24
!
end
[0] Go to the IOS command prompt without saving this config.
[1] Return back to the setup without saving this config.
[2] Save this configuration to nvram and exit.
Enter your selection [2]:2
Building configuration...
[OK]
Use the enabled mode 'configure' command to modify this configuration.
Enter 2 to complete the initial configuration.
```

Logging In to the Switch

When Catalyst switches are configured from the CLI that runs on the console or a remote terminal, the Cisco IOS Software provides a CLI called the EXEC. The EXEC interprets the commands that are entered and carries out the corresponding operations. Figure 2-19 shows the different EXEC modes and prompts of IOS.

Figure 2-19   *OS EXEC Modes*

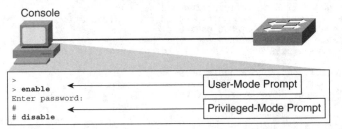

For security purposes, the EXEC has the following two levels of access to commands:

- **User mode:** Typical tasks include those that check the status of the switch, such as some basic **show** commands.

- **Privileged mode:** Typical tasks include those that change the configuration of the switch. This mode is also known as enable mode. If you have the password that gets you to this privileged enable mode, you basically will have access to all possible device configuration commands.

To change from user EXEC mode to privileged EXEC mode, enter the **enable** command. The switch then prompts for the enable password if one is configured. Enter the correct enable password. By default, the enable password is not configured.

> **NOTE** For security reasons, the network device will not echo (not show on the screen) the password that you enter. However, if you are configuring a network device over a modem link or using Telnet, the password is sent over the network connection in plain text. Telnet does not offer a method to secure packets. Secure Shell (SSH) Protocol should be used for remote access.

Configuring a Switch from the Command Line

The Catalyst switch IOS software has different configuration modes, including global configuration mode and interface configuration mode.

To configure global switch parameters such as the switch host name or the switch IP address used for switch management purposes, use global configuration mode. To configure a particular port (interface), use interface configuration mode.

> **NOTE** More switch configuration details are provided throughout this course. This section provides an overview of switch configuration so that you can perform an initial configuration on your switch.

One of the first tasks in configuring a switch is to name it. Naming the switch provides a means to better manage the network by being able to uniquely identify each switch within the network. The name of the switch is considered to be the host name and is the name displayed at the system prompt. The switch name is assigned in global configuration mode. In the following, the switch name is set to SwitchX:

```
>enable
Enter Password:
#config t
(config)#hostname SwitchX
SwitchX(config)#end
SwitchX#
```

The switch's management interface operates as a virtual Layer 3 host within the Layer 2 switch. Remote access to the switch's management interface is accomplished using the Layer 3 protocol and network applications of TCP/IP. Because of this, a Layer 3 address must be assigned to the switch. The management interface resides in VLAN 1. Therefore, the IP address is assigned to what is effectively a virtual interface, one that works just like a physical interface, but with one IP for the entire device, and it is called **interface VLAN 1**.

To configure an IP address and subnet mask for the switch, you must be in VLAN 1 interface configuration mode and then use the **ip address** *configuration* command. An IP address is required on the switch for remote management purposes.

For example, an IP address must be assigned if a Telnet connection is to be used or if the Simple Network Management Protocol (SNMP) will be used to manage the switch.

In addition, just as you would for any interface, you must use the **no shutdown** interface configuration command to make the VLAN 1 interface operational.

To communicate off your network or subnet, you need a default gateway. To configure a default gateway for the switch, use the **ip default-gateway** command. Enter the IP address of the next-hop router interface that is directly connected to the switch where a default gateway is being configured. The default gateway, shown in Figure 2-20, receives IP packets with unresolved destination IP addresses from the switch EXEC processes.

Figure 2-20   *Default Gateway*

After the default gateway is configured, the switch has connectivity to the remote networks that it needs to communicate with.

After the commands to configure the router have been entered, you must save the running configuration to NVRAM with the **copy running-config startup-config** command. If the configuration is not saved to NVRAM and the router is reloaded, the configuration will be lost and the router will revert to the last configuration saved in NVRAM.

Showing the Switch Initial Startup Status

After logging in to a Catalyst switch, the switch initial startup status can be verified using the following switch status commands: **show version**, **show running-config**, and **show interfaces**. This topic describes the switch status commands that can be used to verify the initial switch operation.

Switch status commands are as follows:

- **show version:** Displays the configuration of the system hardware and the currently loaded IOS software version information.

- **show running-config:** Displays the current active running configuration of the switch. This command requires privileged EXEC mode access. The IP address, subnet mask, and default gateway settings are displayed here, as well as all other current running configuration settings.

- **show interfaces:** Displays statistics and status information of all the interfaces on the switch. Both the switch trunks and the switch line ports are considered interfaces. The resulting output varies, depending on the network for which an interface has been configured. Usually this command is entered with the options *type* and *slot/number*, where *type* allows values such as Ethernet and Fast Ethernet, and *slot/number* indicates slot 0 and the port number on the selected interface (for example, E0/1).

Use the **show version** EXEC command to display the configuration of the system hardware and the software version information. Example 2-1 shows the output for the **show version** command.

Example 2-1   show version *Command Output*

```
Switch# show version

Cisco IOS Software, C2960 Software (C2960-LANBASEK9-M), Version 12.2(25)SEE2, RELEASE

SOFTWARE (fc1)
Copyright (c) 1986-2006 by Cisco Systems, Inc.
Compiled Fri 28-Jul-06 11:57 by yenanh
Image text-base: 0x00003000, data-base: 0x00BB7944

ROM: Bootstrap program is C2960 boot loader
BOOTLDR: C2960 Boot Loader (C2960-HBOOT-M) Version 12.2(25r)SEE1, RELEASE SOFTWARE (fc1)

Switch uptime is 24 minutes

System returned to ROM by power-on
System image file is "flash:c2960-lanbasek9-mz.122-25.SEE2/c2960-lanbasek9-mz.122-25
  .SEE2.bin"

cisco WS-C2960-24TT-L (PowerPC405) processor (revision B0) with 61440K/4088K bytes of
  memory.


Processor board ID FOC1052W3XC
Last reset from power-on
1 Virtual Ethernet interface
24 FastEthernet interfaces
2 Gigabit Ethernet interfaces
The password-recovery mechanism is enabled.

! Text omitted

Switch#
```

Table 2-6 describes the highlighted output fields from the **show version** command.

Table 2-6 **show version** *Output Fields*

Output	Description
IOS version	Information identifying the software by name and version (release) number. Always specify the complete release number when reporting a possible software problem. In the example, the switch is running Cisco IOS Release 12.2(25)SEE2.
Switch uptime	Current days and time since the system was last booted. In the example, the switch uptime is 24 minutes.
Switch platform	Shows the hardware platform information including revision and RAM. In the example, the switch is a Cisco 2960 with 24 ports.

The **show interfaces** command, shown in Example 2-2, displays status and statistics information on the network interfaces of the switch.

Example 2-2 **show interfaces** *Command*

```
SwitchX# show interfaces FastEthernet0/2

FastEthernet0/2 is up, line protocol is up (connected)
  Hardware is Fast Ethernet, address is 0008.a445.ce82 (bia 0008.a445.ce82)
  MTU 1500 bytes, BW 10000 Kbit, DLY 1000 usec,
     reliability 255/255, txload 1/255, rxload 1/255
  Encapsulation ARPA, loopback not set
  Keepalive set (10 sec)
  Half-duplex, 10Mb/s
  input flow-control is unsupported output flow-control is unsupported
  ARP type: ARPA, ARP Timeout 04:00:00
  Last input 4w6d, output 00:00:01, output hang never
  Last clearing of "show interface" counters never
  Input queue: 0/75/0/0 (size/max/drops/flushes); Total output drops: 0
  Queueing strategy: fifo
  Output queue: 0/40 (size/max)
  5 minute input rate 0 bits/sec, 0 packets/sec
  5 minute output rate 0 bits/sec, 0 packets/sec
     182979 packets input, 16802150 bytes, 0 no buffer
     Received 49954 broadcasts (0 multicast)
     0 runts, 0 giants, 0 throttles
     0 input errors, 0 CRC, 0 frame, 0 overrun, 8 ignored
     0 watchdog, 20115 multicast, 0 pause input
     0 input packets with dribble condition detected
     3747473 packets output, 353656347 bytes, 0 underruns
```

Table 2-7 shows some fields in the display that are useful for checking on fundamental switch details.

Table 2-7   show interfaces *Output Details*

Output	Description
FastEthernet0/2 is up, line protocol is up	FastEthernet0/2 is up indicates that the interface hardware is functioning correctly at Layer 1. Line protocol is up indicates that the Layer 2 protocol is active (that is, keepalives are being sent and received).
address is 0008.a445.ce82...	Shows the MAC address that identifies the interface hardware.
Half-duplex, 10 Mbps	Shows the type mode of connection. Other possibilities include full-duplex, 100 megabits per second (Mbps).
CRC	Shows that there were "0 CRC" errors. CRC errors can indicate a duplex mismatch or a malfunctioning Ethernet adapter in an attached device.

The **show interfaces** command is used frequently while configuring and monitoring network devices.

MAC Address Table Management

Switches use the MAC address tables to forward traffic between ports. These MAC tables include dynamic, permanent, and static addresses. To view the MAC address table, use the **show mac-address-table** command, as shown in Example 2-3.

Example 2-3   show mac-address-table *Command*

```
SwitchX# show mac-address-table

          Mac Address Table
-------------------------------------------

Vlan    Mac Address       Type        Ports
----    -----------       --------    -----
 All    0008.a445.9b40    STATIC      CPU
 All    0100.0ccc.cccc    STATIC      CPU
 All    0100.0ccc.cccd    STATIC      CPU
 All    0100.0cdd.dddd    STATIC      CPU
   1    0008.e3e8.0440    DYNAMIC     Fa0/2
Total Mac Addresses for this criterion: 5
```

SwitchX#Dynamic addresses are source MAC addresses that are learned by the switch by reading the source MAC address in a frame as it is received by the switch port, and then dropped if they are not refreshed and aged out. The switch provides dynamic addressing by learning the source MAC address of each frame that it receives on each port, and then adding the source MAC address and its associated port number to the MAC address table. As stations are added or removed from the network, the switch updates the MAC address table, adding new entries and aging out those that are currently not in use.

An administrator can specifically assign permanent addresses to certain ports. Unlike dynamic addresses, permanent addresses are not aged out.

The maximum size of the MAC address table varies with different switches. For example, the Catalyst 2960 series switch can store up to 8192 MAC addresses (while less sophisticated switches might not support that many). When the MAC address table is full, traffic for all new unknown addresses is flooded out all ports except for the source port, which is the port that the frame originally came in on.

Summary of Starting a Switch

The key points that were discussed in the previous sections are as follows:

- The startup of a Cisco IOS switch requires verifying the physical installation, powering up the switch, and viewing the Cisco IOS Software output on the console.

- The Cisco IOS switches have several status LEDs that are generally lit in green when the switch is functioning normally but turn amber when there is a malfunction.

- The Catalyst POST is executed only when the switch is powered up.

- During initial startup, if POST test failures are detected, they are reported to the console. If POST completes successfully, the switch can be configured.

- When starting any EXEC mode session on a Cisco IOS switch, either locally or remotely, you begin in user EXEC mode. To change modes, like moving into privileged EXEC enable mode, a password must be entered, assuming that one has been set for securing the "all-access" privileged enable mode.

- The Cisco IOS switch CLI provides a help facility that is similar to the help facility of the router.

- The Catalyst IOS switches can be configured using global and other configuration modes; these modes are similar to the various EXEC modes at the CLI on Cisco routers.

- After logging in to a Catalyst IOS switch, the switch software and hardware status can be verified using the **show version**, **show running-config**, and **show interfaces** commands.

Understanding Switch Security

After physical access has been secured, there is a growing need to ensure that access to the switch ports is secure through any EXEC session connection, such as securing the console (CON) port and securing the Telnet (VTY) ports. In addition, it is important to ensure that unused switch ports do not become security holes. The following sections describe how to mitigate hardware, environmental, electrical, and maintenance-related security threats to Cisco IOS devices.

Physical and Environmental Threats

Improper and incomplete network device installation is an often-overlooked security threat that, if left uncorrected, can have dire results. Just like a typical PC or server configured with default settings presents a security threat, the same is true for Cisco devices. But software-based security configuration measures alone cannot prevent premeditated or even accidental network damage because of poor installation.

Beyond insecure configuration settings, there are four classes of insecure installations or physical access threats:

- **Hardware threats:** The threat of physical damage to the switch or switch hardware

- **Environmental threats:** Threats such as temperature extremes (too hot or too cold) or humidity extremes (too wet or too dry)

- **Electrical threats:** Threats such as voltage spikes, insufficient supply voltage (brownouts), unconditioned power (noise), and total power loss

- **Maintenance threats:** Threats such as poor handling of key electronic components (electrostatic discharge), lack of critical spare parts, poor cabling, and poor labeling

Configuring Password Security

The command-line interface (CLI) is used to configure the password and other console commands. Examples 2-4, 2-5, 2-6, and 2-7 show the various passwords to be configured on a switch.

Example 2-4 *Switch Password Configuration: Console Password Configuration*

```
SwitchX(config)# line console 0
SwitchX(config-line)# login
SwitchX(config-line)# password cisco
```

Example 2-5 *Switch Password Configuration: Virtual Terminal (Telnet) Password Configuration*

```
SwitchX(config)# line vty 0 4
SwitchX(config-line)# login
SwitchX(config-line)# password sanjose
```

Example 2-6 *Switch Password Configuration: Enable Password Configuration*

```
SwitchX(config)# enable password cisco
```

Example 2-7 *Switch Password Configuration: Secret Password Configuration*

```
SwitchX(config)# enable secret sanfran
```

CAUTION   The passwords used in this text are for instructional purposes only.
Passwords used in an actual implementation should meet the requirements of a "strong"
and "complex" password.

You can secure a switch by using passwords to restrict various levels of access. Using
passwords and assigning privilege levels are simple ways of providing both local and
remote terminal access control in a network. Passwords can be established on individual
lines, such as the console, and to the privileged EXEC (enable) mode. Passwords are case
sensitive.

Each Telnet (VTY) port on the switch is known as a virtual type terminal (vty). By default
There are five VTY ports on the switch, allowing five concurrent Telnet sessions, noting that
other Cisco devices might have more than five logical VTY ports. The five total VTY ports
are numbered from 0 through 4 and are referred to all at once as **line vty 0 4** (notice the
space between 0 and 4). By syntax, this would include the range from 0 to 4, so it includes
all five logical VTY ports, 0–4.

Use the **line console 0** command, followed by the **password** and **login** subcommands, to
require login and establish a login password on the console terminal or on a VTY port. By
default, login is not enabled on the console or on VTY ports.

Note that you cannot establish a Telnet connection unless you first set all the vty passwords.
If there are no vty passwords set, when you try to telnet in, you get a "password required
. . . but none set . . ." error message, and your attempt to telnet is rejected.

The **line vty 0 4** command, followed by the **password** and **login** subcommands, requires
login and establishes a login password on incoming Telnet sessions.

Again, for Telnet VTY ports to accept a Telnet EXEC session, you *must* set the vty
passwords.

The **login local** command can be used to enable password checking on a per-user basis
using the username and password specified with the **username** global configuration
command. The **username** command establishes username authentication with encrypted
passwords.

The **enable password** global command restricts access to the privileged EXEC (enable) mode. You can assign an encrypted form of the enable password, called the enable secret password, by entering the **enable secret** command with the desired password at the global configuration mode prompt. If the enable secret password is configured, it is used (and required) instead of the enable password, not in addition to it.

You can also add a further layer of security, which is particularly useful for passwords that ross the network or are stored on a TFTP server. Cisco provides a feature that allows the use of encrypted passwords. To set password encryption, enter the **service password-encryption** command in global configuration mode.

Passwords that are displayed or set after you configure the **service password-encryption** command will be encrypted in the output. This includes the encrypting of the passwords that might otherwise be displayed in plain text on the screen in the terminal output of a **show** command, such as **show run**.

To disable a command, enter **no** before the command. For example, use the **no service password-encryption** command to disable the **service-password encryption** command:

```
SwitchX(config)# service password-encryption
SwitchX(config)# no service password-encryption
```

Configuring the Login Banner

The CLI is used to configure the "message of the day" and other console commands. This banner can be used to warn others that they have accessed a secure device and that they might be monitored.

You can define a customized banner to be displayed before the username and password login prompts by using the **banner login** command in global configuration mode. To disable the login banner, use the **no** form of this command.

When the **banner login** command is entered, follow the command with one or more blank spaces and a delimiting character of any choice. In the example, the delimiting character is a double quotation mark ("). After the banner text has been added, terminate the message with the same delimiting character.

```
SwitchX# banner login " Access for authorized users only. Please enter your
username and password. "
```

> **WARNING**   Use caution when selecting the words that are used in the login banner. Words like *welcome* can imply that access is not restricted and can allow a hacker to defend his actions.

Telnet Versus SSH Access

Telnet is the most common method of accessing a remote network device. However, Telnet is an insecure way of accessing a network device because it passes all command keystrokes, and all output back to the terminal, in unencrypted clear text. Secure Shell (SSH) Protocol is a secure replacement for Telnet that gives the same type of access. Communication between the client and server is encrypted in both SSHv1 and SSHv2. Implement SSHv2 when possible because it uses a more enhanced security encryption algorithm.

First, test the authentication without SSH to make sure that authentication works with the switch. Authentication can be with a local username and password or with an authentication, authorization, and accounting (AAA) server that runs Terminal Access Controller Access Control System Plus (TACACS+) or Remote Authentication Dial-In User Service (RADIUS). (Authentication through the line password is not possible with SSH.) The following example shows local authentication, which lets you use Telnet to get access to the switch with username **cisco** and password **cisco**.

```
!--- The username command create the username and password for the SSH session
username cisco password 0 cisco
ip domain-name mydomain.com
crypto key generate rsa
ip ssh version 2
line vty 0 4
  login local
  transport input ssh
```

To test authentication with SSH, you have to add to the previous configuration statements to enable SSH. Then you can test SSH from the PC and UNIX stations.

If you want to prevent non-SSH connections, add the **transport input ssh** command under the lines to limit the switch to SSH connections only. Straight (non-SSH) Telnets are refused.

```
line vty 0 4
!--- Prevent non-SSH Telnets.
transport input ssh
```

Test to make sure that non-SSH users cannot telnet to the switch.

Port Security Configuration

You can use the port security feature to restrict input to an interface by limiting and identifying MAC addresses of the stations allowed to access the port. When you assign secure MAC addresses to a secure port, the port does not forward packets with source addresses outside the group of defined addresses.

NOTE   Before port security can be activated, the port mode must be set to access using the **switchport mode access** command.

With the Cisco Catalyst 2960 series, use the **switchport port-security** interface command *without* keywords to enable port security on an interface. Use the **switchport port-security** interface command *with* keywords to configure a secure MAC address, a maximum number of secure MAC addresses, or the violation mode. Use the **no** form of this command to disable port security or to set the parameters to their default state. Example 2-8 shows the commands used to configure port security.

Example 2-8 *Configuring Port Security*

```
SwitchX(config)# interface fa0/5
SwitchX(config-if)# switchport mode access
SwitchX(config-if)# switchport port-security
SwitchX(config-if)# switchport port-security maximum 1
SwitchX(config-if)# switchport port-security mac-address sticky
SwitchX(config-if)# switchport port-security violation shutdown
```

A port must be in access mode (not trunk mode) to enable port security.

You can add secure (specific) MAC addresses to the MAC address table after you set the maximum number of secure MAC addresses allowed on a port in these ways:

- Manually configure all the addresses (**switchport port-security mac-address 0008.eeee.eeee**)

- Allow the port to dynamically configure all the addresses (**switchport port-security mac-address sticky**)

- Configure a number of MAC addresses and allow the rest of the addresses to be dynamically configured

You can configure an interface to convert the dynamic MAC addresses to sticky secure MAC addresses and to add them to the running configuration by enabling *sticky learning*. To enable sticky learning, enter the **switchport port-security mac-address sticky** interface configuration command. When you enter this command, the interface converts all the dynamic secure MAC addresses, including those that were dynamically learned before sticky learning was enabled, to sticky secure MAC addresses.

The sticky secure MAC addresses do not automatically become part of the configuration file, which is the startup configuration that is used each time the switch restarts. If you save the sticky secure MAC addresses in the configuration file, when the switch restarts, the interface does not need to relearn these addresses. If you do not save the configuration, the MAC addresses are lost. If sticky learning is disabled, the sticky secure MAC addresses are converted to dynamic secure addresses and are removed from the running configuration. A secure port can have from 1 to 132 associated secure addresses. The total number of available secure addresses on the switch is 1024.

Security violation situations are as follows:

■ The maximum number of secure MAC addresses has been added to the address table, and a station whose MAC address is not in the address table attempts to access the interface.

■ An address learned or configured on one secure interface is seen on another secure interface in the same VLAN.

NOTE   Port security is disabled by default.

On the Catalyst 2960 series, use the **show port-security interface** privileged EXEC command, as shown in Example 2-9, to display the port security settings defined for an interface.

Example 2-9   *Displaying Port Security Settings*

```
SwitchX# show port-security interface fastethernet 0/5

Port Security              : Enabled
Port Status                : Secure-up
Violation Mode             : Shutdown
Aging Time                 : 20 mins
Aging Type                 : Absolute
SecureStatic Address Aging : Disabled
Maximum MAC Addresses      : 1
Total MAC Addresses        : 1
Configured MAC Addresses   : 0
Sticky MAC Addresses       : 0
Last Source Address        : 0000.0000.0000
Security Violation Count   : 0
```

An address violation occurs when a secured port receives a source address that has been assigned to another secured port or when a port tries to learn an address that exceeds its address table size limit, which is set with the **switchport port-security maximum** command.

Table 2-8 lists the parameters that can be used with the **show port-security** command.

Table 2-8   show port-security *Command Parameters*

Command	Description
interface *interface-id*	(Optional) Displays the port security settings for the specified interface
address	(Optional) Displays all the secure addresses on all ports
begin	(Optional) Sets the display to begin with the line that matches the specified expression
exclude	(Optional) Sets the display to exclude lines that match the specified expression
include	(Optional) Sets the display to include lines that match the specified expression
expression	Enters the expression that will be used as a reference point in the output

Use the **show port-security address** command, as shown in Example 2-10, to display the secure MAC addresses for all ports. Use the **show port-security** command without keywords to display the port security settings for the switch.

Example 2-10   show port-security *Commands*

```
SwitchX# sh port-security address

          Secure Mac Address Table
------------------------------------------------------------------
Vlan    Mac Address      Type              Ports   Remaining Age
                                                      (mins)
----    -----------      ----              -----   -------------
 1      0008.dddd.eeee   SecureConfigured  Fa0/5     -
------------------------------------------------------------------
Total Addresses in System (excluding one mac per port)    : 0
SwitchX# sh port-security

Secure Port  MaxSecureAddr  CurrentAddr  SecurityViolation  Security Action
               (Count)        (Count)       (Count)
-----------------------------------------------------------------------
    Fa0/5        1              1              0             Shutdown
-----------------------------------------------------------------------
Total Addresses in System (excluding one mac per port)    : 0
Max Addresses limit in System (excluding one mac per port) : 1024
```

Securing Unused Ports

In a home, an unlocked door can be a security risk. The same is true of an unused port on a switch. A hacker can plug a switch into an unused port and become part of the network. Therefore, unsecured ports can create a security hole. To prevent the issue, you should secure unused ports by disabling unused interfaces (ports).

To disable an interface, use the **shutdown** command in interface configuration mode. To restart, or bring up, a disabled interface, use the **no** form of this command: **no shutdown**.

Summary of Understanding Switch Security

The key points that were discussed in the previous sections are as follows:

■ User and Privileged Passwords can be used to restrict access levels to users that have different access needs for the device.

■ The first level of security is physical.

■ The login banner can be used to display a message before the user is prompted for a username.

■ Port security can be used to limit a MAC address to a port.

■ Unused ports should be shut down.

Maximizing the Benefits of Switching

As devices are added to LANs to accommodate more users, and more bandwidth is required by more networked software applications, maintaining an acceptable level of network performance becomes an increasing challenge. There are a number of ways to enhance switched Ethernet LANs to meet the demands of users for performance and availability.

Microsegmentation

Microsegmentation eliminates the possibility of collisions on the network segment, providing a number of benefits in increasing network performance. Figure 2-21 shows how microsegmentation is accomplished using a switch.

Figure 2-21 *Microsegmentation*

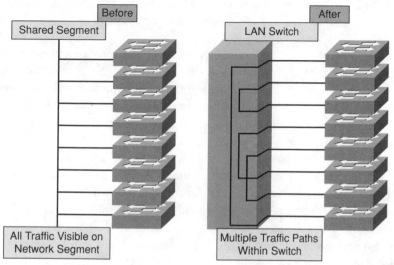

Dedicated Paths Between Sender and Receiver Hosts

Implementing LAN switching provides microsegmentation. Each device on a network segment is connected directly to a switch port and does not have to compete with any other device on the segment for bandwidth. This important function eliminates collisions and increases the effective data rate through full-duplex operation, resulting in a significant increase in available bandwidth.

Example: Getting a Dedicated On-Ramp

Data transmission can be compared to a freeway, with data frames traveling over the freeway like automobiles. Just as automobiles use on-ramps to access the freeway, devices join the network when they want to transmit data. As more and more cars travel on the freeway, however, the on-ramps can become congested, allowing access to only a few cars, and there can even be collisions. If each car had its own on-ramp, however, all the cars would have equal access to the freeway, and there would be no delays or collisions. The microsegmentation that LAN switches provide gives each network device its own "on-ramp" so that the device does not have to compete with other devices to use the network "freeway."

Duplex Communication

Full-duplex communication increases effective bandwidth by allowing both ends of the connection to transmit simultaneously. However, this method of optimizing network performance requires microsegmentation before full-duplex communication can occur.

Half-duplex transmission mode implements Ethernet carrier sense multiple access collision detect (CSMA/CD). The traditional shared LAN operates in half-duplex mode, like with hubs, and is susceptible to transmission collisions across the wire.

Full-duplex Ethernet significantly improves network performance *without* the expense of installing new media. Full-duplex transmission between stations is achieved by using point-to-point Ethernet, Fast Ethernet, and Gigabit Ethernet connections. This arrangement is collision-free. Frames sent by the two connected end nodes cannot collide because the end nodes use two separate circuits in the unshielded twisted-pair (UTP) cable. Each full-duplex connection uses only one port.

Full-duplex port connections are point-to-point links between switches or end nodes, but not between shared hubs. Nodes that are directly attached to a dedicated switch port with network interface cards (NIC) that support full-duplex should be connected to switch ports that are configured to operate in full-duplex mode. Most Ethernet, Fast Ethernet, and Gigabit Ethernet NICs sold today offer full-duplex capability. In full-duplex mode, the collision detect circuit is disabled.

Nodes that are attached to hubs that share their connection to a switch port must operate in half-duplex mode because the end stations must be able to detect collisions.

Figure 2-22 shows how full-duplex can be implemented for bidirectional communication on a switch where it connects to a host but this feature cannot be configured for connectivity for a hub.

Figure 2-22   *Full- and Half-Duplex Connections*

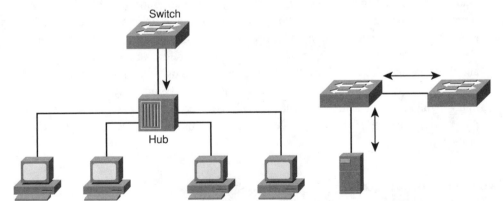

Standard shared Ethernet configuration efficiency is typically rated at 50 to 60 percent of the 10-Mbps bandwidth. Full-duplex Ethernet offers 100 percent efficiency in both directions (10-Mbps transmit and 10-Mbps receive).

Full-Duplex Communication

Because each device on a microsegmented switched LAN is connected directly to a port on a switch, the switch port and that device have a point-to-point connection. In networks with hubs instead of switches, devices can communicate in only one direction at a time because they must compete for the network bandwidth. This type of communication is referred to as half-duplex communication, because it allows data to be either sent or received at one time, but not both. Microsegmented switch ports, however, can provide the devices connected to them with full-duplex-mode communication, allowing the devices to both send and receive data simultaneously. This ability effectively doubles the amount of bandwidth between the devices.

Example: Data Conversations

If you use a voice communication device such as a walkie-talkie, you will be communicating in half-duplex mode. You can talk, but then you must stop talking to hear what the person on the other end of the line is saying. With a telephone, however, you can communicate with someone in full-duplex mode; each person can both talk and hear what the other person says simultaneously.

Duplex Interface Configuration

Example 2-11 shows how to configure the speed and duplex on a 2960 series switch.

Example 2-11   *Configuring Duplex*

```
SwitchX(config)# interface fa0/1
SwitchX(config-if)# duplex {auto | full | half}
SwitchX(config-if)# speed {10 | 100 | 1000 | auto}
```

Use the **duplex** interface configuration command to specify the duplex mode of operation for switch ports.

The duplex parameters on the Cisco Catalyst 2960 series are as follows:

- **auto** sets auto-negotiation of duplex mode.

- **full** sets full-duplex mode.

- **half** sets half-duplex mode.

For Fast Ethernet and 10/100/1000 ports, the default is **auto**. For 100BASE-FX ports, the default is **full**. The 10/100/1000 ports operate in either half-duplex or full-duplex mode when they are set to 10 or 100 Mbps, but when set to 1000 Mbps, they operate only in full-duplex mode.

100BASE-FX ports operate only at 100 Mbps in full-duplex mode.

> **NOTE**   To determine the default duplex mode settings for the Gigabit Interface
> Converter (GBIC) module ports, refer to the documentation that came with your GBIC
> module.

Example: Showing Duplex Options

Verify the duplex settings by using the **show interfaces** command, as shown in
Example 2-12, on the Catalyst 2960 series. The **show interfaces** privileged EXEC
command displays statistics and status for all or specified interfaces.

Example 2-12   *Showing Duplex on an Interface*

```
SwitchX# show interfaces fastethernet0/2

FastEthernet0/2 is up, line protocol is up (connected)
  Hardware is Fast Ethernet, address is 0008.a445.9b42 (bia 0008.a445.9b42)
  MTU 1500 bytes, BW 10000 Kbit, DLY 1000 usec,
     reliability 255/255, txload 1/255, rxload 1/255
  Encapsulation ARPA, loopback not set
  Keepalive set (10 sec)
  Half-duplex, 10Mb/s
  input flow-control is unsupported output flow-control is unsupported
  ARP type: ARPA, ARP Timeout 04:00:00
  Last input 00:00:57, output 00:00:01, output hang never
  Last clearing of "show interface" counters never
  Input queue: 0/75/0/0 (size/max/drops/flushes); Total output drops: 0
  Queueing strategy: fifo
  Output queue: 0/40 (size/max)
  5 minute input rate 0 bits/sec, 0 packets/sec
  5 minute output rate 0 bits/sec, 0 packets/sec
     323479 packets input, 44931071 bytes, 0 no buffer
     Received 98960 broadcasts (0 multicast)
     1 runts, 0 giants, 0 throttles
     1 input errors, 0 CRC, 0 frame, 0 overrun, 0 ignored
     0 watchdog, 36374 multicast, 0 pause input
     0 input packets with dribble condition detected
     1284934 packets output, 103121707 bytes, 0 underruns
     0 output errors, 2 collisions, 6 interface resets
     0 babbles, 0 late collision, 29 deferred
     0 lost carrier, 0 no carrier, 0 PAUSE output
     0 output buffer failures, 0 output buffers swapped out
```

Auto-negotiation can at times produce unpredictable results. Auto-negotiation can happen
when an attached device, which does not support auto-negotiation, is operating in full-
duplex. By default, the Catalyst switch sets the corresponding switch port to half-duplex

mode. This configuration, half-duplex on one end and full-duplex on the other, causes late collision errors at the half-duplex end. To avoid this situation, manually set the duplex parameters of the switch to match the attached device.

If the switch port is in full-duplex mode and the attached device is in half-duplex mode, check for frame check sequence (FCS) errors on the switch full-duplex port.

You can use the **show interfaces** command to check for FCS late collision errors.

Need for Different Media Rates in an Enterprise Network

Large networks include large numbers of end systems, servers, and network devices, and each can require different speeds to be interconnected. This topic describes the reasons for different speed requirements in an enterprise network.

There are a number of higher-speed Ethernet protocols (such as Fast Ethernet and Gigabit Ethernet) that can provide the speed that is required to ensure the performance that is vital to large networks. However, the cost of implementing high-speed connections in all parts of an enterprise network would be very high, and high-speed connections would not be consistently used by all users and devices. Using a hierarchy of Ethernet connectivity, therefore, is usually the most efficient way to supply speed where it will be most effective.

In a typical connectivity hierarchy, the end-user devices are usually referred to as the "access-level" systems, because they are the primary point at which the network is accessed to transmit data. End-user systems are aggregated at the server or workgroup "distribution" level, and if necessary, end-user systems will use the backbone, or "core": level, to reach another distribution device. Higher connectivity speed is usually reserved for those devices that transmit large quantities of data from multiple users, notably at the distribution and core levels. This three-tier hierarchy is shown in Figure 2-23.

Physical Redundancy in an Ethernet LAN

When multiple switches are implemented on the same network and when there are multiple redundant physical connections between the switches, there is a potential for intentional or unintentional physical loops. When loops occur, broadcast storms can be created, propagating frames throughout the network in an endless loop.

Figure 2-23 *Three-Tier Hierarchy of Connectivity*

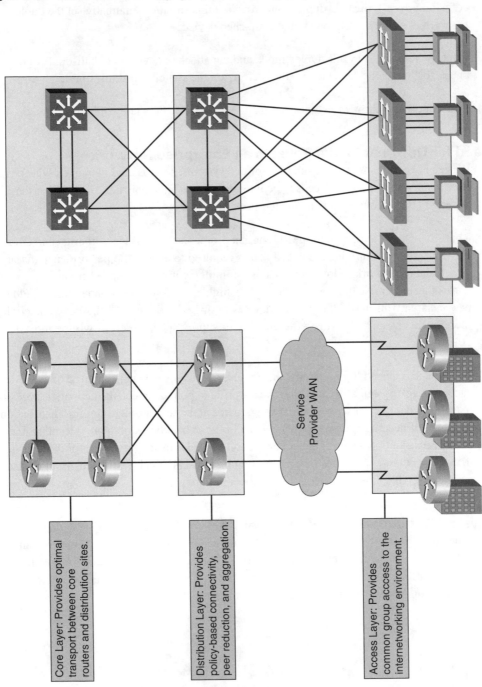

Adding switches to LANs can add the benefit of redundancy, that is, connecting two switches to the same network segments to ensure continual operations in case there are problems with one of the segments. Redundancy can ensure the availability of the network at all times. However, when switches are used for redundancy in a network, there is the potential problem of loops. When a host on one network segment transmits data to a host on another network segment, and the two are connected by two or more switches, each switch receives the data frames, looks up the location of the receiving device, and forwards the frame. Because each switch forwarded the frame, there is a duplication of each frame. This process results in a loop, and the frame circulates between the two paths without being removed from the network. The MAC tables might also be updated with incorrect MAC address port mapping information, resulting in inaccurate forwarding. In addition to basic connectivity problems, the proliferation of broadcast messages in networks with loops represents a serious network problem. Because of how switches operate, any multicast, broadcast, or unknown traffic will be flooded out to all ports except the incoming port. The resulting effect is a "broadcast storm" of traffic being looped endlessly through the network, almost instantly consuming the available bandwidth.

Example: Loops in a Switched Network

This looping problem is demonstrated in Figure 2-24.

Figure 2-24 *Switching Loops in a Network*

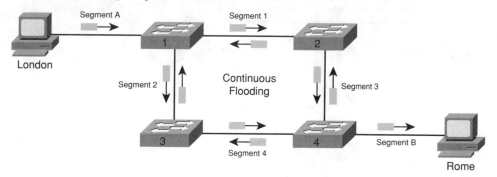

Suppose that a host named London sends a frame to a host named Rome. London resides on network segment A, and Rome resides on network segment B. Redundant connections between switches and hosts are provided to ensure continual operations in the case of a segment failure. For the example shown in Figure 2-24, it is assumed that none of the switches have learned host B's address.

Switch 1 receives the frame destined for host B and floods it out to switches 2 and 3. Both switch 2 and switch 3 receive the frame from London (through switch 1) and correctly learn that London is on segments 1 and 2, respectively. Each switch forwards the frame to switch 4.

Switch 4 receives two copies of the frame from London, one copy through switch 2 and one copy through switch 3. Assume that the frame from switch 2 arrives first. Switch 4 learns that London resides on segment 3. Because switch 4 does not know Rome's MAC address, it forwards the frame from switch 2 to Rome and switch 3. When the frame from switch 3 arrives at switch 4, switch 4 updates its table to indicate that London resides on segment 4. It then forwards the frame to Rome and switch 2.

Switches 2 and 3 now change their internal tables to indicate that London is on segments 3 and 4, respectively. If the initial frame from London were a broadcast frame, both switches would forward the frames endlessly, using all available network bandwidth and blocking the transmission of other packets on both segments. This is called a broadcast storm.

Loop Resolution with Spanning Tree Protocol (STP)

The solution to loops is STP, which manages the physical paths to given network segments. STP provides physical path redundancy, while preventing the undesirable effects of active loops in the network. Spanning Tree Protocol is on by default in Catalyst switches. Figure 2-25 shows how STP prevents loops by blocking on a redundant path link.

Figure 2-25 *STP Prevents Switching Loops*

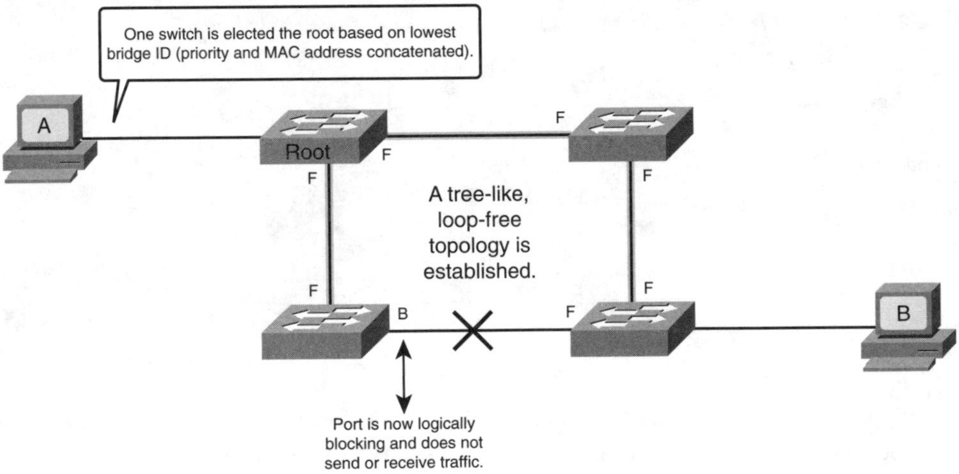

STP behaves as follows:

■ STP forces certain ports into a standby state so that they do not listen to, forward, or flood data frames. The overall effect is that even when multiple physical paths exist for redundancy, there is only one active path to each network segment at any given time.

■ If there is a problem with connectivity to any of the segments within the network, STP will reestablish connectivity by automatically activating a previously inactive path, if one exists.

NOTE   Spanning Tree Protocol is covered in further detail in Interconnecting Cisco
Networking Devices Part 2 (ICND2).

Summary of Maximizing the Benefits of Switching

The key points that were discussed in the previous sections are as follows:

- Switched LANs provide microsegmentation, which means that each device on a
  network segment is connected directly to a switch port and receives its own bandwidth.
  Each device does not have to contend for bandwidth with any other device on the
  network.

- Half-duplex communication in an Ethernet LAN using hubs allows data transmission
  in one direction at a time only (either sending or receiving). The full-duplex
  communication provided by a switch allows both sending and receiving of data
  simultaneously.

- Using a basic core/distribution/access layer three-tier hierarchy of Ethernet
  connectivity is usually the most effective way to provide speed where it will be most
  effective in a campus network, implementing Fast Ethernet and Gigabit Ethernet
  primarily in workgroup and backbone connections.

- Switches provide the valuable feature of redundancy to ensure availability of the
  network, but redundancy can cause loops.

- Loops result when multiple switches are connected through multiple physical paths to
  the same segment and each transmits the same data. The data frames circulate between
  the two or more paths without being removed from the network and can cause
  inaccurate data in the MAC address tables of each switch.

- The solution to loops is STP, which manages the paths to given network segments.
  STP provides path redundancy in an Ethernet LAN while preventing the undesirable
  effects of switching loops in the network.

Troubleshooting Switch Issues

Most issues that affect the switched network are encountered during the original
implementation. Theoretically, after it is installed, a network will continue to operate
without issues. However, that is only true in theory. Things change; cabling gets damaged,
configurations change, and new devices are connected to the switch that require switch
configuration changes. Ongoing maintenance is a fact of life.

Using a Layered Approach

Switches operate at multiple layers of the Open Systems Interconnection (OSI) model. At Layer 1 of the OSI model, switches provide an interface to the physical media. At Layer 2 of the OSI model, they provide switching of frames based on MAC addresses. Therefore, switch problems generally are seen as Layer 1 and Layer 2 issues. Some Layer 3 issues could also result, regarding IP connectivity to the switch for management purposes. The following sections describe using a layered approach to identify common switched network issues.

Identifying and Resolving Media Issues

Media issues are common. It is a fact of life that wiring gets damaged. These are some examples of everyday situations that can cause media issues:

- In an environment using Category 3 wiring, maintenance installs a new air conditioning system that introduces new electromagnetic interference (EMI) sources into the environment.

- In an environment using Category 5 wiring, cabling is run too close to an elevator motor.

- Poor cable management puts a strain on RJ-45 connectors, causing one or more wires to break.

- New applications change network traffic patterns.

- Something as simple as a user connecting a hub to the switch port to connect a second PC can cause an increase in collisions.

Damaged wiring and EMI commonly show up as excessive collisions and noise. Changes in traffic patterns and the installation of a hub will show up as collisions and runt frames. These symptoms are best viewed using the **show interface** command, as shown in Example 2-13.

Example 2-13 *Troubleshooting with the* **show interface** *Command*

```
SwitchX# show interface fastethernet 0/0

Ethernet 0/0 is up, line protocol is up [1]
Hardware is MCI Ethernet, address is aa00.0400.0134 (via 0000.0c00.4369
Internet address is 131.108.1.1, subnet mask is 255.255.255.0
    .
    .
Output Omitted
    .
    .
```

Example 2-13 *Troubleshooting with the* **show interface** *Command (Continued)*

```
2295197 packets input, 305539992 bytes, 0 no buffer
Received 1925500 broadcasts, 0 runts, 0 giants
3 input errors, 3 CRC, 0 frame, 0 overrun, 0 ignored, 0 abort [2]
0 input packets with dribble condition detected
3594664 packets output, 436549843 bytes, 0 underruns
8 output errors, [3]
1790 collisions, [4]
10 interface resets,
0 restarts [5]
```

Table 2-9 explains the highlighted fields in Example 2-13.

Table 2-9 *Highlighted Fields for Troubleshooting*

Callout	Field	Description
1	Interface and line protocol status	Indicates whether the interface hardware is currently active or whether it has been disabled by an administrator. If the interface is shown as "disabled," the device has received more than 5000 errors in a keepalive interval, which is 10 seconds by default. If the line protocol is shown as "down" or "administratively down," the software processes that handle the line protocol consider the interface unusable (because of unsuccessful keepalives) or the interface has been disabled by an administrator.
2	Input errors, including cyclic redundancy check (CRC) errors and framing errors	Total number of errors related to no buffer, runt, giant, CRC, frame, overrun, ignored, and abort. Other input-related errors can also increment the count, so this sum might not balance with the other counts.
3	Output errors	Number of times that the receiver hardware was unable to hand received data to a hardware buffer because the input rate exceeded the receiver's ability to handle the data.
4	Collisions	Number of messages retransmitted because of an Ethernet collision. This is usually the result of an overextended LAN. LANs can become overextended when an Ethernet or transceiver cable is too long or when there are more than two repeaters between stations.
5	Restarts	Number of times that an Ethernet controller has been restarted because of errors.

Identifying and Resolving Common Access Port Issues

Media-related issues can be reported as an access issue. (For example, the user might say, "I can't access the network.") Media issues should be isolated and resolved as indicated in the previous topic. Duplex-related issues result from a mismatch in duplex settings. Speed-related issues result from a mismatch in speed settings.

Use the **show interface** command to verify the duplex settings.

Identifying and Resolving Common Configuration Issues

This topic describes methods of identifying and resolving common configuration issues. The watchword when it comes to configurations is better safe than sorry.

You should always know what you have before you start. When you have a working configuration, keep a copy. For example, keep both a hard copy and an electronic copy—a text file on a PC and/or a copy stored on a TFTP server.

When making changes, before saving the running configuration, verify that the changes accomplish what you wanted and do not cause unexpected issues.

Changes made by an unauthorized person, whether malicious or not, can be disastrous. To ensure that you have secured the configuration, have both the console and VTY ports protected by a strong, complex password. Also, ensure that a strong, complex password has been enabled to enter privileged EXEC mode.

Summary of Troubleshooting Switch Issues

The key points that were discussed in the previous sections are as follows:

- Use the **show interface** command to troubleshoot the following:

    — Media issues

    — Duplex issues

    — Speed issues

- Keep a copy of device configurations.

- Protect the running-config file.

Chapter Summary

The key points that were discussed in this chapter are as follows:

- Ethernet cables and segments can only span a limited physical distance, but there are devices, such as repeaters and hubs, that can be added to an Ethernet LAN to extend the length of LAN segments.

- Bridges and switches divide a LAN into multiple segments. However, switches operate at much higher speeds and support more advanced functionality, performing three major functions in segmenting an Ethernet network: forwarding, filtering, and flooding.

- There are a number of ways in which the performance benefits of switched Ethernet LANs can be enhanced, including microsegmentation and tiered connectivity hierarchies. However, there is a potential for intentional or unintentional physical loops that can be resolved by implementing Spanning Tree Protocol.

- The Cisco IOS CLI is used to communicate the configuration settings and details that implement the network requirements of an organization.

- The startup of a Catalyst switch requires verifying the physical installation, powering up the switch, and viewing the Cisco IOS Software output on the console.

- The CLI is used to configure the device name and passwords and to enter device modes such as global and interface configuration mode.

- Increase switch security by enabling password and port security.

- Most port access problems can be verified by using the **show interface** command.

Review Questions

Use the questions here to review what you learned in this chapter. The correct answers and solutions are found in the appendix, "Answers to Chapter Review Questions."

1. Which of the following statements about the functions of a hub are accurate? (Choose two.)

   a. A hub extends an Ethernet LAN.

   b. A hub reduces the size of a collision domain.

    c. Adding a hub eliminates the need for users on a network segment to compete for the same bandwidth.

    d. A hub is a data link layer device.

    e. A hub amplifies the data signal before retransmitting it.

2. Which of the following statements best describe collisions? (Choose three.)

    a. Collisions occur when two or more stations on a shared media transmit at the same time.

    b. Larger segments are less likely to have collisions.

    c. In a collision, the frames are destroyed, and each station in the segment begins a random timer that must be completed before attempting to retransmit the data.

    d. Adding a hub to a network can improve collision issues.

    e. Collisions are by-products of a shared LAN.

    f. More segments on a network mean greater potential for collisions.

3. Which of these choices best describes a collision domain?

    a. Two or more devices trying to communicate at the same time

    b. Two networks that are connected

    c. Network segments that share the same bandwidth

    d. None of the above

4. What type of hardware will help eliminate collisions?

    a. Repeater

    b. Bridge

    c. Hub

    d. Extender

5. Which of the following factors are typical causes of network congestion? (Choose three.)

    a. High-bandwidth applications

    b. Many network segments

    c. Increasing volume of network traffic

    d. More powerful computer and network technologies

    e. Few network segments

    f. Greater distances for LANs

6. Which of the following are characteristics of a bridge? (Choose three.)

   a. Bridges forward but do not filter data frames between LAN segments.

   b. Bridges maintain MAC address tables.

   c. Bridges extend the distance of the LAN farther than hubs.

   d. Bridges can buffer and forward frames between two or more LAN segments.

   e. Bridges create fewer collision domains.

   f. Bridges operate at Layer 3 of the OSI model.

7. Which of the following are major benefits of adding a bridge to a network? (Choose two.)

   a. Isolating potential network problems to specific segments

   b. Increasing the speed of a network

   c. Extending a LAN to cover greater distances by joining multiple segments

   d. Creating fewer collision domains

   e. Forwarding data frames between LAN segments

8. Match each of the following terms related to the operation of a switch in a network to its description.

   ____ If the switch determines that the destination MAC address of the frame resides on the same network segment as the source, it does not forward the frame.

   ____ If the switch determines that the destination MAC address of the frame is not from the same network as the source, it transmits the frame to the appropriate segment.

   ____ If the switch does *not* have an entry for the destination address, it will transmit the frame out of all ports except the port on which it received the frame.

   a. Flooding

   b. Filtering

   c. Forwarding

9. Which of the following characteristics apply to a switch? (Choose three.)

   a. Uses a table of MAC addresses to determine the port to which the data is to be sent

   b. Connects LAN segments

   c. Reduces the number of collision domains

   d. Increases the number of collision domains

   e. Filters data before forwarding it to its destination on the network

10. Which of the following features differentiate switches from bridges? (Choose three.)

    a. Large frame buffers

    b. Use of a table of MAC addresses to determine the segment to which the data is to be sent

    c. Support for mixed media rates

    d. High port densities

    e. Ability to segment LANs

11. Which of the following statements are accurate about how the network performance of a switch compares to that of a bridge? (Choose three.)

    a. Switches operate at much higher speeds than bridges.

    b. Switches operate at lower speeds than bridges.

    c. Switches support more advanced functionality than bridges.

    d. Switches support less functionality than bridges.

    e. Switches support dedicated communication between devices.

    f. Switches do not support dedicated communication between devices.

12. Which of the following statements about microsegmentation are accurate? (Choose three.)

    a. Implementing a bridge creates microsegmentation.

    b. Microsegmentation increases bandwidth availability.

    c. Each device on a network segment is connected directly to a switch port.

    d. Microsegmentation eliminates collisions.

    e. Microsegmentation limits the number of segments on a network.

    f. Microsegmentation uses half-duplex operation.

13. Match each of the following function descriptions with either full-duplex or half-duplex communication.

    ____ The network sends and receives data frames one at a time, but not simultaneously.

    ____ This communication type effectively doubles the amount of bandwidth between the devices.

    ____ The network sends and receives data frames simultaneously.

    a. Full-duplex communication

    b. Half-duplex communication

14. Match each of the following connectivity functions to the appropriate Ethernet type.

___ At the end-user level, gives high-performance PC workstations 100-Mbps access to a server

___ Not typically used at the end-user level

___ At the workgroup level, provides connectivity between the end user and workgroups

___ At the backbone level, provides interswitch connectivity for low- to medium-volume applications

___ At the workgroup level, provides high-performance connectivity to the enterprise server

___ At the backbone level, provides backbone and interswitch connectivity

___ At the end-user level, provides connectivity between the end user and the user-level switch

___ Provides interswitch connectivity for low- to medium-volume applications

   a. Ethernet 10BASE-T

   b. Fast Ethernet

   c. Gigabit Ethernet

15. When a Cisco device starts up, which of the following does it run to check its hardware?

   a. Flash

   b. RAM

   c. POST

   d. TFTP

16. When a Catalyst switch or Cisco router starts up, what is the first operation performed?

   a. The device performs system startup routines.

   b. The device performs hardware checking routines.

   c. The device attempts to locate other devices on the network.

   d. The device tries to find and apply software configuration settings.

17. Upon initial installation of a Cisco switch or router, the network administrator typically configures the networking devices from a _____.

   a. CD-ROM

   b. TFTP server

    c. console terminal

    d. modem connection

18. If a network administrator is supporting a remote device, the preferred method is to use a modem connection to the _____ of the device for remote configuration.

    a. LAN port

    b. uplink port

    c. console port

    d. auxiliary port

19. Which access level allows a person to access all router commands and can be password protected to allow only authorized individuals to access the router?

    a. User EXEC level

    b. Setup EXEC level

    c. Enable EXEC level

    d. Privileged EXEC level

20. How do you instruct a Cisco device to parse and execute an entered command?

    a. Press the **Send** key.

    b. Press the **Enter** key.

    c. Add a space at the end of the command.

    d. Wait 5 seconds after you enter a command.

21. Which CLI prompt indicates that you are working in privileged EXEC mode?

    a. hostname#

    b. hostname>

    c. hostname-exec>

    d. hostname-config

22. Which command would you enter in the privileged EXEC mode to list the command options?

    a. ?

    b. **init**

    c. **help**

    d. **login**

23. Match each of the following steps of the physical Catalyst switch startup process to its description.

    ___ Step 1

    ___ Step 2

    ___ Step 3

    a.   Attach the power cable plug to the switch power supply socket.

    b.   Observe the boot sequence, including the Cisco IOS Software output text on the console.

    c.   Verify that all cable connections are secure, the terminal is connected to the console port, and the console terminal application is selected.

24. How do you start a Catalyst 2950 series switch?

    a.   Press the On/Off switch.

    b.   Power up the redundant power supply.

    c.   Connect a network cable to another switch on the network.

    d.   Attach the power cable plug to the switch power supply socket.

25. If the POST completes successfully on a Catalyst switch, what display could you see on the console?

    a.   The > prompt

    b.   The privileged EXEC prompt

    c.   The Management Console logon screen

    d.   A list of commands available on the switch

26. What CLI command should you enter to display a list of commands that begin with the letter "c" on a Catalyst switch?

    a.   **c?**

    b.   **c ?**

    c.   **help c**

    d.   **help c***

27. What CLI command should you enter to display the command syntax help so that you can see how to complete a command that begins with "config"?

    a.   **config?**

    b.   **config ?**

    c.   **help config**

    d.   **help config***

28. Which Cisco IOS command correctly configures an IP address and subnet mask on a switch?

    a.   **ip address**

    b.   **ip address 196.125.243.10**

    c.   **196.125.243.10 ip address**

    d.   **ip address 196.125.243.10 255.255.255.0**

29. Which configuration mode do you use to configure a particular port on a switch?

    a.   User mode

    b.   Global configuration mode

    c.   Interface configuration mode

    d.   Controller configuration mode

30. When you use the **show interface** command to display the status and statistics for the interfaces configured on a Catalyst switch, which output field indicates the MAC address that identifies the interface hardware?

    a.   MTU 1500 bytes

    b.   Hardware is . . . 10BaseT

    c.   Address is 0050.BD73.E2C1

    d.   802.1d STP State: Forwarding

31. Which **show** command requires you to have privileged EXEC mode access?

    a.   **show ip**

    b.   **show version**

    c.   **show running**

    d.   **show interfaces**

32. How should you power up a Cisco router?

    a.   Press the **Reset** button.

    b.   Turn the power switch to "On."

    c.   Connect the fiber cable to another router.

    d.   Attach the power cable plug to the router power supply socket.

33. Which of the following would be considered a physical threat? (Choose two.)

    a.   A user leaving a password in her desk

    b.   Someone turning off the power to the switch to block network access

    c.   Someone turning off the air conditioning system in the network closet

    d.   Someone breaking into the cabinet that contains the network documentation

34. Which of the following can be protected with a password? (Choose four.)

    a.   Console access

    b.   VTY access

    c.   TTY access

    d.   User-level access

    e.   EXEC-level access

35. Which of the following is a customized text that is displayed before the username and password login prompts?

    a.   Message of the day

    b.   Login banner

    c.   Access warning

    d.   User banner

    e.   Warning message

36. Which of the following is the most secure method of remotely accessing a network device?

    a.   HTTP

    b.   Telnet

    c.   SSH

    d.   RMON

    e.   SNMP

37. Which of the following is an IOS command that can be used to control access to a switch port based on a MAC address?

    a.   **shutdown**

    b.   **port-security**

    c.   **mac-secure**

    d.   **firewall**

38. Which of the following is an IOS command that can be used to increase the security of unused switch ports?

    a. **shutdown**

    b. **port security**

    c. **mac-secure**

    d. **firewall**

39. Which problem is caused by redundant connections in a network?

    a. Microsegmentation

    b. Loops

    c. Degradation

    d. Collisions

40. Which statement best describes how loops can affect performance in a switched LAN?

    a. Broadcast storms can be created when loops occur, preventing data from being transmitted over the network.

    b. Any multicast, broadcast, or unknown traffic will be flooded out to all ports.

    c. Incorrect information can be updated to the MAC address tables, resulting in inaccurate forwarding of frames.

    d. The loop removes the frame from the network.

41. Which statement accurately describes Spanning Tree Protocol?

    a. STP assigns roles to bridges and ports to ensure that only one forwarding path exists through the network at any given time.

    b. STP automatically keeps the previously inactive path inactive.

    c. STP eliminates the segments in which there are problems.

    d. STP allows ports to listen to, forward, and flood data frames.

42. Which of the following IOS commands is the most useful when troubleshooting media issues?

    a. **show controller**

    b. **show run**

    c. **show interface**

    d. **show counters**

43. Which of the following IOS commands is the most useful when troubleshooting port access issues?

    a.   **show controller**

    b.   **show run**

    c.   **show interface**

    d.   **show counters**

44. Which of the following are methods used to mitigate configuration issues? (Choose three.)

    a.   Secure unused ports.

    b.   Secure the configuration.

    c.   Verify changes before you save.

    d.   Know what you have before you start.

This chapter includes the following sections:

- Chapter Objectives

- Exploring Wireless Networking

- Understanding WLAN Security

- Implementing a WLAN

- Chapter Summary

- Review Questions

CHAPTER 3

Wireless LANs

Historically, LANs have been limited to physical wired segments. With the advent of technologies that utilize infrared (IR) and radio frequency (RF) to carry data, LANs are free from the limitations of a physical media. This chapter describes the reasons for extending the reach of a LAN and the methods that can be used to do so, with a focus on RF wireless access.

Chapter Objectives

Upon completing this chapter, you will be able to describe the wireless LAN (WLAN) environment. This includes being able to meet the following objectives:

- Describe the business drivers and standards that affect WLAN implementation

- Describe WLAN security issues and threat-mitigation methods

- Describe the factors that affect WLAN implementation

Exploring Wireless Networking

Wireless networking technology has developed like most new technologies; business needs drive technology developments, which in turn drive new business needs, which in turn drive new technology developments. To keep this cycle from spinning out of control, several organizations have stepped forward to establish WLAN standards and certifications. This lesson describes the trends and standards that impact WLAN development.

The Business Case for WLAN Service

Productivity is no longer restricted to a fixed work location or a defined time period. People now expect to be connected at any time and place, from the office to the airport or even the home. Traveling employees used to be restricted to pay phones for checking messages and returning a few phone calls between flights. Now employees can check e-mail, voice mail, and the web status of products on personal digital assistants (PDA) while walking to a flight. Figure 3-1 shows the trends involved with wireless networking and mobility.

Figure 3-1   *Wireless Market Trends*

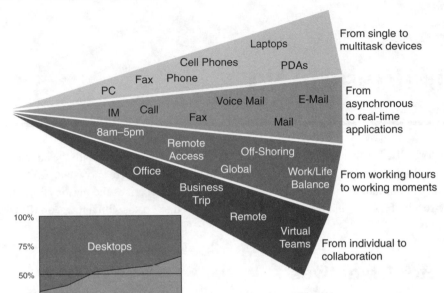

Even at home, people have changed the way they live and learn. The Internet has become a standard in homes, right along with TV and phone service. Even the method of accessing the Internet has quickly moved from temporary modem dialup service to dedicated digital subscriber line (DSL) or cable service, which is always connected and is faster than dialup. In 2005, users of PCs purchased more Wi-Fi–enabled mobile laptops (i.e., products that are based on the IEEE 802.11 standards) than fixed-location desktops.

The most tangible benefit of wireless is the cost reduction. Two situations illustrate cost savings. First, with a wireless infrastructure already in place, savings are realized when moving a person from one location in an office to another, when reorganizing a lab, or when moving from temporary locations or project sites. On average, the IT cost of moving an employee from one location to another where wiring changes are required is $375. For the business case, assume that 15 percent of the staff is moved every year. With a staff of 800, the savings represented by using wireless would be $45,000. The second situation to consider is when a company moves into a new building that does not have a wired infrastructure. In this case, the savings from wireless is even more noticeable because running cables through walls, ceilings, and floors is a labor-intensive process.

Finally, another advantage of using a WLAN is the increase in employee satisfaction brought on by having mobility in their working environment, leading to less turnover and the cost savings of not hiring as many new employees. Employee satisfaction also results in better customer support, which can't be easily quantified, but is a major benefit.

Besides the increase in productivity, WLAN also means better quality in daily work (better responsiveness to customers, a better can-do attitude from employees, and so on) and other benefits that cannot be easily measured.

Differences Between WLANs and LANs

Although WLANs and LANs both provide connectivity between the end users, they have some key differences that include both physical and logical differences between the topologies. In WLANs, radio frequencies are used as the physical layer of the network. Differences also exist in the way the frame is formatted and in the transmission methods, detailed as follows:

■ WLANs use carrier sense multiple access with collision avoidance (CSMA/CA) instead of carrier sense multiple access collision detect (CSMA/CD), which is used by Ethernet LANs. Collision detection is not possible in WLANs, because a sending station cannot receive at the same time that it transmits and, therefore, cannot detect a collision. Instead, WLANs use the Ready To Send (RTS) and Clear To Send (CTS) protocols to avoid collisions.

■ WLANs use a different frame format than wired Ethernet LANs use. WLANs require additional information in the Layer 2 header of the frame.

Radio waves cause problems not found in LANs, such as the following:

■ Connectivity issues occur because of coverage problems, RF transmission, multipath distortion, and interference from other wireless services or other WLANs.

■ Privacy issues occur because radio frequencies can reach outside the facility.

In WLANs, mobile clients connect to the network through an access point, which is the equivalent of a wired Ethernet hub. These connections are characterized as follows:

■ There is no physical connection to the network.

■ The mobile devices are often battery-powered, as opposed to plugged-in LAN devices.

WLANs must meet country-specific RF regulations. The aim of standardization is to make WLANs available worldwide. Because WLANs use radio frequencies, they must follow country-specific regulations of RF power and frequencies. This requirement does not apply to wired LANs.

Radio Frequency Transmission

Radio frequencies range from the AM radio band to frequencies used by cell phones. This section identifies the characteristics of the radio frequency transmissions used by WLANs.

Radio frequencies are radiated into the air by antennas that create radio waves. When radio waves are propagated through objects, they might be absorbed, scattered, or reflected. This absorption, scattering, and reflection can cause areas of low signal strength or low signal quality. Understanding this phenomena and the causes is important when you are building and designing WLAN networks.

The transmission of radio waves is influenced by the following factors:

■ **Reflection:** Occurs when RF waves bounce off objects (for example, metal or glass surfaces)

■ **Scattering:** Occurs when RF waves strike an uneven surface (for example, a rough surface) and are reflected in many directions

■ **Absorption:** Occurs when RF waves are absorbed by objects (for example, walls)

The following rules apply for data transmission over radio waves:

■ Higher data rates have a shorter range because the receiver requires a stronger signal with a better signal-to-noise ratio (SNR) to retrieve the information.

■ Higher transmit power results in a greater range. To double the range, the power has to be increased by a factor of four.

■ Higher data rates require more bandwidth. Increased bandwidth is possible with higher frequencies or more complex modulation.

■ Higher frequencies have a shorter transmission range because they have higher degradation and absorption. This problem can be addressed by more efficient antennas.

Organizations That Standardize WLANs

Several organizations have stepped forward to establish WLAN standards and certifications. This topic identifies the organizations that define WLAN standards.

Regulatory agencies control the use of the RF bands. With the opening of the 900-MHz Industrial, Scientific, and Medical (ISM) band in 1985, the development of WLANs started. New transmissions, modulations, and frequencies must be approved by regulatory agencies. A worldwide consensus is required. Regulatory agencies include the Federal

Communications Commission (FCC) for the United States (http://www.fcc.gov) and the European Telecommunications Standards Institute (ETSI) for Europe (http://www.etsi.org).

The Institute of Electrical and Electronic Engineers (IEEE) defines standards. IEEE 802.11 is part of the 802 networking standardization process. You can download ratified standards from the IEEE website (http://standards.ieee.org/getieee802).

The Wi-Fi Alliance offers certification for interoperability between vendors of 802.11 products. Certification provides a comfort zone for purchasers of these products. It also helps market WLAN technology by promoting interoperability between vendors. Certification includes all three 802.11 RF technologies and Wi-Fi Protected Access (WPA), a security model released in 2003 and ratified in 2004, based on the new security standard IEEE 802.11i, which was ratified in 2004. The Wi-Fi Alliance promotes and influences WLAN standards. A list of ratified products can be found on the Wi-Fi website (http://www.wi-fi.org).

ITU-R Local FCC Wireless

Several unlicensed RF bands exist. Figure 3-2 shows an overview of the FCC bands and where the wireless bands are located.

Figure 3-2 *Wireless Bands*

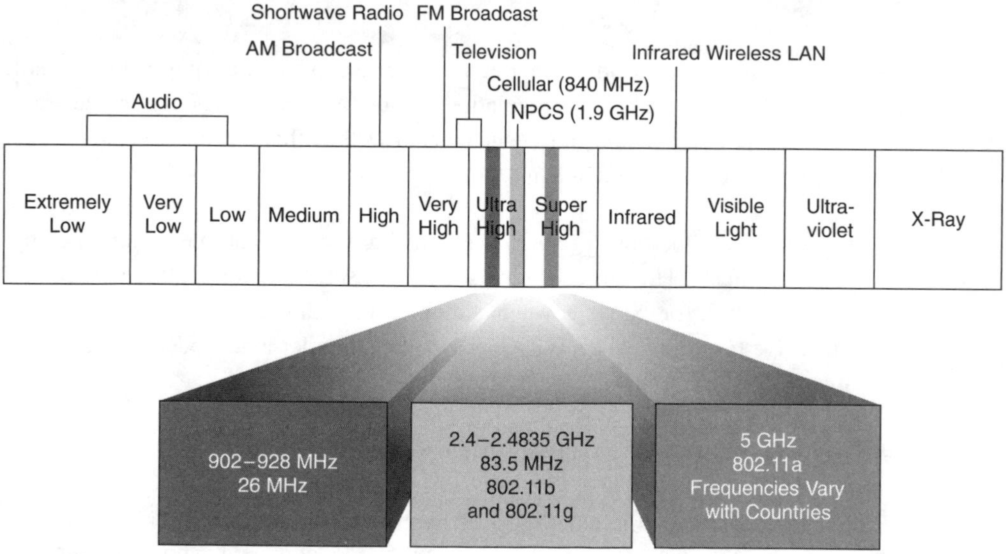

Three unlicensed bands exist: 900 MHz, 2.4 GHz, and 5.7 GHz. The 900-MHz and 2.4-GHz bands are referred to as the ISM bands, and the 5-GHz band is commonly referred to as the Unlicensed National Information Infrastructure (UNII) band.

Frequencies for these bands are as follows:

- **900-MHz band:** 902 MHz to 928 MHz.

- **2.4-GHz band**: 2.400 GHz to 2.483 GHz (in Japan, this band extends to 2.495 GHz.)

- **5-GHz band:** 5.150 GHz to 5.350 GHz, 5.725 GHz to 5.825 GHz, with some countries supporting middle bands between 5.350 GHz and 5.725 GHz. Not all countries permit IEEE 802.11a, and the available spectrum varies widely. The list of countries that permit 802.11a is changing.

Figure 3-2 shows WLAN frequencies. Next to the WLAN frequencies in the spectrum are other wireless services such as cellular phones and Narrowband Personal Communication Services (NPCS). The frequencies used for WLAN are ISM bands.

A license is not required to operate wireless equipment on unlicensed frequency bands. However, no user has exclusive use of any frequency. For example, the 2.4-GHz band is used for WLANs, video transmitters, Bluetooth, microwave ovens, and portable phones. Unlicensed frequency bands offer best-effort use, and interference and degradation are possible.

Even though these frequency bands do not require a license to operate equipment, they still are subject to the local country's code regulations inside the frequencies to regulate areas such as transmitter power, antenna gain (which increases the effective power), and the sum of transmitter loss, cable loss, and antenna gain.

Effective Isotropic Radiated Power (EIRP) is the final unit of measurement monitored by local regulatory agencies. Therefore, caution should be used when attempting to replace a component of a WLAN, for example, when adding or upgrading an antenna to increase range. The possible result could be a WLAN that is illegal under local codes. The equation for calculating EIRP is as follows:

EIRP = transmitter power + antenna gain – cable loss

NOTE   Use only antennas and cables supplied by the original manufacturer listed for the specific access point implementation. Use only qualified technicians who understand the many different requirements of the country's RF regulatory codes.

802.11 Standards Comparison

IEEE standards define the physical layer and the Media Access Control (MAC) sublayer of the data link layer of the OSI model. The original 802.11 wireless standard was completed in June, 1997. It was revised in 1999 to create IEEE 802.11a/b and then reaffirmed in 2003 as IEEE 802.11g.

By design, the standard does not address the upper layers of the OSI model. IEEE 802.11b was defined using Direct Sequence Spread Spectrum (DSSS). DSSS uses just one channel that spreads the data across all frequencies defined by that channel. Table 3-1 shows the different standards and how they compare.

Table 3-1   *802.11 Standards*

Standard	802.11b	802.11a	802.11g	
Frequency band	2.4 GHz	5 GHz	2.4 GHz	
Number of channels	3	Up to 23	3	
Transmission	Direct Sequence Spread Spectrum (DSSS)	Orthogonal Frequency Division Multiplexing (OFDM)	Direct Sequence Spread Spectrum (DSSS)	Orthogonal Frequency Division Multiplexing (OFDM)
Data Rates in Mbps	1, 2, 5.5, 11	6, 9, 12, 18, 24, 36, 48, 54	1, 2, 5.5, 11	6, 9, 12, 18, 24, 36, 48, 54

IEEE 802.11 divided the 2.4-GHz ISM band into 14 channels, but local regulatory agencies such as the FCC designate which channels are allowed, such as channels 1 through 11 in the United States. Each channel in the 2.4 GHz ISM band is 22 MHz wide with 5 MHz separation, resulting in overlap with channels before or after a defined channel. Therefore, a separation of 5 channels is needed to ensure unique nonoverlapping channels. Given the FCC example of 11 channels, the maximum of nonoverlapping frequencies are channels 1, 6, and 11.

Recall that wireless uses half-duplex communication, so the basic throughput is only about half of the data rate. Because of this, the IEEE 802.11b main development goal is to achieve higher data rates within the 2.4-GHz ISM band to continue to increase the Wi-Fi consumer market and encourage consumer acceptance of Wi-Fi.

802.11b defined the usage of DSSS with newer encoding or modulation of Complementary Code Keying (CCK) for higher data rates of 5.5 and 11 Mbps (Barker Coding of 1 and 2 Mbps). 802.11b still uses the same 2.4-GHz ISM band and is backward compatible with prior 802.11 and its associated data rates of 1 and 2 Mbps.

The year that the 802.11b standard was adopted, IEEE developed another standard known as 802.11a. This standard was motivated by the goal of increasing data rates by using a different OFDM spread spectrum and modulation technology and using the less crowded frequency of 5 GHz UNII. The 2.4-GHz ISM band was widely used for all WLAN devices, such as Bluetooth, cordless phones, monitors, video, and home gaming consoles, and it also happens to be the same frequency used by microwave ovens. 802.11a was not as widely known because materials for chip manufacturing were less readily available and initially resulted in higher cost. Most applications satisfied the requirements following the cheaper and more accessible standards of 802.11b.

A more recent development by IEEE maintains usage of the 802.11 MAC and obtains higher data rates in the 2.4-GHz ISM band. The IEEE 802.11g amendment uses the newer OFDM from 802.11a for higher speeds, yet is backward compatible with 802.11b using DSSS, which was already using the same ISM frequency band. DSSS data rates of 1, 2, 5.5, and 11 Mbps are supported, as are OFDM data rates of 6, 9, 12, 18, 24, 48, and 54 Mbps. IEEE requires only mandatory data rates of OFDM using 6, 12, and 24 Mbps, regardless whether it is 802.11a or 802.11g OFDM.

Wi-Fi Certification

Even after the 802.11 standards were established, a need to ensure interoperability among 802.11 products still existed. The Wi-Fi Alliance is a global, nonprofit industry trade association devoted to promoting the growth and acceptance of wireless LANs. One of the primary benefits of the Wi-Fi Alliance is to ensure interoperability among 802.11 products offered by various vendors by providing certification. Figure 3-3 shows an example of the Wi-Fi Alliance certification logo.

Figure 3-3   *Wi-Fi Alliance Certification Logo*

Certified vendor interoperability provides a comfort zone for purchasers. Certification includes all three IEEE 802.11 RF technologies, as well as an early adoption of pending IEEE drafts, such as one that addresses security. The Wi-Fi Alliance adapted the IEEE 802.11i draft security as WPA and then revised it to WPA2 after final release of IEEE 802.11i.

Summary of Exploring Wireless Networking

The following summarizes the key points that were discussed in this section:

■ People now expect to be connected at any time at any place. However, the most tangible benefit of wireless is cost reduction.

■ Both WLANs and LANS use CSMA. However, WLANs use CA, whereas LANs used CD.

■ Radio frequencies are radiated into the air by antennas where they are affected by:

   — Reflection

   — Scattering

   — Absorption

■ The IEEE defines the 802.11 standards.

■ The ITU-R local FCC wireless bands are unlicensed.

■ The 802.11 standards are a set of standards that define the frequencies and radio bands for WLANs.

■ One of the primary benefits of the Wi-Fi Alliance is to ensure interoperability among 802.11 products.

Understanding WLAN Security

As discussed previously, the most tangible benefit of wireless is cost reduction. In addition to increasing productivity, WLANs increase work quality. However, a security breach resulting from a single unsecured access point can negate hours spent securing the corporate network and even ruin an organization. You must understand the security risks of WLANs and how to reduce those risks.

After completing this section, you will be able to describe WLAN security issues and the features available to increase WLAN security.

Wireless LAN Security Threats

With the lower costs of IEEE 802.11b/g systems, it is inevitable that hackers have many more unsecured WLANs from which to choose. Incidents have been reported of people using numerous open source applications to collect and exploit vulnerabilities in the IEEE 802.11 standard security mechanism, Wired Equivalent Privacy (WEP). Wireless sniffers enable network engineers to passively capture data packets so that they can be examined to correct system problems. These same sniffers can be used by hackers to exploit known security weaknesses. Figure 3-4 shows the most common threats to wireless networks.

Figure 3-4   *Wireless LAN Threats*

"WAR DRIVERS"	HACKERS	EMPLOYEES
Find "Open" Networks; Use Them to Gain Free Internet Access	Exploit Weak Privacy Measures to View Sensitive WLAN Info and Even Break into WLANs	Plug Consumer-Grade APs/Gateways into Company Ethernet Ports to Create Own WLANs

"War driving" originally meant using a cellular scanning device to find cell phone numbers to exploit. War driving now also means driving around with a laptop and an 802.11b/g client card to find an 802.11b/g system to exploit.

Most wireless devices sold today are WLAN-ready. End users often do not change default settings, or they implement only standard WEP security, which is not optimal for securing wireless networks. With basic WEP encryption enabled (or, obviously, with no encryption enabled), collecting data and obtaining sensitive network information, such as user login information, account numbers, and personal records, is possible.

A rogue access point (AP) is an AP placed on a WLAN and used to interfere with normal network operations, for example, with denial of service (DoS) attacks. If a rogue AP is programmed with the correct WEP key, client data could be captured. A rogue AP also could be configured to provide unauthorized users with information such as MAC addresses of clients (both wireless and wired), to capture and spoof data packets, or, at worst, to gain access to servers and files. A simple and common version of a rogue AP is one installed by employees with authorization. Employees install access points intended for home use without the necessary security configuration on the enterprise network, causing a security risk for the network.

Mitigating Security Threats

To secure a WLAN, the following components are required:

- **Authentication:** To ensure that legitimate clients and users access the network via trusted access points

- **Encryption:** To provide privacy and confidentiality

- **Intrusion Detection Systems (IDS) and Intrusion Protection Systems (IPS):** To protect from security risks and availability

The fundamental solution for wireless security is authentication and encryption to protect the wireless data transmission. These two wireless security solutions can be implemented in degrees; however, both apply to small office/home office (SOHO) and large enterprise wireless networks. Larger enterprise networks need the additional levels of security offered by an IPS monitor. Current IPS systems do not only detect wireless network attacks, but also provide basic protection against unauthorized clients and access points. Many enterprise networks use IPS for protection not primarily against outside threats, but mainly against unintentional unsecured access points installed by employees desiring the mobility and benefits of wireless.

Evolution of Wireless LAN Security

Almost as soon as the first WLAN standards were established, hackers began trying to exploit weaknesses. To counter this threat, WLAN standards evolved to provide more security. Figure 3-5 shows the evolution of WLAN security.

Figure 3-5 *Evolution of Wireless LAN Security*

1997	2001	2003	2004 to Present
WEP	802.1x EAP	WPA	802.11i/WPA2
• Basic Encryption • No Strong Authentication • Static, Breakable Keys • Not Scalable • MAC Filters and SSID Cloaking Also Used to Complement WEP	• Dynamic Keys • Improved Encryption • User Authentication • 802.1x EAP (LEAP, PEAP) • RADIUS	• Standardized • Improved Encryption • Strong, User Authentication (e.g., LEAP, PEAP, EAP-FAST)	• AES Strong Encryption • Authentication • Dynamic Key Management

Initially, 802.11 security defined only 64-bit static WEP keys for both encryption and authentication. The 64-bit key contained the actual 40-bit key plus a 24-bit initialization vector. The authentication method was not strong, and the keys were eventually compromised. Because the keys were administered statically, this method of security was not scalable to large enterprise environments. Companies tried to counteract this weakness with techniques such as Service Set Identifier (SSID) and MAC address filtering.

The SSID is a network-naming scheme and configurable parameter that both the client and the AP must share. If the access point is configured to broadcast its SSID, the client associates with the access point using the SSID advertised by the access point. An access point can be configured to not broadcast the SSID (SSID cloaking) to provide a first level of security. The belief is that if the access point does not advertise itself, it is harder for hackers to find it. To allow the client to learn the access point SSID, 802.11 allows wireless clients to use a null string (no value entered in the SSID field), thereby requesting that the access point broadcast its SSID. However, this technique renders the security effort ineffective because hackers need only send a null string until they find an access point.

Access points also support filtering using a MAC address. Tables are manually constructed on the AP to allow or disallow clients based upon their physical hardware address. However, MAC addresses are easily spoofed, and MAC address filtering is not considered a security feature.

While 802.11 committees began the process of upgrading WLAN security, enterprise customers needed wireless security immediately to enable deployment. Driven by customer demand, Cisco introduced early proprietary enhancements to RC4-based WEP encryption. Cisco implemented Temporal Key Integrity Protocol (TKIP) per-packet keying or hashing and Cisco Message Integrity Check (Cisco MIC) to protect WEP keys. Cisco also adapted 802.1x wired authentication protocols to wireless and dynamic keys using Cisco Lightweight Extensible Authentication Protocol (Cisco LEAP) to a centralized database.

Soon after the Cisco wireless security implementation, the Wi-Fi Alliance introduced WPA as an interim solution that was a subset of the expected IEEE 802.11i security standard for WLANs using 802.1x authentication and improvements to WEP encryption. The newer key-hashing TKIP versus Cisco Key Integrity Protocol and message integrity check (MIC versus Cisco MIC) had similar features but were not compatible.

Today, 802.11i has been ratified, and Advanced Encryption Standard (AES) has replaced WEP as the latest and most secure method of encrypting data. Wireless Intrusion Detection Systems are available to identify and protect the WLAN from attacks. The Wi-Fi Alliance certifies 802.11i devices under WPA2.

Wireless Client Association

In the client association process, access points send out beacons announcing one or more SSIDs, data rates, and other information. The client sends out a probe and scans all the channels and listens for beacons and responses to the probes from the access points. The client associates to the access point that has the strongest signal. If the signal becomes low, the client repeats the scan to associate with another access point (this process is called roaming). During association, the SSID, MAC address, and security settings are sent from the client to the access point and checked by the access point. Figure 3-6 illustrates the client association process.

Figure 3-6   *Client Association*

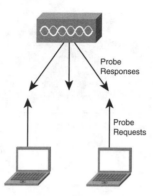

A wireless client's association to a selected access point is actually the second step in a two-step process. First, authentication and then association must occur before an 802.11 client can pass traffic through the access point to another host on the network. Client authentication in this initial process is not the same as network authentication (entering username and password to get access to the network). Client authentication is simply the first step (followed by association) between the wireless client and access point, and it establishes communication. The 802.11 standard specifies only two different methods of authentication: open authentication and shared key authentication. Open authentication is simply the exchange of four "hello" type packets with no client or access point verification, to allow ease of connectivity. Shared key authentication uses a statically defined WEP key, known between the client and access point, for verification. This same key might or might not be used to encrypt the actual data passing between a wireless client and an access point based on user configuration.

How 802.1x Works on WLANs

The access point, acting as the authenticator at the enterprise edge, allows the client to associate using open authentication. The access point then encapsulates any 802.1x traffic bound for the authentication server and sends it to the server. All other network traffic is blocked, meaning that all other attempts to access network resources are blocked. Figure 3-7 shows how 802.1x functions on a wireless network.

Upon receiving RADIUS traffic bound for the client, the access point encapsulates it and sends the information to the client. Although the server authenticates the client as a valid network user, this process allows the client to validate the server as well, ensuring that the client is not logging into a phony server.

Figure 3-7   *802.1x Authentication*

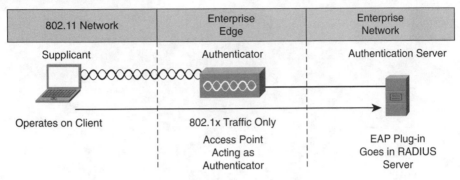

While an enterprise network uses a centralized authentication server, smaller offices or business might simply use the access point with preshared keys as the authentication server for wireless clients.

WPA and WPA2 Modes

WPA provides authentication support via 802.1x and a preshared key (PSK); 802.1x is recommended for enterprise deployments. WPA provides encryption support via TKIP. TKIP includes MIC and per-packet keying (PPK) via initialization vector hashing and broadcast key rotation.

In comparison to WPA, WPA2 authentication is not changed, but the encryption used is AES-Counter with CBC MAC Protocol (AES-CCMP). Table 3-2 compares the two WPA modes.

Table 3-2   *WPA Modes*

	WPA	WPA2
Enterprise Mode (Business, Education, Government)	Authentication: IEEE 802.1x/ EAP Encryption: TKIP/MIC	Authentication: IEEE 802.1x/ EAP Encryption: AES-CCMP
Personal Mode (SOHO, Home/Personal)	Authentication: PSK Encryption: TKIP/MIC	Authentication: PSK Encryption: AES-CCMP

Enterprise Mode

Enterprise Mode is a term given to products that are tested to be interoperable in both PSK and 802.1x/Extensible Authentication Protocol (EAP) modes of operation for authentication.

When 802.1x is used, an authentication, authorization, and accounting (AAA) server (the Remote Authentication Dial-In User Service (RADIUS) protocol for authentication and key management and centralized management of user credentials) is required. Enterprise Mode is targeted to enterprise environments.

NOTE   While Cisco configuration typically uses RADIUS for authentication, the IEEE standard supports RADIUS, Terminal Access Controller Access Control System (TACACS+), DIAMETER, and Common Open Policy Service (COPS) as AAA services.

Personal Mode

Personal Mode is a term given to products tested to be interoperable in the PSK-only mode of operation for authentication. It requires manual configuration of a preshared key on the AP and clients. PSK authenticates users via a password, or identifying code, on both the client station and the AP. No authentication server is needed. Personal Mode is targeted to SOHO environments.

Summary of Understanding WLAN Security

The following summarizes the key points that were discussed in this lesson:

- With 802.1x, the access point, acting as the authenticator at the enterprise edge, allows the client to associate using open authentication.

- WPA provides authentication support via IEEE 802.1x and PSK.

    — Enterprise Mode is a term given to products that are tested to be interoperable in both PSK and IEEE 802.1x/EAP modes of operation for authentication.

    — Personal Mode is a term given to products tested to be interoperable in the PSK-only mode of operation for authentication.

Implementing a WLAN

Implementing a WLAN involves more than selecting the desired standard and selecting a security mechanism. Access point placement can have more effect on throughput than standards. You need to understand how the efficiency of a WLAN is affected by such issues as topology, distance, and access point location.

Upon completing this lesson, you will be able to describe the factors affecting the implementation of a WLAN.

802.11 Topology Building Blocks

Figure 3-8 shows the original standard-defined 802.11 topologies: workgroup (ad hoc), infrastructure, and Extended Services Set. The other topologies such as repeaters, bridges, and workgroup bridges are vendor-specific extensions.

Figure 3-8   *802.11 Building Blocks*

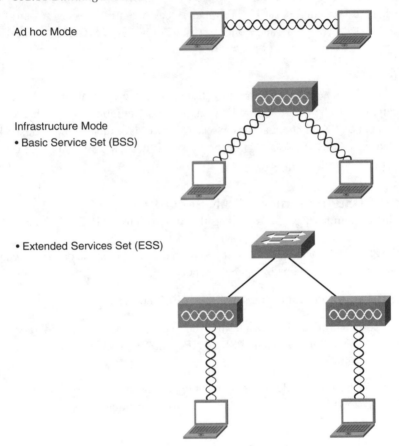

The following list describes these different building blocks.

- **Ad hoc mode:** Independent Basic Service Set (IBSS) is the ad hoc topology mode. Mobile clients connect directly without an intermediate access point. Operating systems such as Windows have made this peer-to-peer network easy to set up. This setup can be used for a small office (or home office) to allow a laptop to be connected to the main PC or for several people to simply share files. The coverage is limited. Everyone must be able to hear everyone else. An access point is not required. A drawback of peer-to-peer networks is that they are difficult to secure.

■ **Infrastructure mode:** In infrastructure mode, clients connect through an access point. There are two infrastructure modes:

— **Basic Service Set (BSS):** The communication devices that create a BSS are mobile clients using a single access point to connect to each other or to wired network resources. The Basic Service Set Identifier (BSSID) is the Layer 2 MAC address of the BSS access point's radio card. While the BSS is the single building block for wireless topology and the BSS access point is uniquely identified through a BSSID, the wireless network itself is advertised through a SSID, which announces the availability of the wireless network to mobile clients. The SSID is a wireless network name that is user configurable and can be made up of as many as 32 case-sensitive characters.

— **Extended Services Set (ESS):** The wireless topology is extended with two or more BSSs connected by a distribution system (DS) or a wired infrastructure. An ESS generally includes a common SSID to allow roaming from access point to access point without requiring client configuration.

BSA Wireless Topology

A Basic Service Area (BSA) is the physical area of RF coverage provided by an access point in a BSS. This area is dependent on the RF created with variations caused by access point power output, antenna type, and physical surroundings affecting the RF. While the BSS is the topology building block and the BSA is the actual coverage pattern, the two terms are used interchangeably in basic wireless discussions. Figure 3-9 shows a BSA topology.

The access point attaches to the Ethernet backbone and communicates with all the wireless devices in the cell area. The access point is the master for the cell and controls traffic flow to and from the network. The remote devices do not communicate directly with each other; they communicate only with the access point. The access point is user-configurable with its unique RF channel and wireless SSID name.

The access point broadcasts the name of the wireless cell in the SSID through beacons. Beacons are broadcasts that access points send to announce the available services. It is used to logically separate WLANs. It must match exactly between the client and the access point. However, clients can be configured without an SSID (null-SSID), then detect all access points, and learn the SSID from the beacons of the access points. A common example of the discovery process is the one used by the integrated Windows Zero Configuration (WZC) utility when a wireless laptop is used at a new location. The user is shown a display of the newly found wireless service and asked to connect or supply appropriate keying material to join. SSID broadcasts can be disabled on the access point, but this approach does not work if the client needs to see the SSID in the beacon.

Figure 3-9 *BSA Topology*

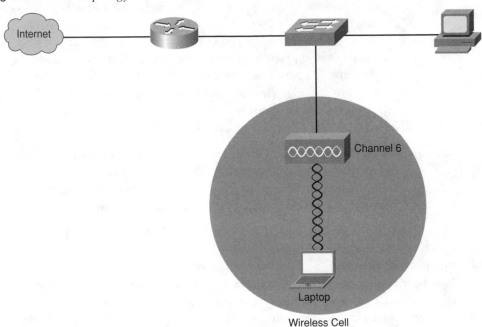

If a single cell does not provide enough coverage, any number of cells can be added to extend the range. This range is known as an Extended Service Area (ESA). Figure 3-10 shows an ESA topology.

It is recommended that ESA cells have 10 to 15 percent overlap to allow remote users to roam without losing RF connections. For wireless voice networks, an overlap of 15 to 20 percent is recommended. Bordering cells should be set to different nonoverlapping channels for best performance.

Wireless Topology Data Rates

WLAN clients have the ability to shift data rates while moving. This strategy allows the same client operating at 11 Mbps to shift to 5.5 Mbps, then 2 Mbps, and finally still communicate in the outside ring at 1 Mbps. This rate-shifting happens without losing the connection and without any interaction from the user. Rate-shifting also happens on a transmission-by-transmission basis; therefore, the access point has the ability to support multiple clients at multiple speeds depending upon the location of each client. Figure 3-11 shows data rates at different distances from the access point.

Figure 3-10 *ESA Topology*

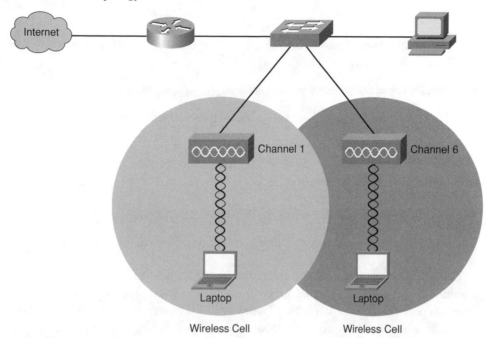

Figure 3-11 *Wireless Data Rates*

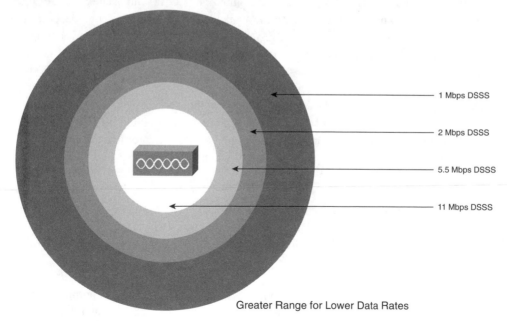

The following outlines the characteristics of data rates as they apply to client devices and signal strength:

■   Higher data rates require stronger signals at the receiver. Therefore, lower data rates have a greater range.

■   Wireless clients always try to communicate with the highest possible data rate.

■   The client reduces the data rate only if transmission errors and transmission retries occur.

This approach outlined in the previous list provides the highest total throughput within the wireless cell. Figure 3-11 is for IEEE 802.11b; however, the same concept applies to IEEE 802.11a or IEEE 802.11g data rates.

Access Point Configuration

This topic describes the factors that should be considered when implementing a WLAN.

Wireless access points can be configured through a command-line interface (CLI), or more commonly through a browser GUI. However, the mode of configuration of the basic wireless parameters is the same. Basic wireless access point parameters include SSID, RF channel with optional power, and authentication (security), whereas basic wireless client parameters include only authentication. Wireless clients need fewer parameters because a wireless network interface card (NIC) scans all the available RF it can to locate the RF channel (meaning an IEEE 802.11b/g card cannot scan 5 GHz) and usually initiates the connection with a null-SSID to discover the available SSIDs. Therefore, by 802.11 design, if you are using open authentication, the result is plug-and-play. When security is configured with PSKs for older WEP or current WPA, remember that the key must be an exact match to allow connectivity.

Depending on the hardware chosen for the access point, it might be capable of two frequencies, 2.4 GHz ISM band and 5 GHz UNII band, and all three IEEE 802.11a/b/g implementations. The features of the access point usually allow for fine adjustment of parameters such as which frequencies to offer, which radio to enable, and which IEEE standard to use on that RF.

When 802.11b wireless clients are mixed with 802.11g wireless clients, throughput is decreased because the access point must implement a protection RTS/CTS protocol. Hence, if you implement only one IEEE wireless client type, throughput is greater than if you use a mixed mode.

After you configure the basic required wireless parameters of the access point, additional fundamental wired side parameters must be configured for the default router and Dynamic Host Configuration Protocol (DHCP) server. Given a pre-existing LAN, a default router is needed to exit the network, and a DHCP server is needed to lease IP addresses to wired PCs. The access point simply uses the existing router and DHCP servers for relaying IP addresses to wireless clients. Because the network has been expanded, verify that the existing DHCP IP address scope is large enough to accommodate the new wireless client additions. If this is a new installation with all router and access point functions in the same hardware, then you simply configure all parameters in the same hardware.

Steps to Implement a Wireless Network

The basic approach to wireless implementation (as with any basic networking) is to gradually configure and test incrementally, following these steps:

Step 1   Before implementing any wireless, verify pre-existing network and Internet access for the wired hosts.

Step 2   Implement wireless with only a single access point and a single client, without wireless security.

Step 3   Verify that the wireless client has received a DHCP IP address and can ping the local wired default router and then browse to the external Internet.

Step 4   Finally, configure wireless security with WPA/WPA2. Only use WEP if hardware equipment does not support WPA/WPA2.

Wireless Clients

Currently, many form factors exist to add wireless to existing laptops. The most common are Universal Serial Bus (USB) devices with self-contained fixed antenna software and wireless supplicant software, both of which enable wireless hardware usage and provide security options for authentication and encryption. Most new laptops contain some form of wireless. This availability of wireless technology has increased the wireless market and improved ease of use. Newer Windows operating systems have a basic wireless supplicant client (WZC). WZC enables wireless plug-and-play by discovering SSIDs being broadcasted and allowing the user to simply type the matching security PSK for such items as WEP or WPA. The basic features of WZC satisfy more simple SOHO environments.

Large enterprise networks require more advanced wireless client features than those of native operating systems. In 2000, Cisco started a program of value-add feature enhancements through a royalty-free certification program. Over 95 percent of Wi-Fi–enabled laptops shipped today are Cisco Compatible Extensions compliant. The details and status of versions and features can be found on http://www.cisco.com/go/ciscocompatible/wireless. Table 3-3 shows a summary of versions and features:

Table 3-3 *Versions and Features*

Version	Topic	Example
V1	Security	Wi-Fi compliant; 802.1x, LEAP, Cisco Key Integrity Protocol
V2	Scaling	WPA, access point–assisted roaming
V3	Performance and security	WPA2, Wi-Fi Multimedia (WMM)
V4	Voice over WLAN	Call Admission Control (CAC), voice metrics, UPSD
V5	Management and IPS	Management Frame Protection (MFP), client reporting

Enterprise networks typically manage one set of wired clients and another set of wireless clients. Cisco offers a full-featured supplicant for both wired and wireless clients called Cisco Secure Services Client. The benefit to users is a single client for wired or wireless connectivity and security.

See http://www.cisco.com/go/ciscocompatible/wireless for additional information.

Wireless Troubleshooting

If you follow the recommended steps for implementing a wireless network, the divide-and-conquer technique via incremental configuration will most likely lead to a problem. These are the most common causes of configuration problems:

■   Configuring a defined SSID on the client (versus its discovery method of SSID) that does not match the access point (inclusive of case sensitivity)

■   Configuring incompatible security methods

Both the wireless client and access point must match for authentication method, EAP or PSK, and encryption method (TKIP or AES).

Other common problems resulting from initial RF installation can sometimes be identified by answering the following questions:

■   Is the radio enabled on both the access point and client for the correct RF (2.4 GHz ISM or 5 GHz UNII)?

■   Is an external antenna connected and facing the correct direction (straight upward for dipole)?

■   Is the antenna location too high or too low relative to wireless clients (within 20 vertical feet)?

■   Are there metal objects in the room reflecting RF and causing poor performance?

■   Is the AP the client is attempting to reach at too great of a distance?

The first step in troubleshooting a suspected wireless issue is to break the environment into wired network versus wireless network. Then, further divide the wireless network into configuration versus RF issues. Begin by verifying the proper operation of the existing wired infrastructure and associated services. Verify that other pre-existing Ethernet-attached hosts can renew their DHCP addresses and reach the Internet.

Then co-locate both the access point and wireless client together to verify configuration and eliminate the possibility of RF issues. Always start the wireless client on open authentication and establish connectivity. Then, implement the desired wireless security.

If the wireless client is operational at this point, then only RF-related issues remain. First, consider whether metal obstructions exist. If so, move the obstruction or change the location of the access point. If the distance is too great, consider adding another access point using the same SSID, but a unique RF channel. Lastly, consider the RF environment. Just as a wired network can become congested with traffic, so can RF for 2.4 GHz (more often than 5 GHz). Check for other sources of wireless devices using 2.4 GHz.

If performance issues seem to relate to time of day, that would indicate RF interference from a device. An example would be slow performance at lunchtime in an office located near a microwave oven used by employees. While most microwaves jam RF channel 11, other microwaves jam all RF channels. Another cause of problems could be RF devices that hop frequencies, such as Frequency Hopping Spread Spectrum (FHSS) used in cordless phones. Because there can be many sources of RF interference, always start with co-locating the access point and wireless client and then move the wireless client until you can reproduce the problem. Most wireless clients have supplicant software that helps troubleshoot by presenting relative RF signal strength and quality.

Summary of Implementing a WLAN

The following summarizes the key points that were discussed in this lesson:

- Ad hoc mode: Clients connect directly without an intermediate access point.

- Infrastructure mode: Clients connect through an access point. There are two modes:

    — Basic Service Set (BSS)

    — Extended Services Set (ESS)

- BSS wireless topology:

    — Basic Service Area (BSA)

    — Extended Service Area (ESA)

- Wireless access points can be configured through a command-line interface or more commonly a browser GUI.

- The basic approach to wireless implementation is to gradually configure and test incrementally.

- Currently, many form factors exist to add wireless to existing laptops:

    — Windows Zero Configuration

    — Cisco Compatible Extensions

    — Cisco Secure Services Client

- Troubleshooting wireless by breaking the environment into wired network versus wireless network.

Chapter Summary

The different 802.11 standards identify the characters of the transmissions used by WLANs, while the Wi-Fi certification ensures compatibility between devices.

To address common threats to WLAN services, security has evolved to include 802.1x and WPA/WPA2.

Wireless implementations are affected by distance, speed, and form factors.

Review Questions

Use the questions here to review what you learned in this chapter. The correct answers can be found in the appendix, "Answers to Chapter Review Questions."

1. What is the most tangible benefit of wireless implementation?

    a. Cost reduction

    b. Increased mobility

    c. Better productivity

    d. Improved security

2. What method does a WLAN use to control transmissions?

    a. CSMA/CA (carrier sense multiple access with collision avoidance)

    b. CSMA/CD (carrier sense multiple access collision detect)

    c.   CSMA/CR (carrier sense multiple access with collision rejection)

    d.   CSMA/CW (carrier sense multiple access with collision weighting)

3. Match each factor that influences the transmission of radio waves to its correct description.

    ___Occurs when RF waves bounce off metal or glass surfaces

    ___Occurs when RF waves are soaked up by walls

    ___Occurs when RF waves strike an uneven surface and are reflected in many directions

    a.   absorption

    b.   reflection

    c.   scattering

4. Which regulatory agency controls the 801.11 standard that governs WLANs?

    a.   Wi-Fi Alliance

    b.   IEEE

    c.   EMA

    d.   WISC

5. Which organization offers certification for interoperability among vendors of 802.11 products?

    a.   Wi-Fi

    b.   IEEE

    c.   EMA

    d.   WISC

6. Which two are the unlicensed bands used by WLANs?

    a.   2.4-MHz band

    b.   900-MHz band

    c.   2.4-GHz band

    d.   5-GHz band

    e.   900-GHz band

7. Which two of the 802.11 standards has the highest possible data rates?

   a. 802.11

   b. 802.11a

   c. 802.11b

   d. 802.11d

   e. 802.11g

8. Which 802.11 standard transmits using the 5-GHz band?

   a. 802.11

   b. 802.11a

   c. 802.11b

   d. 802.11d

   e. 802.11g

9. Which is true about the Wi-Fi Alliance organization?

   a. It is a global standards organization that controls the compatibility of Wi-Fi products.

   b. It operates only in the United States and ensures the compatibility of Wi-Fi products.

   c. It is a global, nonprofit industry trade association devoted to promoting the growth and acceptance of wireless LANs.

   d. It is a global, nonprofit industry trade association devoted to promoting the installation of wireless LANs in retail locations.

10. What is a rogue access point?

   a. An access point that has an open WEP key

   b. An access point that is broadcasting its SSID

   c. An unsecured access point that has been placed on a WLAN

   d. An access point that has had a hardware failure that causes it to endlessly broadcast its SSID

11. Which three are the steps to secure a WLAN?

   a. Encryption for providing privacy and confidentiality

   b. Authentication to ensure that legitimate clients and users access the network via trusted access points

c. Controls to transmit power to limit the access point access range to the property boundaries of the parent organization

d. Protection from security risks and availability with intrusion detection and intrusion protection systems for WLANs

12. Which standard provides the strongest level of WLAN security?

    a. EAP

    b. WEP

    c. WPA

    d. 802.11i/WPA2

13. What factor determines which access point a client associates with?

    a. The access point with the lowest SSID

    b. The access point with the highest SSID

    c. The access point whose SSID is received first

    d. The access point that is received with the strongest signal

14. When you are using 802.11x, how is the client authenticated?

    a. The client is authenticated against a local database stored on the access point.

    b. The access point forwards all network traffic to the server where it is either authenticated or blocked.

    c. The access point encapsulates any 802.1x traffic bound for the authentication server and sends it to the server.

    d. The client encapsulates the 802.1x authentication traffic before sending it to the access point. This causes the access point to forward it to the server.

15. Which is true when comparing WPA and WPA2?

    a. WPA uses preshared keys whereas WPA 2 uses PSK.

    b. WPA uses EAP authentication whereas WPA 2 uses 802.11x.

    c. WPA uses a Personal Mode whereas WPA 2 uses an Enterprise Mode.

    d. WPA uses TKIP/MIC encryption whereas WPA 2 uses AES-CCMP encryption.

16. Match each of the following 802.11 topologies to its description.

    ___Mobile clients connect directly without an intermediate access point.

    ___The communication devices use a single access point for connectivity to each other or to wired network resources.

    ___The wireless topology is two or more service sets connected by a distribution system (DS) or, more commonly, a wired infrastructure.

    a. Ad hoc mode

    b. Basic Service Set (BSS)

    c. Extended Services Set (ESS)

17. What does the physical area of radio frequency coverage provided by an access point define?

    a. The RF service area

    b. The basic service area

    c. The ad hoc service area

    d. The extended services area

18. When implementing Extended Service Areas, how much overlap is suggested?

    a. 5 to 10 percent

    b. 10 to 15 percent

    c. 15 to 20 percent

    d. 25 to 30 percent

19. What strategy enables a client to communicate while moving?

    a. The ability to shift data rates

    b. The ability to vary transmit levels

    c. The ability to match the transmit level to the receive level

    d. The ability to perform error correction as the signal level changes

20. Which three are basic wireless access point parameters?

    a. SSID

    b. Authentication

    c.   Data exchange rates

    d.   Transmit band selection

    e.   RF channel with optional power

21. When implementing a WLAN, when should you use WEP?

    a.   Only if an AAA server is available

    b.   When you need the increased security of WEP

    c.   When you are planning to enable 802.11x authentication

    d.   Only if the hardware equipment does not support WPA

22. Match the wireless client to its description.

        ___Full-featured supplicant for both wired and wireless client

        ___Windows operating systems basic wireless supplicant client

        ___More advanced wireless client features than those of native operating system

    a.   WZC

    b.   Cisco Compatible Extensions

    c.   Cisco Secure Services Client

This chapter includes the following sections:

CHAPTER 4

LAN Connections

In addition to connecting multiple devices in a network, the networks themselves can be connected. In fact, the Internet is a collection of connected networks. The concept of connected networks is a common communication infrastructure in large organizations. Connecting networks with diverse devices, architectures, and protocols requires more sophisticated components than simple local-area networks (LAN). Routers are the devices used in this more complex networking environment, and a suite of protocols known as TCP/IP governs how data is transmitted. This chapter describes the functions of routers in connecting networks and describes how routers transmit data through networks using TCP/IP.

Chapter Objectives

Upon completing this chapter, you will be able to connect multiple networks by creating a default gateway. This ability includes being able to meet these objectives:

- Describe the function of routing in the network model

- Convert a decimal number into a binary number and a binary number into decimal format

- Describe how IP constructs network addresses

- Start a router and use the CLI to configure and monitor the router

- Implement a basic configuration for a Cisco router

- Describe the packet flow from one host to another through a router

- Implement basic router security

- Describe basic SDM features

- Use SDM to enable a DHCP server on the router

- Remotely access a router using Telnet and SSH

Exploring the Functions of Routing

Routing is the process that forwards data packets between networks or subnetworks using a Layer 3 device: a router or gateway. The routing process uses network routing tables, protocols, and algorithms to determine the most efficient path for forwarding the IP packet. Routers greatly expand the scalability of networks by terminating Layer 2 collisions and broadcast domains. Understanding how routers function will help you understand the broader topic of how networks are connected and how data is transmitted over networks. The following sections describe the operation of routers.

Routers

A router or gateway is a network device that determines the optimal path for transmitting data from one network to another. A router is a specialized computing device running programs and algorithms that aid in the optimal delivery of network traffic. Certain characteristics are common to all routers. Figure 4-1 shows a picture of various Cisco 2800 series routers.

Figure 4-1   *Cisco 28000 Series Routers*

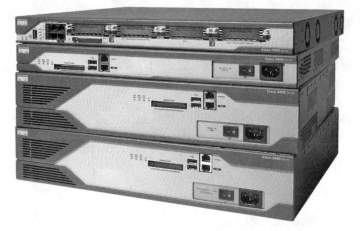

Routers are essential components of large networks that use TCP/IP, because routers provide the ability to accommodate growth across wide geographical areas. The following characteristics are common to all routers:

■   Routers have these components, which are also found in computers and switches:

— CPU

— Motherboard

— RAM

— ROM

- Routers have network adapters to which IP addresses are assigned.

- Routers can have these types of ports:

    — **Console port:** The router uses a console port for the attachment of a terminal used for management, configuration, and control. A console port might not be found on all routers.

    — **Network port:** The router has a number of network ports, including different LAN or WAN media ports.

Routers have the following two key functions:

- **Path determination:** Routers must maintain their routing tables and ensure that other routers know about changes in the network. Routers do this by using a routing protocol to communicate the network information to other routers from a routing table on the router. It is possible to statically populate the routing tables, but statically populating does not scale and leads to problems when the network topology changes, either by design or as a result of outages.

- **Packet forwarding:** Routers use the routing table to determine where to forward packets. Routers forward packets through a network interface toward the destination network identified by the destination IP address in the packet.

Path Determination

During the path determination part of transmitting data over a network, routers evaluate the available paths to remote destinations. This section describes how routers determine the most efficient path for forwarding packets.

There can be many paths to get from one network to another. These paths, also known as routes, can have many different characteristics, such as speed, latency, and media type. The purpose of a router is to communicate with other routers to learn and select the best path, as shown in Figure 4-2.

Figure 4-2   *Routers Perform Path Selection*

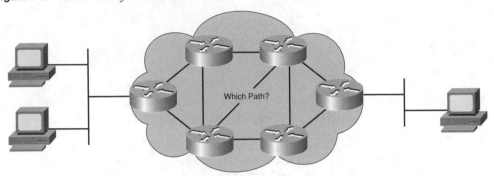

These routes are held in routing tables within the software of the router and are then used to determine where to send a packet based on the destination addressing. The following three types of entries in routing tables can be used to select the best path to a remote destination:

■   **Static routing:** This type of routing requires that you manually enter route information into a routing table.

■   **Dynamic routing:** This type of routing builds a routing table dynamically, using routing information that is obtained from routing protocols.

■   **Default routing:** This type of routing replaces the need to hold an explicit route to every network. The default route entry can be either statically configured or learned from a dynamic routing protocol.

The routing table holds only one entry per network. If there is more than one source of information regarding paths to a particular destination network, the routing process needs to be able to select which source of information should be used in the routing table. Multiple sources come from having multiple dynamic routing protocols running, and from static and default information being available. The routing protocols use different metrics to measure the distance and desirability of a path to a destination network. Because it is not possible to directly select from information provided by different routing protocols, the Cisco routing process assigns a weight, known as the administrative distance, to each source of information. The best, most trusted source has the lowest number.

Routing Tables

As part of the path determination process, the routing process builds a routing table that identifies known networks and knows how to reach them. Figure 4-3 shows how a routing table maintains network locations.

Figure 4-3 *Routing Tables*

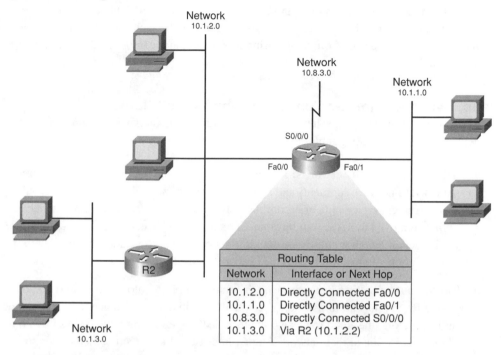

Routing metrics vary depending on the routing protocol used. Figure 4-3 shows how routers keep a table of information used to decide how to forward packets.

Routing Table Information

The routing table consists of an ordered list of "known" network addresses—that is, those addresses that have been learned dynamically by the routing process or the statically configured, directly connected networks. Routing tables also include information on destinations and next-hop associations. These associations tell a router that a particular destination is either directly connected to the router or that it can be reached through another router, called the next-hop router, on the way to the final destination. When a router receives an incoming packet, it uses the destination address and searches the routing table to find the best path. If no entry can be found, the router will discard the packet after sending an Internet Control Message Protocol (ICMP) message to the source address of the packet.

In Figure 4-3, the routing table of the router in the middle shows that when it receives a packet with a destination address on the 10.1.3.0 network, it must forward the packet to R2.

Routing Update Messages

Routers communicate with each other and maintain their routing tables by transmitting routing update messages. Depending on the particular routing protocol, routing update messages can be sent periodically or only when there is a change in the network topology. The information contained in the routing update messages includes the destination networks that the router can reach and the routing metric to reach each destination. By analyzing routing updates from neighboring routers, a router can build and maintain its routing table.

Static, Dynamic, Directly Connected, and Default Routes

Routers can learn about other networks through static, dynamic, directly connected, and default routes. The routing tables can be populated by the following methods:

- **Directly connected networks:** This entry comes from having router interfaces directly attached to network segments and is the most certain method of populating a routing table. If the interface fails or is administratively shut down, the entry for that network will be removed from the routing table. The administrative distance is 0 and, therefore, will preempt all other entries for that destination network, because the entry with the lowest administrative distance is the best, most trusted source.

- **Static routes:** Static routes are manually entered directly into the configuration of a router by a system administrator. The default administrative distance for a static route is 1; therefore, the static routes will be included in the routing table unless there is a direct connection to that network. Static routes can be an effective method for small, simple networks that do not change frequently.

- **Dynamic routes:** Dynamic routes are learned by the router, and the information is responsive to changes in the network so that it is constantly being updated. There is, however, always a lag between the time that a network changes and when all the routers become aware of the change. The time delay for a router to match a network change is called convergence time. The shorter the convergence time, the better, and different routing protocols perform differently in this regard. Larger networks require the dynamic routing method because there are usually many addresses and constant changes, which, if not acted upon immediately, would result in loss of connectivity.

- **Default route:** A default route is used when no explicit path to a destination is found in the routing table. The default route can be manually inserted or populated from a dynamic routing protocol.

Dynamic Routing Protocols

Some routing protocols use their own rules and metrics to build and update routing tables automatically. These protocols are known as dynamic routing protocols because they can adjust dynamically to changes in the network topology.

Routing Metrics

When a routing protocol updates a routing table, the primary objective of the protocol is to determine the best information to include in the table. The routing algorithm generates a number, called the metric value, for each path through the network. Sophisticated routing protocols can base route selection on multiple metrics, combining them in a single metric. Typically, the smaller the metric number, the better the path. Figure 4-4 shows some network criteria that can be used to establish metrics.

Figure 4-4   *Establishing Routing Metrics*

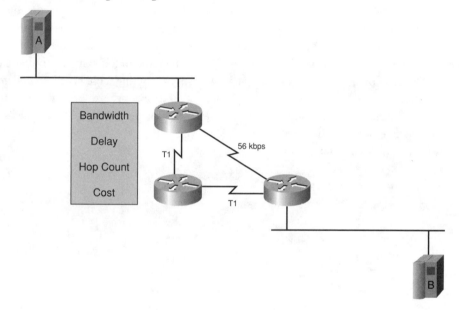

Metrics can be based on either a single characteristic or several characteristics of a path. The metrics that are most commonly used by routing protocols are as follows:

- **Bandwidth:** The data capacity of a link (the connection between two network devices)

- **Delay:** The length of time required to move a packet along each link from source to destination—depends on the bandwidth of intermediate links, port queues at each router, network congestion, and physical distance

- **Hop count:** The number of routers that a packet must travel through before reaching its destination (In Figure 4-4, the hop count from host A to host B would be 1 or 2 depending on the path.)

- **Cost:** An arbitrary value assigned by a network administrator or operating system, usually based on bandwidth, administrator preference, or other measurement

Routing Methods

In addition to the metrics used to select paths, there are also a variety of routing protocol methods. Most routing protocols are designed around one of the following two routing methods: distance vector or link-state.

Distance vector routing: In distance vector routing, a router does not have to know the entire path to every network segment; the router only has to know the direction, or vector, in which to send the packet. The distance vector routing approach determines the direction (vector) and distance (hop count) to any network in the internetwork. Distance vector algorithms periodically (such as every 30 seconds by default for Routing Information Protocol [RIP]) send all or portions of their routing table to their adjacent neighbors. Routers running a distance vector routing protocol will send periodic updates, even if there are no changes in the network. By receiving the routing table of a neighbor, a router can verify all the known routes and make changes to its local routing table based on updated information received from the neighboring router. This process is also known as "routing by rumor," because the understanding that a router has of the network topology is based on the perspective of the routing table of a neighbor router. Figure 4-5 shows how distance vector protocols determine routes.

Figure 4-5 *Distance Vector Protocols*

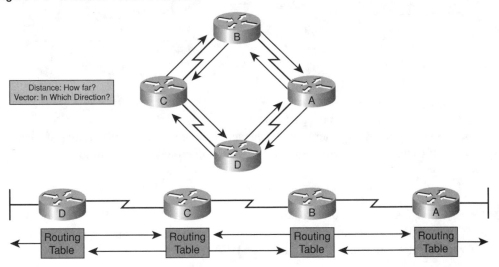

An example of a distance vector protocol is RIP, which is a commonly used routing protocol that uses hop count as its routing metric.

Link-state routing: In link-state routing, each router tries to build its own internal map of the network topology. Each router sends messages into the network when it first becomes active, listing the routers to which it is directly connected and providing information about whether the link to each router is active. The other routers use this information to build a map of the network topology and then use the map to choose the best destination. Link-state routing protocols respond quickly to network changes, sending triggered updates when a network change has occurred and sending periodic updates (link-state refreshes) at long time intervals, such as every 30 minutes.

When a link changes state, the device that detected the change creates an update message regarding that link (route), and that update message is propagated to all routers (running the same routing protocol). Each router takes a copy of the update message, updates its routing tables, and forwards the update message to all neighboring routers. This flooding of the update message is required to ensure that all routers update their databases before creating an updated routing table that reflects the new topology. Figure 4-6 shows how link-state protocols determine routes.

Figure 4-6 *Link-State Protocols*

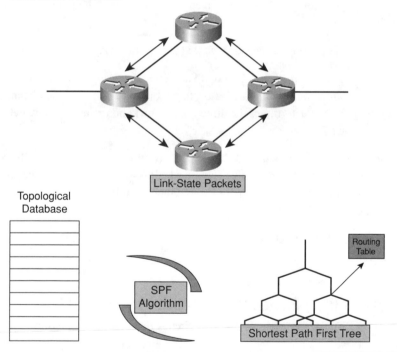

Examples of link-state routing protocols are Open Shortest Path First (OSPF) and Intermediate System–to–Intermediate System **(**IS-IS).

NOTE   Cisco developed the Enhanced Interior Gateway Routing Protocol (EIGRP), which combines the best features of distance vector and link-state routing protocols.

Summary of Exploring the Functions of Routing

The following list summarizes the key points that were discussed in the previous sections:

- Routers have certain components that are also found in computers and switches. These components include the CPU, motherboard, RAM, and ROM.

- Routers have two primary functions in the IP packet delivery process: maintaining routing tables and determining the best path to use to forward packets.

- Routers determine the optimal path for forwarding IP packets between networks. Routers can use different types of routes to reach the destination networks, including static, dynamic, directly connected, and default routes.

- Routing tables provide an ordered list of best paths to known networks and include information such as destination, next-hop associations, and routing metrics.

- Routing algorithms process the received updates and populate the routing table with the best route.

- Commonly used routing metrics include bandwidth, delay, hop count, and cost.

- Distance vector routing protocols build and update routing tables automatically by sending all or some portion of their routing table to neighbors. The distance vector routing approach determines the direction (vector) and distance to any network in the internetwork.

- Link-state routing protocols build and update routing tables automatically, running the shortest path first (SPF) algorithms against the link-state database to determine the best paths, and flood routing information about their own links to all the routers in the network.

- Cisco developed EIGRP, which combines the best features of distance vector and link-state routing protocols.

Understanding Binary Numbering

All computers function using a system of switches that can be in one of two positions, on or off. This is called a binary system, with "off" being represented by the digit 0 and "on" being represented by the digit 1. A binary number will include only the digits 0 and 1.

Network device addresses also use this binary system to define their location on the network. The IP address is based on a dotted decimal notation of a binary number. You must have a basic understanding of the mathematical properties of a binary system to understand networking. The following sections describe the mathematics involved in the binary numbering system and explain how to convert a decimal (base 10) number to a binary (base 2) number and vice versa.

Decimal and Binary Systems

The decimal (base 10) system is the numbering system used in everyday mathematics, and the binary (base 2) system is the foundation of computer operations.

In the decimal system, the digits are 0, 1, 2, 3, 4, 5, 6, 7, 8, and 9. When quantities higher than 9 are required, the decimal system begins with 10 and continues all the way to 99. Then the decimal system begins again with 100, and so on, with each column to the left raising the exponent by 1.

The binary system uses only the digits 0 and 1. Therefore, the first digit is 0, followed by 1. If a quantity higher than 1 is required, the binary system goes to 10, followed by 11. The binary system continues with 100, 101, 110, 111, 1000, and so on. Table 4-1 shows the binary equivalents of the decimal numbers 0 through 19.

Table 4-1   *Decimal Versus Binary Numbers*

Decimal Number	Binary Number
0	0
1	1
2	10
3	11
4	100
5	101
6	110
7	111
8	1000
9	1001
10	1010
11	1011
12	1100
13	1101
14	1110

continues

Table 4-1 *Decimal Versus Binary Numbers (Continued)*

Decimal Number	Binary Number
15	1111
16	10000
17	10001
18	10010
19	10011

Least Significant Bit and Most Significant Bit

Most people are accustomed to the decimal numbering system. While the base number is important in any numbering system, it is the position of a digit that confers value. The number 10 is represented by a 1 in the tens position and a 0 in the ones position. The number 100 is represented by a 1 in the hundreds position, a 0 in the tens position, and a 0 in the ones position.

In a binary number, the digit on the rightmost side is the least significant bit (LSB), and the digit on the leftmost side is the most significant bit (MSB). The significance of any digits in between these sides is based on their proximity to either the LSB or the MSB. Figure 4-7 shows the relationships of bit significance to the values for base 10 and base 2 numbering systems.

Figure 4-7 *Bit Significance*

Base-10 Decimal Conversion - 63204829

	MSB							LSB
Base^{Exponent}	10^7	10^6	10^5	10^4	10^3	10^2	10^1	10^0
Column Value	6	3	2	0	4	8	2	9
Decimal Weight	10000000	1000000	100000	10000	1000	100	10	1
Column Weight	60000000	3000000	200000	0	4000	800	20	9

60000000 + 3000000 + 200000 + 0 + 4000 + 800 + 20 + 9 = 63204829

Base-2 Binary Conversion - 1110100 (233)

	MSB							LSB
Base^{Exponent}	2^7	2^6	2^5	2^4	2^3	2^2	2^1	2^0
Column Value	1	1	1	0	1	0	0	1
Decimal Weight	128	64	32	16	8	4	2	1
Column Weight	128	64	32	0	8	0	0	1

128 + 64 + 32 + 0 + 8 + 0 + 0 + 1 = 233

Base 2 Conversion System

Understanding the base 2 system is important because an IP version 4 (IPv4) address consists of 32 binary bits. Each digit is 1 bit. The 32 bits are divided into four sets of 8 bits, called octets. A dot (period) is placed between each set to separate them. (A byte is another name for 8 bits; however, for the purposes of this module, 8 bits will be referred to as an octet.)

The various classes of addresses are based on the octet boundaries, so it is helpful to get used to such groupings. It is also an ease-of-use issue, because 8-bit binary numbers are easier to convert than 32-bit binary numbers. When converting a binary IP address, you only convert one octet at a time. The highest possible binary octet is 11111111, which converts to the decimal number 255. The lowest possible binary octet is 00000000, which is the decimal number 0. That means that with 8 bits, you can have 256 different number combinations, 0 to 255 inclusive.

Powers of 2

To understand how binary numbers are used in IP addressing, you must understand the mathematical process of converting a decimal number to a binary number and vice versa.

Calculator batteries run down and charts can be misplaced, but if you know the mathematical principles, a piece of paper and pencil are all that you need to convert binary numbers to decimal numbers and to convert decimal numbers to binary numbers. There are charts available to help with decimal-to-binary conversion, showing, for example, $2^0 =$ decimal 1, $2^1 =$ decimal 2, $2^2 =$ decimal 4, and so on. Table 4-2 illustrates which decimal numbers are produced for powers of 2.

Table 4-2 *Powers of 2*

Power of 2	Calculation	Value
2^0	Mathematical identity	1
2^1	2	2
2^2	2*2	4
2^3	2*2*2	8
2^4	2*2*2*2	16
2^5	2*2*2*2*2	32
2^6	2*2*2*2*2*2	64
2^7	2*2*2*2*2*2*2	128

Decimal-to-Binary Conversion

Decimal numbers can be converted to binary numbers through a specific process, as shown in Figure 4-8.

Figure 4-8 *Decimal-to-Binary Conversion*

Base^{Exponent}	2^7	2^6	2^5	2^4	2^3	2^2	2^1	2^0
Place Value	128	64	32	16	8	4	2	1
Example: Convert Decimal 35 to Binary	0	0	1	0	0	0	1	1

$$35 \quad = \qquad\qquad\qquad 2^5 \qquad\qquad + \qquad\qquad\qquad 2^1 + 2^0$$
$$35 \quad = \qquad\qquad\qquad (32 * 1) \qquad + \qquad\qquad (2 * 1) + (1 * 1)$$
$$35 \quad = \quad 0 \ + \ 0 \ + \ 1 \ + \ 0 \ + \ 0 \ + \ 0 \ + \ 1 \ + \ 1$$
$$35 \quad = \quad \underline{00100011}$$

This example shows a simple binary conversion of the decimal number 35. The base exponent line shows base 2 numbers and their exponents ($2 * 2 = 4 * 2 = 8$, and so on). The decimal value of the base exponent number is listed in the second row, and the binary number is displayed in the third row. The table describes the steps to determine the binary number. Notice that the first 2 bits of the binary number are 0s; these are known as leading 0s. In reality, the decimal number 35 would only be a 6-bit binary number. Because IP addresses are laid out as four sets of octets, the binary number is made into an octet by placing 0s to the left of the 6-bit number.

The steps used in converting the number 35 to a binary number are as follows:

Step 1 Looking at Figure 4-8, what is the greatest power of 2 that is less than or equal to 35? 128 does not go into 35, so place a 0 in that column.

Step 2 64 does not go into 35, so place a 0 in that column.

Step 3 2^5 (32) is smaller than 35. 32 goes into 35 one time. Place a 1 in that column.

Step 4 Calculate how much is left over by subtracting 32 from 35. The result is 3.

Step 5 Check to see whether 16 (the next lower power of 2) fits into 3. Because it does not, a 0 is placed in that column.

Step 6 The value of the next number is 8, which is larger than 3, so a 0 is placed in that column, too.

Step 7 The next value is 4, which is still larger than 3, so it too receives a 0.

Step 8 The next value is 2, which is smaller than 3. Because 2 fits into 3 one time, place a 1 in that column.

Step 9   Subtract 2 from 3, and the result is 1.

Step 10   The decimal value of the last bit is 1, which fits in the remaining number. Therefore, place a 1 in the last column. The binary equivalent of the decimal number 35 is 00100011.

Binary-to-Decimal Conversion

As with decimal-to-binary conversion, there is usually more than one way to convert binary numbers to decimal numbers. You can convert binary numbers to decimal numbers using the positional values based on the powers of 2 and identifying the columns with nonzero values, which contribute to the final numerical value. Figure 4-9 illustrates this process.

Figure 4-9   *Binary-to-Decimal Conversion*

Base^{Exponent}	2^7	2^6	2^5	2^4	2^3	2^2	2^1	2^0
Place Value	128	64	32	16	8	4	2	1
Example: Binary Number	1	0	1	1	1	0	0	1
Decimal Number Total: 185	128	0	32	16	8	0	0	1

1 0 1 1 1 0 0 1 = (128 * 1) + (64 * 0) + (32 * 1) + (16 * 1) + (8 * 1) + (4 * 0) + (2 * 0) + (1 * 1)
1 0 1 1 1 0 0 1 = 128 + 0 + 32 + 16 + 8 + 0 + 0 + 1
1 0 1 1 1 0 0 1 = <u>185</u>

The steps used for converting the binary number 10111001 to a decimal number are as follows:

Step 1   Find the place value that corresponds to any 1 bit in the binary number, according to its position. For example, as shown in Figure 4-9, the binary bit in the 2^7 column is 1, so the decimal total is 128.

Step 2   There is a 0 in the 2^6 (64) column. The decimal equation is $128 + 0 = 128$.

Step 3   There is now a 1 in the 2^5 (32) column. The decimal equation becomes $128 + 32 = 160$.

Step 4   There is a 1 in the 2^4 (16) column. Adding the value to the decimal total gives $160 + 16 = 176$.

Step 5   The next column, 2^3, has a 1, so add the value 8 to the decimal total, giving $176 + 8 = 184$.

Step 6   There are 0s in the 2^2 and 2^1 columns. Add 0s to the decimal total: $184 + 0 + 0 = 184$.

Step 7   Finally, there is a 1 in the 2^0 (1) column. Now, add 1 to 184. The result is 185. The decimal equivalent of the binary number 10111001 is 185.

Summary of Understanding Binary Numbering

The following list summarizes the key points that were discussed in the previous sections:

■   All computers operate using a binary system.

■   Binary systems (base 2) use only the numerals 0 and 1.

■   Decimal systems (base 10) use the numerals 0 through 9.

■   Using the powers of 2, a binary number can be converted into a decimal number.

■   Using the powers of 2, a decimal number can be converted into a binary number.

Constructing a Network Addressing Scheme

Subnetworks, also known as subnets, are very common in all but the smallest of network environments, segmenting the network into smaller divisions that have their own addresses. To create subnet addresses, some of the bits used for the host portion of an IP address are "borrowed" to create the subnet address. The following sections describe how subnets function and how they are computed.

Subnetworks

Network administrators often need to divide networks, especially large networks, into subnetworks, or subnets, to provide addressing flexibility. This topic describes the purposes and functions of subnets and their addressing schemes.

A company that occupies a three-story building might have a network divided by floors, with each floor divided into offices. Think of the building as the network, the floors as the three subnets, and the offices as the individual host addresses.

A subnet segments the hosts within the network. With no subnets, the network has a flat topology. A flat topology has a short routing table and relies on Layer 2 MAC addresses to deliver packets. MAC addresses have no hierarchical structure. As the network grows, the use of the network bandwidth becomes less and less efficient.

The disadvantages of a flat network are as follows:

■   All devices share the same bandwidth.

■   All devices share the same Layer 2 broadcast domain.

■   It is difficult to apply security policies because there are no boundaries between devices.

On an Ethernet network connected by hubs, every host on the same physical network sees all the packets on the network. On a switch-connected network, the host sees all broadcasts. In heavy traffic situations, on a shared segment connected by hubs, there can be many collisions caused by two or more devices transmitting simultaneously. The devices detect the collision, stop transmitting, and then begin transmitting at a random interval later. To users, this process is perceived as the network slowing down. Routers can be used in these situations to separate networks by breaking the network into multiple subnets. Figure 4-10 shows an example of a small network broken into three separate subnets.

Figure 4-10   *Network Subnets*

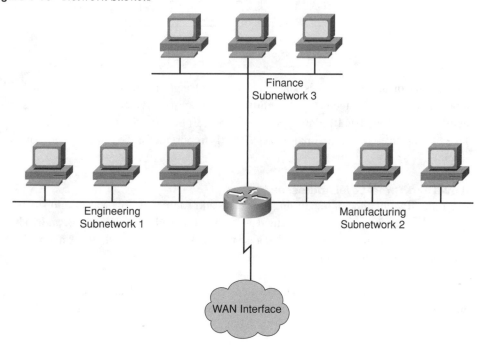

The advantages of subnetting a network are as follows:

- Smaller networks are easier to manage and map to geographical or functional requirements.

- Overall network traffic is reduced, which can improve performance.

- You can more easily apply network security measures at the interconnections between subnets than throughout the entire network.

In multiple-network environments, each subnetwork can be connected to the Internet through a single router, as shown in Figure 4-10. In this example, the network is subdivided into multiple subnetworks. The actual details of the internal network environment and how the network is divided into multiple subnetworks are inconsequential to other IP networks.

IP addresses provide an identifier for both the network and the host of an IP subnet. As Figure 4-11 illustrates, the router must have some way of determining how much of the address is the network portion.

Figure 4-11   *Determining Network Addresses*

Each device on an IP network is configured with both an IP address and a subnet mask. The subnet mask identifies the network-significant portion of an IP address. The network-significant portion of an IP address is, simply, the part that identifies what network the host device is on (that is, the network address). This is important for the routing operation to be efficient.

Two-Level and Three-Level Addresses

When the IPv4 method of identifying addresses and address classes was developed, a two-level address (network and host) seemed sufficient. Each address class (A, B, and C) had a default mask associated with it, and because the mask was predefined, it was not necessary to explicitly configure the mask.

As the number of network-connected devices grew, it became clear that this was an inefficient use of network addresses. To overcome this problem, a third level of addressing, consisting of subnets, was developed.

A subnet address includes the original classful network portion plus a subnet field. This is also known as the extended network prefix. The subnet field and the host field are created from the original classful host portion. To create a subnet address, you can borrow bits from the original host field and designate them as the subnet field.

However, subnets cannot work without a way to identify the part of the address that is network significant and the part that is host significant. For this reason, explicit subnet masks need to be configured.

Subnet Creation

The subnet address is created by taking address bits from the host portion of Class A, Class B, and Class C addresses. Usually a network administrator assigns the subnet address locally. Like IP addresses, each subnet address must be unique.

When creating subnets, many potential individual host addresses (endpoints) are lost. For this reason, you must pay close attention to the percentage of addresses that are lost when you create subnets. The algorithm used to compute the number of subnets uses powers of 2.

When taking (borrowing) bits from the host field, it is important to note that the number of additional subnets that are being created will double each time one more bit is borrowed. Borrowing 1 bit creates two possible subnets ($2^1 = 2$). Borrowing 2 bits creates four possible subnets ($2^2 = 4$). Borrowing 3 bits creates eight possible subnets ($2^3 = 8$), and so on.

Each time another bit is borrowed from the host field, the number of possible subnets created *increases* by a power of 2 and the number of individual possible host addresses on each subnet *decreases* by a power of 2. Some examples are as follows:

- Using 1 bit for the subnet field results in 2 possible subnets ($2^1 = 2$).

- Using 2 bits for the subnet field results in 4 possible subnets ($2^2 = 4$).

- Using 3 bits for the subnet field results in 8 possible subnets ($2^3 = 8$).

- Using 4 bits for the subnet field results in 16 possible subnets ($2^4 = 16$).

- Using 5 bits for the subnet field results in 32 possible subnets ($2^5 = 32$).

- Using 6 bits for the subnet field results in 64 possible subnets ($2^6 = 64$).

In general, the following formula can be used to calculate the number of usable subnets, given the number of subnet bits used:

$$\text{Number of subnets} = 2^s \text{ (where } s \text{ is the number of subnet bits borrowed)}$$

Computing Usable Subnetworks and Hosts

One of the decisions you must make when creating subnets is to determine the optimal number of subnets and hosts. To accomplish this, you need to understand the classes of IP networks and know how to use the bits within these classes to create networks and allocate address space for hosts. This is done by borrowing bits from the host field in a network address space.

Computing Hosts for a Class C Subnetwork

Each time 1 bit is borrowed from a host field, there is one less bit remaining in the host field that can be used for host numbers, and the number of host addresses that can be assigned decreases by a power of 2.

As an example, consider a Class C network address in which all 8 bits in the last octet are used for the host ID. Therefore, there are 256 possible numbers. The actual number of possible addresses available to assign to hosts is 254 (256 − 2 reserved addresses).

Now, imagine that this Class C network is divided into subnets. If 2 bits are borrowed from the default 8-bit host field, the size of the host field decreases to 6 bits. All possible combinations of 0s and 1s that could occur in the remaining 6 bits produce a total number of possible hosts that could be assigned in each subnet. This number, which formerly was 256, is now 64. (You "borrowed" 2 bits to make subnets from 8 host bits total in a Class C network, so with 6 bits remaining for hosts, $2^6 = 64$.) The number of usable host numbers decreases to 62 (64 − 2).

In the same Class C network, if 3 bits are borrowed, the size of the host field decreases to 5 bits, and the total number of assignable hosts for each subnet decreases to 32 (2^5). The number of usable host numbers decreases to 30 (32 − 2). The number of possible host addresses that can be assigned to a subnet is related to the number of subnets that have been created. In a Class C network, for example, with 3 bits borrowed to make subnets, the usable subnets created are 8, each having 30 ($2^5 = 32 − 2 = 30$) usable host addresses. Figure 4-12 shows the number of subnets and hosts that can be computed in a Class C address space by borrowing host bits.

Figure 4-12 *Borrowing Bits in a Class C Network Address Space*

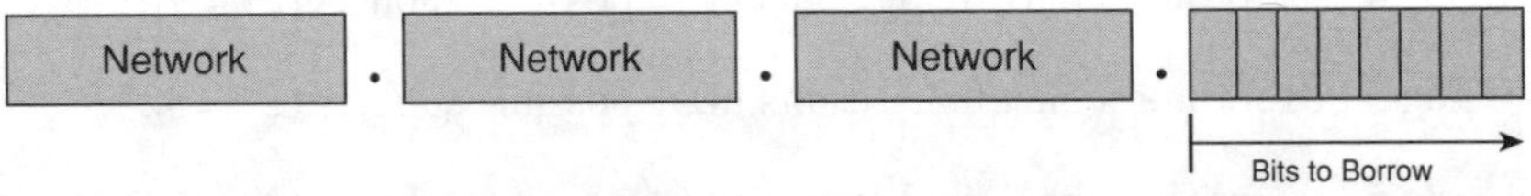

Number of Bits Borrowed (s)	Number of Subnets Possible (2^s)	Number of Bits Remaining in Host ID (8-s=h)	Number of Hosts Possible Per Subnet (2^h-2)
1	2	7	126
2	4	6	62
3	8	5	30
4	16	4	14
5	32	3	6
6	64	2	2
7	128	1	2

Computing Hosts for a Class B Subnetwork

Now consider a Class B network address, in which 16 bits are used for the network ID and 16 bits are used for the host ID. Therefore, there are 65,536 (2^{16}) possible addresses available to assign to hosts (65,534 usable addresses, after subtracting the 2 addresses, the broadcast and the subnet addresses, that cannot be used).

Now, imagine that this Class B network is divided into subnets. If 2 bits are borrowed from the default 16-bit host field, the size of the host field decreases to 14 bits. All possible combinations of 0s and 1s that could occur in the remaining 14 bits produce a total number of possible hosts that could be assigned in each subnet. Thus, the number of hosts assigned to each subnet is now 16,382.

In the same Class B network, if 3 bits are borrowed, making the mask 3 bits longer, the size of the host field decreases from 16 bits to 13 bits, because you borrowed 3 bits to make subnets, and now the total number of host addresses for each subnet decreases to 8192 (2^{13}). The number of usable host numbers decreases to 8190 (8192 − 2). In this Class B network, for example, the usable subnets created are 6 ($2^3 = 8 - 2$), each having 8190 (8192 − 2) usable host addresses. Figure 4-13 shows the number of subnets and hosts that can be computed in a Class B address space by borrowing host bits.

Figure 4-13 *Borrowing Bits in a Class B Network Address Space*

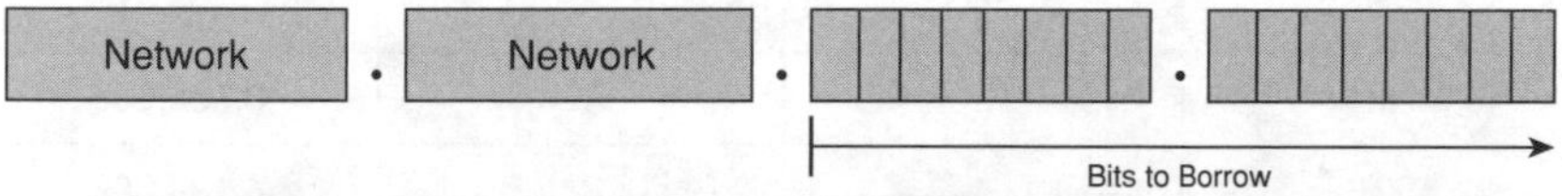

Number of Bits Borrowed (s)	Number of Subnets Possible (2^s)	Number of Bits Remaining in Host ID (16-s=h)	Number of Hosts Possible Per Subnet (2^h-2)
1	2	15	32,766
2	4	14	16.382
3	8	13	8,190
4	16	12	4,094
5	32	11	2,046
6	64	10	1,022
7	128	9	510
...	...	...	...

Computing Hosts for a Class A Subnetwork

Finally, consider a Class A network address, in which by default 8 bits are used for the network ID and 24 bits are used for the host ID. Therefore, there are 16,777,216 (2^{24}) possible addresses available to assign to hosts (16,777,214 usable addresses, after subtracting the 2 addresses, the broadcast and the subnet addresses, that cannot be used).

Now, imagine that this Class A network is divided into subnets. If 6 bits are borrowed from the default 24-bit host field, the size of the host field decreases to 18 bits. All possible combinations of 0s and 1s that could occur in the remaining 18 bits produce a total number of possible hosts that could be assigned in each subnet. This number is now 262,142, while it was formerly 16,777,216. The number of usable hosts decreases to 262,140 (262,142 – 2). Figure 4-14 shows the number of subnets and hosts that can be computed in a Class A address space by borrowing host bits.

Figure 4-14 *Borrowing Bits in a Class A Network Address Space*

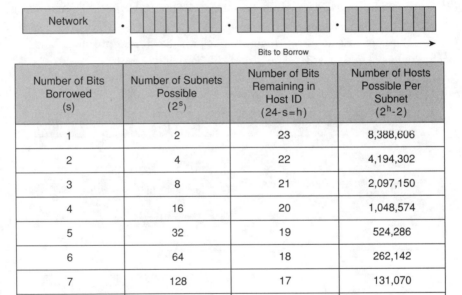

Number of Bits Borrowed (s)	Number of Subnets Possible (2^s)	Number of Bits Remaining in Host ID (24-s=h)	Number of Hosts Possible Per Subnet (2^h-2)
1	2	23	8,388,606
2	4	22	4,194,302
3	8	21	2,097,150
4	16	20	1,048,574
5	32	19	524,286
6	64	18	262,142
7	128	17	131,070
...	...	...	...

How End Systems Use Subnet Masks

The end system uses the subnet mask to compare the network portion of the local network address with the destination network address of the packet to be sent. Before an end system can send a packet to its destination, it must first determine whether the destination address is on the local network. This is done by comparing the bits in the destination address with the network bits of the sending station. Figure 4-15 shows how host A and host B are local because their subnetwork addresses are both 10.1.1.0.

Figure 4-15 *Local Hosts*

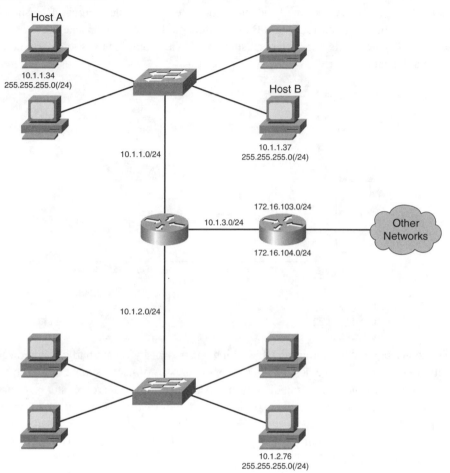

Because these hosts are on the same subnet, the source end system will use the Address Resolution Protocol (ARP) process to bind the destination IP address to the destination MAC address. If it was not on the same subnet, the packet (frame) must be forwarded to the MAC address of the default gateway, the router on the subnet, for transmission to the destination network.

How Routers Use Subnet Masks

The subnet mask identifies the network-significant part of an IP address. Routers, like all IP hosts, need this information to determine how to get a packet to the desired destination. When a device determines that a packet does not belong on the local subnet (which would called off-net), it will send the packet to the router (its default gateway) on its subnet. The router must then determine where to send the packet.

All routers have routing tables. Depending on the location of the router in the network hierarchy, the table can be small and simple or large and complex. Figure 4-16 shows a packet traveling from host A to host B on different networks. As the packet travels between the adjoining networks, the routers must reference their routing tables to determine where to send the packet next.

Figure 4-16   *Routing Tables*

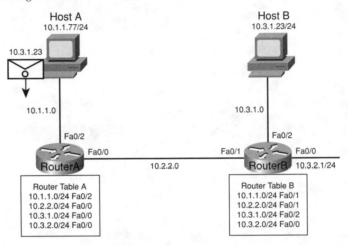

The router populates the routing table with the network-significant part of all known networks, to compare the destination network addresses of packets that need to be forwarded. If the network is not directly attached to the router, the router stores the address of the next-hop router to which the packet should be forwarded. For routers to function without the need to store *all* destination networks in their tables, they use a default route to which packets not matching any entry in the route table are forwarded. The following step list describes this behavior.

Step 1   Host A determines that the destination network is off-net and requires the use of its default gateway router (Router A). So host A must ARP for, and deliver the frame to, Router A.

> **NOTE**   Router A has a route to the destination network 10.3.1.0 and forwards the packet to Router B through the indicated interface.

Step 2   Because the 10.3.1.0/24 network is directly connected to Router B interface Fa0/2, Router B will use ARP to determine the MAC address of host B.

When configuring routers, each interface is connected to a different network or subnet segment. An available host address from each different network or subnet must be assigned to the interface of the router that connects to that network or subnet. In Figure 4-17, RouterA has two Ethernet interfaces one connected to the host network and one to the network connecting RouterA to RouterB.

Figure 4-17 *IP Addressing on a Router Interface*

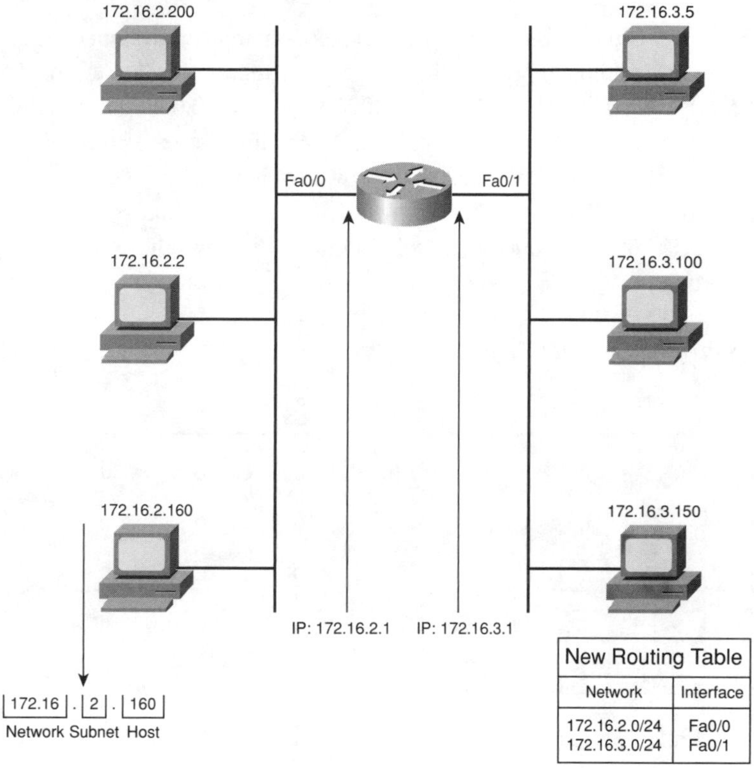

The interface that is connected to the 172.16.2.0 subnetwork is assigned the IP address of 172.16.2.1, and the other interface that is connected to the 172.16.3.0 subnetwork is assigned the IP address of 172.16.3.1. All the attached hosts need to have their addresses within the range of the subnet. Any host configured with an address outside of this would *not* be reachable.

Mechanics of Subnet Mask Operation

Although subnet masks use the same format as IP addresses, they are not IP addresses themselves. Each subnet mask is 32 bits long, divided into four octets, and is usually represented in the dotted decimal notation like IP addresses. In their binary representation, subnet masks have all 1s in the network and subnetwork portions (on the left) and all 0s in the host portion (on the right).

There are only eight valid subnet mask values per octet. The subnet field always immediately follows the network number. That is, the borrowed bits must be the first *n* bits, starting with the most significant bit (MSB) of the default host field, where *n* is the desired size of the new subnet field. The subnet mask is the tool used by the router to determine which bits are routing (network and subnet) bits and which bits are host bits.

If all 8 bits in any octet are binary 1s, the octet has a decimal equivalent of 255. This is why there is a 255 in a decimal representation of a default subnet. In Class A, the default subnet mask is 255.0.0.0 in decimal, 11111111.00000000.00000000.00000000 in binary, and /8 in shorthand; all three mean the same thing. If the three highest-order bits (bits to the left) from the next highest-order host octet are borrowed (add three more 1s to the default mask), they add up to 224 (128 + 64 + 32). This translates to 255.224.0.0, or 11111111.**111**00000.00000000.00000000. Figure 4-18 shows the common values used in subnet masking.

Figure 4-18 *Subnet Mask Octet Values*

128	64	32	16	8	4	2	1		
1	0	0	0	0	0	0	0	=	128
1	1	0	0	0	0	0	0	=	192
1	1	1	0	0	0	0	0	=	224
1	1	1	1	0	0	0	0	=	240
1	1	1	1	1	0	0	0	=	248
1	1	1	1	1	1	0	0	=	252
1	1	1	1	1	1	1	0	=	254
1	1	1	1	1	1	1	1	=	255

With IP addressing, the subnet mask identifies the network addressing information that is necessary to send packets toward their final destinations. The subnet mask identifies which bits within the IP address are the network and subnet bits.

Figure 4-19 shows the default subnet masks for Class A, Class B, and Class C addresses. The subnet mask itself is indicated with 1s in the binary notation for the mask, with all other bits indicated as 0s.

Figure 4-19 *Class A, B, and C Default Subnet Masks*

```
Example Class A Address (Decimal):    10.0.0.0
Example Class A Address (Binary):     00001010.00000000.00000000.00000000
Default Class A Mask (Binary):        11111111.00000000.00000000.00000000
Default Class A Mask (Decimal):       255.0.0.0
Default Classful Prefix Length:       /8
```

```
Example Class B Address (Decimal):    172.16.0.0
Example Class B Address (Binary):     10010001.10101000.00000000.00000000
Default Class B Mask (Binary):        11111111.11111111.00000000.00000000
Default Class B Mask (Decimal):       255.255.0.0
Default Classful Prefix Length:       /16
```

```
Example Class C Address (Decimal):    192.168.42.0
Example Class C Address (Binary):     11000000.10101000.00101010.00000000
Default Class C Mask (Binary):        11111111.11111111.11111111.00000000
Default Class C Mask (Decimal):       255.255.255.0
Default Classful Prefix Length:       /24
```

Applying Subnet Mask Operation

Most network administrators work with existing networks, complete with subnets and subnet masks in place. Network administrators need to be able to determine, from an existing IP address, which part of the address is the network and which part is the subnet. Applying the subnet mask operation provides this information.

The procedure described in the following steps explains how to select the number of subnets you need for a particular network and then apply a mask to implement subnets:

Step 1 Determine the IP address for your network as assigned by the registry authority. Assume that you are assigned a Class B address of 172.16.0.0.

Step 2 Based on your organization and administrative requirements and structure, determine the number of subnets required for the network. Be sure to plan for future growth. Assume that you are managing a worldwide network in 25 countries. Each country has an average of four locations. Therefore, you will need 100 subnets.

Step 3 Based on the address class and the number of subnets you selected, determine the number of bits you need to borrow from the host ID. To create 100 subnets, you need to borrow 7 bits ($2^7 = 128$).

Step 4   Determine the binary and decimal values of the subnet mask you select. For a Class B address with 16 bits in the network ID, when you borrow 7 bits, the mask is /23. Binary value of the mask: 11111111.11111111.11111110.00000000. Decimal value of the mask: 255.255.254.0.

Step 5   Apply the subnet mask for the network IP address to determine the subnet and host addresses. You will also determine the network and broadcast addresses for each subnet.

Step 6   Assign subnet addresses to specific subnets on your network.

Determining the Network Addressing Scheme

When working in a classful networking environment that uses fixed-length subnet masks, you can determine the entire network addressing based on a single IP address and its corresponding subnet mask. Figure 4-20 shows an example of the first three steps, given the following network address and mask:

- Network address: 192.168.221.37

- Subnet mask: 255.255.255.248

Figure 4-20   *Determining the Addressing Scheme, Steps 1–3*

IP Address: 192.168.221.37   Subnet Mask /29

Step	Description	Example
1.	Write the octet that is being split in binary.	4th Octet: 00100101
2.	Write the mask or classful prefix length in binary.	Assigned Mask: 255.255.255.248 (/29) 4th Octet: 11111000
3.	Draw a line to delineate the significant bits in the assigned IP address. Cross out the mask so you can view the significant bits in the IP address.	Split Octet (Binary): 00100|101 Split Mask (Binary): 11111|000

After using the subnet mask to determine the significant bits used in the host address portion, you will use Steps 4 through 8 to determine the subnetwork network address, broadcast address, first host address, last host address, and next subnet address. This is illustrated in Figure 4-21.

Figure 4-21 *Determining the Addressing Scheme, Steps 4–8*

Step	Description	Example
4.	Copy the significant bits four times.	00100 **000** (Network Address) 00100 **001** (First Address in Subnet) 00100 **110** (Last Address in Subnet)
5.	In the first line, define the network address by placing all zeros in the significant bit.	00100 **111** (Broadcast Address)?
		Completed Subnet Addresses
6.	In the last line, define the broadcast address by placing all ones in the significant bits.	Network Address: 192.168.221.32 Subnet Mask: 255.255.255.248 First Subnet: 192.168.221.32 First Host Address: 192.168.221.33
7.	In the middle lines, define the first and last host number.	Last Host Address: 192.168.221.38 Broadcast Address: 192.168.221.39 Next Subnet: 192.168.221.40
8.	Increment the subnet bits by one.	00101000 (Next Subnet)

After converting the addresses from binary to decimal, the addresses for the subnets are as follows:

- Subnet address: 192.168.221.32

- First host address: 192.168.221.33

- Last host address: 192.168.221.38

- Broadcast address: 192.168.221.39

- Next subnet address: 192.168.221.40

Notice that the range of the address block, including the subnet address and directed broadcast address in this example, is from 192.168.221.32 through 192.168.221.39, which includes eight addresses. The address block is the same size as the number of host bits ($2^h = 2^3 = 8$).

Class C Example

In Figure 4-22, we will determine the addressing for a Class C network with a nondefault mask. Given the address of 192.168.5.139 and knowing that the subnet mask is 255.255.255.224, the subnet number is 11111111.11111111.11111111.11100000, or /27.

Figure 4-22　*Class C Addresses with Nondefault Mask*

IP Address 192.168.5.139　　　Subnet Mask 255.255.255.224

IP Address	192	168	5	139	
IP Address	11000000	10101000	00000101	100|01011	
Subnet Mask	11111111	11111111	11111111	111|00000	/27
Subnetwork	11000000	10101000	00000101	10000000	
Subnetwork	192	168	5	128	
First Host	192	168	5	10000001=129	
Last Host	192	168	5	10011110=158	
Directed Broadcast	192	168	5	10011111=159	
Next Subnet	192	168	5	10100000=160	

The following outlines the steps and shows the details of each operation in the eight-step process:

Step 1　Write the octet that is being split in binary (10001011).

Step 2　Write the mask bits of the same octet (11100000).

Step 3　Draw a vertical line to delineate the network-significant bits in the assigned IP address. Put a line under the mask so that you can view the significant bits in the IP address (10000000).

Step 4　Copy the significant bits four times.

Step 5　In the first line, define the network address by placing 0s in the remaining host bits (10000000).

Step 6　In the last line, define the directed broadcast address by placing all 1s in the host bits (10011111).

Step 7　In the middle lines, define the first and last host ID for this subnet: 10000001 and 10011110.

Step 8　Increment the subnet bits by 1 to determine the next subnet address. Repeat Steps 4 through 8 for all subnets (10100000).

Table 4-3 shows the range of subnets and broadcast addresses that would be available with the given subnet mask. Note that the subnet in Figure 4-22 is subnet 4 in the following table.

Table 4-3 *Subnet Addresses Table*

Subnet No.	Subnet ID	Host Range	Broadcast Address
1	192.168.5.32	192.168.5.33 to 192.168.5.62	192.168.5.63
2	192.168.5.64	192.168.5.65 to 192.168.5.94	192.168.5.95
3	192.168.5.96	192.168.5.97 to 192.168.5.126	192.168.5.127
4	192.168.5.128	192.168.5.129 to 192.168.5.158	192.168.5.159
5	192.168.5.160	192.168.5.161 to 192.168.5.190	192.168.5.191
6	192.168.5.192	192.168.5.193 to 192.168.5.222	192.168.5.223

Class B Example

In Figure 4-23, we will determine the addressing for a Class B network with a nondefault mask. Given the address of 172.16.139.46 and knowing that the subnet mask is 255.255.240.0, or /20, you can determine the subnet and host addresses for this network.

Figure 4-23 *Class B Address with Nondefault Subnet Mask*

IP Address 172.16.139.46   Subnet Mask /20

IP Address	172	16	139	46	
IP Address	10101100	00010000	1000|1011	00101110	
Subnet Mask	11111111	11111111	1111|0000	00000000	/20
Subnetwork	10101100	00010000	10000000	00000000	
Subnetwork	172	16	128	0	
First Host	172	16	10000000	00000001=128.1	
Last Host	172	16	10001111	11111110=143.254	
Directed Broadcast	172	16	10001111	11111111=143.255	
Next Subnet	172	16	10010000	00000000=144.0	

The following outlines the steps and shows the details of each operation in the eight-step process:

Step 1   Write the octet that is being split in binary (10001011).

Step 2   Write the mask bits of the same octet (11110000).

Step 3   Draw a vertical line to delineate the network-significant bits in the assigned IP address. Put a line under the mask so that you can view the significant bits in the IP address (10000000).

Step 4   Copy the significant bits four times.

Step 5   In the first line, define the network address by placing 0s in the remaining host bits (10000000.00000000).

Step 6   In the last line, define the directed broadcast address by placing all 1s in the host bits (10011111.11111111).

Step 7   In the middle lines, define the first and last host ID for this subnet— 10000000.00000001 and 10011111.11111110.

Step 8   Increment the subnet bits by 1 to determine the next subnet address. Repeat Steps 4 through 8 for all subnets (10100000.00000000).

Table 4-4 shows the range of subnets and broadcast addresses that would be available with the given subnet mask.

Table 4-4   *Subnet Addresses Table*

Subnet No.	Subnet ID	Host Range	Broadcast
All 0s	172.16.0.0	172.16.0.1 to 172.16.15.254	172.16.15.255
1	172.16.16.0	172.16.16.1 to 172.16.31.254	172.16.31.255
2	172.16.32.0	172.16.32.1 to 172.16.47.254	172.16.47.255
13	172.16.208.0	172.16.208.1 to 172.16.223.254	172.16.223.255
14	172.16.224.0	172.16.224.1 to 172.16.239.254	172.16.239.255
All 1s	172.16.240.0	172.16.240.1 to 172.16.255.254	172.16.255.255

Class A Example

In Figure 4-24, we will determine the addressing for a Class A network with a nondefault mask. Given the address of 10.172.16.211 and knowing that the subnet mask is /18, you can determine the subnet and host addresses for this network.

Figure 4-24 *Class A Address with Nondefault Subnet Mask*

IP Address 10.172.16.211   Subnet Mask /18

IP Address	10	172	16	211	
IP Address	00001010	10101100	00|010000	11010011	
Subnet Mask	11111111	11111111	11|000000	00000000	/18
Subnetwork	00001010	10101100	00000000	00000000	
Subnetwork	10	172	0	0	
First Host	10	172	00000000	00000001=0.1	
Last Host	10	172	00111111	11111110=63.254	
Directed Broadcast	10	172	00111111	11111111=63.255	
Next Subnet	10	172	01000000	00000000=64.0	

The following outlines the steps and shows the details of each operation in the eight-step process:

Step 1 Write the octet that is being split in binary (00010000).

Step 2 Write the mask bits of the same octet (11000000).

Step 3 Draw a vertical line to delineate the network-significant bits in the assigned IP address. Put a line under the mask so that you can view the significant bits in the IP address (00000000).

Step 4 Copy the significant bits four times.

Step 5 In the first line, define the network address by placing 0s in the remaining host bits (00000000.00000000).

Step 6 In the last line, define the directed broadcast address by placing all 1s in the host bits (00111111.11111111).

Step 7 In the middle lines, define the first and last host ID for this subnet—00000000.00000001 and 00111111.11111110.

Step 8 Increment the subnet bits by 1 to determine the next subnet address. Repeat Steps 4 through 8 for all subnets (01000000.00000000).

Table 4-5 shows the range of subnets and broadcast addresses that would be available with the given subnet mask.

Table 4-5 *Subnet Addresses Table*

Subnet No.	Subnet ID	Host Range	Broadcast
All 0s	10.0.0.0	10.0.0.1 to 10.0.63.254	10.0.63.255
1	10.0.64.0	10.0.64.1 to 10.0.127.254	10.0.127.255
2	10.0.128.0	10.0.128.1 to 10.0.191.254	10.0.191.255
1021	10.255.64.0	10.255.64.1 to 10.255.127.254	10.255.127.255
1022	10.255.128.0	10.255.128.1 to 10.255.191.254	10.255.191.255
All 1s	10.255.192.0	10.255.192.1 to 10.255.255.254	10.255.255.255

Summary of Constructing a Network Addressing Scheme

The following list summarizes the key points that were discussed in the previous sections:

■ Networks, particularly large ones, are often divided into smaller subnetworks, or subnets. Subnets can improve network performance and control.

■ A subnet address extends the network portion and is created by borrowing bits from the original host portion and designating them as the subnet field.

■ Determining the optimal number of subnets and hosts depends on the type of network and the number of host addresses required.

■ The algorithm for computing a number of subnets is 2^s, where s is the number of subnet bits.

■ The subnet mask is the tool that the router uses to determine which bits are routing (network and subnet) bits and which bits are host bits.

■ End systems use subnet masks to compare the network portion of the local network addresses with the destination addresses of the packets to be sent.

■ Routers use subnet masks to determine whether the network portion of an IP address is on the corresponding routing table or whether the packet needs to be sent to the next router.

■ Determining the subnetwork and host addresses using a subnet mask is accomplished through this procedure:

— Write the octet being split in binary.

— Write the mask in binary, and draw a line to delineate the significant bits.

— Place a line under the mask so that you can view the significant bits.

— Copy the subnet bits four times.

— Define the network address by placing all 0s in the host bits.

— Define the broadcast address by placing all 1s in the host bits.

— Define the first and last host numbers.

— Increment the subnet bits by 1.

Starting a Cisco Router

A Cisco router goes through its startup when it is first turned on and there is no configuration saved. When the startup is completed, you can enter the initial software configuration. Recognizing correct router startup is the first step in installing a Cisco router. The router must start successfully and have a valid configuration to operate on the network. This lesson describes how the router starts up and explains how to verify its initial operation.

Initial Startup of a Cisco Router

The startup of a Cisco router requires verifying the physical installation, powering up the router, and viewing the Cisco IOS Software output on the console. To start router operations, the router completes the following tasks:

- Runs the power-on self test (POST) to test the hardware

- Finds and loads the Cisco IOS Software that the router uses for its operating system

- Finds and applies the configuration statements about router-specific attributes, protocol functions, and interface addresses

When a Cisco router powers up, it performs a POST. During the POST, the router executes diagnostics to verify the basic operation of the CPU, memory, and interface circuitry.

After verifying the hardware functions, the router proceeds with software initialization, during which it finds and loads the Cisco IOS image, and then finds and loads the configuration file, if one exists.

The following lists the steps required for the initial startup of a Cisco router:

Step 1   Before starting the router, verify the following:

— All network cable connections are secure.

> — Your terminal is connected to the console port.

> — Your console terminal application, such as HyperTerminal, is selected.

Step 2 Push the power switch to "On" or plug in the device if there is no On/Off switch.

Step 3 Observe the boot sequence and the Cisco IOS Software output on the console.

Initial Setup of a Cisco Router

When the router starts up, it looks for a device configuration file. If it does not find one, the router executes a question-driven initial configuration routine, called "setup." Setup is a prompt-driven program that allows a minimal device configuration. After a router completes the POST and loads a Cisco IOS image, it looks for a device configuration file in its NVRAM. The NVRAM of the router is a type of memory that retains its contents even when power is turned off. If the router has a startup configuration file in NVRAM, the user-mode prompt appears after entering the console password, if one has been set.

When starting a new Cisco router, there is no configuration file. If no valid configuration file exists in NVRAM, the operating system executes a question-driven initial configuration routine, referred to as the system configuration dialog, or setup mode.

Setup mode is not intended for entering complex protocol features in the router. Use setup mode to bring up a minimal configuration. Rather than using the setup mode, you can use other various configuration modes to configure the router.

The primary purpose of the setup mode is to rapidly bring up a minimal-feature configuration for any router that cannot find its configuration from some other source. Setup mode can be entered when the router boots up without a configuration, or it can be entered at any time after the router is booted and operational, by entering the **setup** privileged EXEC mode command. Example 4-1 shows how to enter setup from the privileged EXEC mode prompt.

Example 4-1 *Entering Setup*

```
Router# setup


        --- System Configuration Dialog ---

Continue with configuration dialog? [yes/no]: yes

At any point you may enter a question mark '?' for help.
Use ctrl-c to abort configuration dialog at any prompt.
```

Example 4-1   *Entering Setup (Continued)*

```
Default settings are in square brackets '[]'.


Basic management setup configures only enough connectivity
for management of the system, extended setup will ask you
to configure each interface on the system

Would you like to enter basic management setup? [yes/no]: no
```

For many of the prompts in the dialog of the **setup** command facility, default answers appear in square brackets ([ ]) following the question. Pressing **Enter** allows the use of the defaults.

When prompted with "Would you like to enter basic management setup?" the system configuration dialog can be discontinued by entering **no** at the prompt. To begin the initial configuration process, enter **yes**. Normally, you enter **no** at the "basic management setup" prompt so that extended setup can be entered to configure more specific system parameters.

Pressing **Ctrl-C** will terminate the process and start over at any time. When using the command form of setup (Router# **setup**), **Ctrl-C** returns to the privileged EXEC prompt (Router#).

If you enter **yes** at the "Would you like to enter basic management setup?" prompt, you are prompted with "First, would you like to see the current interface summary?" Enter **yes** to view the router interfaces. Example 4-2 shows the output indicating the current status of each router interface. This information includes the interface IP address and current configuration.

Example 4-2   *Current Status of Interfaces*

```
Any interface listed with OK? value "NO" does not have a valid configuration

Interface              IP-Address      OK? Method Status        Protocol
FastEthernet0/0        unassigned      NO  uncot  up            up
FastEthernet0/1        unassigned      NO  unset  up            up
Serial0/0/0            unassigned      NO  unset  up            up
Serial0/0/1            unassigned      NO  unset  down
```

Continuing through the setup dialog, you are prompted for global parameters. Enter the global parameters at the prompts, using the configuration values that were determined for the router.

The first global parameter sets the router host name. This host name will precede Cisco IOS prompts for all configuration modes. The default router name is shown between the square brackets as [Router].

Use the next global parameters shown to set the various passwords used on the router. Example 4-3 illustrates the default settings in brackets and shows entering global parameters.

Example 4-3　*Default Settings and Global Parameters*

```
Configuring global parameters:

  Enter host name [Router]:RouterA

The enable secret is a password used to protect access to privileged EC and configuration
modes. This password, after entered, becomes encrypted in the configuration.
  Enter enable secret: Cisco1

The enable password is used when you do not specify an enable secret password, with some
older software versions, and some boot images.
  Enter enable password: SanFran3

The virtual terminal password is used to protect access to the router over a network
interface.
  Enter virtual terminal password: Sanj0se
  Configure SNMP Network Management? [no]:
```

Continuing through the setup dialog, you are prompted for additional global parameters. Enter the global parameters at the prompts, using the configuration values that were determined for your router. The example shows the prompts for routing protocols as they appear during setup.

If you enter **yes** at a prompt to indicate that you want to configure a protocol, additional subordinate prompts appear about that protocol. Example 4-4 illustrates this feature.

Example 4-4　*Additional Configuration Prompts*

```
Configure IP? [yes]:
    Configure RIP routing? [yes]: no
Configure CLNS? [no]:
  Configure bridging? [no]:
```

Continuing through the setup dialog, you are prompted for parameters for each installed interface. Use the configuration values that were determined for the interface to enter the proper parameters at the prompts. Example 4-5 illustrates the configuration of interface FastEthernet 0/0.

Example 4-5 *Configuring Interface FastEthernet 0/0*

```
Configuring interface parameters:

Do you want to configure FastEthernet0/0 interface? [yes]:
  Use the 100 Base-TX (RJ-45) connector? [yes]:
  Operate in full-duplex mode? [no]:
  Configure IP on this interface? [yes]:
    IP address for this interface: 10.2.2.11
    Subnet mask for this interface [255.0.0.0] : 255.255.255.0
    Class A network is 10.0.0.0, 24 subnet bits; mask is /24

Do you want to configure FastEthernet0/1 interface? [yes]: no

Do you want to configure Serial0/0/0 interface? [yes]: no

Do you want to configure Serial0/0/1 interface? [yes]: no
```

A newer feature in Cisco IOS is Cisco AutoSecure. Cisco AutoSecure is a Cisco IOS security CLI command feature that is used to disable services most often used to attack routers and networks. You can deploy one of these two modes, depending on your needs:

■ **Interactive mode:** Prompts the user with options to enable and disable services and other security features

■ **Noninteractive mode:** Automatically executes a Cisco AutoSecure command with the recommended Cisco default settings

CAUTION   Cisco AutoSecure attempts to ensure maximum security by disabling the services most commonly used by hackers to attack a router. However, some of these services might be needed for successful operation in your network. For this reason, you should not use the Cisco AutoSecure feature until you fully understand its operations and the requirements of your network.

Cisco AutoSecure performs the following functions:

■ Disables these global services:

— Finger

— Packet assembler/disassembler (PAD)

— Small servers

— BOOTP servers

- — HTTP service

- — Identification Service

- — Cisco Discovery Protocol

- — Network Time Protocol (NTP)

- — Source routing

■ Enables these global services:

- — Password encryption service

- — Tuning of scheduler interval and allocation

- — TCP synwait time

- — TCP keepalive messages

- — Security policy database (SPD) configuration

- — Internet Control Message Protocol (ICMP) unreachable messages

■ Disables these services per interface:

- — ICMP

- — Proxy Address Resolution Protocol (ARP)

- — Directed broadcast

- — Maintenance Operation Protocol (MOP) service

- — ICMP unreachables

- — ICMP mask reply messages

■ Provides logging for security, including these functions:

- — Enables sequence numbers and timestamp

- — Provides a console log

- — Sets log buffered size

- — Provides an interactive dialogue to configure the logging server IP address

■ Secures access to the router, including these functions:

- — Checks for a banner and provides the ability to add text for automatic configuration

- — Login and password

— Transport input and output

— **exec-timeout** commands

— Local authentication, authorization, and accounting (AAA)

— Secure Shell (SSH) timeouts and **ssh authentication-retries** commands

— Enables only SSH and Secure Copy Protocol (SCP) for access and file transfers to and from the router

— Disables Simple Network Management Protocol (SNMP) if not being used

■ Secures the forwarding plane, including these functions:

— Enables Cisco Express Forwarding or distributed Cisco Express Forwarding on the router, when available

— Antispoofing

— Blocks all Internet Assigned Numbers Authority (IANA) reserved IP address blocks

— Blocks private address blocks, if customer desires

— Installs a default route to Null0, if a default route is not being used

— Configures a TCP intercept for a connection timeout, if the TCP intercept feature is available and the user desires

— Starts an interactive configuration for Context-Based Access Control (CBAC) on interfaces facing the Internet, when using a Cisco IOS Firewall image

— Enables NetFlow on software forwarding platforms

When you complete the configuration process for all installed interfaces on the router, the **setup** command shows the configuration command script that was created, as shown in Example 4-6.

Example 4-6 *Configuration Command Script*

```
The following configuration command script was created:

hostname RouterX
enable secret 5 $1$aNMG$kV3mxjlWDRGXmfwjEBNAf1
enable password cisco
line vty 0 4
password sanjose
no snmp-server
```

continues

Example 4-6   *Configuration Command Script (Continued)*

```
!
ip routing
no clns routing
no bridge 1
!
interface FastEthernet0/0
media-type 100BaseX
half-duplex
ip address 10.2.2.11 255.255.255.0
no mop enabled
!
interface FastEthernet0/1
shutdown
no ip address
!
interface Serial0/0/0
shutdown
no ip address
!
interface Serial0/0/1
shutdown
no ip address
dialer-list 1 protocol ip permit
!
end
[0] Go to the IOS command prompt without saving this config.
[1] Return back to the setup without saving this config.
[2] Save this configuration to nvram and exit.

Enter your selection [2]: 2
```

The **setup** command offers the following three choices:

- **[0]:** Go to the EXEC prompt without saving the created configuration.

- **[1]:** Go back to the beginning of setup without saving the created configuration.

- **[2]:** Accept the created configuration, save it to NVRAM, and exit to the EXEC mode.

If you choose **[2]**, the configuration is executed and saved to NVRAM, and the system is ready to use. To modify the configuration, you must reconfigure it manually.

The script file generated by the **setup** command is additive. You can turn features *on* with the **setup** command, but not *off*. In addition, the **setup** command does not support many of the advanced features of the router or those features that require a more complex configuration.

Logging In to the Cisco Router

When you configure a Cisco router from the CLI on a console or remote terminal, the Cisco IOS Software provides a command interpreter called the EXEC. The EXEC interprets the commands that are entered and carries out the corresponding operations. You must log in to the router before entering an EXEC command.

After you have configured a Cisco router from the setup utility, you can reconfigure it or add to the configuration from the user interface that runs on the router console or auxiliary port. You can also configure a Cisco router using a remote-access application such as SSH.

For security purposes, the EXEC has the following two levels of access to commands:

- **User mode:** Typical tasks include those that check the router status.

- **Privileged mode:** Typical tasks include those that change the router configuration.

When you first log in to the router, a user-mode prompt is displayed. EXEC commands available in user mode are a subset of the EXEC commands available in privileged mode. These commands provide a means to display information without changing router configuration settings.

To access the full set of commands, you must enable the privileged mode with the **enable** command and supply the enable password, if it is configured.

NOTE   The enable password is displayed in clear text using the **show run** command. The secret password is encrypted, so it is not displayed in clear text. If both the enable and secret passwords are configured, the secret password will override the enable password.

The EXEC prompt then displays as a pound sign (#) while in the privileged mode. From the privileged level, you can access global configuration mode and the other specific configuration modes, such as interface, subinterface, line, router, route-map, and several others.

Use the **disable** command to return to the user EXEC mode from the privileged EXEC mode. Use the **exit** or **logout** command to end the current session. Figure 4-25 illustrates the navigation through these modes.

Figure 4-25　*User Mode Navigation*

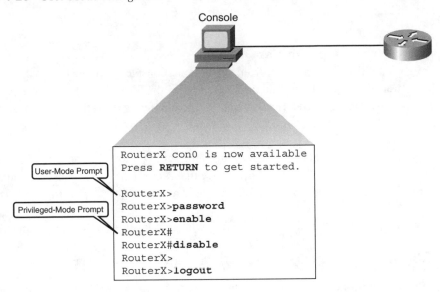

You can enter a question mark (**?**) at the user-mode prompt or the privileged-mode prompt to display a list of commands available in the current mode. Example 4-7 shows help at the user-mode prompt.

Example 4-7　*Getting Help in User Mode*

```
RouterX> ?

Exec commands:
  access-enable    Create a temporary Access-List entry
  access-profile   Apply user-profile to interface
  clear            Reset functions
  connect          Open a terminal connection
  disable          Turn off privileged commands
  disconnect       Disconnect an existing network connection
  enable           Turn on privileged commands
  exit             Exit from the EXEC
  help             Description of the interactive help system
  lat              Open a lat connection
  lock             Lock the terminal
  login            Log in as a particular user
  logout           Exit from the EXEC
-- More --
```

NOTE　The available commands vary with different Cisco IOS Software versions.

Notice the -- More -- at the bottom of the sample display. This indicates that multiple screens are available as output. Additional commands follow, and you can perform any of the following tasks:

■ Press the **Spacebar** to display the next available screen.

■ Press the **Return** key (or, on some keyboards, the **Enter** key) to display the next line.

■ Press any other key to return to the prompt.

Enter the **enable** user-mode command to access privileged EXEC mode. Normally, if an enable password has been configured, you must also enter the enable password before you can access privileged EXEC mode.

Enter the **?** command at the privileged-mode prompt to display a list of the available privileged EXEC commands. Example 4-8 shows privileged-mode help.

Example 4-8 *Getting Help in Privileged Mode*

```
RouterX# ?

Exec commands:
  access-enable    Create a temporary Access-List entry
  access-profile   Apply user-profile to interface
  access-template  Create a temporary Access-List entry
  bfe              For manual emergency modes setting
  cd               Change current directory
  clear            Reset functions
  clock            Manage the system clock
  configure        Enter configuration mode
  connect          Open a terminal connection
  copy             Copy from one file to another
  debug            Debugging functions (see also 'undebug')
  delete           Delete a file
  dir              List files on a filesystem
  disable          Turn off privileged commands
  disconnect       Disconnect an existing network connection
  enable           Turn on privileged commands
  erase            Erase a filesystem
  exit             Exit from the EXEC
  help             Description of the interactive help system
-- More --
```

NOTE   The available commands vary with different Cisco IOS Software versions.

Showing the Router Initial Startup Status

After logging in to a Cisco router, the router hardware and software status can be verified by using the following router status commands: **show version**, **show running-config**, and **show startup-config**.

Use the **show version** EXEC command to display the configuration of the system hardware, the software version, the memory size, and the configuration register setting. Example 4-9 shows the output from a **show version** command.

Example 4-9   **show version** *Command Output*

```
Cisco IOS Software, 2800 Software (C2800NM-ADVIPSERVICESK9-M), Version 12.4(12), RELEASE
SOFTWARE (fc1)
Technical Support: http://www.cisco.com/techsupport
Copyright (c) 1986-2006 by Cisco Systems, Inc.
Compiled Fri 17-Nov-06 12:02 by prod_rel_team


ROM: System Bootstrap, Version 12.4(13r)T, RELEASE SOFTWARE (fc1)


RouterX uptime is 2 days, 21 hours, 15 minutes
System returned to ROM by power-on
System image file is "flash:c2800nm-advipservicesk9-mz.124-12.bin"



This product contains cryptographic features and is subject to United States and local
country laws governing import, export, transfer and use. Delivery of Cisco cryptographic
products does not imply third-party authority to import, export, distribute or use
encryption. Importers, exporters, distributors and users are responsible for compliance
with U.S. and local country laws. By using this product you agree to comply with
applicable laws and regulations. If you are unable to comply with U.S. and local laws,
return this product immediately.


A summary of U.S. laws governing Cisco cryptographic products may be found at:
http://www.cisco.com/wwl/export/crypto/tool/stqrg.html


If you require further assistance please contact us by sending email to
export@cisco.com.


Cisco 2811 (revision 53.50) with 249856K/12288K bytes of memory.
Processor board ID FTX1107A6BB
2 FastEthernet interfaces
2 Serial(sync/async) interfaces
1 Virtual Private Network (VPN) Module
DRAM configuration is 64 bits wide with parity enabled.
239K bytes of non-volatile configuration memory.
62720K bytes of ATA CompactFlash (Read/Write)
```

Example 4-9 **show version** *Command Output (Continued)*

```
Configuration register is 0x2102

RouterX#
```

In the example, the RAM is assigned with 249,856 KB available for main memory and 12,288 KB available for I/O memory (shared by all the interfaces). The I/O memory is used for holding packets while they are in the process of being routed.

The router has two Fast Ethernet interfaces and two serial interfaces. This is useful for confirming that the expected interfaces are recognized at startup and are functioning, from a hardware perspective.

The router has 239 KB used for startup configuration storage in the NVRAM and 62,720 KB of flash storage for the Cisco IOS Software image.

Summary of Starting a Cisco Router

The following list summarizes the key points that were discussed in the previous sections:

- The router startup sequence is similar to the startup sequence of the Catalyst switch. The router first performs the POST, and then the router finds and loads the Cisco IOS image. Finally, it finds and loads the device configuration file.

- Use the **enable** command to access the privileged EXEC mode from the user EXEC mode.

- After logging in to a Cisco router, the initial startup status of a router can be verified using the router status commands **show version**, **show running-config**, and **show**.

Configuring a Cisco Router

When the hardware installation is complete and the Cisco router has the initial configuration, you can begin configuring the router for a specific internetwork. You must be familiar with the Cisco IOS command-line interface (CLI), its modes, and its operation before configuring more advanced features such as IP routing. The following sections describe how to implement a basic configuration for a Cisco router.

Cisco Router Configuration Modes

From privileged EXEC mode, you can enter global configuration mode, providing access to the specific router configuration modes. Figure 4-26 illustrates the different configuration modes and shows how to navigate them.

Figure 4-26 *Navigating Configuration Modes*

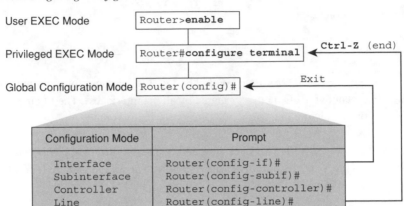

The first step in configuring a Cisco router is to use the setup utility. Setup allows you to create a basic initial configuration. For more complex and specific configurations, you can use the CLI to enter terminal configuration mode.

From the privileged EXEC mode, you can enter the global configuration mode with the **configure terminal** command. From the global configuration mode, you can access the specific configuration modes, which include the following:

- **Interface:** Supports commands that configure operations on a per-interface basis

- **Subinterface:** Supports commands that configure multiple virtual interfaces on a single physical interface

- **Controller:** Supports commands that configure controllers (for example, E1 and T1 controllers)

- **Line:** Supports commands that configure the operation of a terminal line; for example, the console or the vty ports

- **Router:** Supports commands that configure an IP routing protocol

If you enter the **exit** command, the router will back out one level, eventually logging out. In general, you can enter the **exit** command from one of the specific configuration modes to return to global configuration mode. Press **Ctrl-Z** to leave the configuration mode completely and return the router to the privileged EXEC mode.

In terminal configuration mode, an incremental compiler is invoked. Each configuration command entered is parsed as soon as the **Enter** key is pressed.

If there are no syntax errors, the command is executed and stored in the running configuration, and it is effective immediately.

Commands that affect the entire router are called global commands. The **hostname** and **enable password** commands are examples of global commands.

Commands that point to or indicate a process or interface that will be configured are called major commands. When entered, major commands cause the CLI to enter a specific configuration mode. Major commands have no effect unless a subcommand that supplies the configuration entry is immediately entered. For example, the major command **interface serial 0** has no effect unless it is followed by a subcommand that tells what is to be done to that interface.

The following are examples of some major commands and subcommands that go with them:

```
Router(config)# interface serial 0 (major command)
Router(config-if)# shutdown (subcommand)
Router(config-if)# line console 0 (major command)
Router(config-line)# password cisco (subcommand)
Router(config-line)# router rip (major command)
Router(config-router)# network 10.0.0.0 (subcommand)
```

Notice that entering a major command switches from one configuration mode to another. It is not necessary to return to the global configuration mode first before entering another configuration mode.

After you enter the commands to configure the router, you must save the running configuration to NVRAM with the **copy running-config startup-config** command. If the configuration is not saved to NVRAM and the router is reloaded, the configuration will be lost and the router will revert to the last configuration saved in NVRAM. Example 4-10 shows saving the configuration file to startup.

Example 4-10 *Saving Configuration File*

```
Router#
Router# copy running-config startup-config

Destination filename [startup-config]?
Building configuration…

Router#
```

Configuring a Cisco Router from the CLI

The configuration mode of the CLI is used to configure the router name, password, and other console commands.

One of the first tasks in configuring a router is to name it. Naming the router helps you to better manage the network by enabling you to uniquely identify each router within the network. The name of the router is considered to be the host name and is the name displayed at the system prompt. If no name is configured, the default router name is Router. The router name is assigned in global configuration mode. In Example 4-11, the router name is set to RouterA.

Example 4-11 *Assigning the Router Name*

```
Router(config)# hostname RouterA

RouterA(config)#
RouterA(config)# banner motd #  You have entered a secured system Authorized access only!#
```

You can configure a message-of-the-day (MOTD) banner to be displayed on all connected terminals. This banner is displayed at login and is useful for conveying messages, such as impending system shutdowns that might affect network users. When you enter the **banner motd** command, follow the command with one or more blank spaces and a delimiting character of any choice. In the example, the delimiting character is a pound sign (#). After entering the banner text, terminate the message with the same delimiting character.

You can also add a description to an interface to help remember specific information about that interface, such as the network serviced by that interface. This description is meant solely as a comment to help identify how the interface is being used. The description will appear in the output when the configuration information that exists in router memory is displayed, as well as in a **show interfaces** command display.

Other useful console-line commands include the **exec-timeout** command. In the following example, the **exec-timeout** command sets the timeout for the console EXEC session to 20 minutes and 30 seconds, which changes the session from the default timeout of 10 minutes.

The **logging synchronous** console-line command is useful when console messages are being displayed while you are attempting to input EXEC or configuration commands. Instead of the console messages being interspersed with the input, the input is redisplayed on a single line at the end of each console message that "interrupts" the input. This makes reading the input and the messages much easier. Example 4-12 shows how to configure these console settings.

Example 4-12 *Configuring Console Settings*

```
RouterA(config)# line console 0
RouterA(config-line)# exec-timeout 20 30
RouterA(config-line)# logging synchronous
```

CAUTION	Setting the exec-timeout settings too high can be a security risk.

Configuring Cisco Router Interfaces

The main function of a router is to forward packets from one network device to another. To do that, you must define the characteristics of the interfaces through which the packets are received and sent.

The router interface characteristics include, but are not limited to, the IP address of the interface, the data-link encapsulation method, media type, bandwidth, and clock rate.

You can enable many features on a per-interface basis. Interface configuration-mode commands modify the operation of Ethernet, serial, and many other interface types. When you enter the **interface** command, you must define the interface type and number. The number is assigned to each interface based on the physical location of the interface hardware in the router and is used to identify each interface.

This identification is critical when there are multiple interfaces of the same type in a single router. Examples of an interface type and number are as follows:

```
Router(config)# interface serial 0
Router(config)# interface fa 0/0
```

An interface in a Cisco 2800 and 3800 Series Integrated Services Router, or other modular router, is specified by the physical slot in the router and port number on the module in that slot, as follows:

```
Router(config)# interface fa 1/0
```

To quit the interface configuration mode, enter the **exit** command at the Router (config-if) # prompt.

To add a description to an interface configuration, use the **description** command in interface configuration mode. To remove the description, use the **no description** command. The description will show up when using the **show interface** command.

You might want to disable an interface to perform hardware maintenance on a specific interface or segment of a network. You might also want to disable an interface if a problem exists on a specific segment of the network and you must isolate that segment from the rest of the network.

The **shutdown** subcommand administratively turns off an interface. To reinstate the interface, use the **no shutdown** subcommand. Example 4-13 shows the commands and output for these commands.

Example 4-13 *Disabling and Enabling Serial Interfaces*

```
RouterX# configure terminal
RouterX(config)# interface serial 0
RouterX(config-if)# shutdown

%LINK-5-CHANGED: Interface Serial0, changed state to administratively down
%LINEPROTO-5-UPDOWN: Line protocol on Interface Serial0, changed state to down
RouterX# configure terminal
RouterX(config)# interface serial 0
RouterX(config-if)# no shutdown

%LINK-3-UPDOWN:  Interface Serial0, changed state to up
%LINEPROTO-5-UPDOWN: Line Protocol on Interface Serial0, changed state to up
```

When an interface is first configured, unless in setup mode, you must administratively enable the interface before it can be used to transmit and receive packets. Use the **no shutdown** subcommand to allow the Cisco IOS Software to use the interface.

Configuring the Cisco Router IP Address

Each interface on a Cisco router must have its own IP address to uniquely identify it on the network. Figure 4-27 illustrates unique IP addresses for each network attached to the router.

Figure 4-27 *Interface Addresses*

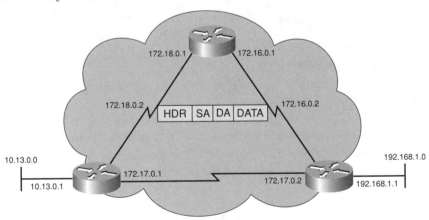

To configure an interface on a Cisco router, follow these steps:

Step 1   Enter global configuration mode using the **configure terminal** command:

```
Router# configure terminal
```

Step 2   Identify the specific interface that requires an IP address by using the **interface** *type slot/port* command:

```
Router(config)# interface fa 0/0
```

Step 3 Set the IP address and subnet mask for the interface by using the **ip address** *ip-address mask* command:

```
Router(config-if)# ip address 192.168.1.1 255.255.255.0
```

Step 4 Enable the interface to change the state from administratively down to up by using the **no shutdown** command:

```
Router(config-if)# no shutdown
```

Step 5 Exit configuration mode for the interface by using the **exit** command:

```
Router(config-if)# exit
```

Verifying the Interface Configuration

When you have completed the router interface configuration, you can verify the configuration by using the **show interfaces** command.

The **show interfaces** command displays the status and statistics of all network interfaces on the router. Alternatively, the status for a specific interface can be displayed by using the **show interfaces type slot** command. Example 4-14 shows common output for the **show interfaces** command.

Example 4-14 show interfaces *Command Output*

```
RouterA# show interfaces

Ethernet0 is up, line protocol is up
  Hardware is Lance, address is 00e0.1e5d.ae2f (bia 00e0.1e5d.ae2f)
  Internet address is 10.1.1.11/24
  MTU 1500 bytes, BW 10000 Kbit, DLY 1000 usec, rely 255/255, load 1/255
  Encapsulation ARPA, loopback not set, keepalive set (10 sec)
  ARP type: ARPA, ARP Timeout 04:00:00
  Last input 00:00:07, output 00:00:08, output hang never
  Last clearing of "show interface" counters never
  Queueing strategy: fifo
  Output queue 0/40, 0 drops; input queue 0/75, 0 drops
  5 minute input rate 0 bits/sec, 0 packets/sec
  5 minute output rate 0 bits/sec, 0 packets/sec
     81833 packets input, 27556491 bytes, 0 no buffer
     Received 42308 broadcasts, 0 runts, 0 giants, 0 throttles
     1 input errors, 0 CRC, 0 frame, 0 overrun, 1 ignored, 0 abort
     0 input packets with dribble condition detected
     55794 packets output, 3929696 bytes, 0 underruns
     0 output errors, 0 collisions, 1 interface resets
     0 babbles, 0 late collision, 4 deferred
     0 lost carrier, 0 no carrier
     0 output buffer failures, 0 output buffers swapped out
```

Output fields for an Ethernet interface and their meanings are shown in Table 4-6.

Table 4-6 **show interfaces** *Output Field Descriptions*

Output	Description
Ethernet . . . is {up | down | administratively down}	Indicates whether the interface hardware is currently active or down, or whether an administrator has taken it down.
line protocol is {up | down}	Indicates whether the software processes that handle the line protocol consider the interface usable (that is, whether keepalives are successful). If the interface misses three consecutive keepalives, the line protocol is marked as down.
Hardware	Hardware type (for example, MCI Ethernet, serial communications interface [SCI], cBus Ethernet) and address.
Internet address	IP address followed by the prefix length (subnet mask).
MTU	Maximum transmission unit (MTU) of the interface.
BW	Bandwidth of the interface, in kilobits per second. The bandwidth parameter is used to compute routing protocol metrics and other calculations.
DLY	Delay of the interface, in microseconds.
rely	Reliability of the interface as a fraction of 255 (255/255 is 100 percent reliability), calculated as an exponential average over 5 minutes.
load	Load on the interface as a fraction of 255 (255/255 is completely saturated), calculated as an exponential average over 5 minutes.
Encapsulation	Encapsulation method assigned to an interface.
keepalive	Indicates whether keepalives are set.
ARP type:	Type of Address Resolution Protocol (ARP) assigned.
loopback	Indicates whether loopback is set.
Last input	Number of hours, minutes, and seconds since the last packet was successfully received by an interface. Useful for knowing when a dead interface failed.
output	Number of hours, minutes, and seconds since the last packet was successfully transmitted by an interface. Useful for knowing when a dead interface failed.

Table 4-6   **show interfaces** *Output Field Descriptions (Continued)*

Output	Description
output hang	Number of hours, minutes, and seconds (or never) since the interface was last reset because of a transmission that took too long. When the number of hours in any of the previous fields exceeds 24 hours, the number of days and hours is printed. If that field overflows, asterisks are printed.
Last clearing	Time at which the counters that measure cumulative statistics shown in this report (such as number of bytes transmitted and received) were last reset to 0. Note that variables that might affect routing (for example, load and reliability) are not cleared when the counters are cleared. Asterisks indicate elapsed time too large to be displayed.
Output queue, input queue, drops	Number of packets in output and input queues. Each number is followed by a slash (/), the maximum size of the queue, and the number of packets dropped because of a full queue.
Five minute input rate, Five minute output rate	Average number of bits and packets transmitted per second in the last 5 minutes. If the interface is not in promiscuous mode, it senses network traffic that it sends and receives (rather than all network traffic). The 5-minute input and output rates should be used only as an approximation of traffic per second during a given 5-minute period. These rates are exponentially weighted averages with a time constant of 5 minutes. A period of four time constants must pass before the average will be within 2 percent of the instantaneous rate of a uniform stream of traffic over that period.
packets input	Total number of error-free packets received by the system.
bytes input	Total number of bytes, including data and MAC encapsulation, in the error-free packets received by the system.
no buffers	Number of received packets discarded because there was no buffer space in the main system. Compare with "ignored count." Broadcast storms on Ethernet are often responsible for no input buffer events.
Received...broadcasts	Total number of broadcast or multicast packets received by the interface. The number of broadcasts should be kept as low as practicable. An approximate threshold is less than 20 percent of the total number of input packets.

continues

Table 4-6 **show interfaces** *Output Field Descriptions (Continued)*

Output	Description
runts	Number of Ethernet frames that are discarded because they are smaller than the minimum Ethernet frame size. Any Ethernet frame that is less than 64 bytes is considered a runt. Runts are usually caused by collisions. If there is more than 1 runt per million bytes received, it should be investigated.
giants	Number of Ethernet frames that are discarded because they exceed the maximum Ethernet frame size. Any Ethernet frame that is larger than 1518 bytes is considered a giant.
input error	Includes runts, giants, no buffer, cyclic redundancy check (CRC), frame, overrun, and ignored counts. Other input-related errors can also cause the input error count to be increased, and some datagrams can have more than one error. Therefore, this sum might not balance with the sum of enumerated input error counts.
CRC	CRC generated by the originating LAN station or far-end device does not match the checksum calculated from the data received. On a LAN, this usually indicates noise or transmission problems on the LAN interface or the LAN bus itself. A high number of CRCs is usually the result of collisions or a station transmitting bad data.
frame	Number of packets received incorrectly having a CRC error and a noninteger number of octets. On a LAN, this is usually the result of collisions or a malfunctioning Ethernet device.
overrun	Number of times the receiver hardware was unable to hand-receive data to a hardware buffer because the input rate exceeded the ability of the receiver to handle the data.
ignored	Number of received packets ignored by the interface because the interface hardware ran low on internal buffers. These buffers are different from the system buffers mentioned in the buffer description. Broadcast storms and bursts of noise can cause the ignored count to be increased.
input packets with dribble condition detected	Dribble bit error indicates that a frame is slightly too long. This frame error counter is incremented just for informational purposes; the router accepts the frame.
packets output	Total number of messages transmitted by the system.
bytes	Total number of bytes, including data and MAC encapsulation, transmitted by the system.
underruns	Number of times that the transmitter has been running faster than the router can handle. This might never be reported on some interfaces.

Table 4-6   **show interfaces** *Output Field Descriptions (Continued)*

Output	Description
output errors	Sum of all errors that prevented the final transmission of datagrams out of the interface being examined. Note that this might not balance with the sum of the enumerated output errors, because some datagrams might have more than one error, and others might have errors that do not fall into any of the specifically tabulated categories.
collisions	Number of messages retransmitted because of an Ethernet collision. This is usually the result of an overextended LAN (Ethernet or transceiver cable too long, more than two repeaters between stations, or too many cascaded multiport transceivers). A packet that collides is counted only once in output packets.
interface resets	Number of times an interface has been completely reset. This can happen if packets queued for transmission were not sent within several seconds. On a serial line, this can be caused by a malfunctioning modem that is not supplying the transmit clock signal, or it can be caused by a cable problem. If the system notices that the carrier detect line of a serial interface is up, but the line protocol is down, it periodically resets the interface in an effort to restart it. Interface resets can also occur when an interface is looped back or shut down.

One of the most important elements of the **show interfaces** command output is the display of the line and data-link protocol status. For other types of interfaces, the meanings of the status line can be slightly different. Figure 4-28 highlights the key output for this command.

Figure 4-28   *Interface State*

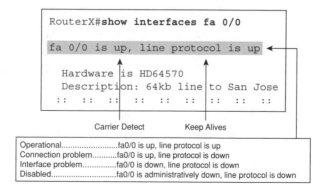

The first parameter refers to the hardware layer and essentially reflects whether the interface is receiving the carrier detect signal from the other end (the data communications equipment [DCE]). The second parameter refers to the data link layer and reflects whether the data link layer protocol keepalives are being received.

Based on the output of the **show interfaces** command, possible problems can be fixed as follows:

- If the interface is up and the line protocol is down, a problem exists. Some possible causes include the following:

    — No keepalives

    — Mismatch in encapsulation type

- If both the line protocol and the interface are down, a cable might never have been attached when the router was powered up, or some other interface problem must exist. For example, in a back-to-back connection, the other end of the connection might be administratively down.

- If the interface is administratively down, it has been manually disabled (the **shutdown** command has been issued) in the active configuration.

After configuring a serial interface, use the **show interface serial** command to verify the changes.

Summary of Configuring a Cisco Router

The following list summarizes the key points that were discussed in the previous sections:

- From the privileged EXEC mode, the global configuration mode can be entered, providing access to other configuration modes such as the interface configuration mode or line configuration mode.

- The main function of a router is to relay packets from one network device to another. To do this, the characteristics of the interfaces through which the packets are received and sent must be defined. Interface characteristics such as the IP address and bandwidth are configured using the interface configuration mode.

- In a TCP/IP environment, end stations communicate seamlessly with servers or other end stations. This communication occurs because each node using the TCP/IP protocol suite has a unique 32-bit logical IP address.

- When the router interface configuration has been completed, it can be verified by using **show** commands.

Exploring the Packet Delivery Process

Understanding the packet delivery process is a fundamental part of understanding Cisco networking devices. You must understand host-to-host communications and routers to administer a network. The following sections describe host-to-host communications through a router by providing a graphic representation.

Layer 2 Addressing

Host-to-host communications require Layer 2 MAC addresses to form an Ethernet frame to be sent onto the wire. MAC addresses are assigned to end devices such as hosts. The physical interfaces on a router provide a Layer 3 function and are assigned a MAC address. These addresses are fundamental in the end-to-end delivery process. Figure 4-29 shows the Layer 2 addressing that will be used during this discussion.

Figure 4-29   *Layer 2 Addressing*

L2 = 0800:0222:2222   L2 = 0800:0333:2222   L2 = 0800:0333:1111   L2 = 0800:0222:1111

Layer 3 Addressing

To be able to move data from one network to another, there must be some type of Layer 3 addressing that can uniquely identify both the network and the host. For this example, we will be using IP as the Layer 3 addressing. Figure 4-30 shows the Layer 3 addressing for each device along the path. The router has its own Layer 3 address on each interface. This will be the gateway address for the client on each subnet and, along with a subnet mask, will identify connected networks to the router.

Figure 4-30   *Layer 3 Addressing*

L3 = 192.168.3.1   L3 = 192.168.3.2   L3 = 192.168.4.1   L3 = 192.168.4.2

Host-to-Host Packet Delivery

The steps to deliver an IP packet over a routed network are similar to the steps to send a letter through a mail delivery service. The key is to know the sender's source address and the destination address of the data. There are a number of steps involved in delivering an IP packet over a routed network. The next several figures give you a graphical understanding of the process.

Note from earlier discussion that an IP host determines the network it belongs to from its IP address and subnet mask. The host will send any packet that is not destined for the local IP network to the default gateway. The default gateway is the address of the local router, which must be configured on hosts (PCs, servers, and so on).

In Figure 4-31, host 192.168.3.1 has application data that it wants to send to host 192.168.4.2. The application selects a User Datagram Protocol (UDP) as the transport for this data, indicating that the reliability of delivery is unimportant for this application or handled by application.

Figure 4-31 *Application Sends Data to Transport Stack*

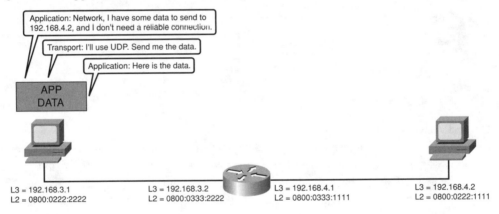

Because it is not necessary to set up a session, the application can start sending data. UDP prepends a UDP header and passes the protocol data unit (PDU) to IP (Layer 3) with an instruction to send the PDU to 192.168.4.2. IP encapsulates the PDU in a Layer 3 packet and passes it to Layer 2. This process is illustrated in Figure 4-32.

This example differs from previous examples of sending packets (now called frames) at Layer 2 because the two hosts are on different segments: 192.168.3.0/24 and 192.168.4.0/24. Because the host is configured with an IP address and a subnet mask, it understands that 192.168.4.0 is on a different network. Because it does not know how to get to this network, it must send the frame to its default gateway, where the frame can be forwarded. If the host does not have a Layer 2 mapping for the default gateway, the host uses the standard ARP process to obtain the mapping for the router. Figure 4-33 shows this process.

Figure 4-32 *Transport Sends Data to IP Stack*

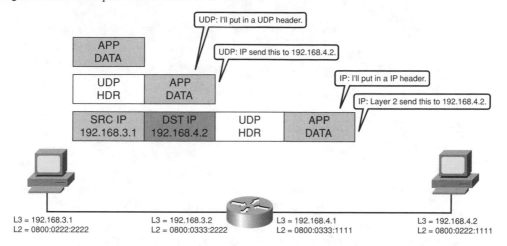

Figure 4-33 *Determine Host Is on a Different Subnet*

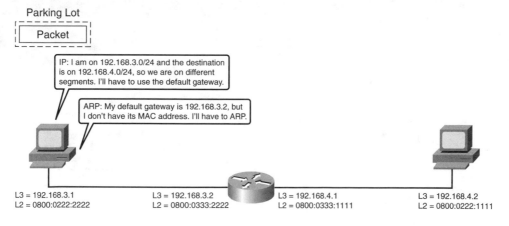

The user has programmed the IP address of 192.168.3.2 as the default gateway. Host 192.168.3.1 sends out the ARP request, and it is received by the router. Figure 4-34 shows the PC sending out an ARP request.

Figure 4-34 *ARP Request for Router*

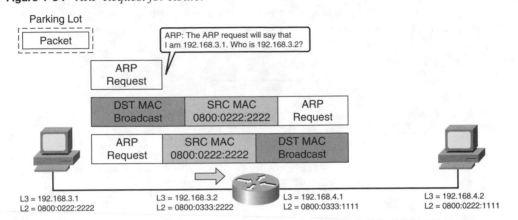

Because an ARP is a Layer 2 broadcast frame, it is not forwarded by the router to the other segment. The router interface on the local segment will, however, send the ARP to the router CPU to be processed. The router processes the ARP request like any other host. Figure 4-35 shows the router processing the ARP request.

Figure 4-35 *Router Processes ARP Request*

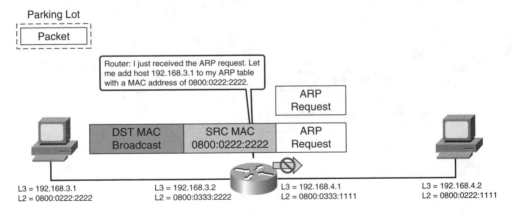

The router will update its ARP table with the address of the PC and will then send a response to the ARP request, as shown in Figure 4-36.

Figure 4-36 *Router Responds to ARP Request*

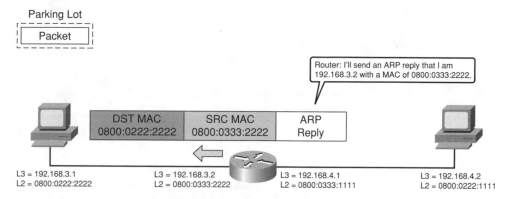

The destination host receives the ARP request. The device can now form a Layer 2 frame to put on the wire. Because the destination host is off network, the Layer 3 address will be mapped to the router's MAC address in the frame. Figure 4-37 shows this step.

Figure 4-37 *Off-Net Layer 3 Mapped to Gateway Layer 2*

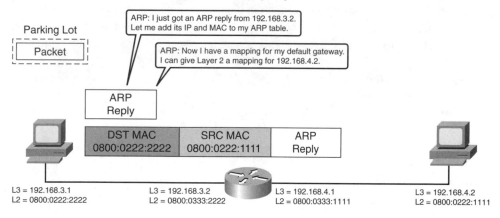

The pending frame is sent with the local host IP address and MAC address as the source. However, the destination IP address is that of the remote host, but the destination MAC address is that of the default gateway. Figure 4-38 shows the frame being sent to the router.

Figure 4-38 *Frame Sent to Router*

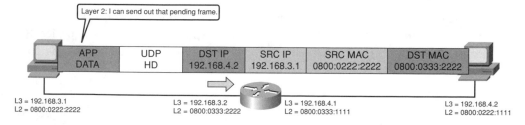

When the frame is received by the router, the router recognizes its own MAC address and processes the frame. At Layer 3, the router sees that the destination IP address is not its address, and it passes all packets that are for nonlocal destinations to the routing process. This is illustrated in Figure 4-39.

Figure 4-39 *Router Process Frame*

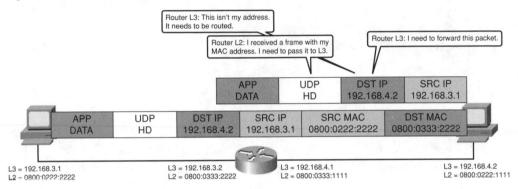

The routing process looks up the destination IP address in its routing table. In this example, the destination segment is directly connected. Because of this, the routing process can pass the packet directly to Layer 2 for the appropriate interface. This is shown in Figure 4-40.

Figure 4-40 *Routing Table Lookup*

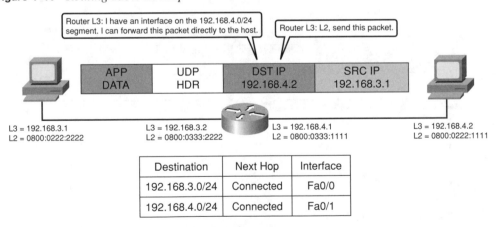

The router will then have to send the packet out the destination interface using Ethernet. This will require that the router know the destination MAC address of the end device. If it does not know the Layer 2 address, it will use the ARP process to obtain the mapping for the IP address and the MAC address. This is shown in Figure 4-41.

Figure 4-41 *Router Performs ARP for End Station*

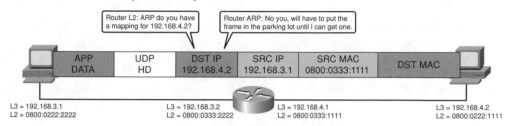

The ARP is sent from the router to the end workstation. Layer 2 will use the ARP process to obtain the mapping for the IP address and the MAC address, as shown in Figure 4-42.

Figure 4-42 *ARP*

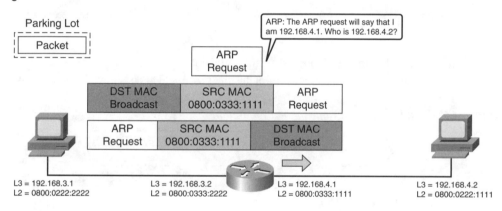

The host receives the frame containing the ARP request and passes the request to the ARP process, as shown in Figure 4-43.

Figure 4-43 *Host Receives ARP*

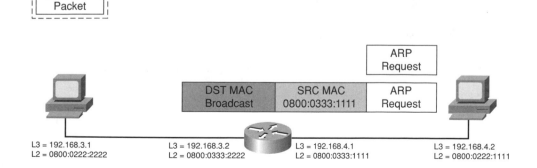

The host responds to the ARP request, as shown in Figure 4-44.

Figure 4-44 *Host Responds to ARP*

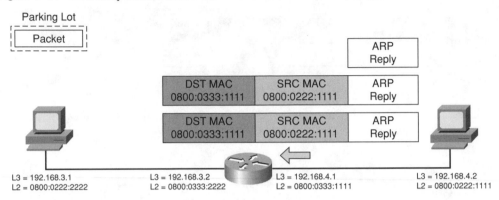

When the router has the MAC address of the end station of the end device, the frame is forwarded to the destination, which completes the process. This is shown in Figure 4-45.

Figure 4-45 *Router Delivers Frame to the End Station*

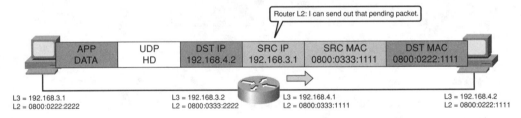

Using the show ip arp Command

From the EXEC mode of the router, you can use the **show ip arp** command to verify that the router has the appropriate Layer 2 mappings.

To display the ARP cache, use the **show ip arp** EXEC command, as follows:

show ip arp [*ip-address*] [*host-name*] [*mac-address*] [*interface type number*]

The command syntax is described in Table 4-7.

Table 4-7   **show ip arp** *Command Syntax Description*

Syntax	Description
ip-address	(Optional) ARP entries matching this IP address are displayed.
host-name	(Optional) Host name.
mac-address	(Optional) 48-bit MAC address.
interface type number	(Optional) ARP entries learned through this interface type and number are displayed.

ARP establishes correspondence between network addresses (an IP address, for example) and LAN hardware addresses (Ethernet addresses). A record of each correspondence is kept in a cache for a predetermined amount of time and then discarded.

Example 4-15 displays the **show ip arp** command, and Table 4-8 describes the sample output.

Example 4-15   **show ip arp** *Command Output*

```
Router# show ip arp

Protocol Address          Age(min)   Hardware Addr    Type      Interface
Internet  172.69.233.229     -         0000.0c59.f892   ARPA      Ethernet0/0
Internet  172.69.233.218     -         0000.0c07.ac00   ARPA      Ethernet0/0
Internet  172.69.233.19      -         0000.0c63.1300   ARPA      Ethernet0/0
Internet  172.69.233.309     -         0000.0c36.6965   ARPA      Ethernet0/0
Internet  172.19.168.11      -         0000.0c63.1300   ARPA      Ethernet0/0
Internet  172.19.168.254     9        0000.0c36.6965   ARPA      Ethernet0/0
```

Table 4-8   **show ip arp** *Command Output Fields*

Field	Description
Protocol	Protocol for network address in the Address field.
Address	The network address that corresponds to the Hardware Address.
Age (min)	Age in minutes of the cache entry. A hyphen (-) means that the address is local.
Hardware Addr	LAN hardware address of a MAC address that corresponds to the network address.

continues

Table 4-8   **show ip arp** *Command Output Fields (Continued)*

Field	Description
Type	Indicates the encapsulation type that the Cisco IOS Software is using in the network address in this entry. Possible values include the following: • Advanced Research Projects Agency (ARPA) • Subnetwork Access Protocol (SNAP) • Session Announcement Protocol (SAP)
Interface	Indicates the interface associated with this network address.

Using Common Cisco IOS Tools

The Cisco IOS Software has many common IP tools to be used for troubleshooting and verification of network connectivity. The most common tools used are ping and traceroute.

To diagnose basic network connectivity, you can use the **ping** command in user EXEC or privileged EXEC mode. The **ping** command sends out an ICMP echo request to an end station to verify reachability. The command structure is as follows:

ping [*protocol* {*host-name* | *system-address*}]

The command syntax is described in Table 4-9.

Table 4-9   **ping** *Command Syntax Description*

Syntax	Description
protocol	(Optional) Protocol keyword: **appletalk**, **atm**, **clns**, **decnet**, **ipx**, or **srb.** If a specific protocol is not specified, a basic ping will be sent using IP (IPv4). For extended options for ping over IP, see the documentation for the **ping ip** command.
host-name	Host name of the system to ping. If a *host-name* or *system-address* is not specified at the command line, it will be required in the ping system dialog.
system-address	Address of the system to ping. If a *host-name* or *system-address* is not specified at the command line, it will be required in the ping system dialog.

To discover the routes that packets will take when traveling to their destination address, you can use the **traceroute** command in user EXEC or privileged EXEC mode. The command structure is as follows:

traceroute [*protocol*] *destination*

The command syntax is described in Table 4-10.

Table 4-10   **traceroute** *Command Syntax Description*

Syntax	Description
protocol	(Optional) Protocol keyword: **appletalk**, **clns**, **ip**, **ipv6**, **ipx**, **oldvines**, or **vines**. When not specified, the *protocol* argument is based on an examination by the software of the format of the *destination* argument.
destination	(Optional in privileged EXEC mode; required in user EXEC mode) The destination address or host name for which you want to trace the route. The software determines the default parameters for the appropriate protocol, and the tracing action begins.

Summary of Exploring the Packet Delivery Process

The following list summarizes the key points that were discussed in the previous sections:

- If the hosts are not on the same segment, the frame is sent to the default gateway.

- Packets sent to the default gateway will have the local host source and remote host destination IP address.

- Frames sent to the default gateway will have the local host source and the default gateway MAC address.

- A router will change the Layer 2 address as needed but will not change the Layer 3 address.

- The **show ip arp** command displays the mapping between network addresses and MAC addresses that the router has learned.

- IOS connectivity tools:

    — Ping

    — Traceroute

Understanding Cisco Router Security

After you secure physical access to your network, you must ensure that access to the Cisco router through the console and vty ports is secure. In addition, you must ensure that unused router ports do not become a security risk. The following sections describe router security.

Physical and Environmental Threats

Improper and incomplete network device installation is an often-overlooked security threat. Software-based security measures alone cannot prevent network damage because of poor installation. This topic describes how to mitigate hardware, environmental, electrical, and maintenance-related security threats to Cisco routers.

There are four classes of insecure installations or physical access threats, as follows:

- **Hardware threats:** Threats of physical damage to the router or router hardware

- **Environmental threats:** Threats such as temperature extremes (too hot or too cold) or humidity extremes (too wet or too dry)

- **Electrical threats:** Threats such as voltage spikes, insufficient supply voltage (brownouts), unconditioned power (noise), and total power loss

- **Maintenance threats:** Threats such as poor handling of key electrical components (electrostatic discharge), lack of critical spare parts, poor cabling, poor labeling, and so on

Configuring Password Security

You can use the command-line interface (CLI) to configure the password and other console commands.

> **CAUTION**   The passwords used here are for instructional purposes only. Passwords used in an actual implementation should meet the requirements of a "strong" password.

You can secure a router by using a password to restrict access. Using a password and assigning privilege levels are simple ways to provide terminal access control in a network. A password can be established on individual lines, such as the console, and to the privileged EXEC mode. Passwords are case sensitive.

Each Telnet port on the router is known as a vty terminal. There are a default of five vty ports on the router, allowing five concurrent Telnet sessions. On the router, the vty ports are numbered from 0 through 4.

You can use the **line console 0** command followed by the **login** and **password** subcommands to require login and establish a login password on a console terminal or a vty port. By default, login is not enabled on a console port.

You can use the **line vty 0 4** command followed by the **login** and **password** subcommands to require login and establish a login password on incoming Telnet sessions.

You can use the **login local** command to enable password checking on a per-user basis using the username and password specified with the **username** global configuration command. The **username** command establishes username authentication with passwords.

The **enable password** global command restricts access to the privileged EXEC mode. You can assign an encrypted form of the **enable password** command, called the enable secret password, by entering the **enable secret** command with the desired password at the global configuration mode prompt. If the enable secret password is configured, it is used rather than the **enable password** command, not in addition to it.

You can also add a further layer of security, which is particularly useful for passwords that cross the network or are stored on a TFTP server. Cisco provides a feature that allows the use of encrypted passwords. To set password encryption, enter the **service password-encryption** command in global configuration mode.

Passwords that are displayed or set after you configure the **service password-encryption** command will be encrypted.

To disable a command, enter **no** before the command. For example, use the **no service password-encryption** command to disable password encryption.

Configuring the Login Banner

You can use the CLI to configure the message-of-the-day and other console commands. This topic describes some essential configuration tasks to enable the login banner.

To define a customized banner to be displayed before the username and password login prompts, you can use the **banner login** command in global configuration mode. To disable the login banner, you can use the **no banner login** command.

When you enter the **banner login** command, follow the command with one or more blank spaces and a delimiting character. After the banner text has been added, terminate the message with the same delimiting character.

> **WARNING**   Be careful when selecting the words that are used in the login banner. Words like *welcome* can imply that access is not restricted and allow a hacker to defend his actions.

Telnet and SSH Access

Telnet is the most common method of accessing a network device. However, Telnet is an insecure way of accessing a network. SSH is a secure replacement for Telnet that gives the same type of access. Communication between the client and server is encrypted in both

SSH version 1 and SSH version 2. Implement SSH version 2, if possible, because it uses a more enhanced security encryption algorithm. When encryption is enabled, a Rivest, Shamir, and Adleman (RSA) encryption key must be generated on the router. In addition, an IP domain must be assigned to the router.

When implementing SSH, first test the authentication without SSH to make sure that authentication works with the router before you add SSH. Example 4-16 shows local authentication, which allows you to telnet into the router with the username **cisco** and password **cisco**.

Example 4-16 *Local Authentication*

```
!--- The username command create the username and password for the SSH session
username cisco password 0 cisco
ip domain-name mydomain.com
crypto key generate rsa
ip ssh version 2
line vty 0 4
  login local
```

To test authentication with SSH, you must add to the previous statements to enable SSH. Then test SSH from the PC and UNIX stations.

To prevent non-SSH connections, add the **transport input ssh** command to limit the router to SSH connections only. Straight (non-SSH) Telnets are refused.

```
line vty 0 4
!--- Prevent non-SSH Telnets.
transport input ssh
```

Test to ensure that non-SSH users cannot telnet to the router.

Summary of Understanding Cisco Router Security

The following list summarizes the key points that were discussed in the previous sections:

- Passwords can be used to restrict access.

- The first level of security is physical.

- The login banner can be used to display a message before the user is prompted for a username.

- Remote access can be configured using Telnet or SSH.

Using the Cisco SDM

The Cisco Router and Security Device Manager (Cisco SDM) is an easy-to-use, Java-based device-management tool, designed for configuring LAN, WAN, and security features on a router. The following sections describe how to use the Cisco SDM.

Upon completing this lesson, you will be able to describe the features of the Cisco SDM. This ability includes being able to meet these objectives:

- Describe the features of Cisco SDM

- Explain how to use the elements of the Cisco SDM interface

- Explain the function of each of the five Cisco SDM wizards

Cisco SDM Overview

Cisco Secure Device Manager (SDM) is an intuitive, web-based device-management tool for Cisco IOS Software–based routers. Cisco SDM simplifies router and security configuration by using wizards, which help you quickly and easily deploy, configure, and monitor a Cisco router without requiring knowledge of command-line interface (CLI) commands. Cisco SDM is supported on Cisco 830 series, Cisco 1700 series, Cisco 1800 series, Cisco 2600XM, Cisco 2800 series, Cisco 3600 series, Cisco 3700 series, and Cisco 3800 series routers and on selected Cisco 7200 series and Cisco 7301 routers.

Cisco SDM allows you to easily configure routing, switching, security, and quality of service (QoS) services on Cisco routers while helping to enable proactive management through performance monitoring. Whether you are deploying a new router or installing the Cisco SDM on an existing router, you can now remotely configure and monitor these routers without using the Cisco IOS Software CLI. The Cisco SDM GUI aids nonexpert users of Cisco IOS Software in day-to-day operations, provides easy-to-use smart wizards, automates router security management, and assists you through comprehensive online help and tutorials. Figure 4-46 shows the home page of the SDM.

Cisco SDM smart wizards guide you step by step through router and security configuration by systematically configuring LAN and WAN interfaces, firewalls, intrusion prevention systems (IPS), and IP security (IPsec) virtual private networks (VPN). Cisco SDM wizards can intelligently detect incorrect configurations and propose fixes, such as allowing DHCP traffic through a firewall if the WAN interface is DHCP addressed. Online help in the Cisco SDM contains appropriate background information, in addition to step-by-step procedures to help you enter correct data in the Cisco SDM. Networking and security terms, and other definitions that you might need, are included in an online glossary.

Figure 4-46 *SDM Home Screen*

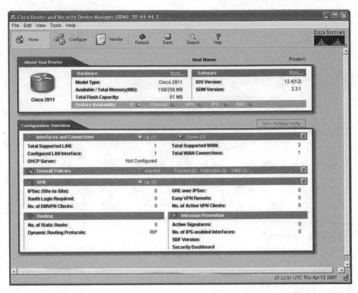

For network professionals familiar with Cisco IOS Software and its security features, Cisco SDM offers advanced configuration tools to allow you to quickly configure and fine-tune router security features, allowing you to review the commands generated by Cisco SDM before delivering the configuration changes to the router.

Cisco SDM helps you configure and monitor routers from remote locations using Secure Socket Layer (SSL) and Secure Shell version 2 (SSHv2) connections. This technology helps enable a secure connection over the Internet between the user browser and the router. When deployed at a branch office, a Cisco SDM–enabled router can be configured and monitored from corporate headquarters, reducing the need for experienced network administrators at the branch office.

Cisco SDM is supported on a number of Cisco routers and the associated Cisco IOS Software versions.

Always consult the latest information regarding Cisco SDM router and Cisco IOS Software release support at http://www.cisco.com/go/sdm.

Cisco SDM comes preinstalled on several Cisco router models manufactured in June 2003 or later that were purchased with the VPN bundle.

If you have a router that does not have Cisco SDM installed, and you would like to use Cisco SDM, you must download it from Cisco.com and install it on your router. Ensure that your router contains enough flash memory to support both your existing flash file structure and the Cisco SDM files. Installing Cisco SDM on a Cisco router is beyond the scope of this course.

Configuring Your Router to Support Cisco SDM

You can install and run Cisco SDM on a router that is already in use without disrupting network traffic, but you must ensure that a few configuration settings are present in the router configuration file.

Access the CLI using Telnet or the console connection to modify the existing configuration before installing Cisco SDM on your router. Follow these steps:

Step 1   Enable the HTTP and HTTPS servers on your router by entering the following commands in global configuration mode:

```
Router# configure terminal

Enter configuration commands, one per line. End with CNTL/Z.
Router(config)# ip http server
Router(config)# ip http secure-server
Router(config)# ip http authentication local
Router(config)# ip http timeout-policy idle 600 life 86400 requests 10000
```

> **NOTE**   If the router supports HTTPS, the HTTPS server will be enabled. If not, the HTTP server will be enabled. HTTPS is supported in all images that support the crypto IPsec feature set, starting from Cisco IOS Release 12.25(T).

Step 2   Create a user account defined with privilege level 15 (enable privileges). Enter the following command in global configuration mode, replacing *username* and *password* with the strings that you want to use:

```
Router(config)# username username privilege 15 secret 0 password
```

For example, if you chose the username **tomato** and the password **vegetable**, you would enter the following:

```
Router(config)# username tomato privilege 15 secret 0 vegetable
```

You will use this username and password to log in to Cisco SDM.

Step 3   Configure SSH and Telnet for local login and privilege level 15. Use the following commands:

```
Router(config)# line vty 0 4
Router(config-line)# privilege level 15
Router(config-line)# login local
Router(config-line)# transport input telnet ssh
Router(config-line)# exit
```

Start Cisco SDM

Cisco SDM is stored in the router flash memory. It is invoked by executing an HTML file in the router archive, which then loads the signed Cisco SDM Java file. To launch Cisco SDM, complete the following steps:

Step 1   From your browser, enter the following URL:

https://<*router IP address*>

The https:// designation specifies that SSL protocol be used for a secure connection.

The http:// designation can be used if SSL is not available.

Step 2   The Cisco SDM home page will appear in the browser window. The username and password dialog box will appear. The type and shape of the dialog box will depend on the type of browser that you are using. Enter the username and password for the privileged (privilege level 15) account on your router.

The Cisco SDM Java applet will begin loading to your PC's web browser.

Step 3   Cisco SDM is a signed Java applet. This can cause your browser to display a security warning. Accept the certificate.

Cisco SDM displays the Launch page.

When the Launch window appears, Cisco SDM displays the Cisco SDM home page. The home page gives you a snapshot of the router configuration and the features that the Cisco IOS image supports. Cisco SDM starts in Wizard mode, in which you can perform configuration tasks using a sequence of windows that break the configuration task into manageable steps. Figure 4-47 shows the SDM home page.

The home page supplies basic information about the router hardware, software, and configuration, and contains the following sections:

- **Host Name:** This is the configured name of the router.

- **About Your Router:** This area shows basic information about your router hardware and software, and contains the fields shown in Table 4-11.

Figure 4-47 *SDM Home Page*

Menu Bar
Tool Bar

Router
Information

Configuration
Overview

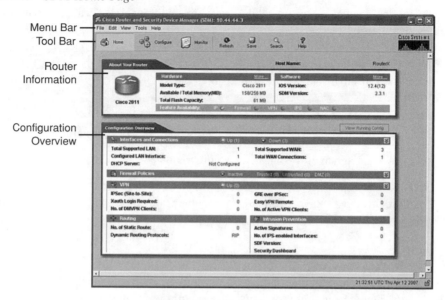

Table 4-11 *Router Information*

Hardware	Description
Model Type	Shows the router model number.
Available/Total Memory	Available RAM and total RAM.
Total Flash Capacity	Flash plus webflash memory (if applicable).
Software	**Description**
IOS Version	The version of Cisco IOS Software that is currently running on the router.
Cisco SDM Version	The version of Cisco SDM software that is currently running on the router.
Feature Availability	The features available in the Cisco IOS image that the router is using are designated by a check mark. The features that Cisco SDM checks for are IP, firewall, VPN, and IPS.

More Link

The More link displays a pop-up window providing additional hardware and software details, as follows:

■ **Hardware Details:** In addition to the information presented in the About Your Router window, this tab displays information about the following:

— Where the router boots from—flash memory or the configuration file

— Whether the router has accelerators, such as VPN accelerators

— A diagram of the hardware configuration

■ **Software Details:** In addition to the information presented in the About Your Router section, this tab displays information about the feature sets included in the Cisco IOS image.

Configuration Overview

This section of the home page summarizes the configuration settings that have been made. To view the running configuration, click **View Running Config**.

The Interfaces and Connections area shows the following information:

■ **Up:** The number of connections that are up.

■ **Down:** The number of connections that are down.

■ **Double arrow:** Click to display or hide details.

■ **Total Supported LAN:** Shows the total number of LAN interfaces that are present in the router.

■ **Total Supported WAN:** The number of Cisco SDM–supported WAN interfaces that are present on the router.

■ **Configured LAN Interfaces:** The number of supported LAN interfaces currently configured on the router.

■ **Total WAN Connections:** The total number of Cisco SDM–supported WAN connections that are present on the router.

■ **DHCP Server:** Configured and not configured.

■ **DHCP Pool (Detail View):** If one pool is configured, this area shows the starting and ending address of the DHCP pool. If multiple pools are configured, it shows a list of configured pool names.

- **Number of DHCP Clients (Detail View):** Current number of clients leasing addresses.

- **Interface:** Name of the configured interface, as follows:

    — **Type:** Interface type

    — **IP Mask:** IP address and subnet mask

    — **Description:** Description of the interface

The Firewall Policies area shows the following information:

- **Active:** A firewall is in place.

- **Inactive:** No firewall is in place.

- **Trusted:** The number of trusted (inside) interfaces.

- **Untrusted:** The number of untrusted (outside) interfaces.

- **DMZ:** The number of demilitarized zone (DMZ) interfaces.

- **Double arrow:** Click to display or hide details.

- **Interface:** The name of the interface to which a firewall has been applied.

- **Firewall icon:** Whether the interface is designated as an inside or an outside interface.

- **NAT:** The name or number of the Network Address Translation (NAT) rule applied to this interface.

- **Inspection Rule:** The names or numbers of the inbound and outbound inspection rules.

- **Access Rule:** The names or numbers of the inbound and outbound access rules.

The VPN area shows the following information:

- **Up:** The number of active VPN connections.

- **Double arrow:** Click to display or hide details.

- **IPsec (Site-to-Site):** The number of configured site-to-site VPN connections.

- **GRE over IPsec:** The number of configured Generic Routing Encapsulation (GRE) over IPsec connections.

- **XAUTH Login Required:** The number of Cisco Easy VPN connections awaiting an Extended Authentication (XAUTH) login.

> **NOTE**   Some VPN servers or concentrators authenticate clients using XAUTH. This shows the number of VPN tunnels awaiting an XAUTH login. If any Cisco Easy VPN tunnel is waiting for an XAUTH login, a separate message panel is shown with a Login button. Click **Login** to enter the credentials for the tunnel.
>
> If XAUTH has been configured for a tunnel, it will not begin to function until the login and password have been supplied. There is no timeout after which it will stop waiting; it will wait indefinitely for this information.

- **Easy VPN Remote:** The number of configured Cisco Easy VPN Remote connections.

- **No. of DMVPN Clients:** If the router is configured as a Dynamic Multipoint VPN (DMVPN) hub, the number of DMVPN clients.

- **No. of Active VPN Clients:** If this router is functioning as an Easy VPN Server, the number of Easy VPN clients with active connections.

- **Interface:** The name of an interface with a configured VPN connection.

- **IPsec Policy:** The name of the IPsec policy associated with the VPN connection.

The Routing area shows the following information:

- **No. of Static Routes:** The number of static routes configured on the router.

- **Dynamic Routing Protocols:** Lists any dynamic routing protocols that are configured on the router.

The Intrusion Prevention area shows the following information:

- **Active Signatures:** The number of active signatures that the router is using. These can be built-in, or they can be loaded from a remote location.

- **No. of IPS-Enabled Interfaces:** The number of router interfaces on which IPS has been enabled.

Cisco SDM Wizards

The following wizards are included in Cisco SDM:

- **LAN wizard:** Used to configure the LAN interfaces and DHCP.

- **WAN wizard:** Used to configure PPP, Frame Relay, and High-Level Data Link Control (HDLC) WAN interfaces. Check http://www.cisco.com/go/sdm for the latest information about wizards and the interfaces they support.

- **Firewall wizards**

- **VPN wizards**

- **Security Audit wizards:** There are these two options:

    — The router security audit wizard

    — An easy one-step router security lockdown wizard

- **QoS:** Quality of service wizard.

> **NOTE**   At the end of each wizard procedure, all changes are automatically delivered to the router using Cisco SDM–generated CLI commands. You can choose whether or not to preview the commands to be sent. The default is to not preview the commands.

Summary of Using the Cisco SDM

The following list summarizes the key points that were discussed in the previous sections:

- Cisco SDM is a useful tool for configuring Cisco access routers.

- Cisco SDM contains several easy-to-use wizards for efficient configuration of Cisco access routers.

- Cisco SDM allows you to customize Cisco access router configurations using advanced features.

Using a Cisco Router as a DHCP Server

Originally, network administrators had to manually configure the host address, default gateway, and other network parameters on each host. However, DHCP provides configuration parameters to IP hosts. DHCP consists of these two components:

- A protocol for delivering host-specific configuration parameters from a DHCP server to a host

- A mechanism for allocating network addresses to hosts

Understanding DHCP

DHCP is built on a client-server model. The DHCP server hosts allocate network addresses and deliver configuration parameters to dynamically configured hosts. The term *client* refers to a host requesting initialization parameters from a DHCP server.

DHCP supports these three mechanisms for IP address allocation:

- **Automatic allocation:** DHCP assigns a permanent IP address to a client.

- **Dynamic allocation:** DHCP assigns an IP address to a client for a limited period of time (or until the client explicitly relinquishes the address).

- **Manual allocation:** A client IP address is assigned by the network administrator, and DHCP is used simply to convey the assigned address to the client.

Dynamic allocation is the only one of the three mechanisms that allows automatic reuse of an address that is no longer needed by the client to which it was assigned. Dynamic allocation is particularly useful for assigning an address to a client that will be connected to the network only temporarily, or for sharing a limited pool of IP addresses among a group of clients that do not need permanent IP addresses. Dynamic allocation can also be a good choice for assigning an IP address to a new client being permanently connected to a network in which IP addresses are sufficiently scarce that it is important to reclaim them when old clients are retired.

DHCPDISCOVER

When a DHCP client boots up for the first time, it transmits a DHCPDISCOVER message on its local physical subnet. Because the client has no way of knowing the subnet to which it belongs, the DHCPDISCOVER is an all-subnets (all-hosts) broadcast (destination IP address of 255.255.255.255). The client does not have a configured IP address; therefore, the source IP address of 0.0.0.0 is used.

DHCPOFFER

A DHCP server that receives a DHCPDISCOVER message can respond with a DHCPOFFER message, which contains initial configuration information for the client. For example, the DHCP server provides the requested IP address. The subnet mask and default gateway are specified in the options field, subnet mask, and router options, respectively. Other common options in the DHCPOFFER message include IP address lease time, renewal time, domain name server, and NetBIOS Name Service (Microsoft Windows Internet Name Service [Microsoft WINS]).

DHCPREQUEST

After the client receives a DHCPOFFER message, it responds with a DHCPREQUEST message, indicating its intent to accept the parameters in the DHCPOFFER.

DHCPACK

After the DHCP server receives the DHCPREQUEST message, it acknowledges the request with a DHCPACK message, thus completing the initialization process.

Using a Cisco Router as a DHCP Server

Cisco routers running Cisco IOS Software provide full support for a router to be a DHCP server. The Cisco IOS DHCP server is a full DHCP server implementation that assigns and manages IP addresses from specified address pools within the router to DHCP clients. You can configure a DHCP server to assign additional parameters, such as the IP address of the Domain Name System (DNS) server and the default router.

The Cisco IOS DHCP server accepts address assignment requests and renewals and assigns the addresses from predefined groups of addresses contained within DHCP address pools. These address pools can also be configured to supply additional information to the requesting client, such as the IP address of the DNS server, the default router, and other configuration parameters. The Cisco IOS DHCP server can accept broadcasts from locally attached LAN segments or from DHCP requests that have been forwarded by other DHCP relay agents within the network.

Using Cisco SDM to Enable the DHCP Server Function

This topic describes how to use the Cisco Router and Security Device Manager (SDM) to enable the DHCP server function on the router. Figure 4-48 shows how to configure DHCP from SDM.

Figure 4-48 *Using SDM to Enable DHCP*

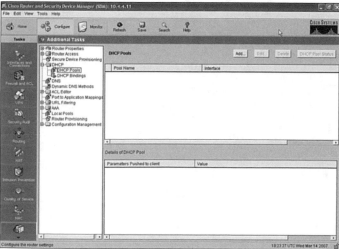

For this example, you will enable the DHCP server for the 10.4.4.11/24 interface using a pool of addresses from 10.4.4.100 through 10.4.4.200. This router will be advertised as the default router (default gateway to the clients).

The DHCP server function is enabled on the Additional Tasks tab. Click **DHCP Pools** in the directory. Then click **Add** to create the new DHCP pool.

The Add DHCP Pool window allows you to configure the DHCP IP address pool. The IP addresses that the DHCP server assigns are drawn from a common pool that you configure by specifying the starting and ending IP addresses in the range. The Add DHCP Pool window shows the following fields:

■ **DHCP Pool Name:** A character string that identifies the DHCP pool.

■ **DHCP Pool Network** and **Subnet Mask:** The IP addresses that the DHCP server assigns are drawn from a common pool that you configure by specifying the starting IP address in the range and the ending address in the range.

The address range that you specify should be within the following private address ranges:

■ 10.0.0.0 to 10.255.255.255

■ 172.16.0.0 to 172.31.255.255

■ 192.168.0.0 to 192.168.255.255

The address range that you specify must also be in the same subnet as the IP address of the LAN interface. With a /24 mask, the range can represent a maximum of 254 addresses. The following examples are valid ranges with a /24 mask:

■ 10.1.1.1 to 10.1.1.254 (assuming LAN IP address is in the 10.1.1.0/24 subnet)

■ 172.16.1.1 to 172.16.1.254 (assuming LAN IP address is in the 172.16.1.0/24 subnet)

SDM configures the router to automatically exclude the LAN interface IP address in the pool.

You must not use the following reserved addresses in the range of addresses that you specify:

■ The network or subnetwork IP address.

■ The broadcast address on the network.

- **Starting IP:** Enter the beginning of the range of IP addresses for the DHCP server to use in assigning addresses to devices on the LAN. This is the lowest-numbered IP address in the range.

- **Ending IP:** Enter the highest-numbered IP address in the range of IP addresses.

- **Lease Length:** The amount of time that the client can use the assigned address before it must be renewed.

- **DHCP Options:** Use this pane to configure DHCP options that will be sent to hosts on the LAN that request IP addresses from the router. These are not options for the router that you are configuring; these are parameters that will be sent to the requesting hosts on the LAN. To set these properties for the router, click **Additional Tasks** on the SDM category bar, click **DHCP**, and configure these settings in the DHCP Pool window.

- **DNS Server1:** The DNS server is typically a server that maps a known device name with its IP address. If you have a DNS server configured for your network, enter the IP address for the server here.

- **DNS Server2:** If there is an additional DNS server on the network, you can enter the IP address for that server in this field.

- **Domain Name:** The DHCP server that you are configuring on this router will provide services to other devices within this domain. Enter the name of the domain.

- **WINS Server1:** Some clients might require Microsoft WINS to connect to devices on the Internet. If there is a Microsoft WINS server on the network, enter the IP address for the server in this field.

- **WINS Server2:** If there is an additional Microsoft WINS server on the network, enter the IP address for the server in this field.

- **Default Router:** The IP address that will be provided to the client for use as the default gateway.

- **Import All DHCP Options into the DHCP Server Database:** This check box allows the DHCP options to be imported from a higher-level server, and is typically used in conjunction with an Internet DHCP server.

Monitoring DHCP Server Functions

You can check the DHCP configuration parameters from the DHCP Pools tab. You can also view additional information on the leased addresses by clicking **DHCP Pool Status**.

The DHCP Pool Status window shows a list of the currently leased addresses, as shown in Figure 4-49.

Figure 4-49 *DHCP Pool Status*

To display address conflicts found by a DHCP server when addresses are offered to the client, use the **show ip dhcp conflict** command in user EXEC or privileged EXEC mode:

show ip dhcp conflict [*ip-address*]

The server uses ping to detect conflicts. The client uses Gratuitous Address Resolution Protocol (ARP) to detect clients. If an address conflict is detected, the address is removed from the pool and the address is not assigned until an administrator resolves the conflict.

Example 4-17 displays the detection method and detection time for all IP addresses offered by the DHCP server that have conflicts with other devices. Table 4-12 outlines the field descriptions.

Example 4-17 *Detection Method and Detection Time*

```
Router# show ip dhcp conflict

IP address      Detection Method      Detection time
172.16.1.32     Ping                  Feb 16 1998 12:28 PM
172.16.1.64     Gratuitous ARP        Feb 23 1998 08:12 AM
```

Table 4-12 **show ip dhcp conflict** *Command Field Descriptions*

Field	Description
IP address	The IP address of the host as recorded on the DHCP server
Detection Method	The manner in which the IP addresses of the hosts were found on the DHCP server, which can be a ping or a gratuitous ARP
Detection time	The date and time when the conflict was found

Summary Using a Cisco Router as a DHCP Server

The following list summarizes the key points that were discussed in the previous sections:

- DHCP is built on a client-server model.

- DHCP server hosts allocate network addresses and deliver configuration parameters.

- Cisco IOS Software includes Dynamic Host Configuration Protocol (DHCP) server.

- SDM can be used to configure DHCP server on the router.

- Required configuration items are as follows:

  — Pool name

  — Pool network and subnet

  — Starting and ending addresses

- SDM can be used to monitor DHCP server on the router.

- The **show ip dhcp conflict** command can be used to find conflicts.

Accessing Remote Devices

During routine maintenance, it is often desirable to access a device from another device. Cisco IOS Software provides a set of tools for this purpose. The following sections describe methods that you can use to access remote devices.

Establishing a Telnet or SSH Connection

Telnet or Secure Shell (SSH) applications are useful for connecting to remote devices. One way to obtain information about a remote network device is to connect to it using either the Telnet or SSH applications. Telnet and SSH are virtual terminal protocols that are part of the TCP/IP suite. The protocols allow connections and remote console sessions from one network device to one or more other remote devices. Figure 4-50 shows how to telnet to another device.

Telnet on Cisco routers varies slightly from Telnet on most Cisco Catalyst switches.

Telnet

To log on to a host that supports Telnet, use the **telnet** EXEC command:

```
RouterA# telnet host
```

Figure 4-50 *Telneting to Another Device*

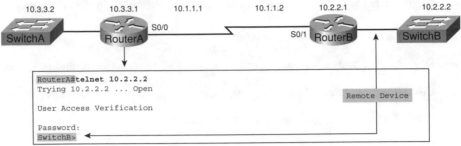

SSH

To start an encrypted session with a remote networking device, use the **ssh** user EXEC command:

```
RouterA# ssh ip address
```

With Cisco IOS Software installed on a router, the IP address or host name of the target device is all that is required to establish a Telnet connection. The **telnet** command placed before the target IP address or host name is used to open a Telnet connection from a Catalyst switch.

For both routers and switches, a prompt for console login signifies a successful Telnet connection, if login is enabled on the vty ports on the remote device. When you are logged in to the remote device, the console prompt indicates which device is active on the console. The console prompt uses the host name of the device.

Use the **show sessions** command on the originating router or switch to verify Telnet connectivity and to display a list of hosts to which a connection has been established. This command displays the host name, IP address, byte count, amount of time the device has been idle, and connection name assigned to the session. If multiple sessions are in progress, the asterisk (*) indicates which was the last session and to which session the user will return to if the **Enter** key is pressed.

In Figure 4-51, using the **show sessions** command on Router A, the output shows that Router A has a suspended Telnet session with Router B. Then use the **show users** command on Router B to determine the last active session. The output shows that the user who was connected to the console port had the last active session.

Use the **show users** command to learn whether the console port is active and to list all active Telnet sessions with the IP address or IP alias of the originating host on the local device. In the **show users** output, the "con" line represents the local console and the "vty" line represents a remote connection. The "11" next to the vty value in Figure 4-51 indicates the vty line number, not its port number. If there are multiple users, the asterisk (*) denotes the current terminal session user.

Figure 4-51   show sessions *Command*

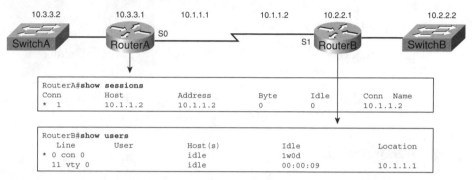

To display the status of SSH server connections, use the **show ssh** command in privileged EXEC mode, as shown in Example 4-18.

Example 4-18   show ssh *Command*

```
RouterB# show ssh

Connection     Version     Encryption     State              Username
0              1.5         3DES           Session Started    guest
```

Suspending and Resuming a Telnet Session

After connecting to a remote device, you might want to access a local device without terminating the Telnet session. Telnet allows temporary suspension and resumption of a remote session.

Figure 4-52 shows a Telnet session from Router A to Router B. The key sequence shown is entered to suspend the session. The output indicates that the Telnet session has been suspended.

Figure 4-52 *Suspending a Telnet Session*

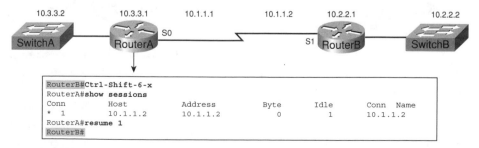

To suspend a Telnet session and escape from the remote target system back to a local switch or router, use the command **Ctrl-Shift-6** or **Ctrl-^** (depending on your keyboard); then follow either command by the character **x**.

The methods to reestablish a suspended Telnet session are as follows:

- Press the **Enter** key.

- Enter the **resume** command if there is only one session. (Entering **resume** without *session number* will resume the last active session.)

- Enter the **resume** *session number* command to reconnect to a specific Telnet session. (Enter the **show sessions** command to find the session number.)

Closing a Telnet Session

You can end a Telnet session on a Cisco device by using the **exit**, **logout**, **disconnect**, or **clear** command. Figure 4-53 illustrates closing a Telnet connection.

Figure 4-53 *Closing a Telnet Connection*

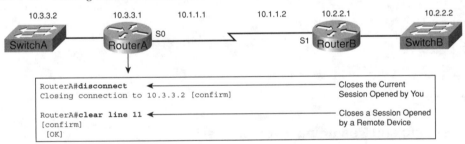

You can close a Telnet session on a Cisco network device by using one of the following methods:

- From a remote device, by using the **exit** or **logout** command to log out from the console session and return the session to the local device

- From the local device, by using the **disconnect** command (when there are multiple sessions) or the **disconnect session** *session number* command to disconnect a single session

If a Telnet session from a remote user is causing bandwidth or other types of problems, you should close the session. Alternatively, network staff can terminate the session from their console. To close a Telnet session from a foreign host, use the **clear line** *line number* command. The *line number* corresponds to the vty port of the incoming Telnet session. The **show sessions** command determines the *line number*. At the other end of the connection, the user will get a notice that the connection was "closed by a foreign host."

Alternate Connectivity Tests

The **ping** and **traceroute** commands provide information about connectivity with and the path to remote devices. This topic describes the use of the **ping** and **traceroute** commands.

You can verify connectivity to local and remote networks by using ping and traceroute. Example 4-19 shows how these commands are used, along with some typical output.

Example 4-19   ping *and* **traceroute** *Commands*

```
RouterA# ping 10.1.1.10

Type escape sequence to abort.
Sending 5, 100-byte ICMP Echos to 10.1.1.10, timeout is 2 seconds:
!!!!!
Success rate is 100 percent (5/5), round-trip min/avg/max = 4/4/4 ms

RouterA# trace 192.168.101.101

Type escape sequence to abort.
Tracing the route to 192.168.101.101

  1 p1r1 (192.168.1.49) 20 msec 16 msec 16 msec
  2 p1r2 (192.168.1.18) 48 msec *  44 msec
RouterA#
```

Detailed information about how these tools operate are as follows:

- The **ping** command verifies network connectivity. Ping tells the minimum, average, and maximum times it takes for ping packets to find the specified system and return. This can validate the reliability of the path to a specified system.

Table 4-13 lists possible output characters from the **ping** command output.

Table 4-13   ping *Command Output characters*

Character	Description
!	Indicates receipt of a reply
.	Indicates that the network server timed out while waiting for a reply
U	Indicates that a destination unreachable protocol data unit (PDU) was received
Q	Indicates source quench (destination too busy)
M	Could not fragment
?	Unknown packet type
&	Packet lifetime exceeded

■ The **traceroute** command shows the routes that the packets take between network devices. A device, such as a router or switch, sends out a sequence of User Datagram Protocol (UDP) datagrams to an invalid port address at the remote host. Three datagrams are sent, each with a Time to Live (TTL) field value set to 1. The TTL value of 1 causes the datagram to time out as soon as it hits the first router in the path. The router then responds with an Internet Control Message Protocol (ICMP) Time Exceeded Message (TEM), indicating that the datagram has expired.

■ Another three UDP messages are then sent, each with the TTL value set to 2, which causes the second router to return ICMP TEMs. This process continues until the packets reach the other destination. Because these datagrams are trying to access an invalid port at the destination host, ICMP Port Unreachable messages are received, indicating an unreachable port and signaling the traceroute program that it is finished. The purpose is to record the source of each ICMP TEM, to provide a trace of the path that the packet took to reach the destination.

Table 4-14 lists the characters that can appear in the **traceroute** command output.

Table 4-14   traceroute *Command Output*

Character	Description
nn msec	For each node, the round-trip time (RTT) in milliseconds for the specified number of probes
*	Probe timed out
A	Administratively prohibited (for example, access-list)
Q	Source quench (destination too busy)
I	User-interrupted test
U	Port unreachable
H	Host unreachable
N	Network unreachable
P	Protocol unreachable
T	Timeout
?	Unknown packet type

NOTE   If IP domain name lookup is enabled, the router will attempt to reconcile each IP address to a name, which can cause the **traceroute** command to slow down.

Summary of Accessing Remote Devices

The following list summarizes the key points that were discussed in the previous sections:

■ After being connected to a remote device, network staff might want to access a local device without terminating the Telnet session. Telnet allows temporary suspension and then resumption of a remote session.

■ Ending a Telnet session on a Cisco device uses the **exit**, **logout**, **disconnect**, or **clear** command.

■ The **ping** and **trace** commands provide information about the connectivity with and path to remote devices.

Chapter Summary

The following list summarizes the key points that were discussed in this chapter:

■ Routers operate at Layer 3, and their function is path determination.

■ Binary numbers are based on the "powers of 2."

■ IP addressing:

— Dotted decimal representation of a binary string

— Identifies the network, subnet, and host

■ Routers have a startup process where they test the hardware and load the operating system and configuration.

■ Basic router configuration is usually done through the console port using CLI and consists of the following:

— Host address

— Interface IP addressing

■ Router have the similar hardware, environmental, electrical, and maintenance-related security threats as switches.

■ Basic router security consists of the following:

— Login banner

— Telnet versus SSH

■   The Cisco IOS DHCP server is a full DHCP server that can be configured using SDM.

■   Cisco IOS provides a set of tools for remote accessing and testing:

— Telnet

— SSH

— ping

— traceroute

Review Questions

Use the questions here to review what you learned in this chapter. The correct answers are found in the appendix, "Answers to Chapter Review Questions."

1.   Which of the following components are common to routers, switches, and computers? (Choose three.)

a.   RAM

b.   CPU

c.   Motherboard

d.   Keyboard

2.   Which of the following types of ports do routers have? (Choose two.)

a.   Printer

b.   Console

c.   Network

d.   CD-ROM

e.   USB

3.   Which of the following statements best describe the functions of a router in a network? (Choose two.)

a.   Routers maintain their routing tables and ensure that other routers know of changes in the network.

b.   Routers use the routing table to determine where to forward packets.

c.   Routers strengthen the signal over large distances in a network.

d.   Routers create larger collision domains.

e.   Routers use ICMP to communicate network information from their own routing table with other routers.

4. Which of the following statements about the path determination process are accurate? (Choose three.)

    a. Routers evaluate the available paths to a destination.

    b. The routing process uses metrics and administrative distances when evaluating network paths.

    c. Dynamic routing occurs when the network administrator configures information on each router.

    d. Dynamic routing occurs when information is learned using routing information that is obtained from routing protocols.

    e. A default route holds an explicit route to every network.

    f. The routing table holds multiple entries per network.

5. Arrange the following steps of the routing process in the correct order.

    __ Step 1

    __ Step 2

    __ Step 3

    __ Step 4

    __ Step 5

    a. The router deencapsulates the frame and uses the protocol information of the frame to determine that the network layer packet will pass to the IP process.

    b. If the destination network is on a directly attached network, the router will use the ARP process to obtain the MAC address of the host and forward it to the network segment. If the network is reachable through another router, the router will use the MAC address of the next-hop router and forward the packet out the interface indicated in the routing table.

    c. The router checks the destination address in the IP header. Either the packet is destined for the router itself or it needs to be forwarded. If the packet needs to be forwarded, the router searches its routing table to determine where to send the packet.

    d. The outgoing interface process encapsulates the packet appropriately to the media and sends the packet onto the network segment.

    e. The router receives a packet on one of its interfaces.

6. Which of the following contains routing information that helps a router in determining the routing path? (Choose three.)

    a. IP address

    b. MAC address

    c.   Routing table

    d.   Routing protocol

7. Which of the following statements describe the function of routing tables? (Choose three.)

    a.   Routing tables provide an ordered list of known network addresses.

    b.   Routing tables are maintained through the transmission of MAC addresses.

    c.   Routing tables contain metrics that are used to determine the desirability of the route.

    d.   Routing table associations tell a router that a particular destination is either directly connected to the router or that it can be reached through another router (the next-hop router) on the way to the final destination.

    e.   When a router receives an incoming packet, it uses the source address and searches the routing table to find the best path for the data from that source.

    f.   Although routing protocols vary, routing metrics do not.

8. Match each of the following method of populating a routing table to its definition.

    ___ This entry comes from having interfaces attached to network segments. This entry is obviously the most certain; if the interface fails or is administratively shut down, the entry for that network will be removed from the routing table.

    ___ This is an optional entry that is used when no explicit path to a destination is found in the routing table. This entry can be manually inserted or be populated from a dynamic routing protocol.

    ___ These routes are entered manually by a system administrator directly into the configuration of a router.

    ___ These routes are learned by the router, and the information is responsive to changes in the network so that the router is constantly being updated.

    a.   Static routing

    b.   Dynamic routing

    c.   Default route

    d.   Directly connected network

9. Which of the following metrics are most commonly used by routing protocols to determine a network path? (Choose three.)

    a.   Hop count

    b.   Bandwidth

    c.   Delay

    d.   Packet length

    e.   Distance

    f.   Quantity

10. Which of the following statements accurately describe a distance vector protocol? (Choose three.)

    a.   IGRP was developed by Cisco to address the issues associated with routing in medium-size LANs.

    b.   Examples of this protocol include RIP and IGRP.

    c.   This protocol determines the direction (vector) and distance (hop count) to any network in the internetwork.

    d.   Using this protocol, a router needs to know the entire path to every network segment.

    e.   This process is also known as "routing by rumor."

    f.   Routers running the distance vector routing protocol send periodic updates only when there are changes in the network.

11. Which of the following statements accurately describe a link-state routing protocol? (Choose three.)

    a.   The link-state database is used to calculate the paths with the highest bandwidths on the network.

    b.   Link-state routing protocols respond quickly to network changes.

    c.   In link-state routing protocols, each router periodically sends messages to the network, listing the routers to which it is directly connected and also information about whether the link to each router is active.

    d.   Link-state routing protocols send periodic updates (link-state refreshes) at long time intervals, approximately once every 30 minutes.

    e.   In link-state routing protocols, every router tries to build its own internal map of the network topology.

    f.   Link-state routing protocols send periodic updates even if no network changes have occurred.

12. All computers function using the _____.

    a.   base 10 system

    b.   decimal system

    c.   numeric system

    d.   binary system

13. The decimal number 10 converts to the binary number _____.

    a. 10

    b. 1010

    c. 110

    d. 1000

14. Which of the following binary octets has an LSB of 0?

    a. 01100011

    b. 10100101

    c. 10011010

    d. 10011001

15. IP addresses are represented using _____.

    a. 32-bit binary numbers

    b. 16-bit decimal numbers

    c. 8-bit binary numbers

    d. 8 sets of 4-bit decimal numbers

16. 2 to the fifth power is _____.

    a. 2 * 5

    b. 128

    c. 2 multiplied by itself 5 times

    d. None of the above

17. The decimal number 205 converted into a binary number is _____.

    a. 11011101

    b. 11001001

    c. 110001019

    d. 11001101

18. The decimal number 452 converted into a binary number, using successive division by 2, is _____.

    a. 111000100

    b. 110000100

    c. 111001100

    d. 101000100

19. What is the decimal equivalent of the binary number 11000111?

    a.   218

    b.   199

    c.   179

    d.   208

20. The binary number 11101000111 converted into a decimal number, using powers of 2, is _____.

    a.   1183

    b.   1873

    c.   1638

    d.   1863

21. How many octets does a Class A network have in the host field?

    a.   3

    b.   2

    c.   1

    d.   4

22. What is the practical minimum number of bits that can be borrowed to form a subnet?

    a.   1

    b.   2

    c.   3

    d.   4

23. Using six subnet bits, how many usable subnets are created?

    a.   58

    b.   60

    c.   64

24. How many host addresses can be used in a Class C network?

    a.   253

    b.   254

    c.   255

    d.   256

25. What is the maximum number of bits that can be borrowed to create a subnet for a Class C network?

   a. 2

   b. 4

   c. 6

   d. 8

26. A subnet mask tells the router to look at which portions of an IP address?

   a. Mask and host bits

   b. Host and network bits

   c. Host and subnet bits

   d. Network and subnet bits

27. If a router does not match the appropriate address portions to a number in its routing table, it _____.

   a. sends the packet back to the sender

   b. passes the packet to the next router in the hierarchy

   c. adds that number to its table

   d. discards the packet

28. Which of the following subnet masks falls on octet boundaries?

   a. 255.0.0.0

   b. 255.255.0.0

   c. 255.255.255.0

   d. All of the above

29. Which of the following are binary default subnet masks? (Choose two.)

   a. 11111111.00000000.00000000.00000000

   b. 11111111.11111111.01000000.00000000

   c. 11111111.11111111.11111111.00000000

   d. 255.255.224.0

30. Which part of the IP address 172.17.128.47 does the subnet mask 255.255.0.0 tell the router to look for?

   a. 172.17.128.47

   b. 172.17.128

    c. 172.17

    d. 10.172.47

31. 255.255.224.0 translates into the binary number _____.

    a. 11111111.00000000.11100000.00000000

    b. 11111111.11100000.00000000.00000000

    c. 11111111.11111111.11100000.00000000

    d. 11111111.11111111.11110000.00000000

32. To see how many bits you should borrow from the host portion of the network address to give you the number of subnets you need, you should _____.

    a. subtract the number of subnets you need from the host portion

    b. add the bit values from right to left until the total (decimal value) is just greater than the number of subnets you need

    c. add the bit values from left to right until the total (decimal value) is just greater than the number of subnets you need

    d. None of the above

33. How should you power up a Cisco router?

    a. Press the **Reset** button.

    b. Turn the power switch to "On."

    c. Connect the fiber cable to another router.

    d. Attach the power cable plug to the router power supply socket.

34. When you start a Cisco router, what should you see on the console?

    a. Cisco IOS debug messages

    b. The Diagnostic Console menu

    c. Cisco IOS Software output text

    d. A graphical picture showing the real-time status of the LED

35. What is the primary purpose of setup mode on a Cisco router?

    a. To display the current router configuration

    b. To complete hardware and interface testing

    c. To bring up a minimal feature configuration

    d. To fully configure a Cisco router for IP routing

36. Which statement best describes what the user EXEC mode commands allow you to configure on a Cisco router?

   a. You cannot configure anything; the user mode commands are used to display information.

   b. The user EXEC mode allows you to perform global configuration tasks that affect the entire router.

   c. The user EXEC mode commands allow you to enter a secret password so that you can configure the router.

   d. The user EXEC mode commands allow you to configure interfaces, subinterfaces, lines, and routers.

37. Which Cisco IOS command is used to return to user EXEC mode from the privileged EXEC mode?

   a. exit

   b. quit

   c. disable

   d. userexec

38. Match each type of help available with the Cisco IOS CLI to its description.

     __ Context-sensitive help

     __ Console error messages

     __ Command history buffer

   a. Provides a list of commands and arguments associated with a specific command

   b. Allows recall of long or complex commands or entries for reentry, review, or correction

   c. Identifies problems with router commands incorrectly entered so that you can alter or correct them

39. What information does the **show running-config** command provide on a Cisco router?

   a. Current (running) configuration in RAM

   b. System hardware and names of configuration files

   c. Amount of NVRAM used to store the configuration

   d. Version of Cisco IOS Software running on the router

40. Which Cisco IOS command displays the configuration of the system hardware and the software version information?

   a.   **show version**

   b.   **show interfaces**

   c.   **show startup-config**

   d.   **show running-config**

41. Match each of the following router prompts to its configuration mode.

   ___ Line

   ___ Router

   ___ Interface

   ___ Controller

   ___ Subinterface

   a.   Router(config-if)#

   b.   Router(config-line)#

   c.   Router(config-subif)#

   d.   Router(config-router)#

   e.   Router(config-controller)#

42. If you enter a major command on a Cisco router, what happens?

   a.   The router returns you to user EXEC mode.

   b.   The router returns a list of possible commands.

   c.   The router invokes a global configuration command.

   d.   The router switches you from one configuration mode to another.

43. Which Cisco IOS command creates a message to be displayed upon router login?

   a.   **hostname** *hostname*

   b.   **banner motd** *message*

   c.   **hostname interface description**

   d.   **description interface description**

44. If both the **enable secret** and the **enable password** commands are configured on your router, how do you get to the # prompt?

   a.   Enter the **enable secret** command.

   b.   Enter the **enable password** command.

    c.   Enter either the **enable secret** or the **enable password** command.

    d.   Enter both the **enable secret** and the **enable password** commands.

45. Which Cisco IOS command do you use to set the console session timeout to 15 minutes and 30 seconds?

    a.   **set exec timeout 15 30**

    b.   **console timeout 15 30**

    c.   **timeout 15 30**

    d.   **exec-timeout 15 30**

46. Which Cisco IOS command configures a serial port in slot 0, port 1 on a modular router?

    a.   **interface serial 0-1**

    b.   **interface serial 0 1**

    c.   **interface serial 0/1**

    d.   **interface serial 0.1**

47. Which Cisco IOS command should you use to set the clock speed to 64 kbps on a serial interface on a Cisco router?

    a.   **clock rate 64**

    b.   **clock speed 64**

    c.   **clock rate 64000**

    d.   **clock speed 64000**

48. A serial interface displays "Serial1 is up, line protocol is down." Which of the following situations can cause this error? (Choose two.)

    a.   The clock rate has not been set.

    b.   The interface has been manually disabled.

    c.   No cable is attached to the serial interface.

    d.   There are no keepalives.

    e.   There is a mismatch in the encapsulation type.

49. Which of the following would be considered a physical threat? (Choose two.)

    a.   A user leaving his password in his desk

    b.   Someone turning off the power to the switch to block network access

    c.   Someone turning off the air conditioning system in the network closet

    d.   Someone breaking into the cabinet that contains the network documentation

50. Which of the following can be protected with a password? (Choose four.)

    a. Console access

    b. vty access

    c. tty access

    d. User-level access

    e. EXEC-level access

51. Which of the following is a customized text that is displayed before the username and password login prompts?

    a. Message-of-the-day banner

    b. Login banner

    c. Access warning

    d. User banner

    e. Warning message

52. Which of the following is the most secure method of remotely accessing a network device?

    a. HTTP

    b. Telnet

    c. SSH

    d. RMON

    e. SNMP

53. Which of the following describes the Cisco Router and Security Device Manager?

    a. It is a PC-based management system that can be used to configure features such as a DHCP server.

    b. It is a web-based management system that can be used to configure features such as a DHCP server.

    c. It is a server-based management system that can be used to configure features such as a DHCP server.

    d. It is a client-based management system that can be used to configure features such as a DHCP server.

54. Where do the Cisco Router and Security Device Manager files reside?

    a. The PC

    b. The router

    c.   The local client

    d.   A network server

55. Which of the following are functions of DHCP? (Choose two.)

    a.   DHCP dynamically assigns host names to client devices.

    b.   DHCP dynamically assigns IP addresses to client devices.

    c.   DHCP dynamically assigns a default gateway to client devices.

    d.   DHCP dynamically assigns security access levels to client devices.

56. Which of the following describes the DHCP server provided by the Cisco IOS?

    a.   It is a full DHCP server.

    b.   Its support is limited to assigning IP addresses to clients.

    c.   It must obtain its DHCP information from a master DHCP server.

    d.   It has limited DHCP support and can only assign IP addresses and default gateways to clients.

57. Which of the following are required DHCP parameters when configuring a DHCP server on a Cisco router? (Choose four.)

    a.   Pool name

    b.   Lease time

    c.   Domain name

    d.   Default router

    e.   DNS server addresses

    f.   WINS server addresses

    g.   DHCP network and subnet

    h.   Starting and ending addresses

58. Which command can be used to see whether an address in the DHCP pool is already in use by another device?

    a.   **sh ip dhcp bindings**

    b.   **sh ip dhcp database**

    c.   **sh ip dhcp mapping**

    d.   **sh ip dhcp conflicts**

59. Which of the following is a Cisco IOS tool that can be used for secure remote access to another device?

    a. SSH

    b. SDM

    c. ping

    d. Telnet

    e. traceroute

60. Which command would you use to see who has Telnet sessions to your router?

    a. **show user**

    b. **show telnet**

    c. **show sessions**

    d. **show connections**

61. Which of the following would you use to suspend a Telnet session?

    a. **end** keyword

    b. **suspend** keyword

    c. **Ctrl-Shift-6**, **x** key sequence

    d. **Ctrl-Shift-Del** key sequence

This chapter includes the following sections:

- Chapter Objectives

- Understanding WAN Technologies

- Enabling the Internet Connection

- Enabling Static Routing

- Configuring Serial Encapsulation

- Enabling RIP

- Chapter Summary

- Review Questions

CHAPTER 5

WAN Connections

When sites are located at different geographic locations, a WAN provides interconnections between the sites. WANs are most often charge-for-service networks, enabling you to access resources across a wide geographical area. Several types of WANs exist, including point-to-point leased lines, circuit-switched networks, and packet-switched networks. Also, many physical network devices are used in the WAN, as well as many access and encapsulation technologies such as digital subscriber line (DSL), Frame Relay, Asynchronous Transfer Mode (ATM), Point-to-Point Protocol (PPP), and High-Level Data Link Control (HDLC). This chapter focuses on HDLC and PPP WAN access technologies.

When sites are interconnected, a way to get information to the correct site is needed. Routing is the process by which information gets from one location to another. You need to understand how the various routing protocols determine IP routes. This chapter describes the features and operation of static routing, default routing, and Routing Information Protocol (RIP).

As organization's merge, addresses sometimes become limited or addressing conflicts arise. One of the most common addressing issues occurs when a network using private addressing is connected to the Internet, which uses public addressing. Network Address Translation (NAT) and Port Address Translation (PAT) are two protocols that you can use to address these types of issues.

It is becoming common to interconnect small sites via the Internet. In these implementations, it is not unusual for the Internet service provider (ISP) to dynamically assign the interface address using DHCP. To be compatible with this implementation, a router can act as a DHCP client.

Chapter Objectives

Upon completing this chapter, you will be able to define the characteristics, functions, and components of a WAN. This ability includes being able to meet these objectives:

- Describe WANs and their major devices and technologies

- Configure a router to act as an interface to the Internet using the DHCP client and PAT features of a Cisco IOS router

- Configure and verify static and dynamic routing

- Configure and verify serial ports using HDLC and PPP encapsulation

- Configure and verify RIP routing

Understanding WAN Technologies

As an enterprise grows beyond a single location, it becomes necessary to interconnect LANs in various locations to form a WAN. Several technologies are involved in the functioning of WANs, including hardware devices and software functions. This lesson describes the functions and characteristics of WANs and contrasts them with LANs. The lesson also explores how WANs relate to the Open Systems Interconnection (OSI) reference model in their design and function, which major hardware components are typically seen in WAN environments, and how data is managed in a WAN through multiplexing.

What Is a WAN?

A WAN is a data communications network that operates beyond the geographical scope of a LAN.

WANs use facilities provided by a service provider, or carrier, such as a telephone or cable company. They connect the locations of an organization to each other, to locations of other organizations, to external services, and to remote users. WANs generally carry a variety of traffic types, such as voice, data, and video. Figure 5-1 shows how the WAN provides interconnectivity between the campus LAN and remote sites.

Here are the three major characteristics of WANs:

- WANs connect devices that are separated by wide geographical areas.

- WANs use the services of carriers, such as telephone companies, cable companies, satellite systems, and network providers.

- WANs use serial connections of various types to provide access to bandwidth over large geographical areas.

Figure 5-1 *WAN Connectivity*

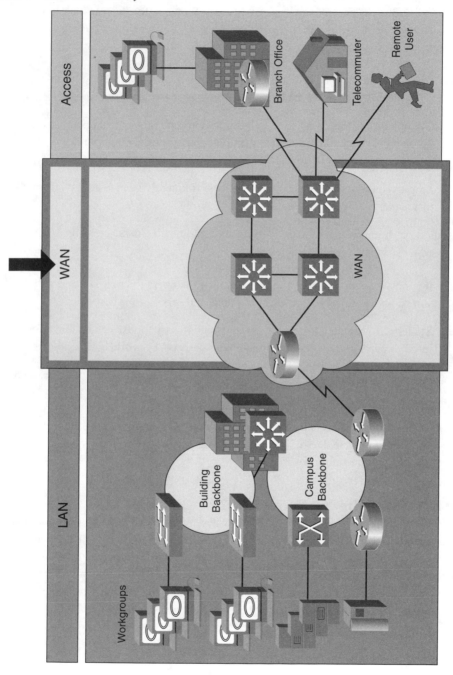

Why Are WANs Necessary?

LAN technologies provide both speed and cost-efficiency for the transmission of data in organizations in relatively small geographical areas. However, other business needs require communication among remote users, including the following:

- People in the regional or branch offices of an organization need to be able to communicate and share data.

- Organizations often want to share information with other organizations across large distances. For example, software manufacturers routinely communicate product and promotion information to distributors that sell their products to end users.

- Employees who travel on company business frequently need to access information that resides on their corporate networks.

In addition, home computer users need to send and receive data across increasingly larger distances. Here are some examples:

- It is now common in many households for consumers to communicate with banks, stores, and a variety of providers of goods and services via computers.

- Students do research for classes by accessing library indexes and publications located in other parts of their country and in other parts of the world.

Figure 5-2 shows the variety of ways that WAN users connect to corporate resources.

Because it is obviously not feasible to connect computers across a country or around the world with cables, different technologies have evolved to support this need to connect these geographically diverse devices. WANs allow organizations and individuals to meet their wide-area communication needs.

How Is a WAN Different from a LAN?

WANs are different from LANs in several ways. Whereas a LAN connects computers, peripherals, and other devices in a single building or other small geographical area, a WAN enables the transmission of data across broad geographical distances. In addition, a company or organization must subscribe to an outside WAN service provider to use WAN carrier network services. LANs are typically owned by the company or organization that uses them. Table 5-1 compares the differences between the WAN and LAN.

Figure 5-2 *WAN Connectivity*

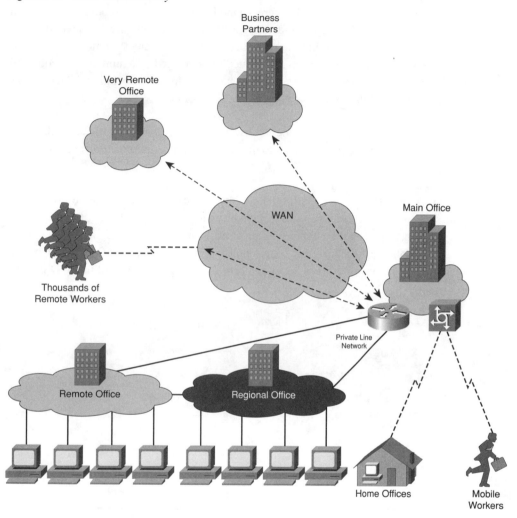

Table 5-1 *LAN/WAN Comparisons*

	WANs	LANs
Area	Wide geographic area	Single building or campus covering small geographical area
Ownership	Subscription to outside service provider	Owned by organization

WAN Access and the OSI Reference Model

WANs function in relation to the OSI reference model. Their function focuses primarily on Layer 1 and Layer 2. WAN access standards typically describe both physical layer delivery methods and data link layer requirements, including physical addressing, flow control, and encapsulation. WAN access standards are defined and managed by a number of recognized authorities, including the ISO, the Telecommunications Industry Association (TIA), and the Electronics Industry Alliance (EIA).

The physical layer (OSI Layer 1) protocols describe how to provide electrical, mechanical, operational, and functional connections to the services of a communications service provider.

The data link layer (OSI Layer 2) protocols define how data is encapsulated for transmission toward a remote location and the mechanisms for transferring the resulting frames. A variety of different technologies are used, such as Frame Relay and ATM. Some of these protocols use the same basic framing mechanism, HDLC, an ISO standard, or one of its subsets or variants. Figure 5-3 shows where WAN technologies fall in the OSI reference model.

Figure 5-3   *OSI Layers Where the WAN Operates*

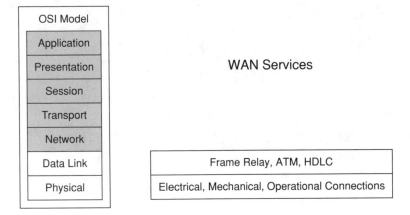

WAN Devices

Several devices operate at the physical layer in a WAN. The following devices are used for WAN access:

- **Routers:** Routers provide internetworking and WAN access interface ports.

- **Communication servers:** Communication servers concentrate dial-in and dial-out user communications.

- **Modems or digital service units (DSU)/channel service units(CSU):** In analog lines, modems convert the digital signal of the sending device into analog format for transmission over an analog line and then convert this digital signal back to digital form so that it can be received and processed by the receiving device on the network. For digital lines, a DSU and a CSU are required. The two are often combined into a single piece of equipment, called the DSU/CSU. The DSU/CSU can also be built into the interface card in the router.

- **WAN networking devices:** Other devices, such as ATM switches, Frame Relay switches, public switched telephone network (PSTN) switches, and core routers, are also used within the cloud to support the access services.

Devices on the subscriber premises are referred to as customer premises equipment (CPE). The subscriber owns the CPE or leases the CPE from the service provider. A copper or fiber cable connects the CPE to the nearest exchange or central office (CO) of the service provider. This cabling is often called the local loop, or "last mile." Transmission of analog data (such as a telephone call) is connected locally to other local loops, or nonlocally through a trunk to a primary center. Analog data then goes to a sectional center and on to a regional or international carrier center as the call travels to its destination.

For the local loop to carry data, however, a device such as a modem or DSU/CSU is needed to prepare the data for transmission. Devices that put data on the local loop are called data communications equipment (DCE). The customer devices that pass the data to the DCE are called data terminal equipment (DTE). The DCE primarily provides an interface for the DTE into the communication link on the WAN cloud.

The WAN access physical layer describes the interface between the DTE and the DCE. Figure 5-4 shows the location of DTE and DCE equipment and some Layer 1 connectivity supported between those devices.

WAN Cabling

Cisco routers support the EIA/TIA-232, EIA/TIA-449, V.35, X.21, and EIA/TIA-530 standards for serial connections.

When you order the cable, you receive a shielded serial transition cable that has the appropriate connector for the standard you specify. For some Cisco routers, the router end of the shielded serial transition cable has a DB-60 connector, which connects to the DB-60 port on a serial WAN interface card (WIC). Because five different cable types are supported with this port, the port is sometimes called a five-in-one serial port. The other end of the serial transition cable is available with the connector that is appropriate for the standard you specify. The documentation for the device to which you want to connect should indicate the standard for that device.

Figure 5-4   *DTE and DCE*

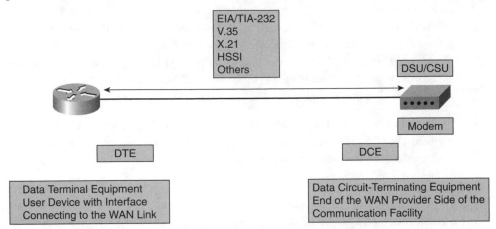

Your CPE, in this case a router, is the DTE. The data DCE, commonly a modem or a DSU/CSU, is the device that converts the user data from the DTE into a form acceptable to the WAN service provider. The synchronous serial port on the router is configured as DTE or DCE (except EIA/TIA-530, which is DTE only) depending on the attached cable, which is ordered as either DTE or DCE to match the router configuration. If the port is configured as DTE (the default setting), it requires external clocking from the DCE device. Figure 5-5 shows the variety of WAN connectors that can be used on a Cisco router.

Figure 5-5   *WAN Cables*

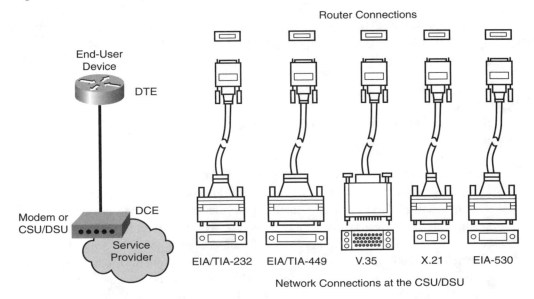

NOTE   To support higher densities in a smaller form factor, Cisco introduced a smart serial cable. The serial end of the smart serial cable is a 26-pin connector. It is much smaller than the DB-60 connector that connects to a five-in-one serial port. These transition cables support the same five serial standards, are available in either DTE or DCE configuration, and are used with two-port serial connections and two-port asynchronous and synchronous WICs.

The Role of Routers in WANs

An enterprise WAN is actually a collection of separate but connected LANs, and routers play a central role in transmitting data through this interconnected network.

Routers have both LAN and WAN interfaces, and whereas a router segments LANs, it is also used as the WAN access connection device. The functions and role of a router in accessing the WAN can be best understood by looking at the types of connections available on the router.

Three basic types of connections on a router exist: LAN interfaces, WAN interfaces, and management ports. LAN interfaces enable the router to connect to the LAN media through Ethernet or some other LAN technology, such as Token Ring or ATM.

WAN connections are made through a WAN interface on a router to a service provider to a distant site or to the Internet. These might be serial connections or any number of other WAN interfaces. With some types of WAN interfaces, an external device such as a DSU/CSU or modem (such as an analog modem, cable modem, or DSL modem) is required to connect the router to the local point of presence (POP) of the service provider. The physical demarcation point is the place where the responsibility for the connection changes from the user to the service provider. This is important because when problems arise, both sides of the link need to prove that the problem either resides with them or not. Figure 5-6 illustrates how a router interconnects different LANs through a WAN segment.

The management ports provide a text-based connection that allows for configuration and troubleshooting of a router. The common management interfaces are the console and auxiliary ports. These ports are connected to a communications port on a computer. The computer must run a terminal emulation program to provide a text-based session with the router, which enables you to manage the device.

Figure 5-6   *Routers Use the WAN to Connect Remote LANs*

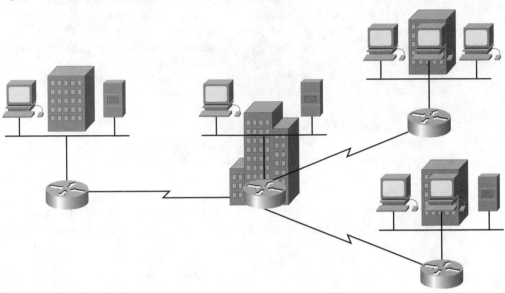

WAN Data Link Layer Protocols

In addition to physical layer devices, WANs require data link layer protocols to establish the link across the communication line from the sending to the receiving device.

Data link layer protocols define how data is encapsulated for transmission to remote sites and the mechanisms for transferring the resulting frames. A variety of different technologies, such as ISDN, Frame Relay, or ATM, are used. Many of these protocols use the same basic framing mechanism, HDLC, an ISO standard, or one of its subsets or variants. ATM is the most different because it uses small, fixed-size cells of 53 bytes (48 bytes for data).

The WAN data link layer protocols are as follows:

- HDLC

- PPP

- Frame Relay (Link Access Procedure for Frame Relay [LAPF])

- ATM

WAN Communication Link Options

WANs are accessed in a number of ways, depending on the data transmission requirements for the WAN. Figure 5-7 maps out the different WAN connectivity options.

Figure 5-7   *WAN Connectivity Options*

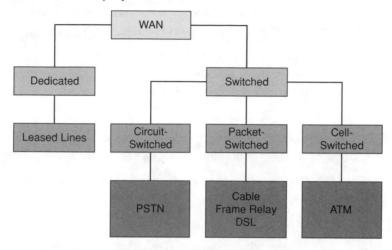

Two major categories of communication links for WANs exist: dedicated and switched. Within each category, individual types of communication link options exist, as follows:

- **Dedicated communication links:** When permanent dedicated connections are required, point-to-point lines are used with various capacities that are limited only by the underlying physical facilities and the willingness of users to pay for these dedicated lines. A point-to-point link provides a pre-established WAN communications path from the customer premises through the provider network to a remote destination. Point-to-point lines are usually leased from a carrier and are also called leased lines.

- **Circuit-switched communication links:** Circuit switching dynamically establishes a dedicated virtual connection for voice or data between a sender and a receiver. Before communication can start, you need to establish the connection through the network of the service provider.

- **Packet-switched communication links:** Many WAN users do not make efficient use of the fixed bandwidth that is available with dedicated, switched, or permanent circuits because the data flow fluctuates. Communications providers have data networks available to more appropriately service these users. In packet-switched networks, the data is transmitted in labeled cells, frames, or packets.

Summary of Understanding WAN Technologies

The following list summarizes the key points that were discussed in this lesson.

- A WAN has three major characteristics: the connection of devices that are separated by wide geographical distances; the use of the services of carriers, such as telephone companies, cable companies, satellite systems, and network providers; and the use of serial connections of various types to access bandwidth over large geographic areas.

- Many business and home needs require communication among remote users, including communication between users in remote company locations, data sharing among different organizations, access to corporate information by traveling workers, and access to Internet.

- LANs connect computers, peripherals, and other devices in a single building or other small geographic area; WANs transmit data across broad geographic distances.

- A company, organization, or individual must subscribe to an outside WAN service provider to use WAN network services, whereas LANs are owned typically by the company, organization, or individual that uses them.

- WAN access functions in relation to the OSI reference model; the WAN function focuses primarily on Layer 1 and Layer 2.

- The major types of devices used for WAN access environments include routers, communication servers, modems (DSU/CSUs).

- Routers have both LAN and WAN interfaces, and whereas a router segments LANs, it is also used as the WAN connection device.

- The data link layer protocols define how data is encapsulated for transmission toward remote sites in a WAN environment and the mechanisms for transferring the resulting frames.

Enabling the Internet Connection

It is common for small sites to use the Internet to connect to other sites. The Internet service is obtained through an ISP. The physical connection is usually provided using either DSL or cable technology with packet switching.

In some cases, the ISP provides a static address for the interface that is connected to the Internet. In other cases, this address is provided using DHCP.

Two scalability challenges facing the Internet are the depletion of the registered IP version 4 (IPv4) address space and scaling in routing. Cisco IOS Network Address Translation

(NAT) and Port Address Translation (PAT) are mechanisms for conserving registered IP addresses in large networks, and they also simplify IP addressing tasks. NAT and PAT translate IP addresses within private internal networks to legal IP addresses for transport over public external networks such as the Internet without requiring a registered subnet address. Incoming traffic is translated for delivery within the inside network.

This translation of IP addresses eliminates the need for host renumbering and allows the same IP address range to be used in multiple intranets, networks that exists within a companies' boundaries. This section describes the features of NAT and PAT and how to configure NAT and PAT on Cisco routers.

Packet-Switched Communication Links

Packet switching is a switching method in which no dedicated path between source and destination endpoints exists, allowing for the sharing of connection links and common carrier resources for data transmission.

Packet-switched networks send data packets over different routes of a shared public network to reach the same destination. Instead of providing a dedicated communication path, the carrier provides a network to its subscribers and ensures that data received from one site exits toward another specific site. However, the route that the packets take to reach the destination site varies. When the packets reach their destination, it is the responsibility of the receiving protocol to ensure that they are reassembled in order.

Packet switching enables you to reduce the number of links to the network, and it allows the carrier to make more efficient use of its infrastructure so that the overall cost is generally lower than with discrete point-to-point lines, or leased lines. In a packet-switching environment, many customer networks connect to the network of the carrier. The carrier can then, depending on the technology, create virtual circuits between customer sites. When the customer is not using the full bandwidth on its virtual circuit, the carrier, through statistical multiplexing, can make that unused bandwidth available to another customer. Figure 5-8 shows an example of virtual circuits through a packet-switched network.

Figure 5-8 *Packet Switching*

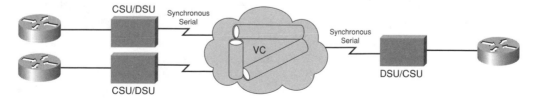

Digital Subscriber Line

DSL technology is an always-on connection technology that uses existing twisted-pair telephone lines to transport high-bandwidth data and provides IP services to subscribers. A DSL modem converts an Ethernet signal from users to a DSL signal to the CO. Figure 5-9 shows an example of DSL connectivity from a remote site through a service provider.

Figure 5-9 *DSL Connectivity*

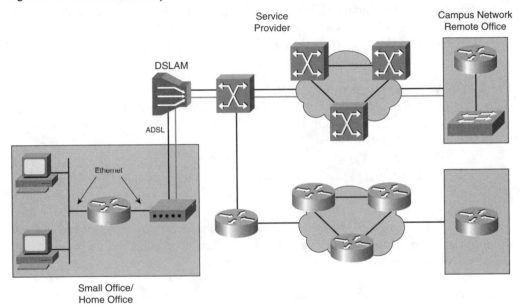

DSL technology allows a service provider to offer high-speed network services, up to and exceeding the speed of a T1 connection, to customers, using installed local-loop copper lines. DSL technology allows the local-loop line to be used for normal telephone voice connection, plus an always-on connection for instant network connectivity. Multiple DSL are multiplexed into a single, high-capacity link by the use of a DSL access multiplexer (DSLAM) at the provider location. DSLAMs incorporate time-division multiplexing (TDM) technology to aggregate many subscriber lines into a less cumbersome single medium, generally a T3 (DS3) connection. Current DSL technologies use sophisticated coding and modulation techniques to achieve data rates up to 8.192 Mbps.

The voice channel of a standard consumer telephone covers the frequency range of 330 Hz to 3.3 kHz. A frequency range, or window, of 4 kHz is regarded as the requirement for any voice transmission on the local loop. Asymmetric DSL (ADSL) technologies place upstream (upload) and downstream (download) data transmissions at frequencies above this 4-kHz window, which allows both voice and data transmissions to occur simultaneously on a DSL service.

DSL availability is far from universal, and a wide variety of types, standards, and emerging standards exist. DSL is now a popular choice for enterprise IT departments to support home workers. Generally, a subscriber cannot choose to connect to an enterprise network directly, but must first connect to an ISP, and an IP connection is made through the Internet to the enterprise. Security risks are incurred in this process.

DSL Types and Standards

The two basic types of DSL technologies are as follows:

- **Asymmetric DSL (ADSL):** Provides higher download bandwidth than upload bandwidth

- **Symmetric DSL (SDSL):** Provides the same capacity of bandwidth in both directions

Figure 5-10 illustrates the difference between ADSL and SDSL.

Figure 5-10 *Asymmetric Versus Symmetric DSL*

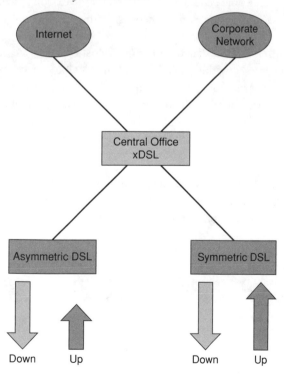

All forms of DSL services are categorized as asymmetric or symmetric, but several varieties of each type exist. ADSL includes the following forms:

- ADSL

- Consumer DSL (CDSL), also called G.Lite or G.992.2

- Very-high-data-rate DSL (VDSL)

SDSL includes the following forms:

- SDSL

- High-data-rate DSL (HDSL)

- ISDN DSL (IDSL)

- Symmetric high-bit-rate DSL (G.shdsl)

DSL service can be added incrementally in any area. A service provider can upgrade bandwidth to coincide with a growth in numbers of subscribers. DSL is also backward compatible with analog voice and makes good use of the existing local loop, which means that it is easy to use DSL service simultaneously with normal phone service.

However, DSL suffers from distance limitations. Most DSL service offerings currently require the customer to be within 18,000 feet of the CO location of the provider, and the older, longer loops present problems. Also, upstream (upload) speed is usually considerably slower than the downstream (download) speed. The always-on technology of DSL also can present security risks because potential hackers have greater access.

Cable

Another technology that has become increasingly popular as a WAN communications access option is the IP over Ethernet Internet service delivered by cable networks. Figure 5-11 shows typical cable connectivity.

Figure 5-11 *Cable Connectivity*

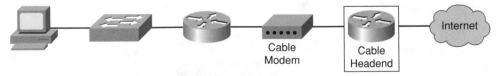

Cable Modem

Cable Headend

Internet

Originally, cable was a one-directional medium designed to carry broadcast analog video channels to the customers, or subscribers. During the 1990s, with the introduction of direct broadcast satellite (DBS) and DSL technology, however, cable operators experienced a serious challenge to their existence by competing technologies. DBS operators marketed more choices and better quality entertainment products through digital technology, and the existing local exchange carriers (LEC) in cities that offered a combination of voice, video, and data by means of DSL.

Fearing loss of market share, and facing the need to offer advanced services to remain economically viable, key multiple service operators (MSO) formed the Multimedia Cable Network System Partners Ltd. (MCNS), with the purpose of defining a product and system standard capable of providing data and future services over cable television (CATV) plants. MCNS proposed a packet-based (IP) solution in contention with a cell-based (ATM) solution promoted by IEEE 802.14. MCNS partners included Comcast Cable Communications, Cox Communications, Tele-Communications, Time Warner Cable, MediaOne, Rogers Cablesystems, and Cable Television Laboratories (CableLabs).

Global Internet: The Largest WAN

The Internet can be thought of as a WAN that spans the globe. In the 1960s, researchers at the U.S. Department of Defense wanted to build a command-and-control network by linking several of their computing facilities around the country. This early WAN could be vulnerable, however, to natural disaster or military attack. Therefore, it was necessary to ensure that if part of the network was destroyed, the rest of the system would still function. Thus, the network would have no central authority, and the computers running it could automatically reroute the flow of information around any broken links.

The Department of Defense researchers devised a way to break messages into parts, sending each part separately to its destination, where the message would be reassembled. This method of data transmission is now known as a packet system.

This packet system, which was made public by the military in 1964, was also being researched at the Massachusetts Institute of Technology (MIT), the University of California, Los Angeles (UCLA), and the National Physical Laboratory in the United Kingdom. In the fall of 1969, UCLA installed the first computer on this network. Several months later, four computers were on this network, which was named the Advanced Research Projects Agency Network (ARPANET).

In 1972, the first e-mail messaging software was developed so that ARPANET developers could more easily communicate and coordinate on projects. Later that year, a program that allowed users to read, file, forward, and respond to messages was developed.

Throughout the 1970s and 1980s, the network expanded as technology became more sophisticated. In 1984, the Domain Name System (DNS) was introduced and gave the world domain suffixes (such as .edu, .com, .gov, and .org) and a series of country codes. This system made the Internet much more manageable. Without DNS, users had to remember the IP address of every Internet site they wanted to visit, a long series of numbers, instead of a string of words.

In 1989, Timothy Berners-Lee began work on a means to better facilitate communication among physicists around the world, based on the concept of hypertext, which would allow electronic documents to be linked directly to each other. The eventual result of linking documents was the World Wide Web. Standard formatting languages, such as HTML and its variants, allow web pages to display formatted text, graphics, and multimedia. A web browser can read and display HTML documents and can access and download related files and software.

The web was popularized by the 1993 release of a graphical, easy-to-use browser called Mosaic. Therefore, although the web began as just one component of the Internet, it is clearly the most popular, and the two are now nearly synonymous.

Throughout the 1990s, personal computers (PC) became more powerful and less expensive, allowing millions of people to buy them for their homes and offices. ISPs, such as America Online (AOL), CompuServe, and many local providers, began offering affordable dialup connections to the Internet. To accommodate the need for increased speed, cable service providers began to offer access through cable network facilities and technologies.

Today, the Internet has grown into the largest network on the earth, providing access to information and communication for business and home users. The Internet can be seen as a network of networks, consisting of a worldwide mesh of hundreds of thousands of networks, owned and operated by millions of companies and individuals all over the world, all connected to thousands of ISPs. Figure 5-12 illustrates how the Internet provides connectivity between different businesses and organizations across a WAN.

Obtaining an Interface Address from a DHCP Server

An ISP sometimes provides a static address for an interface that is connected to the Internet. In other cases, this address is provided using DHCP.

If the ISP uses DHCP to provide interface addressing, no manual address can be configured. Instead, the interface is configured to operate as a DHCP client.

Figure 5-12   *The Internet Connects via WAN*

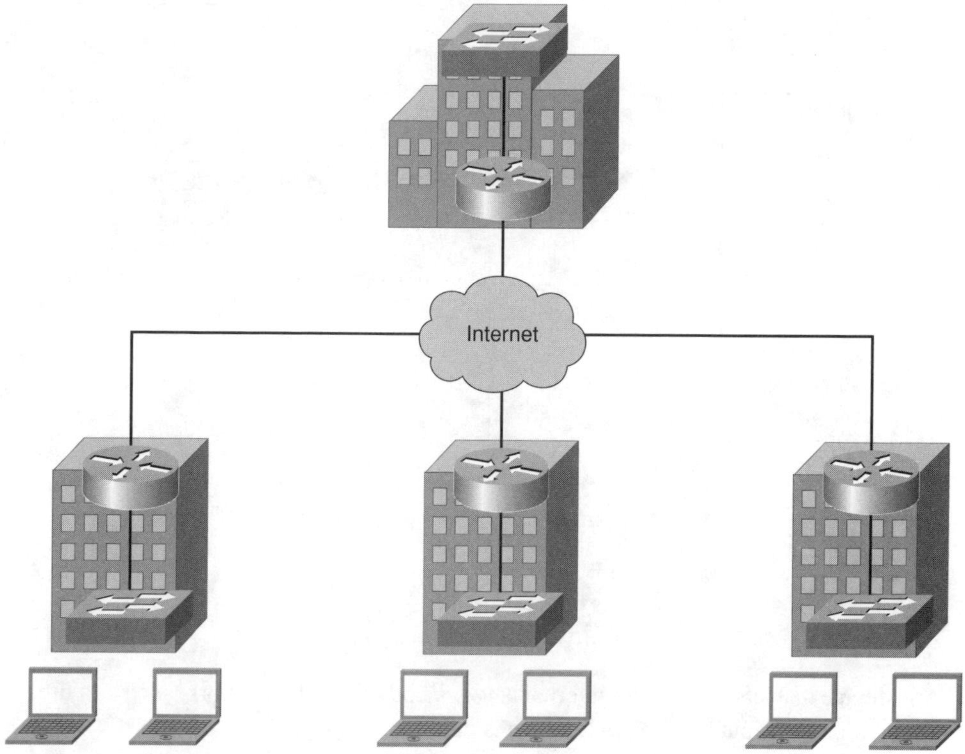

Introducing NAT and PAT

Small networks are commonly implemented using private IP addressing. When connecting this type of network to public networks such as the Internet, you need a method to convert the private IP addressing to public addressing. NAT operates on a Cisco router and is designed for IP address simplification and conservation. NAT enables private IP intranets that use nonregistered IP addresses to connect to the Internet. Usually, NAT connects two networks together and translates the private (inside local) addresses in the internal network into public addresses (inside global) before packets are forwarded to another network. You can configure NAT to advertise only one address for the entire network to the outside world. Advertising only one address effectively hides the internal network from the world, thus providing additional security. Figure 5-13 shows how NAT changes and tracks addressing between interfaces.

Figure 5-13 *NAT Translations*

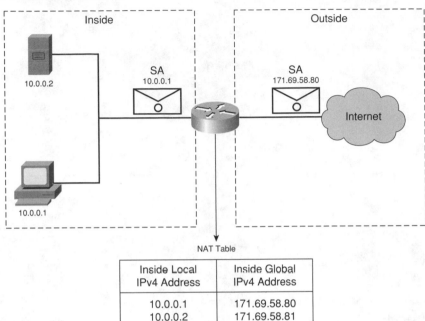

Inside Local IPv4 Address	Inside Global IPv4 Address
10.0.0.1	171.69.58.80
10.0.0.2	171.69.58.81

Any device that sits between an internal network and the public network, such as a firewall, a router, or a computer, uses NAT, which is defined in RFC 1631.

In NAT terminology, the "inside network" is the set of networks that are subject to translation. The "outside network" refers to all other addresses. Usually these are valid addresses located on the Internet.

Cisco defines the following NAT terms:

- **Inside local address:** The IP address assigned to a host on the inside network. The inside local address is likely *not* an IP address assigned by the Internet Assigned Numbers Authority (IANA) or service provider.

- **Inside global address:** A legitimate IP address assigned by the NIC or service provider that represents one or more inside local IP addresses to the outside world.

- **Outside local address:** The IP address of an outside host as it appears to the inside network. Not necessarily legitimate, the outside local address is allocated from an address space routable on the inside.

- **Outside global address:** The IP address assigned to a host on the outside network by the host owner. The outside global address is allocated from a globally routable address or network space.

One of the main features of NAT is static PAT, which is also referred to as overload in Cisco IOS configuration. Several internal addresses can be translated using NAT into just one or a few external addresses by using PAT.

PAT uses unique source port numbers on the inside global IP address to distinguish between translations. Because the port number is encoded in 16 bits, the total number of internal addresses that NAT can translate into one external address is, theoretically, as many as 65,536 addresses. PAT attempts to preserve the original source port. If the source port is already allocated, PAT attempts to find the first available port number. It starts from the beginning of the appropriate port group, 0–511, 512–1023, or 1024–65535. If PAT does not find a port that is available from the appropriate port group and if more than one external IP address is configured, PAT moves to the next IP address and tries to allocate the original source port again. PAT continues trying to allocate the original source port until it runs out of available ports and external IP addresses. Figure 5-14 shows how a single address can be used to translate for multiple addresses.

Figure 5-14 *PAT Translations*

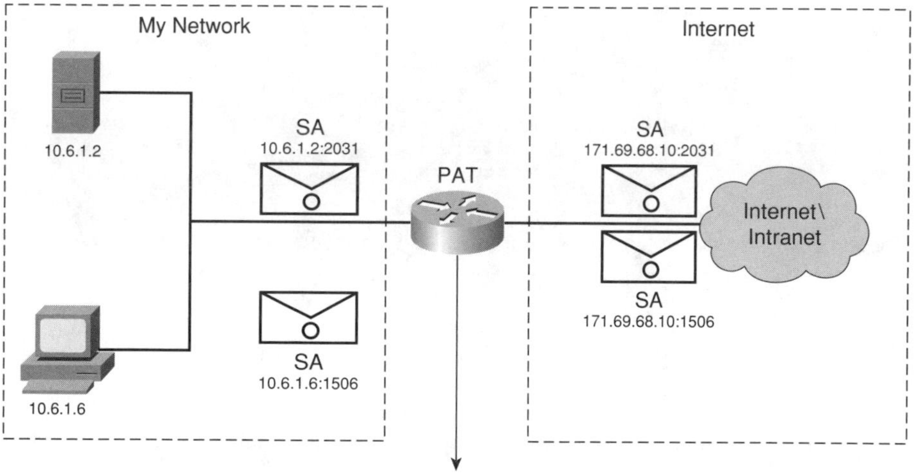

Inside Local IPv4 Address	Inside Global IPv4 Address
10.6.1.2:2031	171.69.68.10:2031
10.6.1.6:1506	171.69.68.10:1506

Translating Inside Source Addresses

You can translate your own IP addresses into globally unique IP addresses when you are communicating outside your network. You can configure static or dynamic inside source translation.

Example: Translating Inside Source Addresses

Figure 5-15 illustrates a router that is translating a source address inside a network into a source address outside the network.

Figure 5-15 *Translating Inside Source Address (NAT)*

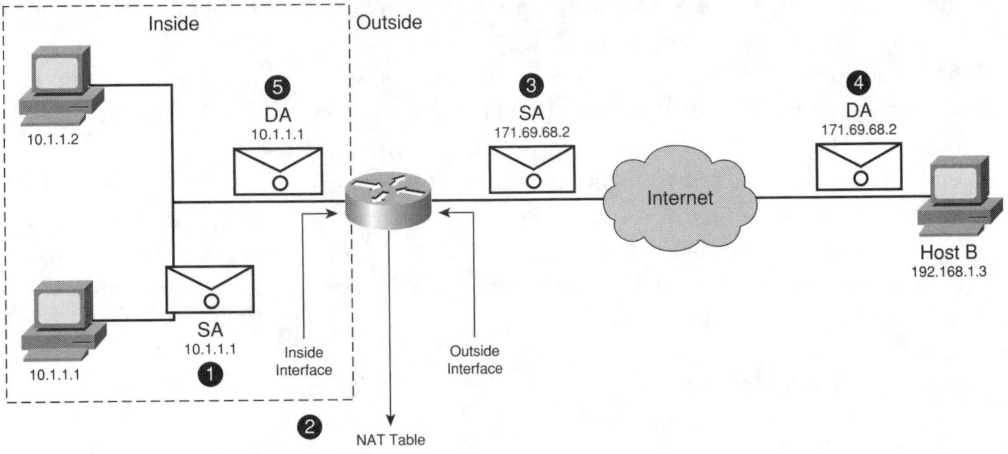

Inside Local IP Address	Inside Global IP Address
10.1.1.2 10.1.1.1	2.2.2.3 171.69.68.2

The steps for translating an inside source address are as follows:

Step 1 The user at host 10.1.1.1 opens a connection to host B.

Step 2 The first packet that the router receives from host 10.1.1.1 causes the router to check its NAT table.

- If a static translation entry was configured, the router goes to Step 3.
- If no static translation entry exists, the router determines that the source address 10.1.1.1 (SA 10.1.1.1) must be translated dynamically. The router then selects a legal, global address from the dynamic address pool and creates a translation entry (in this example, 171.69.68.2). This type of entry is called a simple entry.

Step 3 The router replaces the inside local source address of host 10.1.1.1 with the translation entry global address and forwards the packet.

Step 4 Host B receives the packet and responds to host 10.1.1.1 by using the inside global IP destination address 171.69.68.2 (DA 171.69.68.2).

Step 5   When the router receives the packet with the inside global IP address, the router performs a NAT table lookup by using the inside global address as a key. The router then translates the address back to the inside local address of host 10.1.1.1 and forwards the packet to host 10.1.1.1. Host 10.1.1.1 receives the packet and continues the conversation. The router performs Steps 2 through 5 for each packet.

You can conserve addresses in the inside global address pool by allowing the router to use one inside global address for many inside local addresses. When this overloading is configured, the router maintains enough information from higher-level protocols, for example, TCP or User Datagram Protocol (UDP) port numbers, to translate the inside global address back into the correct inside local address. When multiple inside local addresses map to one inside global address, the TCP or UDP port numbers of each inside host distinguish between the local addresses.

Example: Overloading an Inside Global Address

Figure 5-16 illustrates NAT operation when one inside global address represents multiple inside local addresses. The TCP port numbers act as differentiators. Both host B and host C think they are talking to a single host at address 171.69.68.2. They are actually talking to different hosts; the port number is the differentiator. In fact, many inside hosts could share the inside global IP address by using many port numbers.

Figure 5-16   *Overloading an Inside Global Address (PAT)*

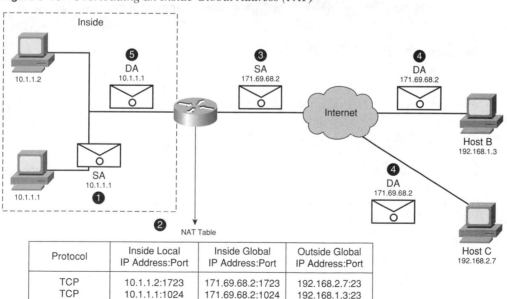

Protocol	Inside Local IP Address:Port	Inside Global IP Address:Port	Outside Global IP Address:Port
TCP	10.1.1.2:1723	171.69.68.2:1723	192.168.2.7:23
TCP	10.1.1.1:1024	171.69.68.2:1024	192.168.1.3:23

The router performs the following process in overloading inside global addresses:

Step 1   The user at host 10.1.1.1 opens a connection to host B. The first packet that the router receives from host 10.1.1.1 causes the router to check its NAT table.

Step 2   If no translation entry exists, the router determines that address 10.1.1.1 must be translated and sets up a translation of inside local address 10.1.1.1 into a legal inside global address. If overloading is enabled and another translation is active, the router reuses the inside global address from that translation and saves enough information to be able to translate back. This type of entry is called an extended entry.

Step 3   The router replaces the inside local source address 10.1.1.1 with the selected inside global address and forwards the packet.

Step 4   Host B receives the packet and responds to host 10.1.1.1 by using the inside global IP address 171.69.68.2.

Step 5   When the router receives the packet with the inside global IP address, the router performs a NAT table lookup. Using the inside global address and port and outside global address and port as a key, the router translates the address back into the inside local address 10.1.1.1 and forwards the packet to host 10.1.1.1. Host 10.1.1.1 receives the packet and continues the conversation. The router performs Steps 2 through 5 for each packet.

Configuring the DHCP Client and PAT

For a router that connects to the Internet where the provider gives you an address via DHCP, such as DSL or cable connectivity, you need to configure the router as a DHCP client and to perform PAT on the inside private address. The first thing you need to do is determine what interface the DHCP client is to be configured on. Figure 5-17 shows the private and public addresses for this example.

In this implementation, you configure the WAN interface (fa0/1) as a DCHP client so that it get its IP address, default gateway, and default routing from the Internet DHCP server. In addition, you enable PAT to translate the internal private addressing to the external public addressing. For this example, you use Security Device Manager (SDM) to configure DHCP.

Figure 5-17 *Identifying Inside and Outside Interfaces*

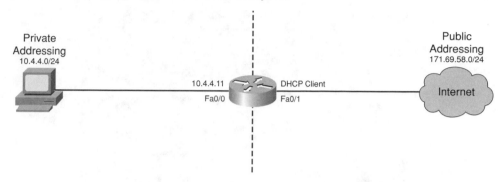

To begin configuring the DHCP client interface, click the **Interfaces and Connections** tab. Check the **Ethernet (PPPoE or Unencapsulated Routing)** radio button, and then click the **Create New Connection** button. This is shown in Figure 5-18.

Figure 5-18 *Configuring the Ethernet Interface*

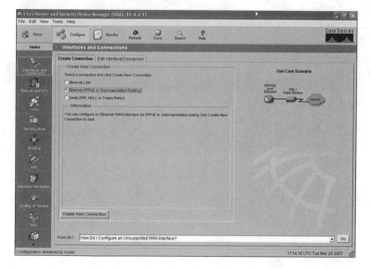

Clicking the **Create New Connection** button opens the WAN Wizard for further configuration. Figure 5-19 shows the wizard welcome window. Click **Next** to continue.

Figure 5-19   *WAN Wizard*

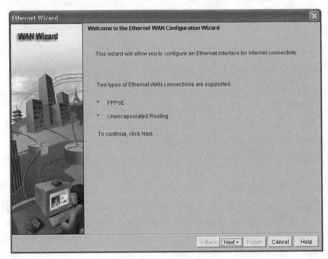

If the ISP uses PPP over Ethernet (PPPoE), click the check box, and then click **Next**. These options are shown in Figure 5-20.

Figure 5-20   *PPPOE Configuration*

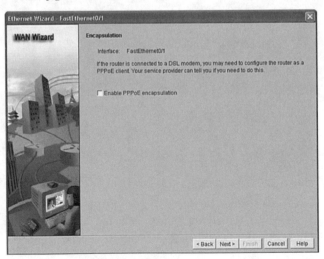

Click the **Dynamic (DHCP Client)** radio button and enter the hostname as shown in Figure 5-21.

Figure 5-21 *DHCP Configuration*

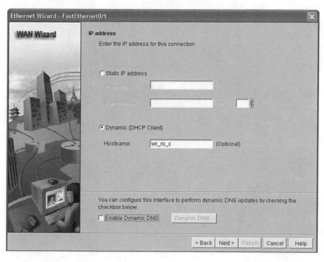

Check the **Port Address Translation** check box and choose the inside interface in the drop-down list as shown in Figure 5-22.

Figure 5-22 *PAT Configuration*

When you are finished, the wizard provides a summary of the configuration, as shown in Figure 5-23.

Figure 5-23 *Configuration Summary*

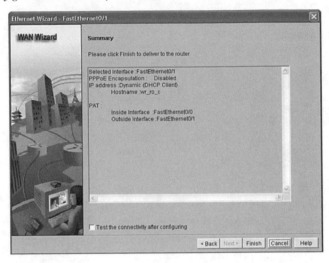

Verifying the DHCP Client Configuration

You can use the Interfaces and Connections window in SDM to verify that the DHCP client is obtaining an address from the DHCP server. This is shown in Figure 5-24.

Figure 5-24 *Configuration Verification*

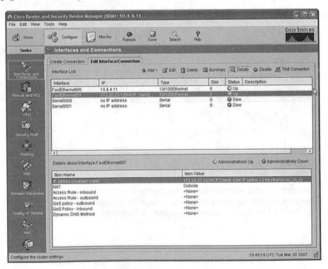

> **NOTE**   The client IP address might not display in the window immediately, and you might need to refresh the window.

Verifying the NAT and PAT Configuration

You can verify the NAT and PAT configuration with the command **show ip nat translation**. Its output follows:

```
RouterX# show ip nat translations
      Pro Inside global      Inside local       Outside local      Outside global

      - - -                  172.16.131.1       10.10.10.1         - - -
```

Table 5-2 shows the commands that you can use in EXEC mode to display and manage translation information.

Table 5-2   *Useful NAT Management Commands*

Command	Description
show ip nat translations	Displays active translations
clear ip nat translation *	Clears all dynamic address translation entries from the NAT translation table

After you have configured NAT, verify that it operates as expected. You can do this by using the **show** and **clear** commands.

By default, dynamic address translations time out from the NAT and PAT translation tables at some time after a period of nonuse. When port translation is not configured, translation entries time out after 24 hours unless you reconfigure them with the **ip nat translation** command. You can clear the entries before the timeout by using the **clear** command listed in the Table 5-2.

Alternatively, you can use the **show run** command and look for NAT, ACL, interface, or pool commands with the required values.

Summary of Enabling the Internet Connection

This topic summarizes the key points that were discussed in this section.

- Packet-switched networks send data packets over different routes of a shared public network owned by a carrier to reach the same destination. The route that the packets take to reach the destination site, however, varies.

- DSL comes in several varieties, including ADSL, SDSL, HDSL, IDSL, and CDSL. DSL has both advantages (speed, always on, and so on) and disadvantages (availability).

- The global Internet grew from a U.S. Department of Defense plan to build a command-and-control network in the 1960s to its present state as the largest WAN on earth, with multiple ways to access it and multiple communication, research, and commercial uses.

- An interface can get its IP address from a DHCP server.

- NAT enables private IP internetworks that use nonregistered IP addresses to connect to the Internet.

- You can translate your own IP addresses into globally unique IP addresses when you are communicating outside of your network.

- Overloading is a form of dynamic NAT that maps multiple unregistered IP addresses to a single registered IP address (many-to-one) by using different ports, known also as PAT.

- After NAT is configured, the **clear** and **show** commands can be used to verify that it operates as expected.

Enabling Static Routing

Routing is the process of determining where to send data packets destined for addresses outside the local network. Routers gather and maintain routing information to enable the transmission and receipt of such data packets.

Conceptually, routing information takes the form of entries in a routing table, with one entry for each identified route. You can statically (manually) configure the entries in the routing table, or the router can use a routing protocol to create and maintain the routing table dynamically to accommodate network changes when they occur.

To manage an IP network effectively, you must understand the operation of both static and dynamic routing and the impact that they have on an IP network. This lesson introduces IP static routing.

Routing Overview

To be able to route anything, a router, or any entity that performs routing, must do the following:

- **Identify the destination address:** Determine the destination (or address) of the item that needs to be routed.

- **Identify sources of routing information:** Determine from which sources (other routers) the router can learn the paths to given destinations.

- **Identify routes:** Determine the initial possible routes, or paths, to the intended destination.

- **Select routes:** Select the best path to the intended destination.

- **Maintain and verify routing information:** Determine if the known paths to the destination are the most current.

The routing information that a router obtains from other routers is placed in its routing table. The router relies on this table to tell it which interfaces to use when forwarding addressed packets. Figure 5-25 shows that the router on the left uses interface s0/0/0 to get to the 172.16.1.0 subnet.

Figure 5-25 *Routes to Destination*

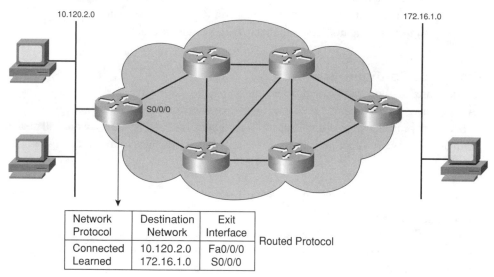

If the destination network is directly connected, the router already knows which interface to use when forwarding packets. If destination networks are not directly attached, the router must learn the best route to use when forwarding packets.

The destination information can be learned in two ways:

- You can enter routing information manually.

- You can collect routing information through the dynamic routing process that runs in the routers.

Static and Dynamic Route Comparison

Routers can forward packets over static routes or dynamic routes based on the router configuration. The two ways to tell the router where to forward packets to destination networks that are not directly connected are as follows:

■ **Static route:** The router learns routes when an administrator manually configures the static route. The administrator must manually update this static route entry whenever an internetwork topology change requires an update. Static routes are user-defined routes that specify the path that packets take when moving between a source and a destination. These administrator-defined routes allow very precise control over the routing behavior of the IP internetwork.

■ **Dynamic route:** The router dynamically learns routes after an administrator configures a routing protocol that helps determine routes. Unlike the situation with static routes, after the network administrator enables dynamic routing, the routing process automatically updates route knowledge whenever new topology information is received. The router learns and maintains routes to the remote destinations by exchanging routing updates with other routers in the internetwork.

Static Route Configuration

Static routes are commonly used when you are routing from a network to a stub network. A stub network (sometimes called a leaf node) is a network accessed by a single route. Static routes can also be useful for specifying a "gateway of last resort" to which all packets with an unknown destination address are sent. Following is the syntax for configuring a static route:

```
RouterX(config)# ip route network [mask] {address ¦ interface}[distance] [permanent]
```

Example: Understanding Static Routes

In Figure 5-26, router A is configured with a static route to reach the 172.16.1.0 subnet via the serial interface of router A given either configuration method. Router B is configured with a static or default route to reach the networks behind router A via the serial interface of router B.

> **NOTE**   The static route is configured for connectivity to remote networks that are not directly connected to your router. For end-to-end connectivity, a static route must be configured in both directions.

Figure 5-26 *Static Route Example*

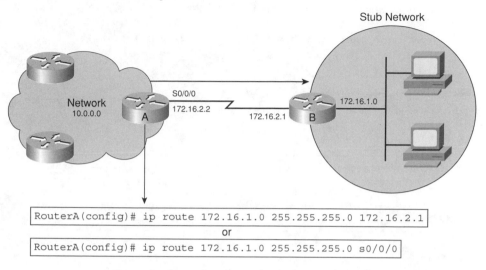

```
RouterA(config)# ip route 172.16.1.0 255.255.255.0 172.16.2.1
```
                                     or
```
RouterA(config)# ip route 172.16.1.0 255.255.255.0 s0/0/0
```

To configure a static route, enter the **ip route** command in global configuration mode. The parameters identified in Table 5-3 further define the static route. A static route allows manual configuration of the routing table. No dynamic changes to the routing table entry occur as long as the path is active.

Table 5-3 lists the **ip route** command parameters and gives descriptions of them.

Table 5-3   ip route *Parameters*

ip route Command Parameters	Description
network	Destination network, subnetwork, or host.
mask	Subnet mask.
address	IP address of the next hop router.
interface	Name of the interface to use to get to the destination network. The interface should be a point-to-point interface. The command does not work properly if the interface is multi-access (for example, a shared media Ethernet interface).
distance	(Optional) Defines the administrative distance.
permanent	(Optional) Specifies that the route will not be removed, even if the interface shuts down.

Example: Configuring Static Routes

In this example, the static route is configured as follows:

```
Router(config)#ip route 172.16.1.0 255.255.255.0 172.16.2.1
```

or

```
Router(config)#ip route 172.16.1.0 255.255.255.0 s0/0/0
```

Table 5-4 lists the **ip route** command parameters for this example.

Table 5-4   *Static Route Example Parameters*

ip route Command Parameters	Description
ip route	Identifies the static route.
172.16.1.0	IP address of a static route to the destination subnetwork.
255.255.255.0	Indicates the subnet mask. There are 8 bits of subnetting in effect.
172.16.2.1	IP address of the next hop router in the path to the destination.
s0/0/0	Optional: If next hop address is not used, then the interface to send the packet out can be used instead.

The assignment of a static route to reach the stub network 172.16.1.0 is proper for router A because only one way to reach that network exists.

Default Route Forwarding Configuration

You should use a default route in situations in which the route from a source to a destination is not known or when it is not feasible for the router to maintain many routes in its routing table, such as the one shown in Figure 5-27.

Use the **ip route** command to configure default route forwarding. In Figure 5-27, router B is configured to forward all packets that do not have the destination network listed in the router B routing table to router A.

In the default route example, the default route is configured as follows:

```
Router(config)# ip route 0.0.0.0 0.0.0.0 172.16.2.2
```

Figure 5-27 *Using Default Routes*

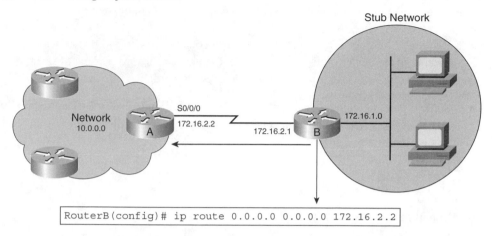

```
RouterB(config)# ip route 0.0.0.0 0.0.0.0 172.16.2.2
```

Table 5-5 lists the **ip route** command parameters for this example.

Table 5-5 *Default Route Example Parameters*

ip route Command Parameters	Description
ip route	Identifies the static route.
0.0.0.0	Routes to networks not on the routing table.
0.0.0.0	Special mask indicating the default route.
172.16.2.2	IP address of the next hop router to be used as the default for packet forwarding.

Static Route Configuration Verification

To verify that you have properly configured static routing, enter the **show ip route** command and look for static routes signified by "S." You should see a verification output as indicated:

```
RouterA# show ip route
Codes: C - connected, S - static, I - IGRP, R - RIP, M - mobile, B - BGP
       D - EIGRP, EX - EIGRP external, O - OSPF, IA - OSPF inter area
       E1 - OSPF external type 1, E2 - OSPF external type 2, E - EGP
       i - IS-IS, L1 - IS-IS level-1, L2 - IS-IS level-2, * - candidate default
       U - per-user static route

Gateway of last resort is 0.0.0.0 to network 0.0.0.0

     10.0.0.0/8 is subnetted, 1 subnets
C       10.1.1.0 is directly connected, Serial0/0/0
S*    0.0.0.0/0 is directly connected, Serial0
```

Summary of Enabling Static Routing

The following summarizes the key points that were discussed in this section:

■ Routing is the process by which items get from one location to another. In networking, a router is the device used to route traffic. Routers can forward packets over static routes or dynamic routes based on the router configuration.

■ Static routers use a route that a network administrator enters into the router manually. Dynamic routes use a router that a network routing protocol adjusts automatically for topology or traffic changes.

■ Unidirectional static routes must be configured to and from a stub network to allow communications to occur.

■ The **ip route** command can be used to configure default route forwarding.

■ The **show ip route** command verifies that static routing is properly configured. Static routes are signified in the command output by "S."

Configuring Serial Encapsulation

You can use serial point-to-point connections to connect your LAN to your service provider WAN. You are likely to have serial point-to-point connections within your network, between your network and a service provider, or both. You need to know how to configure the serial ports for such connections.

Circuit-switched WANs used to be the most common method of connecting remote sites. Because of the bandwidth requirements of modern applications, circuit-switching technology has been relegated to backup solutions and very small home offices. Because of this, this lesson provides only an overview of circuit-switching technology.

One of the most common types of WAN connections is the point-to-point connection. A point-to-point connection is also referred to as a serial connection or leased-line connection, because the lines are leased from a carrier (usually a telephone company) and are dedicated for use by the company leasing the lines. Companies pay for a continuous connection between two remote sites, and the line is continuously active and available. Understanding how point-to-point communication links function to provide access to a WAN is important to an overall understanding of how WANs function.

Frame Relay and ATM are packet-switching technologies used to connect sites. Because of their complexity, only an overview is provided in this lesson. More in-depth coverage of these packet-switching technologies is provided in *Interconnecting Cisco Network Devices, Part 2 (ICND2)*.

This lesson describes the protocols that encapsulate both data link layer and network layer information over serial links and how to configure those links.

Circuit-Switched Communication Links

Switched circuits allow connections to be initiated when transmission is needed and terminated when the transmission is complete. Figure 5-28 shows examples of circuit-switched WAN connections.

Figure 5-28 *Circuit-Switched Communications*

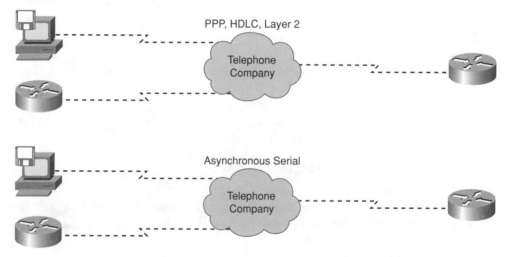

In circuit switching, a dedicated path is established, maintained, and terminated through a carrier network for each communication session. Only the access path is a dedicated physical circuit; the network uses some form of multiplexing technology within the cloud.

Circuit switching operates much like a normal dialup telephone call and is used extensively in telephone company networks. Circuit switching establishes a dedicated physical connection for voice or data between a sender and receiver. Before communication can start, it is necessary to establish the connection by setting the switches through a dialup activity. Whereas point-to-point communication links can accommodate only two sites on a single connection, circuit switching allows multiple sites to connect to the switched network of a carrier and communicate with each other.

An example of a circuit-switched connection is a public switched telephone network (PSTN).

Public Switched Telephone Network

The most common type of circuit-switched WAN communications is the PSTN (also referred to as the plain old telephone service [POTS]).

When intermittent, low-volume data transfers are needed, asynchronous modems and analog dialed telephone lines provide low capacity, on-demand, dedicated switched connections. Traditional telephony uses a copper cable, called the local loop, to connect the telephone handset in the subscriber premises to the telephone network. The signal on the local loop during a call is a continuously varying electronic signal that is a translation of the subscriber voice.

The local loop is not suitable for direct transport of binary computer data, but a modem can send computer data through the voice telephone network. The modem modulates the binary data into an analog signal at the source and, at the destination, demodulates the analog signal to binary data.

The physical characteristics of the local loop and the connection of the local loop to the PSTN limit the rate of the signal. The upper limit is around 53 kbps.

For small businesses, the PSTN can be adequate for the exchange of sales figures, prices, routine reports, and e-mail. Using automatic dialup at night or on weekends for large file transfers and data backup can take advantage of lower off-peak tariffs (line charges). Tariffs are based on the distance between the endpoints, the time of day, and the duration of the call.

Using PSTN has a number of advantages, including the following:

- **Simplicity:** Other than a modem, no additional equipment is required, and analog modems are easy to configure.

- **Availability:** Because a public telephone network is available virtually everywhere, it is easy to locate a telephone service provider, and the maintenance of the telephone system is very high quality, with few instances in which lines are not available.

- **Cost:** The cost associated with the implementation of a PSTN connection link for a WAN is relatively low, consisting primarily of line charges and modems.

Using PSTN also has some disadvantages, including the following:

- **Low data rates:** Because the telephone system was designed to transmit voice data, the transmission rate for large data files is noticeably slow.

- **Relatively long connection setup time:** Because the connection to the PSTN requires a dialup activity, the time required to connect through the WAN is very slow compared to other connection types.

Point-to-Point Communication Links

A point-to-point (or serial) communication link provides a single, established WAN communications path from the customer premises through a carrier network, such as a telephone company, to a remote network. Figure 5-29 shows an example of using a leased line to connect two corporate offices.

Figure 5-29 *Leased Line*

A point-to-point (or serial) line can connect two geographically distant sites, such as a corporate office in New York and a regional office in London. Point-to-point lines are usually leased from a carrier and are therefore often called leased lines. For a point-to-point line, the carrier dedicates fixed transport capacity and facility hardware to the line leased by the customer. The carrier, however, still uses multiplexing technologies within the network.

If the underlying network is based on the T-carrier or E-carrier technologies, the leased line connects to the network of the carrier through a DSU/CSU. The purpose of the DSU/CSU is to provide a clocked signal to the customer equipment interface from the DSU and terminate the channelized transport media of the carrier on the CSU. The CSU also provides diagnostic functions such as a loopback test. Most T1 or E1 TDM interfaces on current routers include approved DSU/CSU capabilities.

Leased lines are a frequently used type of WAN access, and they are generally priced based on the bandwidth required and the distance between the two connected points.

Bandwidth

Bandwidth refers to the rate at which data is transferred over the communication link. The underlying carrier technology depends on the bandwidth available. A difference exists between bandwidth points in the North American (T-carrier) specification and the European (E-carrier) system. Both of these systems are based on the plesiochronous digital hierarchy (PDH) supported in their networks. Optical networks use a different bandwidth hierarchy, which again differs between North America and Europe. In the United States, the Optical Carrier (OC) defines the bandwidth points, and in Europe, the Synchronous Digital Hierarchy (SDH) defines the bandwidth points.

In North America, the bandwidth is usually expressed as a digital service level number (DS0, DS1, and so forth) that technically refers to the rate and format of the signal. The most fundamental line speed is 64 kbps, or DS0, which is the bandwidth required for an uncompressed, digitized phone call.

Serial connection bandwidths can be incrementally increased to accommodate the need for faster transmission. For example, 24 DS0s can be bundled to get a DS1 line (also called a T1 line) with a speed of 1.544 Mbps. Also, 28 DS1s can be bundled to get a DS3 line (also called a T3 line) with a speed of 43.736 Mbps. Figure 5-30 illustrates the different levels of bandwidth.

Figure 5-30   *WAN Bandwidth*

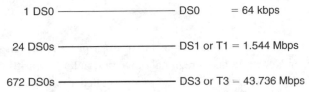

> **NOTE**   E1 (2.048 Mbps) and E3 (34.368 Mbps) are European standards similar to T1 and T3, but they possess different bandwidths and frame structures.

To configure a serial interface, follow these steps:

Step 1   Enter global configuration mode (**configure terminal** command).

Step 2   When in global configuration mode, enter the interface configuration mode. In this example, it is the **interface serial 0/0** command.

Step 3   If a DCE cable is attached, use the **clock rate** *bps* interface configuration command to configure the clock rate for the hardware connections on serial interfaces, such as network interface modules (NIM) and interface processors, to an acceptable bit rate.

Be sure to enter the complete clock speed. For example, a clock rate of 64000 cannot be abbreviated to 64.

On serial links, one side of the link acts as the DCE, and the other side of the link acts as the DTE. By default, Cisco routers are DTE devices, but can be configured as DCE devices. In a "back-to-back" router configuration in which a modem is not used, one of the interfaces must be configured as the DCE to provide a clocking signal. You must specify the clock rate for each DCE interface that is configured in this type of environment. Clock rates in bits per second are as follows: 1200, 2400, 4800, 9600, 19200, 38400, 56000, 64000, 72000, 125000, 148000, 500000, 800000, 1000000, 1300000, 2000000, and 4000000.

Step 4 Enter the specified bandwidth for the interface. The **bandwidth** command overrides the default bandwidth that is displayed in the **show interfaces** command and is used by some routing protocols, such as the Enhanced Interior Gateway Routing Protocol (EIGRP), for routing metric calculations. The router also uses the bandwidth for other types of calculations, such as those required for the Resource Reservation Protocol (RSVP). The default bandwidth for serial lines is T1 speed (1.544 Mbps). The bandwidth entered has no effect on the actual speed of the line.

> **NOTE** The attached serial cable determines the DTE or DCE mode of the Cisco router. Choose the cable to match the network requirement.

The **show controller** command displays information about the physical interface itself. This command is useful with serial interfaces to determine the type of cable connected without the need to physically inspect the cable itself.

The information displayed is determined when the router initially starts and represents only the type of cable that was attached when the router was started. If the cable type is changed after startup, the **show controller** command display doesn't show the cable type of the new cable.

Point-to-Point Communication Considerations

Point-to-point links have been the traditional connection of choice. The advantages to this type of WAN access include the following:

■ **Simplicity:** Point-to-point communication links require minimal expertise to install and maintain.

■ **Quality:** Point-to-point communication links usually offer a high quality of service, provided that they have adequate bandwidth. The dedicated capacity gives no latency or jitter between the endpoints.

■ **Availability:** Constant availability is essential for some applications, such as electronic commerce, and point-to-point communication links provide permanent, dedicated capacity that is always available.

This type of WAN access also has some disadvantages, including the following:

- **Cost:** Point-to-point links are generally the most expensive type of WAN access, and this cost can become significant when they connect many sites. In addition, each endpoint requires an interface on the router, which increases equipment costs.

- **Limited flexibility:** WAN traffic is often variable, and leased lines have a fixed capacity, resulting in the bandwidth of the line seldom being exactly what is needed. Any changes to the leased line generally require a site visit by the ISP or carrier personnel to adjust capacity.

High-Level Data Link Control Protocol

The High-Level Data Link Control (HDLC) protocol is one of two major data-link protocols commonly used with point-to-point WAN connections.

HDLC specifies an encapsulation method for data on synchronous serial data links using frame character and checksum. HDLC supports both point-to-point and multipoint configurations and includes a means for authentication. However, HDLC might not be compatible between devices from different vendors because of the way each vendor might have chosen to implement it.

A Cisco implementation of HDLC exists; it is the default encapsulation for serial lines. Cisco HDLC is streamlined. It has no windowing or flow control, and only point-to-point connections are allowed. The Cisco HDLC implementation includes proprietary extensions in the data field, as shown in Figure 5-31; the extensions allowed multiprotocol support at a time before PPP was specified. Because of the modification, the Cisco HDLC implementation does not interoperate with other HDLC implementations. HDLC encapsulations vary; however, PPP should be used when interoperability is required. Figure 5-31 shows the differences between HDLC and Cisco HDLC.

Configuring HDLC Encapsulation

By default, Cisco devices use the Cisco HDLC serial encapsulation method on synchronous serial lines. However, if the serial interface is configured with another encapsulation protocol and you want to change the encapsulation back to HDLC, enter the interface configuration mode of the interface that you want to change. Use the **encapsulation hdlc** interface configuration command to specify HDLC encapsulation on the interface:

```
RouterA(config-if)# encapsulation hdlc
```

Cisco HDLC is a PPP that can be used on leased lines between two Cisco devices. When you are communicating with a device from another vendor, synchronous PPP is a better option.

Figure 5-31   *HDLC Versus Cisco HDLC*

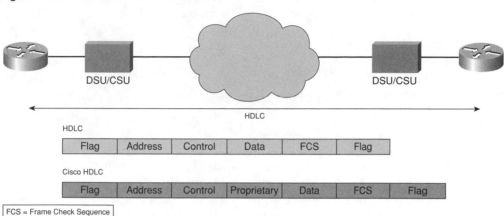

FCS = Frame Check Sequence

Point-to-Point Protocol

PPP originally emerged as an encapsulation protocol for transporting IP traffic over point-to-point links. PPP also established a standard for the assignment and management of IP addresses, asynchronous (start and stop bit) and bit-oriented synchronous encapsulation, network protocol multiplexing, link configuration, link quality testing, error detection, and option negotiation for such capabilities as network layer address negotiation and data-compression negotiation.

PPP provides router-to-router and host-to-network connections over both synchronous and asynchronous circuits. An example of an asynchronous connection is a dialup connection. An example of a synchronous connection is a leased line. Figure 5-32 illustrates using PPP instead of HDLC over a leased line.

Figure 5-32   *PPP*

WAN

PPP
Encapsulation

PPP provides a standard method for transporting multiprotocol datagrams (packets) over point-to-point links. PPP comprises these three main components:

■ A method for encapsulating multiprotocol datagrams

■ A link control protocol (LCP) for establishing, configuring, and testing the data-link connection

■ A family of Network Control Programs (NCP) for establishing and configuring different network layer protocols

PPP provides that an LCP be sufficiently versatile and portable to a wide variety of environments. The LCP is used to automatically determine the encapsulation format option, handle varying limits on sizes of packets, and detect a loopback link and terminate the link. Other optional facilities provided are authentication of the identity of its peer on the link and determination of when a link is functioning properly or failing.

The authentication phase of a PPP session is optional. After the link has been established and the authentication protocol chosen, the peer can be authenticated. If the authentication option is used, authentication takes place before the network layer protocol configuration phase begins.

The authentication options require that the calling side of the link enter authentication information to help ensure that the user has permission from the network administrator to make the call. Peer routers exchange authentication messages. Figure 5-33 shows the basic PPP frame.

Figure 5-33 *PPP Frame*

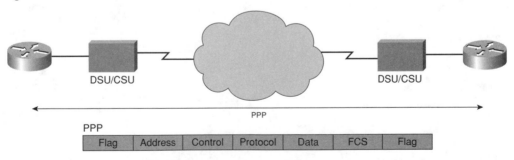

PPP Layered Architecture

Developers designed PPP to make the connection for point-to-point links. PPP, described in RFCs 1661 and 1332, encapsulates network layer protocol information over point-to-point links. RFC 1661 is updated by RFC 2153, "PPP Vendor Extensions."

You can configure PPP on the following types of physical interfaces:

■ Asynchronous serial

■ Synchronous serial

■ Basic Rate Interface (BRI)

■ High-Speed Serial Interface (HSSI)

PPP uses its NCP component to encapsulate and negotiate options for multiple network layer protocols.

PPP uses another of its major components, the LCP, to negotiate and set up control options on the WAN data link.

To enable PPP encapsulation, enter interface configuration mode. Use the **encapsulation ppp** interface configuration command to specify PPP encapsulation on the interface:

```
RouterA(config-if)# encapsulation ppp
```

NOTE   Additional configuration steps are required to enable PPP on an asynchronous serial interface. These steps are not taught in this course. For information about configuring PPP on an asynchronous serial interface, see the *CCNP ISCW Official Exam Certification Guide* book.

Example: PPP Configuration

Figure 5-34 shows a typical example of a PPP configuration.

Figure 5-34 *PPP Configuration*

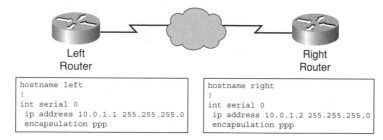

After configuring a serial interface, use the **show interface serial** command to verify the changes:

```
RouterA# show interface s0/0/0
Serial0/0/0 is up, line protocol is up
  Hardware is HD64570
  Internet address is 10.140.1.2/24
```

```
        MTU 1500 bytes, BW 1544 Kbit, DLY 20000 usec, rely 255/255, load 1/255
        Encapsulation PPP, loopback not set, keepalive set (10 sec)
        LCP Open
        Open: IPCP, CDPCP
        Last input 00:00:05, output 00:00:05, output hang never
        Last clearing of "show interface" counters never
        Queueing strategy: fifo
        Output queue 0/40, 0 drops; input queue 0/75, 0 drops
        5 minute input rate 0 bits/sec, 0 packets/sec
        5 minute output rate 0 bits/sec, 0 packets/sec
           38021 packets input, 5656110 bytes, 0 no buffer
           Received 23488 broadcasts, 0 runts, 0 giants, 0 throttles
           0 input errors, 0 CRC, 0 frame, 0 overrun, 0 ignored, 0 abort
           38097 packets output, 2135697 bytes, 0 underruns
           0 output errors, 0 collisions, 6045 interface resets
           0 output buffer failures, 0 output buffers swapped out
           482 carrier transitions
           DCD=up  DSR=up  DTR=up  RTS=up  CTS=up
```

NOTE   Notice in this example that the line is up and the bandwidth is set to 1544 kbps.

Serial Encapsulation Configuration Verification

You need to verify the encapsulation types when configuring WAN connectivity. If the encapsulation is not consistent on each end of a point-to-point link, then the communication between the sites fails.

Use the **show interface** command to verify proper configuration. The following example illustrates a PPP configuration. When HDLC is configured, "Encapsulation HDLC" should be reflected in the output of the **show interface** command. When PPP is configured, you can also use this command to check LCP and NCP states.

```
RouterA# show interface s0/0/0
Serial0/0/0 is up, line protocol is up
  Hardware is HD64570
  Internet address is 10.140.1.2/24
  MTU 1500 bytes, BW 1544 Kbit, DLY 20000 usec, rely 255/255, load 1/255
  Encapsulation PPP, loopback not set, keepalive set (10 sec)
  LCP Open
  Open: IPCP, CDPCP
  Last input 00:00:05, output 00:00:05, output hang never
  Last clearing of "show interface" counters never
  Queueing strategy: fifo
  Output queue 0/40, 0 drops; input queue 0/75, 0 drops
  5 minute input rate 0 bits/sec, 0 packets/sec
  5 minute output rate 0 bits/sec, 0 packets/sec
     38021 packets input, 5656110 bytes, 0 no buffer
     Received 23488 broadcasts, 0 runts, 0 giants, 0 throttles
     0 input errors, 0 CRC, 0 frame, 0 overrun, 0 ignored, 0 abort
     38097 packets output, 2135697 bytes, 0 underruns
     0 output errors, 0 collisions, 6045 interface resets
     0 output buffer failures, 0 output buffers swapped out
     482 carrier transitions
     DCD=up  DSR=up  DTR=up  RTS=up  CTS=up
```

Frame Relay

Frame Relay is a packet-switching protocol that grew in its popularity by being much more cost-effective and thereby replaced older technologies such as X.25 and leased lines. Figure 5-35 illustrates where the Frame Relay protocol operates.

Figure 5-35 *Frame Relay*

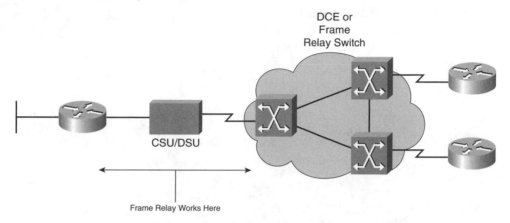

With increasing demand for higher bandwidth and lower latency packet switching, service providers introduced Frame Relay. Frame Relay provides both permanent virtual circuit (PVC) and switched virtual circuit (SVC) service using shared medium-bandwidth connectivity that carries both voice and data traffic. Available data rates are commonly up to 4 Mbps, with some providers offering even higher rates. In addition, Frame Relay is a much simpler protocol that works at the data link layer rather than at the network layer.

Frame Relay implements no error or flow control. The simplified handling of frames leads to reduced latency, and measures taken to avoid frame buildup at intermediate switches help reduce jitter.

Most Frame Relay connections are PVCs rather than SVCs. The connection to the network edge is often a leased line, but dialup connections are available from some providers using ISDN or xDSL lines.

Frame Relay is ideal for connecting enterprise LANs, because a router on the LAN needs only a single WAN interface, even when multiple virtual circuits (VC) are used. The dedicated line to the Frame Relay network edge allows cost-effective connections between widely scattered LANs.

Frame Relay operates over virtual circuits, which are logical connections created to enable communication between two remote devices across a network. VCs provide a bidirectional communications path from one DTE device to another. A data-link connection identifier

(DLCI) within the Frame Relay address header uniquely identifies a virtual circuit. The DLCI is specific only to the router where it is configured. A VC can pass through any number of intermediate DCE devices located within the network. Numerous VCs can be multiplexed into a single physical circuit for access to and transmission across the network. Figure 5-36 illustrates a VC through the Frame Relay cloud.

Figure 5-36 *Frame Relay Virtual Circuit*

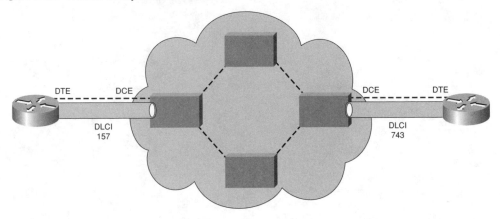

ATM and Cell Switching

ATM is a type of cell-switching connection technology that is capable of transferring voice, video, and data through private and public networks. ATM is used primarily in enterprise LAN backbones or WAN links. Figure 5-37 depicts an ATM connection.

Figure 5-37 *ATM Connectivity*

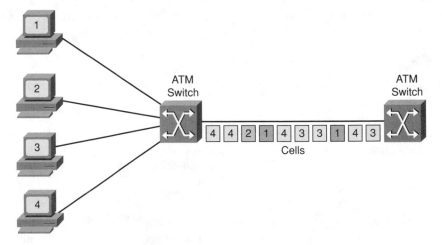

Service providers saw a need for a permanent shared network technology offering low latency and jitter with high bandwidth. Their solution was to leverage the same technology used in their own core network: ATM. ATM has data rates beyond 155 Mbps. Topology diagrams for ATM WANs look similar to other shared technologies, such as X.25 and Frame Relay.

ATM is built on a cell-based architecture rather than on a frame-based architecture. ATM cells are always a fixed length of 53 bytes. The 53-byte ATM cell contains a 5-byte ATM header followed by 48 bytes of ATM payload. Small, fixed-length cells are well suited for carrying voice and video traffic because this traffic is intolerant of delay. Video and voice traffic do not have to wait for a larger data packet to be transmitted.

The 53-byte ATM cell is less efficient than the larger frames and packets of Frame Relay and X.25. Furthermore, the ATM cell has at least 5 bytes of overhead for each 48-byte payload. When the cell is carrying segmented network layer packets, the overhead is higher because the ATM 48-byte data payload might *not* map very well to other packet sizes (64-byte IP packets, for example). A typical ATM line needs almost 20 percent greater bandwidth than Frame Relay to carry the same volume of network layer data.

Like Frame Relay, ATM is implemented using VCs that can be either PVC or SVC. With ATM, the data is divided into small 53-byte cells before it is transmitted. The ATM cell header contains a field called the virtual path identifier/virtual channel identifier (VPI/VCI) that indicates to which VC an ATM cell belongs. At the physical layer, ATM can run over a variety of physical media, including fiber optics using Synchronous Digital Hierarchy (SONET)/Synchronous Digital Hierarchy (SDH) framing and coaxial cable using DS3.

An ATM network includes ATM switches, which are responsible for cell forwarding. The ATM switch receives the incoming cell from an ATM endpoint or another ATM switch. The ATM switch then uses the incoming VPI/VCI to map to the outgoing interface and new VPI/VCI to be used on the next link toward its destination. The ATM cell-switching process is extremely fast and can be programmed in hardware.

An ATM VC is a logical connection created between two ATM endpoints across an ATM network. ATM VCs fall into the two categories of PVC and SVC. VCs provide a bidirectional communications path from one ATM endpoint to another. The VPI/VCI within the ATM cell header uniquely identifies the VCs.

A VC can pass through any number of intermediate ATM switches in the ATM network. Numerous VCs can be multiplexed into a single physical circuit for transmission across the network.

Summary of Configuring Serial Encapsulation

This topic summarizes the key points that were discussed in this lesson.

- A point-to-point (or serial) line can connect two geographically distant sites. These lines are usually leased from a carrier and are, therefore, often called leased lines.

- Bandwidth refers to the rate at which data is transferred over the communication link. In North America, point-to-point leased line bandwidth is typically specified as a DS number (DS0, DS1, and so forth) that technically refers to the rate and format of the signal.

- The HDLC protocol is one of two major data link layer protocols commonly used with point-to-point WAN connections. HDLC supports both point-to-point and multipoint configurations.

- The **encapsulation hdlc** interface configuration command can be used to specify Cisco HDLC encapsulation on the interface.

- PPP lower-level functions use synchronous and asynchronous physical media. PPP higher-level functions carry packets from several network layer protocols using NCPs.

- The **encapsulation ppp** interface configuration command can be used to specify PPP encapsulation on the interface.

- The **show interface** command can be used to verify proper configuration of PPP or HDLC encapsulation.

- Frame Relay data rates are commonly up to 4 Mbps, with some providers offering even higher rates. Frame Relay is a simpler protocol that works at the data link layer rather than at the network layer.

- ATM is a type of cell-switched connection technology that is capable of transferring voice, video, and data through private and public networks. ATM is used primarily in service provider networks and enterprise LAN backbones.

- ATM and Frame Relay VCs can be either PVC or SVC.

Enabling RIP

While static routes provide a method for giving the router information about where networks are located so that they can route packets, they are not scalable. For that information you need to use a dynamic routing protocol. While a lot of different routing protocols exist, the Routing Information Protocol (RIP), which is a distance vector routing protocol, is one of the most enduring of all routing protocols. RIP is a relatively old, but still commonly used, interior gateway protocol created for use in small, homogeneous networks. RIP is also very useful for understanding how dynamic routing protocols operate. This section describes the basic features and operation of RIP and explains how to enable RIP on an IP network.

Dynamic Routing Protocol Overview

A routing protocol defines the rules that are used by a router when it communicates with neighboring routers. Dynamic routing relies on a routing protocol to disseminate knowledge. In contrast, static routing defines the format and use of the fields within a packet. Packets are generally conveyed from end system to end system. Figure 5-38 shows how a router uses a routing protocol to learn the locations of other networks.

Figure 5-38 *Routing Protocols Learn about Networks*

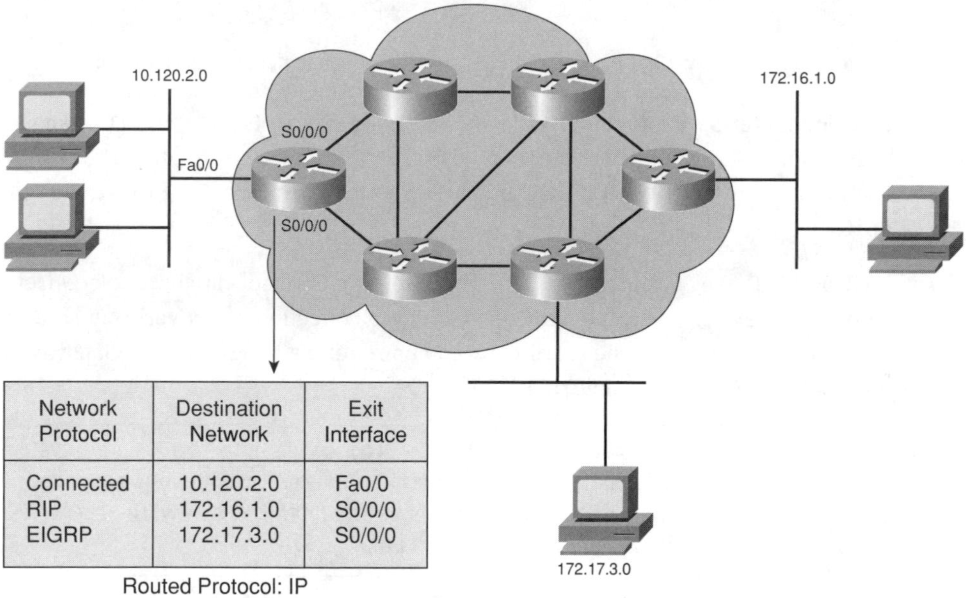

Network Protocol	Destination Network	Exit Interface
Connected	10.120.2.0	Fa0/0
RIP	172.16.1.0	S0/0/0
EIGRP	172.17.3.0	S0/0/0

Routed Protocol: IP
Routing Protocol: RIP, EIGRP

Further examples of the information that routing protocols describe are as follows:

■   How updates are conveyed

■   What knowledge is conveyed

■   When to convey knowledge

■   How to locate recipients of the updates

Figure 5-39 shows the two types of routing protocols, Interior Gateway Protocols and Exterior Gateway Protocols.

Figure 5-39 *Routing Protocol Types*

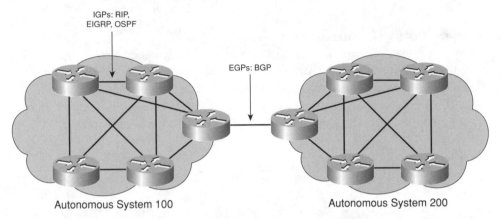

- **Interior Gateway Protocols (IGP):** These routing protocols are used to exchange routing information within an autonomous system. Routing Information Protocol version 1 (RIPv1), RIPv2, EIGRP, and Open Shortest Path First (OSPF) are examples of IGPs.

- **Exterior Gateway Protocols (EGP):** These routing protocols are used to connect autonomous systems. An autonomous system is a collection of networks under a common administration and sharing a common routing strategy. Border Gateway Protocol (BGP) is an example of an EGP.

> **NOTE** The Internet Assigned Numbers Authority (IANA) assigns autonomous system numbers for many jurisdictions. Use of IANA numbering is required if your organization plans to use an EGP, such as BGP. However, it is good practice to be aware of private versus public autonomous system numbering schema.

In addition to types like RIP, OSPF, etc., routing protocols can further be classified as to how the routing protocols operate, as shown in Figure 5-40.

In an autonomous system, most IGP routing algorithms can be classified as conforming to one of the following algorithms:

- **Distance vector:** The distance vector routing approach determines the direction (vector) and distance (hops) to any link in the internetwork.

- **Balanced hybrid:** The balanced hybrid approach combines aspects of link-state and distance vector algorithms.

- **Link state:** The link-state approach, also known as the shortest path first (SPF) algorithm, creates an abstraction of the exact topology of the entire internetwork, or at least of the partition in which the router is situated.

Figure 5-40   *Routing Protocol Algorithms*

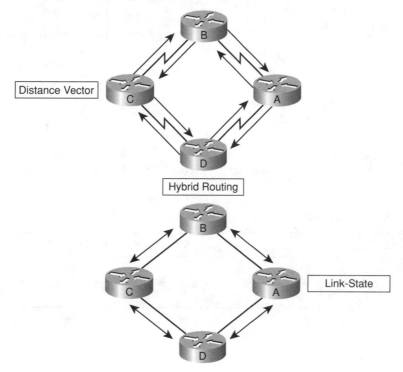

No single best routing algorithm exists for all internetworks. Each routing protocol provides information differently.

Features of Dynamic Routing Protocols

Multiple routing protocols and static routes can be used at the same time. If several sources for routing information exist, an administrative distance value rates the trustworthiness of each routing information source. By specifying administrative distance values, Cisco IOS software can discriminate between sources of routing information.

Example: Administrative Distance

An administrative distance is an integer from 0 to 255. A routing protocol with a lower administrative distance is more trustworthy than one with a higher administrative distance. As shown in Figure 5-41, if router A receives a route to network E from EIGRP and RIP at the same time, router A uses the administrative distance to determine that EIGRP is more trustworthy. Router A would then add the EIGRP route to the routing table.

Figure 5-41 *Administrative Distance*

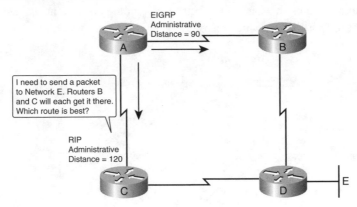

Table 5-6 shows the default administrative distance for selected routing information sources.

Table 5-6 *Default Administrative Distances*

Route Source	Default Distance
Connected interface	0
Static route address	1
EIGRP	90
OSPF	110
RIPv1, RIPv2	120
External EIGRP	170
Unknown or unbelievable	255 (will not be used to pass traffic)

If nondefault values are necessary, you can use Cisco IOS software to configure administrative distance values on a per-router, per-protocol, and per-route basis.

Classful Routing Versus Classless Routing Protocols

Routing protocols are also identified by how they handle IP address space. RIP version 1 is a classful routing protocol. Classful routing is a consequence of the fact that subnet masks are *not* advertised in the routing advertisements that are generated by most distance vector routing protocols.

When a classful routing protocol is used, all subnetworks of the same major network (Class A, B, or C) must use the same subnet mask. Routers that are running a classful routing protocol perform automatic route summarization across network boundaries.

Upon receiving a routing update packet, a router that is running a classful routing protocol takes one of the following actions to determine the network portion of the route:

■ If the routing update information contains the same major network number as is configured on the receiving interface, the router applies the subnet mask that is configured on the receiving interface.

■ If the routing update information contains a major network that is different from that configured on the receiving interface, the router applies the default classful mask (by address class) as follows:

— For Class A addresses, the default classful mask is 255.0.0.0.

— For Class B addresses, the default classful mask is 255.255.0.0.

— For Class C addresses, the default classful mask is 255.255.255.0.

RIP version 2 is a classless routing protocol. Classless routing protocols can be considered second-generation protocols because they are designed to address some of the limitations of the earlier classful routing protocols. One of the most serious limitations in a classful network environment is that the subnet mask is not exchanged during the routing update process, thus requiring the same subnet mask to be used on all subnetworks within the same major network.

Another limitation of the classful approach is the need to automatically summarize to the classful network boundary at major network boundaries.

In the classless environment, the summarization process is controlled manually and can usually be invoked at any bit position within the address. Because subnet routes are propagated throughout the routing domain, manual summarization might be required to keep the size of the routing tables manageable. Classless routing protocols include RIPv2, EIGRP, OSPF, and Intermediate System-to-Intermediate System (IS-IS).

Distance Vector Route Selection

In addition to supporting both classful and classless routing, RIP can be characterized as a distance vector routing protocol. The periodic routing updates that most distance vector routing protocols generate are addressed only to directly connected routing devices. The addressing scheme that is most commonly used is a logical broadcast. Routers that are running a distance vector routing protocol send periodic updates even if no changes exist in the network.

In a pure distance vector environment, the periodic routing update includes a complete routing table. Upon receiving a full routing table from its neighbor, a router can verify all known routes and make changes to the local routing table based on updated information. This process is also known as "routing by rumor" because the router's understanding of the network is based on the neighboring router's perspective of the network topology. Figure 5-42 demonstrates how distance vector protocols operate.

Figure 5-42   *Distance Vector Protocols*

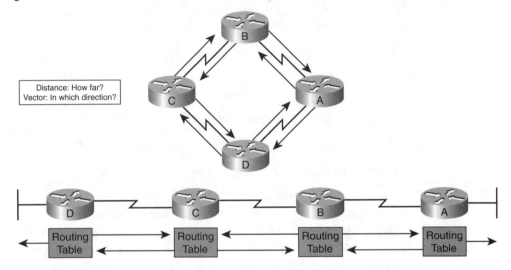

Example: Distance Vector Routing Protocols

Router B receives periodic routing updates from router A. Router B adds a distance vector metric (such as the hop count) to each route learned from router A, increasing the distance vector. Router B then passes its own routing table to its neighbor, router C. This step-by-step process occurs in all directions between directly connected neighbor routers.

Traditionally, distance vector protocols were also classful protocols. RIPv2 and EIGRP are examples of more advanced distance vector protocols that exhibit classless behavior. EIGRP also exhibits some link-state characteristics.

In Figure 5-43, the interface to each directly connected network is shown as having a distance of 0.

Figure 5-43 *Distance Vector Example*

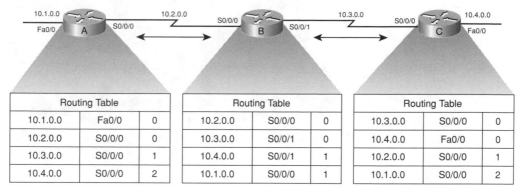

As the distance vector network discovery process continues, routers discover the best path to destination networks that are not directly connected, based on accumulated metrics from each neighbor. Neighboring routers provide information for routes that are not directly connected.

Example: Sources of Information and Discovering Routes

Router A learns about networks that are not directly connected (10.3.0.0 and 10.4.0.0) based on information that it receives from router B. Each network entry in the routing table has an accumulated distance vector to show how far away that network is in a given direction.

RIP Features

The key characteristics of RIP include the following:

■ RIP is a distance vector routing protocol.

■ Hop count is used as the metric for path selection.

■ The maximum allowable hop count is 15.

■ Routing updates are broadcast every 30 seconds by default.

■ RIP is capable of load balancing over as many as 16 equal-cost paths. (Four paths is the default.)

Because of the characteristics of RIP, it always chooses the route with the least number of hops. This is not always, however, the best route, as is shown in Figure 5-44.

Figure 5-44 *RIP Uses Hop Count*

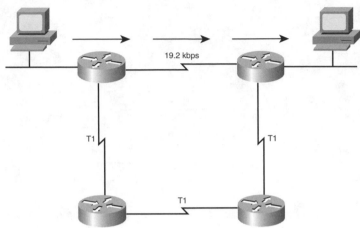

RIPv1 and RIPv2 Comparison

RIP has been around for a long time, but recently RIP version 2 was created to allow for more flexibility with addressing. Both routing protocols are still distance vector, but the versions have a number of differences. Table 5-7 outlines those differences.

Table 5-7 *RIPv1 and RIPv2 Comparison*

Features	RIPv1	RIPv2
Class support	Classful	Classless
Supports variable-length subnet mask (VLSM)	No	Yes
Sends the subnet mask along with the routing update	No	Yes
Communicates with other RIP routers using the following address type	Broadcast	Multicast
RFC definition	RFC 1058	RFCs 1721, 1722, and 2453
Supports manual route summarization	No	Yes
Supports authentication	No	Yes

Defining the maximum number of parallel paths allowed in a routing table enables RIP load balancing. With RIP, the paths must be equal-cost paths. If the maximum number of paths is set to one, load balancing is disabled.

> **NOTE**   Cisco routers support RIPv1 and RIPv2. This course focuses on configuring RIPv2 only.

Dynamic Routing Configuration Tasks

To enable a dynamic routing protocol, you must complete the following steps:

Step 1   Select a routing protocol: RIP, EIGRP, or OSPF.

Step 2   Assign IP network numbers without specifying subnet values (except for OSPF).

You must also assign network or subnet addresses and the appropriate subnet mask to the interfaces.

RIP Configuration

The **router rip** command selects RIP as the routing protocol.

The **network** command assigns a major network number that the router is directly connected to. The RIP routing process associates interface addresses with the advertised network number and begins RIP packet processing on the specified interfaces.

Figure 5-45 shows three routers to be configured to communicate their networks via RIP.

Figure 5-45   *RIP Configuration*

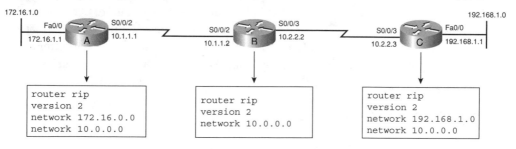

In the example, the router A configuration includes the following:

- **router rip:** Selects RIP as the routing protocol

- **version 2:** Enables RIPv2

- **network 172.16.0.0:** Specifies a directly connected network

- **network 10.0.0.0:** Specifies a directly connected network

The router A interfaces that are connected to networks 172.16.0.0 and 10.0.0.0, or their subnets, are to send and receive RIP updates. These routing updates allow the routers to learn the network topology.

Routers B and C have similar RIP configurations, but with different network numbers specified.

RIP Configuration Verification

The **show ip protocols** command displays values about routing protocols and the routing protocol timer information that is associated with the router.

In the following example, you use the **show ip protocols** command to see that router A, in Figure 5-46, is configured with RIP and sends updated routing table information every 30 seconds. (This interval is configurable.)

Figure 5-46 *Sample RIP Network*

If a router running RIP does not receive an update from another router for 180 seconds or more, it marks the routes that are served by that router as being invalid. Also, in this output you see that the hold-down timer is set to 180 seconds. As a result, an update to a route that was down and is now up stays in the hold-down (possibly down) state until 180 seconds have passed. If still no update occurs after 240 seconds (flush timer), the router removes the routing table entries from the router. The router is injecting routes for the networks that are listed following the "Routing for Networks" line. The router is receiving routes from the neighboring RIP routers that are listed following the "Routing Information Sources" line. The distance default of 120 refers to the administrative distance for an RIP route.

```
RouterA# show ip protocols
Routing Protocol is "rip"
  Sending updates every 30 seconds, next due in 6 seconds
  Invalid after 180 seconds, hold down 180, flushed after 240
  Outgoing update filter list for all interfaces is not set
  Incoming update filter list for all interfaces is not set
  Redistributing: rip
  Default version control: send version 2, receive version 2
    Interface          Send  Recv  Triggered RIP  Key-chain
    FastEthernet0/0      2     2
    Serial0/0/2          2     2
  Automatic network summarization is in effect
  Maximum path: 4
  Routing for Networks:
    10.0.0.0
    172.16.0.0
```

```
   Routing Information Sources:
     Gateway          Distance      Last Update
     10.1.1.2              120      00:00:25
   Distance: (default is 120)

RouterA#
```

Table 5-8 describes the significant fields shown in the display.

Table 5-8 *RIP Verification Fields*

Field	Description
Routing Protocol is "rip"	Specifies the routing protocol used
Sending updates every 30 seconds	Specifies the time between sending updates
next due in 6 seconds	Specifies when the next update is due to be sent
Invalid after 180 seconds	Specifies the value of the invalid parameter
hold down 180	Specifies the current value of the hold-down parameter
flushed after 240	Specifies the time (in seconds) after which the individual routing information is thrown (flushed) out
Outgoing update	Specifies whether the outgoing filtering list has been set
Incoming update	Specifies whether the incoming filtering list has been set
Redistributing	Lists the protocol that is being redistributed
Default version control	Specifies the version of RIP packets that are sent and received
Routing for Networks	Specifies the networks for which the routing process is currently injecting routes
Routing Information Sources	Lists all the routing sources that the Cisco IOS software is using to build its routing table. For each source, you see the following displayed: IP address Administrative distance Time the last update was received from this source

In addition to the **show ip protocols** command, you use the **show ip route** command to display the routes known by router A as well as the methods by which it learned the routes and the last time it received an update. This is shown in the following example.

```
RouterA# show ip route
Codes: C - connected, S - static, I - IGRP, R - RIP, M - mobile, B - BGP
       D - EIGRP, EX - EIGRP external, O - OSPF, IA - OSPF inter area
       N1 - OSPF NSSA external type 1, N2 - OSPF NSSA external type 2
       E1 - OSPF external type 1, E2 - OSPF external type 2, E - EGP
       i - IS-IS, L1 - IS-IS level-1, L2 - IS-IS level-2, * - candidate default
       U - per-user static route, o - ODR
       T - traffic engineered route

Gateway of last resort is not set


     172.16.0.0/24 is subnetted, 1 subnets
C       172.16.1.0 is directly connected, fastethernet0/0
     10.0.0.0/24 is subnetted, 2 subnets
R       10.2.2.0 [120/1] via 10.1.1.2, 00:00:07, Serial0/0/2
C       10.1.1.0 is directly connected, Serial0/0/2
R    192.168.1.0/24 [120/2] via 10.1.1.2, 00:00:07, Serial0/0/2
```

The routing table contains entries for all known networks and subnetworks, and a code that indicates how that information was learned. The output and function of key fields from the **show ip route** command are explained in Table 5-9.

Table 5-9   show ip route *Command Output*

Output	Description
R or C	Identifies the source of the route. For example, a "C" indicates that the route came from a direct connection of the route to a router interface. An "R" indicates that RIP is the protocol that determined the route.
192.168.1.0 10.2.2.0	Indicates the address of the remote network.
120/1	The first number in the brackets is the administrative distance of the information source; the second number is the metric for the route (here, 1 hop).
via 10.1.1.2	Specifies the address of the next hop router to the remote network.
00:00:07	Specifies the amount of time since the route was updated (here, 7 seconds).
Serial0/0/2	Specifies the interface through which the specified network can be reached.

If routing information is not being exchanged (that is, if the output of the **show ip route** command shows no entries that were learned from a routing protocol), use the **show running-config** or **show ip protocols** privileged EXEC commands on the router to check for a possible misconfigured routing protocol.

RIP Configuration Troubleshooting

Use the **debug ip rip** command to display RIP routing updates as they are sent and received. The **no debug all** command turns off all debugging.

```
RouterA# debug ip rip
RIP protocol debugging is on
RouterA#
00:06:24: RIP: received v1 update from 10.1.1.2 on Serial0/0/2
00:06:24:        10.2.2.0 in 1 hops
00:06:24:        192.168.1.0 in 2 hops
00:06:33: RIP: sending v1 update to 255.255.255.255 via FastEthernet0/0 (172.16.1.1)
00:06:34:        network 10.0.0.0, metric 1
00:06:34:        network 192.168.1.0, metric 3
00:06:34: RIP: sending v1 update to 255.255.255.255 via Serial0/0/2 (10.1.1.1)
00:06:34:        network 172.16.0.0, metric 1
```

The following output indicates the source address from which updates were received:

```
RIP: received v1 update from 10.1.1.2 on Serial0/0/2
```

The following output indicates the destination addresses to which updates were sent:

```
RIP: sending v1 update to 255.255.255.255 via FastEthernet0/0 (172.16.1.1)
RIP: sending v1 update to 255.255.255.255 via Serial0/0/2 (10.1.1.1)
```

Example: debug ip rip Command

The example shows that the router being debugged has received updates from one router at source address 10.1.1.2. That router sent information about two destinations in the routing table update. The router being debugged also sent updates, in both cases to broadcast address 255.255.255.255 as the destination. The number in parentheses is the source address that is encapsulated into the IP header.

Other output that you might see from the **debug ip rip** command includes entries such as the following:

```
RIP: broadcasting general request on FastEthernet0/0
RIP: broadcasting general request on FastEthernet1/0
```

Entries like these can appear at startup or when an event occurs, such as an interface transitioning or a user manually clearing the routing table. The following entry is most likely caused by a malformed packet from the transmitter:

```
RIP: bad version 128 from 160.89.80.43
```

Summary of Enabling RIP

The following summarizes the key points that were discussed in this section:

■ Routing is the process by which items get from one location to another.

■ Dynamic routing protocols determine how updates are conveyed, what knowledge is conveyed, when to convey knowledge, and how to locate recipients of the updates.

- A routing protocol that has a lower administrative value is more trustworthy than a protocol that has a higher administrative value.

- Three classes of routing protocols exist: distance vector, link-state, and balanced hybrid.

- RIP is a distance vector routing protocol that uses hop count as the matrix for route selection and broadcasts updates every 30 seconds.

- RIPv1 uses classful routing protocol; RIPv2 uses classless routing protocol. RIPv2 supports VLSM, manual route summarization, and authentication; RIPv1 does not.

- To enable a dynamic routing protocol, first a routing protocol is selected, and then IP network numbers are assigned without values being specified (except OSPF).

- The **router** command starts the routing process. The **network** command allows the routing process to determine which interfaces participate in sending and receiving the routing updates.

Chapter Summary

The following summarizes the key points that were discussed in this chapter:

- A WAN allows the transmission of data across broad geographic distances. A number of technologies are involved in the functions of WANs, including hardware devices, such as routers, communication servers, and modems, and software functions.

- A common type of WAN connection is the point-to-point connection, which is also referred to as a serial or leased-line connection because the lines are leased from a carrier (usually a telephone company) and are dedicated for use by the company leasing the lines.

- Circuit switching allows multiple sites to connect to the switched network of a carrier and communicate with each other. This technology provides a more cost-effective means of WAN connection and includes its own set of technologies, including the PSTN.

- NAT and PAT translate IP addresses within private internal networks into legal IP addresses for transport over public external networks such as the Internet without requiring a registered subnet address.

- A router can get its interface address from a DHCP server.

- Routing information takes the form of entries in a routing table, with one entry for each identified route. The routing table can be updated manually or automatically to accommodate network changes.

- Distance vector routing algorithms enable each router to send all or some portion of its routing table to its neighbors.

- Link-state routing algorithms maintain a complex database of topology information, which routers use to maintain full knowledge of distant routers.

- Balanced hybrid routing algorithms combine aspects of both distance vector and link-state routing.

- RIP is used in small, homogeneous networks.

Review Questions

Use the questions here to review what you learned in this chapter. The correct answers and solutions are found in the appendix, "Answers to Chapter Review Questions."

1. Which three statements accurately describe WANs?

    a. The companies in which WANs are implemented usually own the WANs.

    b. WANs connect devices that are separated by wide geographic areas.

    c. WANs use the services of carriers such as telephone companies, cable companies, satellite systems, and network providers.

    d. WANs generally carry limited types of data at high speeds.

    e. WANs use serial connections of various types to provide access to bandwidth.

    f. WANs connect devices that are in a small geographic area.

2. Which three communications needs do WANs address?

    a. Workers in a small business need to be able to communicate and share data with each other.

    b. Administrative staff within a school need to share schedule information with the teachers.

    c. Organizations often want to share information with other organizations across large distances.

    d. A department needs to share large data files quickly.

    e. Students need to do research for classes by accessing library indexes and publications located in other parts of their country and in other parts of the world.

    f. Workers within a branch of a large company need to share project data with each other.

3. Which two statements accurately describe the difference between LANs and WANs?

    a. A WAN transmits data faster than a LAN.

    b. A LAN transmits data faster than a WAN.

    c. Whereas a LAN connects computers, peripherals, and other devices in a single building or other small geographic area, a WAN transmits data across broad geographic distances.

    d. A company or organization usually owns the hardware and software required for WANs.

    e. LANs span large geographic areas if a LAN administrator configures them correctly.

4. At which OSI layer do WAN protocols describe how to provide electrical, mechanical, operational, and functional connections to the services of a communications service provider?

    a. Layer 1

    b. Layer 2

    c. Layer 3

    d. Layer 4

5. At which OSI layer do WAN protocols define encapsulation of data for transmission toward a remote location and the mechanisms for transferring the resulting frames?

    a. Layer 1

    b. Layer 2

    c. Layer 3

    d. Layer 4

6. Match each type of WAN device to its function.

    ____In analog lines, they convert the digital signal of the sending device into analog format for transmission over an analog line and then convert the signal back to digital form so that the receiving device can receive and process the network signal.

    ____They concentrate dial-in and dial-out user communications.

___They provide internetworking and WAN access interface ports.

___WANs use these to provide access.

a. Routers

b. Communication servers

c. Modems

d. Other networking devices

7. Match each type of connection on a router to its function.

___allow the router to connect to the LAN media through Ethernet or some other LAN technology such as Token Ring or ATM.

___are made through a WAN interface on a router to a service provider to a distant site or to the Internet.

___provide a text-based connection for the configuration and troubleshooting of the router.

a. Management ports

b. LAN interfaces

c. WAN interfaces

8. Which two statements accurately describe data-link protocols in a WAN?

a. Many data link layer protocols use a framing mechanism similar to HDLC.

b. Data link layer protocols determine the cable type to be used in the WAN.

c. ICMP is an example of a data-link protocol.

d. Data link layer protocols define how data is encapsulated for transmission to remote sites, and also the mechanisms for transferring the resulting frames to establish the connection across the communication line from the sending to the receiving device.

e. RIP is an example of a data-link protocol.

9. Match each type of multiplexing to its function.

   ___Time-division multiplexing

   ___Frequency-division multiplexing

   ___Statistical multiplexing

  a. Creates and combines multiple channels on a single line. Bandwidth is allocated for information from each data channel based on the signal frequency of the traffic.

  b. Information from each data channel is allocated bandwidth based on short, pre-assigned time slots, regardless of whether data is available to transmit.

  c. Bandwidth dynamically allocates to any data channel that transmits information.

10. Match each type of communication link to its function in a WAN.

   ___Dedicated communication links

   ___Circuit-switched communication links

   ___Packet-switched communication links

  a. Transmits data in labeled cells, frames, or packets

  b. Provides a pre-established WAN communications path from the customer premises through the provider network to a remote destination

  c. Dynamically establishes a dedicated virtual connection for voice or data between a sender and a receiver

11. Which three statements accurately describe the functions of a packet-switching WAN communication link?

  a. Packet switching is a communication method in which users have a dedicated path between source and destination endpoints.

  b. The route that the packets take to reach the destination site varies.

  c. Packet-switched networks send data packets over different routes of a shared public network owned by a carrier to reach the same destination.

  d. In a packet-switching network, each customer uses the full bandwidth on its virtual circuit.

  e. The PSTN uses packet switching.

  f. The cost of a packet-switched network to the customer is generally lower than with point-to-point leased lines.

12. Which three statements accurately describe DSL?

    a. An ISP is not required to connect enterprise users through DSL.

    b. Current DSL technologies use sophisticated coding and modulation techniques to achieve data rates of up to 10 Mbps.

    c. A subscriber can connect to a DSL enterprise network directly.

    d. DSL technology is a circuit-switched connection technology that uses existing twisted-pair telephone lines to transport high-bandwidth data, such as multimedia and video, to service subscribers.

    e. DSL technology allows use of the local-loop line for normal telephone voice connection and an always-on connection for instant network connectivity.

    f. DSL technologies place upload (upstream) and download (downstream) data transmissions at frequencies above a 4-kHz window, allowing both voice and data transmissions to occur simultaneously on a DSL service.

13. Which two of the following are types of DSL?

    a. ADSL

    b. IDSL

    c. LDSL

    d. D-lite

    e. GDSL

14. Which three statements are considerations for DSL?

    a. DSL is not backward compatible with analog voice connections.

    b. DSL service can be incrementally added in any area.

    c. Most DSL service offerings currently require the customer to be within 10,000 feet of the CO location of the provider.

    d. DSL has distance limitations.

    e. Upstream (upload) speed is usually faster than the downstream (download) speed.

    f. DSL is not universally available in all geographic locations.

15. Which three statements accurately describe cable connections?

   a. Originally, cable was a one-directional medium designed to carry broadcast digital video channels to customers (or subscribers).

   b. Some cable service providers promise data speeds of up to 20 times that of T1 leased lines.

   c. The original purpose of the Multimedia Cable Network System Partners Ltd. was to define a product and system standard capable of providing data and future services over CATV plants.

   d. Cable modems enable two-way, high-speed data transmissions using the same coaxial lines that transmit cable television.

   e. Cable modem access provides speeds superior to leased lines, with lower costs and simpler installation.

   f. Cable modems use the telephone system infrastructure, so local-loop charges apply.

16. Which three statements accurately describe the history of the Internet?

   a. The 1993 release of a graphical, easy-to-use browser called Navigator popularized the web.

   b. U.S. Department of Defense researchers devised a way to break messages into parts, sending each part separately to its destination, where reassembly of the message would take place. Today, this method of data transmission is known as a packet system.

   c. The University of Southern California installed the first computer on the packet system developed by the Department of Defense.

   d. The origin of what has become the Internet began with a need at the Department of Defense for an inventory management network that linked several of their computing facilities around the country.

   e. In 1972, ARPANET developers created the first e-mail messaging software to more easily communicate and coordinate projects.

   f. In 1984, DNS was introduced and gave the world domain suffixes (such as .edu, .com, .gov, and .org) and a series of country codes.

17. Match each NAT term with its definition.

____Static NAT

____Dynamic NAT

____Inside network

____Outside global IP address

a. A set of networks subject to translation using NAT

b. An IP address of an inside host as it appears to the outside network (the translated IP address)

c. A form of NAT that maps an unregistered IP address to a registered IP address on a one-to-one basis

d. A form of NAT that maps an unregistered IP address to a registered IP address from a group of registered IP addresses

18. When you are configuring NAT, what determines the number of simultaneous NAT translations that can be active?

a. The size of the NAT memory queue

b. The number of addresses in the NAT pool

c. The number of unused TCP port numbers

d. The ratio between the number of UDP and TCP sessions

19. When configuring NAT, the Internet interface is considered which of the following?

a. NAT local interface

b. NAT inside interface

c. NAT global interface

d. NAT outside interface

20. The output of which command displays the active translations for a NAT translation table?

    a.   **show ip nat statistics**

    b.   **show ip nat translations**

    c.   **clear ip nat translation ***

    d.   **clear ip nat translation outside**

21. You are troubleshooting a NAT connectivity problem on a Cisco router. You determine that the appropriate translation is not installed in the translation table. Which three actions should you take?

    a.   Determine if you have enough addresses in the NAT pool.

    b.   Run **debug ip nat detailed** to determine the source of the problem.

    c.   Use the **show ip route** command to verify that the selected route exists.

    d.   Verify that the router interfaces are appropriately defined as NAT inside or NAT outside.

    e.   Verify that the ACL referenced by the NAT command is permitting all necessary inside local IP addresses.

22. Which statement most accurately describes static and dynamic routes?

    a.   Dynamic routes are manually configured by a network administrator, whereas static routes are automatically learned and adjusted by a routing protocol.

    b.   Static routes are manually configured by a network administrator, whereas dynamic routes are automatically learned and adjusted by a routing protocol.

    c.   Static routes tell the router how to forward packets to networks that are not directly connected, whereas dynamic routes tell the router how to forward packets to networks that are directly connected.

    d.   Dynamic routes tell the router how to forward packets to networks that are not directly connected, whereas static routes tell the router how to forward packets to networks that are directly connected.

23. What does the command **ip route 186.157.5.0 255.255.255.0 10.1.1.3** specify?

    a.   Both 186.157.5.0 and 10.1.1.3 use a mask of 255.255.255.0.

    b.   The router should use network 186.157.5.0 to get to address 10.1.1.3.

    c. You want the router to trace a route to network 186.157.5.0 via 10.1.1.3.

    d. The router should use address 10.1.1.3 to get to devices on network 186.157.5.0.

24. Which command displays information about static route configuration on a Cisco router?

    a. **show route ip**

    b. **show ip route**

    c. **show ip route static**

    d. **show route ip static**

25. Which of the following protocols is an example of an exterior gateway protocol?

    a. RIP

    b. BGP

    c. IGRP

    d. EIGRP

26. In which situation is an administrative distance required?

    a. When static routes are defined

    b. When dynamic routing is enabled

    c. When the same route is learned via multiple routing protocols

    d. When multiple paths are available to the same destination and they are all learned via the same routing protocol

27. When a router receives a packet with a destination address that is in an unknown subnetwork of a directly attached network, what is the default behavior if the **ip classless** command is not enabled?

    a. Drop the packet

    b. Forward the packet to the default route

    c. Forward the packet to the next hop for the directly attached network

    d. Broadcast the packet through all interfaces except the one on which it was received

28. Which three statements accurately describe the characteristics and functions of circuit-switched networks?

   a. With circuit switching, a dedicated physical circuit is established, maintained, and terminated through a carrier network for each communication session.

   b. Circuit switching allows multiple sites to connect to the switched network of a carrier and communicate with each other.

   c. With circuit switching, communication links can accommodate only two sites on a single connection.

   d. ATM is an example of circuit-switching technology.

   e. ISDN is an example of a circuit-switched network.

   f. Frame Relay is an example of circuit-switching technology.

29. Which three statements describe considerations for PSTN as a communications link?

   a. Other than a modem, no additional equipment is required.

   b. The transmission rate for large data files is fast.

   c. The cost associated with the implementation of a PSTN connection link for a WAN is relatively low.

   d. The maintenance of a public telephone network is very high quality with few instances in which lines are not available.

   e. The time required to connect through the WAN is fast.

   f. No limitations on the signal rate in a PSTN connection exist.

30. Which three statements accurately describe a point-to-point communication link?

   a. A point-to-point (or serial) communication link provides a single, pre-established WAN communications path from the customer premises through a carrier network, such as a telephone company, to a remote network.

   b. Carriers usually lease point-to-point lines, which is why point-to-point lines are often called leased lines.

   c. A point-to-point (or serial) line usually connects two relatively close sites.

   d. For a point-to-point line, the carrier dedicates fixed transport capacity and facility hardware to the line of a customer.

   e. The purpose of a DSU/CSU in a point-to-point communication link is to ensure reliable delivery of data packets over the connection.

   f. Multiplexing technologies are not used in point-to-point communications.

31. Which three statements accurately describe bandwidth available for WAN connections?

    a. In North America, bandwidth is usually expressed as a "DS" number (DS0, DS1, and so forth) that technically refers to the rate and format of the signal.

    b. To get a DS1 line (also called a T1 line), 12 DS0s can be bundled to achieve a total speed of 1.544 Mbps.

    c. The bandwidth on a serial connection can be incrementally increased to accommodate the need for faster transmission.

    d. The most fundamental line speed is 1.544 Mbps (DS1), which is the bandwidth required for an uncompressed, digitized phone call.

    e. Optical networks use a bandwidth hierarchy that differs between North America and Europe. In Europe, the OC defines the bandwidth points, and in North America, the SDH defines the bandwidth points.

    f. Bandwidth refers to the rate at which data is transferred over the communication link.

32. Which three statements describe the functions of HDLC?

    a. HDLC includes support for both point-to-point and multipoint configurations.

    b. HDLC includes a method for authentication.

    c. HDLC is compatible between devices from different vendors.

    d. HDLC specifies an encapsulation method for data on synchronous serial data links using frame character and checksum.

    e. HDLC supports only multipoint configurations.

    f. The Cisco implementation of HDLC includes windowing and flow control.

33. Which three statements describe the function of PPP?

    a. The authentication phase of a PPP session is required.

    b. PPP provides router-to-router and host-to-network connections only over asynchronous circuits.

    c. PPP originally emerged as an encapsulation protocol for transporting IP traffic over point-to-point links.

    d. PPP established a standard for the management of TCP sessions.

    e. PPP provides router-to-router and host-to-network connections over synchronous and asynchronous circuits.

    f. The LCP in PPP is used for establishment, configuration, and testing the data-link connection.

34. Which three statements describe considerations for point-to-point communication links?

    a. Point-to-point communication links require minimal expertise to install and maintain.

    b. Point-to-point communication links usually offer a high quality of service.

    c. Point-to-point communication links provide permanent, dedicated capacity that is always available.

    d. With leased lines, the bandwidth of the line is usually what is needed for communication.

    e. Point-to-point communication links are available on a shared basis.

    f. In point-to-point communication links, endpoints share the interfaces on the router, which decreases equipment costs.

35. Which command enables HDLC?

    a. Router (config)# **hdlc encapsulation**

    b. Router (config)# **encapsulation hdlc**

    c. Router (config-if)# **hdlc encapsulation**

    d. Router (config-if)# **encapsulation hdlc**

36. How does the Cisco-proprietary HDLC make it possible for multiple network layer protocols to share the same serial link?

    a. It adds a new type field.

    b. It subdivides the control field.

    c. It provides for additional values in the FCS field.

    d. It includes protocol information with the data field.

37. In which Cisco command-line interface (CLI) mode do you enter the command to specify PPP authentication?

    a. User mode

    b. ROM monitor mode

c. Global configuration mode

d. Interface configuration mode

38. Which output from the **show interface** command indicates that PPP is configured properly?

   a. Encaps = PPP

   b. PPP encapsulation

   c. Encapsulation PPP

   d. Encapsulation HDLC using PPP

39. Which three statements properly describe Frame Relay?

   a. Frame Relay works at the application layer.

   b. The connection to the network edge is often a leased line, but dialup connections are available from some providers using ISDN or xDSL lines.

   c. Frame Relay implements no error or flow control.

   d. Available data rates for Frame Relay are commonly up to 10 Mbps.

   e. Most Frame Relay connections are SVCs rather than PVCs.

   f. Frame Relay provides both PVC and SVC service using shared medium-bandwidth connectivity that carries both voice and data traffic.

40. Which three statements accurately describe ATM?

   a. ATM is implemented by using virtual circuits.

   b. An ATM network comprises ATM routers, which are responsible for forwarding cells and packets.

   c. Virtual circuits provide a bidirectional communications path from one ATM endpoint to another.

   d. An ATM virtual circuit is a physical circuit-switched connection created between two computer endpoints across an ATM network.

   e. ATM can run only over coaxial cable using DS3.

   f. ATM is a type of cell-switched connection technology that is capable of transferring voice, video, and data through private and public networks.

41. How does a distance vector router learn about paths for networks that are not directly connected?

    a. From the source router

    b. From neighboring routers

    c. From the destination router

    d. A distance vector router learns only about directly connected networks

42. What does a distance vector router send to its neighboring routers as part of a periodic routing table update?

    a. The entire routing table

    b. Information about new routes

    c. Information about routes that have changed

    d. Information about routes that no longer exist

43. What is the maximum allowable hop count for RIP?

    a. 6

    b. 15

    c. 30

    d. 60

44. With RIP, load balancing is performed over multiple paths that have which characteristic?

    a. Equal cost

    b. Equal weight

    c. Equal distance

    d. Equal bandwidth

45. Which command correctly specifies RIP as the routing protocol?

    a. Router(config)#**rip**

    b. Router(config)#**router rip**

c. Router(config-router)#**rip {AS no.}**

d. Router(config-router)#**router rip {AS no.}**

46. What is the default value of the RIP hold-down timer?

a. 30 seconds

b. 60 seconds

c. 90 seconds

d. 180 seconds

This chapter includes the following sections:

- Chapter Objectives

- Discovering Neighbors on the Network

- Managing Cisco Router Startup and Configuration

- Managing Cisco Devices

- Chapter Summary

- Review Questions

CHAPTER 6

Network Environment Management

The network staff is responsible for ensuring that the underlying communications infrastructure is capable of supporting business objectives and associated applications. Network staff is also responsible for managing each device on the network according to best industry practices and for reducing device downtime. This chapter describes commands and processes to determine network operational status, gather information about remote devices, and manage Cisco IOS images, configuration files, and devices on a network.

Chapter Objectives

Upon completing this chapter, you will be able to manage devices on a network. This ability includes being able to meet these objectives:

- Use the CLI to discover neighbors on a network

- Manage router startup and configuration

- Manage Cisco IOS images, configuration files, and devices on the network

Discovering Neighbors on the Network

Most network devices, by definition, do not work in isolation. A Cisco device frequently has other Cisco devices as neighbors on the network, and being able to obtain information about those other devices is important to assist with network design decisions, troubleshooting, and completing equipment changes. The following sections describe how to gather information about the Cisco devices in a network and use that information to create a map of the network environment.

Cisco Discovery Protocol

The Cisco Discovery Protocol (CDP) is an information-gathering tool used by network administrators to obtain information about directly connected Cisco devices.

CDP is a proprietary tool that enables you to access a summary of protocol and address information about other Cisco devices that are directly connected to the Cisco device initiating the CDP commands.

CDP runs over the data link layer connecting the physical media to the upper-layer protocols (ULP). Because CDP operates at the data link layer, two or more Cisco network devices, such as routers that support different network layer protocols (for example, IP and Novell IPX), can learn about each other.

Physical media connecting CDP devices must support Subnetwork Access Protocol (SNAP) encapsulation. These can include all LANs, Frame Relay, other WANs, and ATM networks. This is illustrated by Figure 6-1.

Figure 6-1 *CDP Runs at Layer 2*

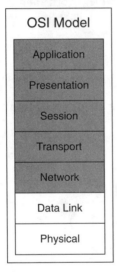

OSI Model
Application
Presentation
Session
Transport
Network
Data Link
Physical

Upper-Layer Entry Addresses	TCP/IP	Novell IPX	AppleTalk	Others
Cisco Proprietary Data-Link Protocol	CDP discovers and displays information about directly connected Cisco devices.			
Media Supporting SNAP	LANs	Frame Relay	ATM	Others

When a Cisco device boots, CDP starts by default, and automatically discovers neighboring Cisco devices running CDP, regardless of which protocol suite is running.

Information Obtained with CDP

Figure 6-2 displays an example of how CDP exchanges information with its directly connected neighbors. You can display the results of this information exchange on a console connected to a network device configured to run CDP on its interfaces.

Figure 6-2 *CDP Works Between Neighbor Devices*

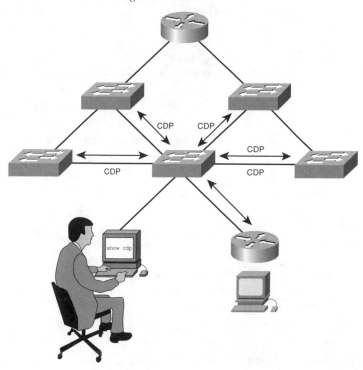

CDP provides the following information about each neighboring device:

- **Device identifiers:** For example, the configured host name of the switch

- **Address list:** Up to one network layer address for each protocol supported

- **Port identifier:** The name of the local port and remote port, in the form of an ASCII character string such as ethernet0

- **Capabilities list:** Supported features; for example, the device acting as a source-route bridge and also as a router

- **Platform:** The hardware platform of the device; for example, Cisco 7200 series router

Notice that the upper router in Figure 6-2 is not connected directly to the console of the administrator. To obtain CDP information about this upper router from the console of the administrator, network staff could use Telnet to connect to a switch connected directly to this target device.

CDP version 2 is the most recent release of the protocol and provides more intelligent device-tracking features. These features include a reporting mechanism that allows more rapid error tracking, thereby reducing costly downtime. Reported error messages can be sent to the console or to a logging server.

Implementation of Cisco Discovery Protocol

You can enable or disable CDP on a router as a whole (global) or on a port-by-port (interface) basis.

You can view CDP information with the **show cdp** command. CDP has several keywords that enable access to different types of information and different levels of detail. It is designed and implemented as a very simple, low-overhead protocol. A CDP packet can be as small as 80 octets, mostly made up of the ASCII strings that represent information. Example 6-1 shows the different **show cdp** options.

Example 6-1   **show cdp** *Options*

```
RouterA# show cdp ?

  entry      Information for specific neighbor entry
  interface  CDP interface status and configuration
  neighbors  CDP neighbor entries
  traffic    CDP statistics
```

CDP functionality is enabled by default on all interfaces (except for Frame Relay multipoint subinterfaces), but can be disabled at the device level. However, some interfaces, such as ATM interfaces, do not support CDP. To prevent other CDP-capable devices from accessing information about a specific device, the **no cdp run** global configuration command is used. To disable CDP on an interface, the **no cdp enable** command is used. To enable CDP on an interface, the **cdp enable** interface configuration command is used. Example 6-2 illustrates how to disable CDP globally and on a per-interface basis.

Example 6-2 *Disabling CDP on an Interface*

```
RouterA(config)# no cdp run

! Disable CDP Globally
RouterA(config)#interface serial0/0/0
RouterA(config-if)#no cdp enable
! Disable CDP on just this interface
```

Using the show cdp neighbors Command

The **show cdp neighbors** command displays information about CDP neighbors. Example 6-3 shows the CDP output for RouterA shown in Figure 6-3.

Figure 6-3 *CDP Neighbor Information*

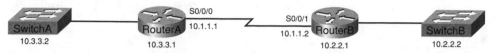

Example 6-3 *CDP Output for RouterA*

```
RouterA# show cdp neighbors

Capability Codes: R - Router, T - Trans Bridge, B - Source Route Bridge
                  S - Switch, H - Host, I - IGMP, r - Repeater

Device ID    Local Intrfce    Holdtme    Capability    Platform    Port ID
SwitchA        fa0/0            122          S I                    WS-C2960-fa0/2
RouterB        s0/0/0           177         R S I        2811           s0/0/1
```

For each CDP neighbor, the following information is displayed:

- Device ID

- Local interface

- Holdtime value, in seconds

- Device capability code

- Hardware platform

- Remote port ID

The holdtime value indicates how long the receiving device should hold the CDP packet before discarding it.

The format of the **show cdp neighbors** output varies between different types of devices, but the available information is generally consistent across devices.

The **show cdp neighbors** command can be used on a Cisco Catalyst switch to display the CDP updates received on the local interfaces. Note that on a switch, the local interface is referred to as the local port.

If you add the *detail* argument to the **show cdp neighbors** command, the resulting output includes additional information, such as the network layer addresses of neighboring devices. The output from the **show cdp neighbors detail** command is identical to that produced by the **show cdp entry *** command.

Monitoring and Maintaining Cisco Discovery Protocol

The **show cdp entry**, **show cdp traffic**, and **show cdp interface** commands display detailed CDP information.

The **show cdp entry** command displays detailed information about neighboring devices. This output is shown in Example 6-4 for RouterA in Figure 6-3.

Example 6-4   *Output of the* **show cdp entry** *Command*

```
Device ID: RouterB
Entry address(es):
  IP address: 10.1.1.2
Platform: Cisco 2811,  Capabilities: Router Switch IGMP
Interface: Serial0/0/0,  Port ID (outgoing port): Serial0/0/1
Holdtime : 155 sec


Version :
Cisco IOS Software, 2800 Software (C2800NM-ADVIPSERVICESK9-M), Version 12.4(12), RELEASE
SOFTWARE (fc1)
Technical Support: http://www.cisco.com/techsupport
Copyright (c) 1986-2006 by Cisco Systems, Inc.
Compiled Fri 17-Nov-06 12:02 by prod_rel_team
```

To display information about a specific neighbor, the command string must include the IP address or device ID of the neighbor. The asterisk (*) is used to display information about all neighbors. The **show cdp entry** command outputs the following:

■   Neighbor device ID

■   Layer 3 protocol information (for example, IP addresses)

■   Device platform

■   Device capabilities

■   Local interface type and outgoing remote port ID

■   Holdtime value, in seconds

■   Cisco IOS Software type and release

The output from this command includes all the Layer 3 addresses of the neighbor device interfaces (up to one Layer 3 address per protocol).

The **show cdp traffic** command displays information about interface traffic. It shows the number of CDP packets sent and received. Example 6-5 shows the output from the **show cdp traffic** command from RouterA in Figure 6-3.

Example 6-5 *Output of the* **show cdp traffic** *Command*

```
RouterA# show cdp traffic

CDP counters :
        Total packets output: 8680, Input: 8678
        Hdr syntax: 0, Chksum error: 0, Encaps failed: 5
        No memory: 0, Invalid packet: 0, Fragmented: 0
        CDP version 1 advertisements output: 0, Input: 0
        CDP version 2 advertisements output: 8680, Input: 8678

RouterA# show cdp interface s0/0/0

Serial0/0/0 is up, line protocol is up
  Encapsulation PPP
  Sending CDP packets every 60 seconds
  Holdtime is 180 seconds
```

This output also displays the number of errors for the following error conditions:

- Syntax error

- Checksum error

- Failed encapsulations

- Out of memory

- Invalid packets

- Fragmented packets

- Number of CDP version 1 packets sent

- Number of CDP version 2 packets sent

The **show cdp interface** command displays the following interface status and configuration information about the local device:

- Line and data-link status of the interface

- Encapsulation type for the interface

- Frequency at which CDP packets are sent (default is 60 seconds)

- Holdtime value, in seconds (default is 180 seconds)

CDP is limited to gathering information about directly connected Cisco neighbors. Other tools, such as Telnet, are available for gathering information about remote devices that are not directly connected.

Creating a Network Map of the Environment

After all the devices on the internetwork have been discovered, it is important to document the network so that it can be readily supported.

Topology documentation is used to validate design guidelines and to aid future design, change, and troubleshooting. Topology documentation should include both logical and physical documentation for the following components:

- Connectivity

- Addressing

- Media types

- Devices

- Rack layouts

- Card assignments

- Cable routing

- Cable identification

- Termination points

- Power information

- Circuit identification information

Figure 6-4 shows an example of the information that can be gathered using CDP.

Figure 6-4   *Documentation Using CDP*

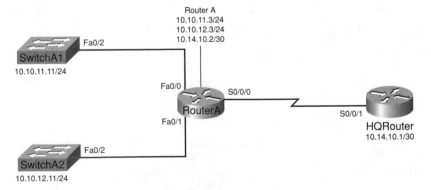

Maintaining accurate network topology documentation is the key to successful configuration management. To create an environment where topology documentation maintenance can occur, the information must be available for updates. Cisco strongly recommends updating topology documentation whenever a network change occurs.

Summary of Discovering Neighbors on the Network

The following list summarizes the key points that were discussed in the previous sections:

- The CDP is an information-gathering tool used by network administrators to get information about directly connected devices.

- CDP exchanges hardware and software device information with its directly connected CDP neighbors.

- CDP on a router can be enabled or disabled as a whole or on a port-by-port basis.

- The **show cdp neighbors** command displays information about the CDP neighbors of a router.

- The **show cdp entry**, **show cdp traffic**, and **show cdp interface** commands display detailed CDP information on a Cisco device.

- Using the information obtained from the **show cdp** commands output, a network topology map can be created to aid troubleshooting.

Managing Cisco Router Startup and Configuration

When a Cisco router boots, it performs a series of steps in a particular order. At several points during the process, the router makes a decision about the next step to take. Knowledge of the boot sequence can be of great help when troubleshooting a Cisco router and also when adjusting its configuration. The following sections describe each step in the router boot sequence.

Stages of the Router Power-On Boot Sequence

When a router boots, it performs a series of steps: performing tests, finding and loading the Cisco IOS Software, finding and loading configurations, and finally, running the Cisco IOS Software.

The sequence of events that occurs during the power-up (boot) process of a router is important. Knowledge of this sequence aids in accomplishing operational tasks and troubleshooting router problems.

When power is initially applied to a router, the events occur in the following order:

Step 1 Perform power-on self test (POST). This is a series of hardware tests that verifies whether all components of the Cisco router are functional. During this test, the router also determines what hardware is present. POST executes from microcode resident in the system ROM.

Step 2 Load and run bootstrap code. Bootstrap code is used to perform subsequent events, such as locating the Cisco IOS Software, loading it, and then running it. When the Cisco IOS Software is loaded and running, the bootstrap code is not used until the next time the router is reloaded or power cycled.

Step 3 The bootstrap code determines where the Cisco IOS Software to be run is located. Normally, the Cisco IOS Software image is located in the flash memory. The configuration register and configuration file determine where the Cisco IOS Software images are located and which image file to use.

Step 4 When the bootstrap code has found the proper image, it then loads that image into RAM and starts the Cisco IOS Software. Some routers do not load the Cisco IOS Software image into RAM, but execute it directly from flash memory.

Step 5 The default is to look in NVRAM for a valid saved configuration file, called startup-config.

Step 6 The desired configuration for the router is loaded and executed. If no configuration exists, the router will enter the setup utility or attempt an AutoInstall to look for a configuration file from a TFTP server.

Internal Router Components

The major internal components of a Cisco router include the interfaces, RAM, ROM, flash memory, NVRAM, and the configuration register.

The major components of a router are shown in Figure 6-5.

Figure 6-5 *Router Components*

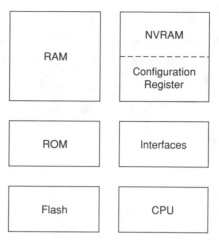

Most of these components are hardware, as follows:

- **CPU:** This is the processor that runs the Cisco IOS and features like route processing.

- **RAM:** This read/write memory contains the software and data structures that enable the router to function. The principal software running in RAM is the Cisco IOS Software image and the running configuration. The RAM also contains the routing tables and packet buffers. RAM is volatile; its memory contents will be lost when power is turned off.

- **ROM:** This type of memory contains microcode for basic functions to start and maintain the router, including bootstrap and POST. The ROM contains the ROM Monitor (ROMMON) used for router disaster recovery functions, such as password recovery. The ROM also contains a subset of Cisco IOS, which is used for Cisco IOS image file recovery, such as when the Cisco IOS image file in flash memory is erased. ROM is nonvolatile; it maintains the memory contents even when the power is off.

- **Flash memory:** Flash read/write memory is primarily used to store the Cisco IOS Software image. Some routers run the Cisco IOS Software image directly from flash memory and do not need to transfer it to RAM. Some routers maintain a subset of the Cisco IOS Software in flash memory rather than in ROM. Flash memory is nonvolatile; it maintains the memory contents even when the power is off.

- **NVRAM:** This read/write memory is mainly used to store the saved configuration file, called the startup-config file. NVRAM uses a built-in battery to maintain the data when power is removed from the router.

- **Configuration register:** The configuration register is used to control how the router boots. The configuration register is part of the NVRAM.

- **Interfaces:** Interfaces are the physical connections to the external world for the router and include the following types, among others:

  — Ethernet, Fast Ethernet, and Gigabit Ethernet

  — Asynchronous and synchronous serial

  — Token Ring

  — FDDI

  — ATM

  — Console and auxiliary ports

As shown in Figure 6-6, three major areas of microcode are generally contained in ROM.

Figure 6-6 *ROM Functions*

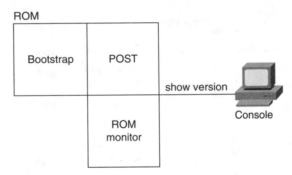

The functions of these areas are as follows:

- **Bootstrap code:** The bootstrap code is used to bring the router up during initialization. It reads the configuration register to determine how to boot, and then, if instructed to do so, loads the Cisco IOS Software.

- **POST:** POST is the microcode used to test the basic functionality of the router hardware and determine which components are present.

- **ROMMON:** This is a low-level operating system normally used for manufacturing, testing, troubleshooting, and password recovery. In ROMMON mode, the router has no routing or IP capabilities.

NOTE Depending on the specific Cisco router platform, the components listed can be stored in flash memory or in bootstrap memory to allow a field upgrade to later versions.

How a Device Locates and Loads Cisco IOS Image and Configuration Files

When a Cisco router boots, it searches for the Cisco IOS image in a specific sequence: the location specified in the configuration register, flash memory, a TFTP server, and ROM.

The bootstrap code is responsible for locating the Cisco IOS Software. It searches for the image according to the following sequence:

1. The bootstrap code checks the boot field of the configuration register. The boot field is the lower 4 bits of the configuration register and is used to specify how the router boots. These bits can point to flash memory for the Cisco IOS image, the startup-config file (if one exists) for commands that tell the router how to boot, or a remote TFTP server. Or, these bits can specify that no Cisco IOS image is to be loaded and to just start the Cisco IOS subset image in ROM. The configuration register bits perform other functions as well, such as selecting the console baud rate and determining whether to use the saved configuration file (startup-config) in NVRAM.

    For example, a configuration register value of 0x2102 (the 0x indicates that the digits that follow are in hexadecimal notation) has a boot field value of 0x2 (the rightmost digit in the register value is 2 and represents the lower 4 bits of the register).

    If the boot field value of the configuration register is from 0x2 to 0xF, the bootstrap code parses the startup-config file in NVRAM for the **boot system** commands that specify the name and location of the Cisco IOS Software image to load. Several **boot system** commands can be entered in sequence to provide a fault-tolerant boot plan.

    The **boot system** command is a global configuration command that allows you to specify the source for the Cisco IOS Software image to load. Some of the syntax options available include the following:

    — **boot system flash** [*filename*]

    — **boot system tftp** [*filename*][*server-address*]

    — **boot system rom**

2. If there are no **boot system** commands in the configuration, the router defaults to loading the first valid Cisco IOS image in flash memory and running it.

3. If no valid Cisco IOS image is found in flash memory, the router attempts to boot from a network TFTP server using the boot field value as part of the Cisco IOS image file name.

NOTE   Booting from a network TFTP server is a seldom-used method of loading a Cisco IOS Software image.

Not every router has a boot helper image, so Steps 4 and 5 do not always follow.

4. By default, if booting from a network TFTP server fails after five tries, the router will boot the boot helper image (the Cisco IOS subset) from ROM. The user can also set bit 13 of the configuration register to 0 to tell the router to try to boot from a TFTP server continuously without booting the Cisco IOS subset from ROM after five unsuccessful tries.

5. If there is no boot helper image or if it is corrupted, the router will boot the ROMMON from ROM.

When the router locates a valid Cisco IOS image file in flash memory, the Cisco IOS image is normally loaded into RAM to run, as shown in Figure 6-7. Some routers, including the Cisco 2500 series routers, do not have sufficient RAM to hold the Cisco IOS image and, therefore, run the Cisco IOS image directly from flash memory.

Figure 6-7   *IOS Is Loaded into RAM*

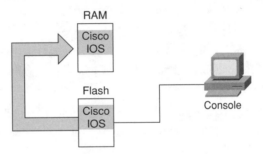

If the image is to be loaded from flash memory into RAM, it must first be decompressed. After the file is decompressed into RAM, it is started. Cisco IOS images that are run from flash memory are not compressed.

After the Cisco IOS Software image is loaded and started, the router must be configured to be useful. If there is an existing saved configuration file (startup-config) in NVRAM, it is executed. If there is no saved configuration file in NVRAM, the router either begins AutoInstall or enters the setup utility.

AutoInstall attempts to download a configuration from a TFTP server. AutoInstall requires a connection to the network and a previously configured TFTP server to respond to the download request.

The setup utility prompts a user at the console for specific configuration information to create a basic initial configuration on the router. Figure 6-8 shows how setup will copy the configuration file into running memory as well as NVRAM.

Figure 6-8 *Startup Copies Config File to RAM and NVRAM*

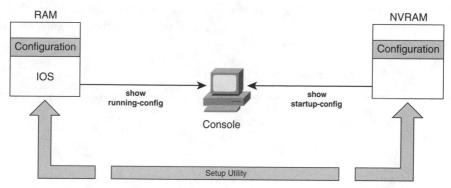

The **show running-config** and **show startup-config** commands are among the most common Cisco IOS Software EXEC commands, because they enable you to see the current running configuration in RAM on the router or the startup configuration commands in the startup-config file in NVRAM that the router will use on the next restart.

If the words "Current configuration" are displayed, the active running configuration from RAM is being displayed.

If there is a message at the top indicating how much nonvolatile memory is being used, the startup configuration file from NVRAM is being displayed. This is shown in Figure 6-9.

Figure 6-9 *Running Versus Startup Configuration*

In RAM

```
RouterX#show running-config
Building configuration...

Current configuration:
!
Version 12.2
!
    -- More --
```

In NVRAM

```
RouterX#show startup-config
Using 1359 out of 32762 bytes
!
Version 12.2
!
    -- More --
```

Configuration Register

The configuration register includes information specifying where to locate the Cisco IOS Software image. You can examine the register with a **show** command, and you can change the register value with the **config-register** global configuration command. This topic describes how to display and change the boot information in the configuration register.

Before altering the configuration register, you should determine how the router is currently loading the software image. The **show version** command will obtain the current configuration register value. The last line of the display contains the configuration register value. This is shown in Example 6-6.

Example 6-6   *Output of the* **show version** *Command*

```
Cisco IOS Software, 2800 Software (C2800NM-IPBASE-M), Version 12.4(5a), RELEASE SOFTWARE
(fc3)
Technical Support: http://www.cisco.com/techsupport
Copyright (c) 1986-2006 by Cisco Systems, Inc.
Compiled Sat 14-Jan-06 03:19 by alnguyen

ROM: System Bootstrap, Version 12.4(1r) [hqluong 1r], RELEASE SOFTWARE (fc1)

RouterX uptime is 1 week, 5 days, 21 hours, 30 minutes
System returned to ROM by reload at 23:04:40 UTC Tue Mar 13 2007
System image file is "flash:c2800nm-ipbase-mz.124-5a.bin"

Cisco 2811 (revision 53.51) with 251904K/10240K bytes of memory.
Processor board ID FTX1013A1DJ
2 FastEthernet interfaces
2 Serial(sync/async) interfaces
DRAM configuration is 64 bits wide with parity enabled.
239K bytes of non-volatile configuration memory.
62720K bytes of ATA CompactFlash (Read/Write)

Configuration register is 0x2102
```

You can change the default configuration register setting with the **config-register** global configuration command, as shown in Example 6-7.

Example 6-7   **config-register** *Command*

```
RouterA# configure terminal
RouterA(config)# config-register 0x2100
RouterA(config)# end

RouterA#
```

The configuration register is a 16-bit register. The lowest 4 bits of the configuration register (bits 3, 2, 1, and 0) form the boot field. A hexadecimal number is used as the argument to set the value of the configuration register. The default value of the configuration register is 0x2102. The boot field would be the last digit in the hexadecimal register. The setting of this field determines how the device boots. This is illustrated in Table 6-1.

Table 6-1 *Configuration Register Values*

Configuration Register Boot Field Value	Meaning
0x0	Use ROMMON mode (manually boot using the **boot** command)
0x1	Automatically boot from ROM (provides Cisco IOS Software subset)
0x2 to 0xF	Examine NVRAM for boot system commands (0x2 default if router has flash)

The guidelines for changing the boot field are as follows:

- The boot field is set to 0 to enter ROMMON mode automatically. This value sets the boot field bits to 0-0-0-0. In the ROMMON mode, the router displays the ">" or "rommon>" prompt, depending on the router processor type. From the ROMMON mode, you can use the **boot** command to manually boot the router.

- The boot field is set to 1 to configure the system to boot the Cisco IOS subset automatically from ROM. This value sets the boot field bits to 0-0-0-1. The router displays the Router(boot)> prompt in this mode.

- The boot field is set to any value from 0x2 to 0xF to configure the system to use the **boot system** commands in the startup-config file in NVRAM. The default is 0x2. These values set the boot field bits to 0-0-1-0 through 1-1-1-1.

The **show version** command is used to verify changes in the configuration register setting. The new configuration register value takes effect when the router reloads.

In Example 6-6, the **show version** command indicates that the current configuration register setting of 0x2104 will be used during the next router reload.

> **NOTE** When using the **config-register** command, all 16 bits of the configuration register are set. Be careful to modify only the bits that you are trying to change, for example, the boot field, and leave the other bits as they are. Remember that the other configuration register bits perform functions that include selecting the console baud rate and determining whether to use the saved configuration in NVRAM.

The **show flash** command displays the contents of flash memory, including the image file names and sizes. This is illustrated in Example 6-8.

Example 6-8 **show flash** *Command*

```
RouterX# sh flash

-#- --length-- -----date/time------ path
1      14951648 Feb 22 2007 21:38:56 +00:00 c2800nm-ipbase-mz.124-5a.bin
2          1823 Dec 14 2006 08:24:54 +00:00 sdmconfig-2811.cfg
3       4734464 Dec 14 2006 08:25:24 +00:00 sdm.tar
4        833024 Dec 14 2006 08:25:38 +00:00 es.tar
5       1052160 Dec 14 2006 08:25:54 +00:00 common.tar
6          1038 Dec 14 2006 08:26:08 +00:00 home.shtml
7        102400 Dec 14 2006 08:26:22 +00:00 home.tar
8        491213 Dec 14 2006 08:26:40 +00:00 128MB.sdf

41836544 bytes available (22179840 bytes used)
```

In the example, the bottom line tells how much flash memory is available. Some of it might already be in use. Flash memory is always read-only.

Summary of Managing Cisco Router Startup and Configuration

The following list summarizes the key points that were discussed in the previous sections:

- When a router boots, it performs tests, finds and loads software, finds and loads configurations, and finally runs the software.

- The major internal components of a router include the CPU, RAM, ROM, flash memory, NVRAM, and the configuration register.

- When a router boots, it searches for the Cisco IOS Software image in a specific sequence: location specified in the configuration register, flash memory, a TFTP server, and ROM.

- The configuration register includes boot information specifying where to locate the Cisco IOS Software image. The register can be examined with a **show version** command, and you can change the register value with the **config-register** global configuration command.

Managing Cisco Devices

Carefully managing Cisco IOS images and configuration files reduces device downtime and maintains best practices. Cisco IOS image files contain the Cisco IOS Software required for a Cisco device to operate, and the device configuration files contain a set of user-defined configuration commands that customize the functionality of a Cisco device.

Cisco IOS File System and Devices

The Cisco IOS File System (Cisco IFS) feature provides a single interface to all the file systems that a router uses. This topic describes the file systems used by a Cisco router. Figure 6-10 shows the various file systems for an IOS device.

Figure 6-10   *IOS File System Devices*

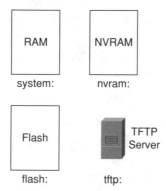

The Cisco IFS feature provides a single interface to all the file systems that a Cisco router uses, including the following:

- Flash memory file systems

- Network file systems: TFTP, Remote Copy Protocol (RCP), and FTP (This lesson only discusses commands used to transfer Cisco IOS images and configuration files to and from a TFTP server.)

- Any other endpoint for reading or writing data (such as NVRAM, the running configuration in RAM, and so on)

One key feature of the Cisco IFS is the use of the URL convention to specify files on network devices and the network.

Table 6-2 contains some commonly used URL prefixes for Cisco file devices.

Table 6-2   *Common URLs for IOS File Devices*

Prefix	Description
bootflash:	Bootflash memory.
flash:	Flash memory. This prefix is available on all platforms. For platforms that do not have a device named flash, the prefix flash: is aliased to slot0. Therefore, the prefix flash: can be used to refer to the main flash memory storage area on all platforms.

continues

Table 6-2 *Common URLs for IOS File Devices (Continued)*

Prefix	Description
flh:	Flash load helper log files.
ftp:	FTP network server.
nvram:	NVRAM.
rcp:	The RCP network server.
slot0:	The first Personal Computer Memory Card International Association (PCMCIA) flash memory card.
slot1:	The second PCMCIA flash memory card.
system:	Contains the system memory, including the current running configuration.
tftp:	TFTP network server.

With Cisco IOS Release 12.0, commands used to copy and transfer configuration and system files changed to include the Cisco IFS specifications.

Table 6-3 contains pre–Cisco IOS Release 12.0 and newer Cisco IOS Release 12.x commands used for configuration file movement and management. Notice that the Cisco IOS Release 12.x commands identify the location of the configuration files following the colon as [[[//*location*]/*directory*]/*filename*], as applicable.

Table 6-3 *IFS Management Files*

Pre–Cisco IOS Release 12.0 Commands	Cisco IOS Release 12.x Commands
configure network (before Cisco IOS Release 10.3) **copy rcp running-config** **copy tftp running-config**	**copy ftp: system:running-config** **copy rcp: system:running-config** **copy tftp: system:running-config**
configure overwrite-network (before Cisco IOS Release 10.3) **copy rcp startup-config** **copy tftp startup-config**	**copy ftp: nvram:startup-config** **copy rcp: nvram:startup-config** **copy tftp: nvram:startup-config**
show configuration (before Cisco IOS Release 10.3) **show startup-config**	**more nvram:startup-config**
write erase (before Cisco IOS Release 10.3) **erase startup-config**	**erase nvram:**

Table 6-3 *IFS Management Files (Continued)*

Pre–Cisco IOS Release 12.0 Commands	Cisco IOS Release 12.x Commands
write memory (before Cisco IOS Release 10.3) **copy running-config startup-config**	**copy system:running-config nvram:startup-config**
write network (before Cisco IOS Release 10.3) **copy running-config rcp** **copy running-config tftp**	**copy system:running-config ftp:** **copy system:running-config rcp:** **copy system:running-config tftp:**
write terminal (before Cisco IOS Release 10.3) **show running-config**	**more system:running-config**

Managing Cisco IOS Images

As any network grows, storage of Cisco IOS images and configuration files on a central TFTP server enables control of the number and revision level of Cisco IOS images and configuration files that must be maintained.

Production internetworks usually span wide areas and contain multiple routers. For any network, it is always prudent to retain a backup copy of the Cisco IOS Software image in case the system image in the router becomes corrupted or accidentally erased.

Widely distributed routers also need a source or backup location for Cisco IOS Software images. Using a network TFTP server allows image and configuration uploads and downloads over the network. The network TFTP server can be another router, a workstation, or a host system. Figure 6-11 illustrates copying files to and from a network server.

Figure 6-11 *Copying IOS Images to a Network Server*

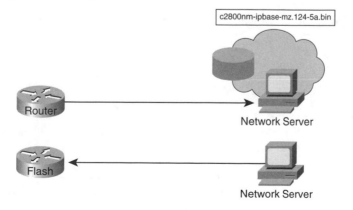

Before copying the Cisco IOS image software from flash memory in the router to the network TFTP server, you should follow these steps:

Step 1   Make sure that you have access to the network TFTP server. You can ping the TFTP server to test connectivity.

Step 2   Verify that the TFTP server has sufficient disk space to accommodate the Cisco IOS Software image. Use the **show flash** command on the router to determine the size of the Cisco IOS image file.

Step 3   Check the filename requirements on the TFTP server. This can differ, depending on whether the server is running Microsoft Windows, UNIX, or another operating system.

Step 4   Create the destination file to receive the upload, if required. This step depends on the network server operating system.

The **show flash** command, shown previously, is an important tool to gather information about the router memory and image file. The **show flash** command can determine the following:

- Total amount of flash memory on the router

- Amount of flash memory available

- Name of all the files stored in the flash memory

The name for the Cisco IOS image file contains multiple parts, each with a specific meaning. For example, the filename c2800nm-ipbase-mz.124-5a.bin, shown earlier in Figure 6-11, contains the following information:

- The first part of the image name identifies the platform on which the image runs. In this example, the platform is c2800.

- The second part of the name specifies where the image runs and whether the file is compressed. In this example, mz indicates that the file runs from RAM and is compressed.

- The third part of the name indicates the version number. In this example, the version number is 124-5a.

- The final part of the name is the file extension. The .bin extension indicates that this is a binary executable file.

The Cisco IOS Software naming conventions, field meaning, image content, and other details are subject to change. You can contact the Cisco sales representative or distribution channel for updates, or refer to Cisco.com.

A software backup image file is created by copying the image file from a router to a network TFTP server. To copy the current system image file from the router to the network TFTP server, use the following command in privileged EXEC mode:

```
Router# copy flash tftp:
```

The **copy flash tftp** command requires you to enter the IP address of the remote host and the name of the source and destination system image files. Example 6-9 shows the output of this command.

Example 6-9 *Output of the* **copy flash tftp** *Command*

```
RouterA# copy flash tftp:

Source filename []? c2800nm-ipbase-mz.124-5a.binAddress or name of remote host []?
10.1.1.1
Destination filename [c2800nm-ipbase-mz.124-5a.bin]
!!!!!!!!!!!!!!!!!!!!!!!!!!!!!!!!!!!!!!!!!!!!!!!!!!!!!!!!!!!!!!!!!!!!!<output omitted>
12094416 bytes copied in 98.858 secs (122341 bytes/sec)
RouterA#
```

The exclamation points (!!!) indicate the copying process from the flash memory of the router to the TFTP server. Each exclamation point means that one User Datagram Protocol (UDP) segment has successfully transferred.

Before updating the flash memory with a new Cisco IOS image, you should back up the current Cisco IOS image to a TFTP server. Backing up provides a fallback in case there is only sufficient space to store one image in the flash memory.

Upgrading a system to a newer software version requires a different system image file to be loaded on the router. Use the following command to download the new image from the network TFTP server:

```
Router# copy tftp flash:
```

The command prompts you for the IP address of the remote host and the name of the source and destination system image file. Enter the appropriate filename of the update image just as it appears on the server. Example 6-10 shows the output of this command.

Example 6-10 *Output of the* **copy tftp flash** *Command*

```
RouterA# copy tftp flash:

Address or name of remote host [10.1.1.1]?
Source filename []? c2800nm-ipbase-mz.124-5a.bin
Destination filename [c2800nm-ipbase-mz.124-5a.bin]
Accessing tftp://10.1.1.1/c2600-js-mz.122-21a.bin...
```

continues

Example 6-10   *Output of the* **copy tftp flash** *Command (Continued)*

```
Erase flash: before copying? [confirm]
Erasing the flash filesystem will remove all files! Continue? [confirm]
Erasing device... eeeeeeeeee (output omitted) ...erased
Erase of flash: complete
Loading c2800nm-ipbase-mz.124-5a.bin from  10.1.1.1 (via Ethernet0/0): !!!!!!!!!!!!!!!!
(output omited)
[OK - 12094416 bytes]
Verifying checksum...  OK (0x45E2)
12094416 bytes copied in 120.465 secs (100398 bytes/sec)
RouterA#
```

After these entries are confirmed, the erase flash prompt appears. Erasing flash memory makes room for the new image. Erase flash memory if there is not sufficient flash memory for more than one Cisco IOS image. If no free flash memory is available, the erase routine is required before new files can be copied. The system informs you of these conditions and prompts for a response.

> **NOTE**   Make sure that the Cisco IOS image loaded is appropriate for the router platform. If the wrong Cisco IOS image is loaded, the router could be made unbootable, requiring ROMMON intervention.

Managing Device Configuration Files

Device configuration files contain a set of user-defined configuration commands that customize the functionality of a Cisco device.

Configuration files contain the Cisco IOS Software commands used to customize the functionality of a Cisco routing device, such as a router, access server, switch, and so on. Commands are parsed, that is, translated and executed, by the Cisco IOS Software when you boot the system from the startup configuration file or when you enter commands at the command-line interface (CLI) in configuration mode.

Configuration files are stored in the following locations:

- The running configuration is stored in RAM.

- The startup configuration is stored in NVRAM.

You can copy configuration files from the router to a file server using FTP, RCP, or TFTP. For example, you can copy configuration files to back up a current configuration file to a server before changing its contents, thereby allowing the original configuration file to be restored from the server. The protocol used depends on which type of server is used. Figure 6-12 shows the various locations in which a configuration file can be stored.

Figure 6-12 *Configuration File Locations*

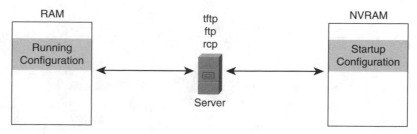

You can copy configuration files from a TFTP, RCP, or FTP server to the running configuration in RAM or to the startup-config file in NVRAM of the router for one of the following reasons:

- To restore a backed-up configuration file.

- To use the configuration file for another router. For example, you might add another router to the network and want it to have a similar configuration as the original router. By copying the file to the network server and making the changes to reflect the configuration requirements of the new router, you can save time by not re-creating the entire file.

- To load the same configuration commands onto all the routers in the network so that all the routers have similar configurations.

Cisco IOS copy Command

The Cisco IOS Software **copy** command is used to move configurations from one component or device to another, such as RAM, NVRAM, or a TFTP server.

In addition to using AutoInstall, the setup utility, or the CLI to load or create a configuration, there are several other sources for configurations that you can use. Figure 6-13 shows the variety of **copy** commands that can be used with the configuration file.

You can use the Cisco IOS Software **copy** command to move configurations from one component or device to another. The **copy** command indicates the source (from where the configuration is to be copied), followed by the destination (to where the configuration is to be copied). For example, in the **copy running-config tftp** command, the running configuration in RAM is copied to a TFTP server.

Use the **copy running-config startup-config** command after a configuration change is made in RAM and must be saved to the startup-config file in NVRAM. Similarly, copy the startup-config file in NVRAM back into RAM with the **copy startup running** command. Notice that you can abbreviate the commands.

Figure 6-13   *Copying the Configuration File*

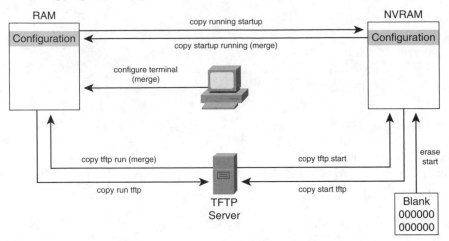

Similar commands exist for copying between a TFTP server and either NVRAM or RAM.

Use the **configure terminal** command to interactively create configurations in RAM from the console or remote terminal.

Use the **erase startup-config** command to delete the saved startup-config file in NVRAM.

Figure 6-14 shows an example of how to use the **copy tftp run** command to merge the running configuration in RAM with a saved configuration file on a TFTP server.

Figure 6-14   *Merging Configuration Files*

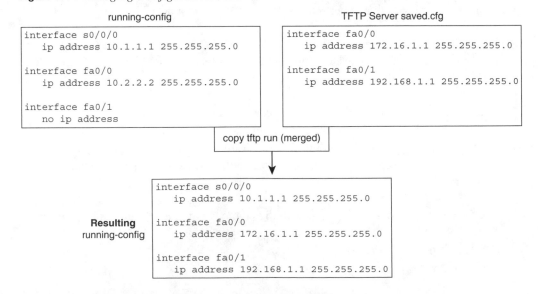

NOTE   When a configuration is copied into RAM from any source, the configuration merges with, or overlays, any existing configuration in RAM, rather than overwriting it. New configuration parameters are added, and changes to existing parameters overwrite the old parameters. Configuration commands that exist in RAM for which there is no corresponding command in NVRAM remain unaffected. Copying the running configuration from RAM into the startup-config file in NVRAM will overwrite the startup-config file in NVRAM.

You can use the TFTP servers to store configurations in a central place, allowing centralized management and updating. Regardless of the size of the network, there should always be a copy of the current running configuration online as a backup. Example 6-11 shows how to transfer, back up, and restore configuration files.

Example 6-11   *Actions for Configuration Files*

```
RouterA# copy running-config: tftp:

Address or name of remote host []? 10.1.1.1
Destination filename [running-config]? wgroa.cfg
.!!
1684 bytes copied in 13.300 secs (129 bytes/sec)

RouterA# copy tftp: running-config:

Address or name of remote host []? 10.1.1.1
Source filename []? wgroa.cfg
Destination filename [running-config]?
Accessing tftp://10.1.1.1/wgroa.cfg...
Loading wgroa.cfg from 10.1.1.1 (via Ethernet0): !
[OK - 1684/3072 bytes]

1684 bytes copied in 17.692 secs (99 bytes/sec)
```

The **copy running-config tftp** command allows the current configuration to be uploaded and saved to a TFTP server. The IP address or name of the TFTP server and the destination filename must be supplied. On the display, a series of exclamation marks show the progress of the upload.

The **copy tftp running-config** command downloads a configuration file from the TFTP server to the running configuration of RAM. Again, the address or name of the TFTP server and the source and destination filename must be supplied. In this case, because you are copying the file to the running configuration, the destination filename should be running-config. This is a merge process, not an overwrite process.

Using show and debug Commands on Cisco Devices

The **show** and **debug** commands are built-in tools for troubleshooting. The **show** command is used to display static information, while the **debug** command is used to display dynamic data and events. Table 6-4 outlines the major differences in these commands.

Table 6-4   **show** *Versus* **debug** *Commands*

	show Commands	debug Commands
Processing Characteristics	Static	Dynamic
Processing Load	Low overhead	High overhead
Primary Use	Gather facts	Observer processes

The **show** and **debug** commands have the following functions:

- **show:** To snapshot problems with interfaces, media, or network performance

- **debug:** To check the flow of protocol traffic for problems, protocol bugs, or misconfigurations

Table 6-5 describes the major differences between the **show** and **debug** commands.

Table 6-5   *Differences Between the* **show** *and* **debug** *Commands*

Command	Description
show	Provides a static collection of information about the status of a network device, neighboring devices, and network performance. Use **show** commands when gathering facts for isolating problems in an internetwork, including problems with interfaces, nodes, media, servers, clients, or applications.
debug	Provides a flow of information about the traffic being seen (or not seen) on an interface, error messages generated by nodes on the network, protocol-specific diagnostic packets, and other useful troubleshooting data. Use **debug** commands when operations on the router or network must be viewed to determine whether events or packets are working properly.

Use **debug** commands to isolate problems, not to monitor normal network operation. Because the high overhead of **debug** commands can disrupt router operation, **debug** commands should be used only when looking for specific types of traffic or problems and when those problems have been narrowed to a likely subset of causes.

The following are some considerations when using **debug** commands:

- Be aware that the **debug** commands can generate too much data that is of little use for a specific problem. Normally, knowledge of the protocol or protocols being debugged is required to properly interpret the debug outputs.

- Because the high CPU overhead of **debug** commands can disrupt network device operation, **debug** commands should be used only when looking for specific types of traffic or problems and when those problems have been narrowed to a likely subset of causes.

- When using the **debug** troubleshooting tools, be aware that output formats vary with each protocol. Some generate a single line of output per packet, whereas others generate multiple lines of output per packet.

- Some **debug** commands generate large amounts of output; others generate only occasional output. Some generate lines of text, and others generate information in field format.

- Use of **debug** commands is suggested for obtaining information about network traffic and router status. Use these commands with great care.

- If you are not sure about the impact of a debug command, check http://www.cisco.com for details or consult with a technical support representative.

Many IOS commands are useful when performing debugs. Table 6-6 lists descriptions of the commands that you can use with a **debug** command.

Table 6-6 *Command Descriptions*

Command	Description
service timestamps	Use this command to add a time stamp to a **debug** or log message. This feature can provide valuable information about when debug elements occurred and the duration of time between events.
show processes	Displays the CPU utilization for each process. This data can influence decisions about using a **debug** command, if it indicates that the production system is already too heavily used for adding a **debug** command.
no debug all	Disables all **debug** commands. This command can free system resources after you finish using debug.
terminal monitor	Displays **debug** output and system error messages for the current terminal and session.

Because the problem condition is an abnormal situation, you might be willing to temporarily trade off efficiency for the opportunity to rapidly diagnose and correct the problem. To effectively use debugging tools, you must consider the following:

- The impact that a troubleshooting tool has on router performance

- The most selective and focused use of the diagnostic tool

- How to minimize the impact of troubleshooting on other processes that compete for resources on the network device

- How to stop the troubleshooting tool when diagnosing is complete so that the router can resume its most efficient switching

It is one thing to use **debug** commands to troubleshoot a lab network that lacks end-user application traffic. It is another thing to use **debug** commands on a production network that users depend on for data flow. Without proper precautions, the impact of a broadly focused **debug** command could make matters worse.

With proper, selective, and temporary use of **debug** commands, you can easily obtain potentially useful information without needing a protocol analyzer or other third-party tool.

Other considerations for using **debug** commands are as follows:

- Ideally, it is best to use **debug** commands during periods of lower network traffic and fewer users. Debugging during these periods reduces the effect on other users.

- When the information you need from the **debug** command is interpreted and the debug (and other related configuration settings, if any) is undone, the router can resume its faster switching. Problem solving can be resumed, a better-targeted action plan created, and the network problem resolved.

All **debug** commands are entered in privileged EXEC mode, and most **debug** commands take no arguments.

> **CAUTION**   Do not use the **debug all** command because this can cause a system to crash.

To list and see a brief description of all the debugging command options, enter the **debug ?** command in privileged EXEC mode.

By default, the network server sends the output from **debug** commands and system error messages to the console. When using this default, you should monitor the debugging output using a virtual terminal connection rather than the console port. To redirect debugging output, you should use the **logging** command options in configuration mode. Possible destinations include the console, vty, internal buffer, and UNIX hosts running a syslog server. The syslog format is compatible with 4.3 Berkeley Software Distribution (4.3 BSD) UNIX and its derivatives.

> **NOTE**   It is important to turn off debugging when you have finished your troubleshooting.

Summary of Managing Cisco Devices

The following list summarizes the key points that were discussed in the previous sections:

- The Cisco IOS File System feature provides a single interface to all the file systems (NVRAM, RAM, TFTP, flash) that a router uses.

- As a network grows, storage of the Cisco IOS Software and configuration files on a central server enables control of the number and revision level of software images and configuration files that must be maintained.

- Having proper backup of the current device configuration stored in a TFTP server can help reduce device downtime.

- The Cisco IOS Software **copy** commands can be used to move configurations from one component or device to another, such as RAM, NVRAM, or a file server.

- Network equipment is often moved from one location to another or removed from the network, or the configuration can change. The process is referred to as adds, moves, and changes.

- The **show** and **debug** commands are built-in tools for troubleshooting. The **show** command is used to display static information, while the **debug** command is used to display dynamic data.

Chapter Summary

The following list summarizes the key points that were discussed in this chapter:

- The CDP is an information-gathering tool used by network administrators to get information about directly connected Cisco devices, including the following for each device: device identifier, address list, port identifier, capabilities list, and platform. You can view this information by using the **show cdp** command.

■ When a router boots up, it performs a series of steps, including performing tests, finding and loading the Cisco IOS Software, finding and loading configurations, and running the Cisco IOS Software.

■ The Cisco IFS feature provides a single interface to all the file systems that a router uses. As any network grows, storage of Cisco IOS images and configuration files on a central TFTP server enables control of the number and revision level of Cisco IOS images and configuration files that must be maintained.

Review Questions

Use the questions in this section to review what you learned in this chapter. The correct answers and solutions are found in the appendix, "Answers to Chapter Review Questions."

1. Which of the following statements are true of Cisco Discovery Protocol? (Choose two.)

    a. Cisco Discovery Protocol is a proprietary protocol.

    b. Cisco Discovery Protocol is an open protocol standard.

    c. Cisco Discovery Protocol discovers information about directly connected Cisco devices.

    d. Cisco Discovery Protocol discovers information about all devices on the network.

    e. Cisco Discovery Protocol runs over the network layer.

2. How could you obtain Cisco Discovery Protocol information about a remote device that is not directly connected?

    a. Use the command **show cdp neighbors** *address*.

    b. Use the command **show cdp neighbors** *hostname*.

    c. Use SSH or Telnet to access a Cisco device connected to the target device.

    d. It is not possible to obtain Cisco Discovery Protocol information about a remote device.

3. Which of the following pieces of information are included in a Cisco Discovery Protocol update packet? (Choose two.)

    a. Platform

    b. Routing updates

    c. Device identifiers

    d. MAC address list

    e. Link speed

4. Which command disables Cisco Discovery Protocol on the device as a whole?

    a. **no run cdp**

    b. **no cdp run**

    c. **no cdp enable**

    d. **no cdp execute**

5. What does the command **cdp enable** do?

    a. Disables Cisco Discovery Protocol on a specific interface

    b. Enables Cisco Discovery Protocol on the device as a whole

    c. Enables Cisco Discovery Protocol on an individual interface

    d. Enables Cisco Discovery Protocol on a specific type of interface

6. Which Cisco IOS command produces the same result as the **show cdp neighbors detail** command?

    a. **show cdp traffic**

    b. **show cdp entry ***

    c. **show cdp neighbors**

    d. **show cdp interface all**

7. Which keyword do you add to the **show cdp neighbors** command to obtain additional information in the output?

    a. **full**

    b. **detail**

    c. **verbose**

    d. **complete**

8. Which Cisco IOS command displays the frequency at which packets are sent?

    a. **show cdp entry**

    b. **show cdp traffic**

    c. **show cdp interface**

    d. **show cdp neighbors**

9. What information is included in the output of the command **show cdp interface**?

   a. Remote port ID

   b. Remote device ID

   c. Encapsulation type

   d. Number of Cisco Discovery Protocol packets sent

10. Which command displays the device platform of a directly connected device?

   a. **show cdp entry**

   b. **show cdp traffic**

   c. **show cdp interface**

   d. **show cdp platform**

11. Which command displays Cisco Discovery Protocol packet checksum errors?

   a. **show cdp entry**

   b. **show cdp traffic**

   c. **show cdp interface**

   d. **show cdp neighbors**

12. Which of the following statements identify the primary uses of a network map? (Choose three.)

   a. Tracks modifications to network design

   b. Creates a software inventory

   c. Tracks changes to the topology

   d. Troubleshoots network problems

   e. Tracks changes in protocol configurations

   f. Implements new configurations

13. Which stage during a Cisco router bootup occurs last?

   a. POST

   b. Find and load Cisco IOS Software

   c. Find and load bootstrap

   d. Find and load configuration

14. Which stage of a Cisco router bootup process verifies that all router components are operational?

    a. POST

    b. Find Cisco IOS Software

    c. Find bootstrap

    d. Find configuration

15. Which Cisco router component is used primarily to store the startup-config file?

    a. RAM

    b. ROM

    c. NVRAM

    d. Flash memory

    e. Configuration register

16. Which of the following is a low-level operating system normally used for manufacturing testing and troubleshooting?

    a. POST

    b. Bootstrap

    c. Mini Cisco IOS

    d. ROMMON

17. During the Cisco router bootup process, what does the router do if the boot field value is 0x2?

    a. Runs ROM monitor

    b. Loads Cisco IOS image from flash memory

    c. Loads Cisco IOS image subset from ROM

    d. Checks the startup-config file for **boot system** commands

18. What happens if the router cannot find a valid startup configuration file in NVRAM during router bootup?

    a. The router enters setup mode.

    b. The router attempts to restart.

    c. The router runs ROM Monitor.

    d. The router performs a shutdown.

19. On most routers, the Cisco IOS Software is loaded into _____ to run, but on some routers, it is run directly from _____.

    a. RAM, NVRAM

    b. RAM, flash memory

    c. flash memory, RAM

    d. NVRAM, flash memory

20. The command **show startup-config** displays the configuration in what location?

    a. ROM

    b. RAM

    c. NVRAM

    d. Flash memory

21. Which bits of the configuration register value make up the boot field?

    a. Lowest octet

    b. Highest octet

    c. Lowest 4 bits

    d. Highest 4 bits

22. Which Cisco IOS command is used to download a copy of the Cisco IOS image file from a TFTP server?

    a. **copy IOS tftp**

    b. **copy tftp flash**

    c. **copy flash tftp**

    d. **backup flash tftp**

23. Given the system image file c2600-js-mz.122-21a.bin, which part of the filename indicates the platform?

    a. mz

    b. js

    c. 122-21a

    d. c2600

24. Which Cisco IOS command displays the amount of memory that is available where the Cisco IOS image is stored on your router?

   a. **show flash**

   b. **show nvram**

   c. **show memory**

   d. **show running-config**

25. Where is the running configuration of the router usually stored?

   a. BIOS

   b. RAM

   c. NVRAM

   d. bootflash

26. Which Cisco IOS command merges a configuration file from NVRAM into the configuration in RAM?

   a. **copy startup running**

   b. **copy running-config tftp**

   c. **copy startup-config RAM**

   d. **copy NVRAM running-config**

27. What does the **copy tftp startup** command do?

   a. Copies the configuration in NVRAM to a TFTP server

   b. Downloads a configuration file from a TFTP file to RAM

   c. Downloads a configuration file from a TFTP server to NVRAM

   d. Merges the configuration in RAM with the configuration file on a TFTP server

28. When you copy a configuration from another source into RAM, what happens to the previous configuration?

   a. It is overwritten.

   b. It is retained in its current state.

   c. It is merged with the new configuration, with the existing configuration taking precedence.

   d. It is merged with the new configuration, with the new configuration taking precedence.

29. You should use **debug** commands to _____ problems, not to monitor normal network operation.

    a. test

    b. repair

    c. isolate

    d. duplicate

30. Why must you be so careful when using **debug** commands?

    a. They are destructive.

    b. They open security holes.

    c. They prevent normal traffic processing.

    d. They can have a negative impact on performance.

31. Which Cisco IOS command will add a time stamp to a debug or log message?

    a. **timestamps debug**

    b. **debug timestamps**

    c. **service timestamps**

    d. **service debug timestamps**

32. Which action can lead to a software reload on a Cisco device?

    a. Disabling a **debug** privileged EXEC command on a heavily used production router

    b. Enabling a **debug** privileged EXEC command on a heavily used production router

    c. Enabling a **debug** privileged EXEC command on a lightly used production router

    d. Disabling a **debug** privileged EXEC command on a lightly used production router

33. Which Cisco IOS command will enable a Telnet session to receive console messages?

    a. **terminal monitor**

    b. **terminal debug monitor**

    c. **terminal debug messages**

    d. **terminal console messages**

34. It is best to use **debug** commands during periods of _____ network traffic and _____ users.

   a. lower, more

   b. lower, fewer

   c. higher, more

   d. higher, fewer

35. On a heavily used production router, enabling a **debug** privileged EXEC command can be _____.

   a. useful

   b. helpful

   c. harmful

   d. difficult

Answers to Chapter Review Questions

Chapter 1

Review Questions

1. A, B, C

2. A

3. C

4. D

5. A

6. A, B, D

7. __D__ 1. speed

    __G__ 2. cost

    __C__ 3. security

    __A__ 4. availability

    __E__ 5. scalability

    __B__ 6. reliability

    __F__ 7. topology

8. A, B

9. C

10. __B__ 1. All of the network devices connect directly to each other in a linear fashion.

    __A__ 2. All of the network devices are directly connected to one central point with no other connections between them.

      D   3. All of the devices on a network are connected in the form of a circle.

      C   4. Each device has a connection to all of the other devices.

      E   5. At least one device maintains multiple connections to other devices.

      F   6. This design adds redundancy to the network.

11. A, B

12. D

13. B, D

14. A, C

15. A, B

16. E 1. physical

      C 2. data link

      A 3. network

      D 4. transport

      G 5. session

      B 6. presentation

      F 7. application

17. F 1. Step 1

      C 2. Step 2

      A 3. Step 3

      B 4. Step 4

      E 5. Step 5

      D 6. Step 6

      G 7. Step 7

      H 8. Step 8

18. B

19.   _B_ 1. network layer

       _A_ 2. data link layer

       _C_ 3. physical layer

20. A

21.   _D_ 1. Provides applications for file transfer, network troubleshooting, and Internet activities, and supports the network

       _B_ 2. Defines how data is formatted for transmission and how access to the network is controlled

       _A_ 3. Defines the electrical, mechanical, procedural, and functional specifications for activating, maintaining, and deactivating the physical link between end systems

       _C_ 4. Provides routing of data from the source to a destination by defining the packet and addressing scheme, moving data between the data link and transport layers, routing packets of data to remote hosts, and performing fragmentation and reassembly of data packets

       _E_ 5. Provides communication services directly to the application processes running on different network hosts

22. B

23. B

24. D

25. B

26. C

27. A, B

28. A, B, F

29. B, D, F

30. A

31. B

32. A, C

33. A, C, D

34. C, D

35. C

36. A

37. D

38. B

39. C

40. A

41. D

42. B

43. B

44. A, C, E

45. D

46. A

47. B

48. D

49.   _D_ 1. Category 1

   _F_ 2. Category 2

   _G_ 3. Category 3

   _E_ 4. Category 4

   _A_ 5. Category 5

   _B_ 6. Category 5e

   _C_ 7. Category 6

50. B, C, D

Chapter 2

Review Questions

1.   A, E

2.   A, C, E

3. C

4. B

5. A, C, E

6. B, D, E

7. A, E

8. _B_ If the switch determines that the destination MAC address of the frame resides on the same network segment as the source, it does not forward the frame.

   _C_ If the switch determines that the destination MAC address of the frame is not from the same network as the source, it transmits the frame to the appropriate segment.

   _A_ If the switch does *not* have an entry for the destination address, it will transmit the frame out of all ports except the port on which it received the frame.

9. A, B, D

10. A, C, D

11. A, C, E

12. B, C, D

13. _B_ The network sends and receives data frames one at a time, but not simultaneously.

   _A_ This communication type effectively doubles the amount of bandwidth between the devices.

   _A_ The network sends and receives data frames simultaneously.

14. _B_ At the end-user level, gives high-performance PC workstations 100-Mbps access to a server

   _C_ Not typically used at the end-user level

   _A_ At the workgroup level, provides connectivity between the end user and workgroups

   _B_ At the backbone level, provides interswitch connectivity for low- to medium-volume applications

   _B_ At the workgroup level, provides high-performance connectivity to the enterprise server

     _C_ At the backbone level, provides backbone and interswitch connectivity

     _A_ At the end-user level, provides connectivity between the end user and the user-level switch

     _C_ Provides interswitch connectivity for low- to medium-volume applications

15. C

16. B

17. B

18. D

19. D

20. B

21. A

22. A

23. _A_ Step 1

     _B_ Step 2

     _C_ Step 3

24. D

25. A

26. A

27. B

28. D

29. C

30. C

31. C

32. B

33. B, C

34. A, B, C, E

35. B

36. C

37. B

38. A

39. B

40. A

41. A

42. C

43. C

44. B, C, D

Chapter 3

Review Questions

1. A

2. A

3. <u>B</u> Occurs when RF waves bounce off metal or glass surfaces

<u>A</u> Occurs when RF waves are soaked up by walls

<u>C</u> Occurs when RF waves strike an uneven surface and are reflected in many directions

4. B

5. A

6. C, D

7. B, E

8. B

9. C

10. C

11. A, B, D

12. D

13. D

14. C

15. D

16. __A__ Mobile clients connect directly without an intermediate access point.

__B__ The communication devices use a single access point for connectivity to each other or to wired network resources.

__C__ The wireless topology is two or more service sets connected by a distribution system (DS) or, more commonly, a wired infrastructure.

17. B

18. B

19. A

20. A, B, E

21. D

22. __C__ Full-featured supplicant for both wired and wireless client

__A__ Windows operating systems basic wireless supplicant client

__B__ More advanced wireless client features than those of native operating system

Chapter 4

Review Questions

1. A, B, C

2. B, C

3. A, B

4. A, B, D

5. __E__ Step 1

__A__ Step 2

__C__ Step 3

__B__ Step 4

__D__ Step 5

6. A, B, C

7. B, C, E

8. _D_ This entry comes from having interfaces attached to network segments. This entry is obviously the most certain; if the interface fails or is administratively shut down, the entry for that network will be removed from the routing table.

    _C_ This is an optional entry that is used when no explicit path to a destination is found in the routing table. This entry can be manually inserted or be populated from a dynamic routing protocol.

    _A_ These routes are entered manually by a system administrator directly into the configuration of a router.

    _B_ These routes are learned by the router, and the information is responsive to changes in the network so that the router is constantly being updated.

9. A, B, C

10. B, C, E

11. B, D, E

12. D

13. B

14. C

15. A

16. C

17. D

18. A

19. B

20. D

21. A

22. A

23. C

24. B

25. C

26. D

27. D

28. D

29. A, C

30. C

31. C

32. D

33. B

34. C

35. C

36. A

37. C

38. _A_ Context-sensitive help

  _C_ Console error messages

  _B_ Command history buffer

39. A

40. A

41. _B_ Line

  _D_ Router

  _A_ Interface

  _E_ Controller

  _C_ Subinterface

42. D

43. B

44. A

45. D

46. C

47. C

48. D, E

49. B, C

50. A, B, C, E

51. B

52. C

53. B

54. B

55. B, C

56. A

57. A, B, G, H

58. D

59. A

60. A

61. C

Chapter 5

Review Questions

1. C, D, F

2. D, F

3. B, C

4. A

5. B

6. __C__ In analog lines, they convert the digital signal of the sending device into analog format for transmission over an analog line and then convert the signal back to digital form so that the receiving device can receive and process the network signal.

   __B__ They concentrate dial-in and dial-out user communications.

   __A__ They provide internetworking and WAN access interface ports.

   __D__ WANs use these to provide access.

7.   _B_ Allow the router to connect to the LAN media through Ethernet or some other LAN technology such as Token Ring or ATM

   _C_ Are made through a WAN interface on a router to a service provider to a distant site or to the Internet

   _A_ Provide a text-based connection for the configuration and troubleshooting of the router

8.   A, D

9.   _B_ Time-division multiplexing

   _A_ Frequency-division multiplexing

   _C_ Statistical multiplexing

10.   _B_ Dedicated communication links

   _C_ Circuit-switched communication links

   _A_ Packet-switched communication links

11.   B, C, F

12.   D, E, F

13.   A, B

14.   B, D, F

15.   C, D, E

16.   B, E, F

17.   Match each NAT term with its definition. (Source: Enabling the Internet Connection)

   _C_ Static NAT

   _D_ Dynamic NAT

   _A_ Inside network

   _B_ Outside global IP address

18.   B

19.   D

20.   B

21. A, D, E

22. B

23. D

24. B

25. B

26. C

27. A

28. A, B, E

29. A, C, D

30. A, B, D

31. A, C, F

32. A, B, D

33. C, E, F

34. A, B, C

35. D

36. A

37. D

38. C

39. B, C, F

40. A, C, F

41. B

42. A

43. B

44. A

45. B

46. D

Chapter 6

Review Questions

1. A, C

2. C

3. A, C

4. B

5. C

6. C

7. B

8. C

9. C

10. A

11. B

12. A, C, D

13. D

14. A

15. C

16. D

17. D

18. A

19. B

20. C

21. C

22. B

23. D

24. A

25. B

26. A

27. C

28. D

29. C

30. D

31. C

32. B

33. A

34. B

35. C

Index

Numerics

SEARCH THOUSANDS OF BOOKS FROM LEADING PUBLISHERS

Safari® Bookshelf is a searchable electronic reference library for IT professionals that features more than 2,000 titles from technical publishers, including Cisco Press.

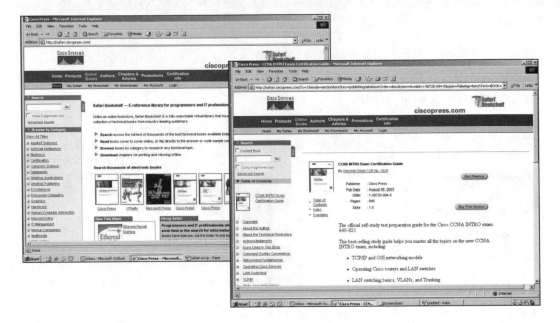

With Safari Bookshelf you can

- **Search** the full text of thousands of technical books, including more than 70 Cisco Press titles from authors such as Wendell Odom, Jeff Doyle, Bill Parkhurst, Sam Halabi, and Karl Solie.

- **Read** the books on My Bookshelf from cover to cover, or just flip to the information you need.

- **Browse** books by category to research any technical topic.

- **Download** chapters for printing and viewing offline.

With a customized library, you'll have access to your books when and where you need them—and all you need is a user name and password.

TRY SAFARI BOOKSHELF FREE FOR 14 DAYS!

You can sign up to get a 10-slot Bookshelf free for the first 14 days.
Visit **http://safari.ciscopress.com** to register.